IRRATIONAL PUBLICS
AND THE FATE OF DEMOCRACY

McGILL-QUEEN'S STUDIES IN THE HISTORY OF IDEAS
Series Editor: Philip J. Cercone

72 The Culturalist Challenge to Liberal Republicanism
Michael Lusztig

73 God and Government: Martin Luther's Political Thought
Jarrett A. Carty

74 The Age of Secularization
Augusto Del Noce
Edited and Translated by Carlo Lancellotti

75 Emancipatory Thinking: Simone de Beauvoir and Contemporary Political Thought
Elaine Stavro

76 Life Embodied: The Promise of Vital Force in Spanish Modernity
Nicolás Fernández-Medina

77 The Aesthetics of Fear in German Romanticism
Paola Mayer

78 Objectively Engaged Journalism: An Ethic
Stephen J.A. Ward

79 Progress, Pluralism, and Politics: Liberalism and Colonialism, Past and Present
David Williams

80 Beyond Tragedy and Eternal Peace: Politics and International Relations in the Thought of Friedrich Nietzsche
Jean-François Drolet

81 Inequality in Canada: The History and Politics of an Idea
Eric W. Sager

82 Attending: An Ethical Art
Warren Heiti

83 Imperial Paradoxes: Training the Senses and Tasting the Eighteenth Century
Robert James Merrett

84 The Problem of Atheism
Augusto Del Noce
Edited and Translated by Carlo Lancellotti

85 The Etruscans in the Modern Imagination
Sam Solecki

86 The Communion of the Book: Milton and the Humanist Revolution in Reading
David Williams

87 Dying for France: Experiencing and Representing the Soldier's Death, 1500–2000
Ian Germani

88 Religion and the Post-revolutionary Mind: Idéologues, Catholic Traditionalists, and Liberals in France
Arthur McCalla

89 The Domination of Nature, New Edition
William Leiss

90 Lines Drawn across the Globe: Reading Richard Hakluyt's *Principal Navigations*
Mary C. Fuller

91 Irrational Publics and the Fate of Democracy
Stephen J.A. Ward

Irrational Publics and the Fate of Democracy

Stephen J.A. Ward

McGill-Queen's University Press
Montreal & Kingston • London • Chicago

ISBN 978-0-2280-2002-8 (cloth)
ISBN 978-0-2280-2003-5 (paper)
ISBN 978-0-2280-2004-2 (ePDF)
ISBN 978-0-2280-2005-9 (ePUB)

Legal deposit fourth quarter 2024
Bibliothèque nationale du Québec

Printed in Canada on acid-free paper that is 100% ancient forest free (100% post-consumer recycled), processed chlorine free

This book has been published with the help of a grant from the Federation for the Humanities and Social Sciences, through the Awards to Scholarly Publications Program, using funds provided by the Social Sciences and Humanities Research Council of Canada.

Funded by the Government of Canada | Financé par le gouvernement du Canada | Canada | Canada Council for the Arts | Conseil des arts du Canada

We acknowledge the support of the Canada Council for the Arts.
Nous remercions le Conseil des arts du Canada de son soutien.

McGill-Queen's University Press in Montreal is on land which long served as a site of meeting and exchange amongst Indigenous Peoples, including the Haudenosaunee and Anishinabeg nations. In Kingston it is situated on the territory of the Haudenosaunee and Anishinaabek. We acknowledge and thank the diverse Indigenous Peoples whose footsteps have marked these territories on which peoples of the world now gather.

Library and Archives Canada Cataloguing in Publication

Title: Irrational publics and the fate of democracy / Stephen J.A. Ward.

Names: Ward, Stephen J. A. (Stephen John Anthony), 1951- author.

Series: McGill-Queen's studies in the history of ideas; 91.

Description: Series statement: McGill-Queen's studies in the history of ideas; 91 | Includes bibliographical references and index.

Identifiers: Canadiana (print) 20240391128 | Canadiana (ebook) 20240391187 | ISBN 9780228020028 (cloth) | ISBN 9780228020035 (paper) | ISBN 9780228020042 (ePDF) | ISBN 9780228020059 (ePUB)

Subjects: LCSH: Irrationalism (Philosophy)—Social aspects. | LCSH: Irrationalism (Philosophy)—History. | LCSH: Democracy.

Classification: LCC B824.2 .W37 2024 | DDC 128/.33—dc23

This book was typeset by Marquis Interscript in 10/13 New Baskerville.

To Nadia, maker of musical worlds

Contents

Acknowledgments

Philosophy employs reason but it does not come from reason. It comes from our encounters with wide, rich experience. Philosophy occurs not in one season but across the seasons of a life, where fresh experience merges with the memory of things past and books read long ago. All is new, yet all is old. Ideas form a dynamic circle that are within and without time.

Along the way, if we are open to the pathway of life – cognitively, emotionally, aesthetically – we may be able to weave the tapestry of ideas into a book of philosophy. The ideas may help, in some small way, to illuminate, but never replace, the questions raised by the original sources of humane existence: life, love, hardship and grief, recovery and renaissance, the passage of time, and the inevitability of death. Through it all, if we are fortunate, we maintain an enthusiasm for experience, knowledge, and love as we approach the journey's end.

I have been so fortunate.

I was fortunate to be brought up in a family that never questioned my esoteric desire to read philosophy – esoteric for a mill and mining town of 16,000 hard-working, honest souls in northern New Brunswick. I was fortunate to have close friends with whom I could lose myself in the pleasures of playing rock music. I have been fortunate to work with the best of democratic journalists and then the best of academic colleagues. I have been fortunate to be married to two intelligent, sensitive, and talented women, Glenda and Nadia, who – despite their own busy careers – understood and understand my intense mental lifestyle of reading and writing. Then reading and writing more. An addict of the idea.

I was fortunate in having university professors who instilled in me a love of history and philosophical inquiry. They challenged me to say something different, never settling for the easy, vacuous opinion. From my first undergraduate course in Socrates and Plato, I knew I had found my intellectual home in philosophy and the history of ideas.

I have come to believe that humans, to be fully themselves, need to search for important, if uncomfortable, truths about themselves and the world. We need to recognize and deal with our rational and the irrational sides, and everything in between. Even where we fail to be utterly honest, as we must as fallible humans, we should persist. When humans give up on being honest with themselves, all is lost.

This book honours that need for honesty, and all who made the tapestry possible.

PART ONE

The Pendulum of Irrationality

1

Irrational Intolerance

What sort of freak then is man! How novel, how monstrous, how chaotic, how paradoxical. What a novelty, what a monster, what a chaos, what a contradiction, what a prodigy! Judge of all things, feeble earthworm, repository of truth, sink of doubt and error, glory and refuse of the universe.

Pascal[1]

Madness is something rare in individuals – but in groups, parties, peoples, and ages it is the rule.

Friedrich Nietzsche[2]

I AM BOTH RATIONAL AND IRRATIONAL. So are you.

So are your society and the times in which you live.

Humans cannot be otherwise. We cannot untangle, separate, and command the rational or irrational strands in the rope of life.

One way to express this entanglement is to say that I, you, and society are not fully rational, or, to turn the phrase around, we are not fully irrational. We are an intimate collage of rational, irrational, and non-rational elements.

The collage that defines our soul is dynamic. It changes over time. The balance of elements changes over the lifetime of an individual or a group. Like a pendulum, people, groups, and societies swing between periods marked by rationality or irrationality. The pendulum also swings in culture between conceptions of rationality and irrationality. These conceptions rise, fall, and return in some other guise. There are times when confidence in human rationality is strong, and times when it is doubted. Or, people prefer to listen to the sirens of extreme irrationality. Individuals and societies are in motion between extremes.

1 Pascal, *Pensées*, section 131, 34.
2 Nietzsche, *Beyond Good and Evil*, Aphorism 156, 103.

Why this is so is the topic of this book.

This book seeks to understand irrationality in the human being and in society. It also seeks to understand the lethal combination of irrationality and intolerance in groups, and how it occurs. First, I approach the topic logically, identifying the meanings of rational and irrationality and how those conceptions are affected by our worldview. Second, I look at the topic culturally. I track the evolution of conceptions of rationality and irrationality and how they have shaped history. Third, I examine examples of extreme irrationalism and their horrendous impact on society. Fourth, and finally, I offer a conceptual framework that helps to explain how extreme irrationality and intolerance arise in the human mind and in society. This leads to a consideration of what we must do to rebuild rational publics for the sake of democracy.

Among the questions I ask are: What is the nature of humans that they should have this deep rational/irrational tension within them? How does philosophy, science, and society change the way humans conceive of their rationality and irrationality? How have elites used the rational–irrational distinction to support reforms or to oppress rivals? How is the rational–irrational distinction related to other basic distinctions: the good and the bad, the beautiful and the ugly, the natural and the unnatural?

I do not ask such questions idly.

It is vitally important that we who wish to live in egalitarian democracies understand how to protect the idea of rationality and how to support rational public spheres. Large parts of Western society are swinging on the pendulum towards irrational and intolerant politics, shaped by charismatic pseudo-populists who appeal to the darkest side of our nature. Responses to the problem of irrational publics will be inadequate unless it is based on a rich understanding of rationality and irrationality – logically, historically, and socially.

This book attempts to contribute to this understanding. It is what a philosopher can contribute.

SECTION 1: LETHAL INTOLERANCE

There is an ambiguity lurking in the emotion-charged term "irrationality" that we need to identify from the start. We use the phrase in at least three different senses: (1) what is irrational is *not part of*, or does not stem from, reason; or (2) what is irrational is *against* reason; or (3) what is irrational is what is *out of touch* with reality, even insane.

In the first sense, there are psychological capacities, such as the capacity to dream, to imagine, or to feel emotion, which interact with, but are not part of, our rational capacity. Its source is not reason. This meaning is neutral. It entails no negative or positive judgment about the capacity. In the second sense, what is irrational is thought to violate basic facts and logic. A negative evaluation is usually part of (2). People who act violently on strong emotion are said to act against reason. In the third sense, someone is irrational because they have lost touch with reality. An action, such as genocide, is called "crazy" because it is the product of deranged minds.[3]

In what follows, I discuss irrationality in all three senses.

Stubborn Irrationality

Despite science, despite super computers stuffed with data, despite gleaming technology and global communication, and despite centres of learning that venerate rational method and objective fact, humans remain stubbornly irrational in two of the three senses of the term. They act against reason and, at times, are moved to act in ways that are so far from reality as to be considered pathological.

Expressions of irrationality are diverse. Humans can dismiss inconvenient facts, ignore deep contradictions among beliefs, live in a world of narcissism and self-deception, employ a pseudo-rationality that cloaks self-interest, fall victim to pathologies of mind and brain, promulgate stereotypes, hate strangers for being strangers, or support hideous pogroms. Humans are susceptible to the striking image and to the rhetoric of demagogues who tap into reservoirs of pent-up emotion. In such charged contexts, the truth, laboriously verified, doesn't stand a chance against the easy, pleasing attraction of emotional untruth.

When we consider the irrational, we may think about people who do violent acts we cannot fathom, such as a terrorist who kills children without blinking an eye or a pilot who intentionally flies a plane full of passengers into a mountain or a person who drives a truck down a city street, running over pedestrians. We think of sociopaths who enjoy tormenting their victims. We call their acts mad and meaningless. Yet,

3 There is also a distinction between the rational and the non-rational. Our digestive system is non-rational because it operates without reasons. But the system is not against reason.

irrationality is not always extreme or bloody. We can be irrational in our ordinary actions. For example, we may refuse to get on an airplane because we overestimate the risk of flying, but we feel comfortable driving dangerous highways. Some people do not cause mayhem, but they act in an abnormal manner that perplexes us.[4] Someone, for no apparent reason, spray paints a masterpiece painting, or some people enjoy sex only if it involves sadomasochistic elements. They seek – rationally? – domination and degradation.

Above all, we can be primitive, despite our postmodern sophistication. Our consciousness remains mired in tribalism, pre-wired into our brains by evolution.[5] We have seen, in recent decades, the killing fields of Cambodia and Vietnam, the bodies of murdered civilians floating in the rivers of Rwanda, and the genocide of Muslims in Kosovo. To a depressing extent, we live in an immoral, unjust world incapable of addressing the most basic of global issues from climate change to sharing resources, let alone to seek peace. We live in a world that, on many days, deserves to be called irrational. Psychiatrist Aaron Beck, who has written extensively on the origins of hatred, states that the "dazzling technological advances of our era are paralleled by a reversion to the savagery of the Dark Ages."[6]

Into the hands of such flawed human creatures – and into the hands of their erratic, power-thirsty leaders – technology places weapons of mass destruction, digital media for terrorists to recruit the confused, and innumerable military means to subjugate others.

Political Cannibalism

The problem of group irrationality is not new.

On 4 August 1672, Johan de Witt, ruler of Holland for twenty years, and his brother Cornelis were shot by The Hague's civic militia.

4 Psychologists define "abnormal" in three ways: (1) statistical: the behaviour is outside the statistical norm, i.e., most people do not act this way; (2) norm violation: the behaviour violates basic social norms; and (3) maladaptive: the actions limit their capacity to flourish. See Getzfeld, *Essentials of Abnormal Psychology*, 1–3.

5 I prefer "pre-wired" to "hard wired" since the former suggests that our neural circuits and psychology can change with experience, while the latter suggests inflexibility. Pre-wired means structured before experience.

6 Beck, *Prisoners of Hate*, 3.

The assassinations occurred amid a disastrous year of military defeats to French and English forces. Johan de Witt was blamed for neglecting the Dutch army. On 4 August he resigned as grand pensionary but his critics were not satisfied. They arrested Cornelis, a leading soldier, on trumped up charges of treason and tortured him. Refusing to confess to being a traitor, Cornelis was sentenced to exile. When Johan went to visit Cornelis in jail, they were shot.

But assassination was not enough. Not by far. A mob attacked and mutilated their bodies. They (or what was left of their bodies) were lynched on a nearby public giblet. Pieces of their bodies, such as their livers, were roasted and eaten in an act of political cannibalism.

Examples of group irrationalism across history are not hard to find. They include extreme tribalism, antisemitism, and racism. For example, there is the phenomenon of social contagion where irrational acts spread among groups. It may take hold of a group of troubled young people, causing a rash of suicides.[7] The Mỹ Lai Massacre by US troops in 1968 during the Vietnam War is an example of a military unit losing their rationality due to contagion. In a mad fervour, they killed civilians, raped young women, and disemboweled pregnant women. The soldiers lost their rationality and humanity.

In what sense are groups irrational? As we will see, in several ways: (a) in their dogmatic persistence in fixed and biased beliefs immune to counterfacts and reality; (b) in the extremity of their emotions and in their hostile attitudes toward others, based on race, religion, or ethnicity; and (c) in their willingness to support, or participate in, extremely harmful acts against innocent people and peaceful groups, which they slander as enemies of the state. I treat the "isms" of irrational intolerance – tribalism, racism – as a sign of social pathology. This view was summarized some time ago with respect to antisemitism:

> Anti-Semitism in whatever form it appears is a symptom of social pathology, indicating a form of social disorganization that menaces the stability, if not the very foundation of a culture, even beyond the suffering that it entails for its victims.[8]

7 See, for example, Kravetz, *Strange Contagion.*

8 Ackerman and Jahoda, *Anti-Semitism and Emotional Disorder*, 2.

Irrational intolerance is a motivator that no lawmaker or social scientist can ignore. But how to respond? Prejudice seems resistant to rational treatment, the historical record, and fact. New generations seem to learn little from history. Bloody battles and inhuman persecution fade in memory. It is easy to fall back on old attitudes: that the people are an irrational mob that needs authoritarian leaders with firm laws. Before we embrace such negativity, we need to ask: Why do intolerant publics exist?

Scholars and citizens have a duty to improve their understanding of how extreme irrationality and evil are possible for humans. Historian Ian Kershaw wrote his biography of Hitler because of "the continuing duty to seek understanding of how Hitler was possible," since those conditions and causes will arise again.[9] American psychologist Robert Jay Lifton spent a lifetime probing the sources of extreme group violence, from apocalyptic cults to the willingness of German doctors to participate in Nazi experiments in extermination camps. Perhaps we can never understand it completely. As a survivor of Auschwitz said to Lifton about his probe into Nazi doctors, "The professor wants to understand what cannot be understood."[10]

Yet, we must try to understand as much as we can. It is too easy to dismiss genocide and war atrocities as horrible acts by people who are not in any way like us. The Nazis, it might be thought, were a minority of demonic, crazy people who somehow obtained political power. A bunch of thugs.[11] To the contrary, I argue that horrific actions are expressions of general human capacities. The capacity for evil is deep inside us, part of human nature.

We are all potential thugs.

9 Kershaw, *Hitler: Hubris*, xiv.

10 Cited in Lifton, *The Nazis Doctors*, 13.

11 Bertolt Brecht, in his 1941 play *The Resistible Rise of Arturo Ui*, depicts the rise of Ui, a fictional 1930s Chicago mobster, and his attempts to control the cauliflower racket by killing the opposition. The play is a satirical allegory of the rise of Adolf Hitler and the Nazi Party in Germany prior to the Second World War. Both Ui and Hitler lead a bunch of thugs.

Episodic History of Ideas

This is a book in philosophy of history, or the history of ideas, at the group or social level. "Ideas" is defined liberally to include norms, ideologies, and important or dominant ways of thinking. It is deliberately transdisciplinary because, as a work of philosophy, I am not doing science or delving into only one discipline in the humanities. Instead, I take a broad view of what current science, the humanities, and other forms of knowledge can tell us about the causes, history, and triggers of irrational groups.

Part of my method can be called "episodic" in the sense that I use outstanding examples of irrational people and publics across Western history to explain my perspective. I link the examples together through causal hypotheses and historical context. Another part of my method is philosophical synthesis. I bring together notions from evolutionary theory, anthropology, psychology, history, and art. I construct a theory of the evolutionary causes of social irrationality and a model that shows how irrational traits are triggered by current society and media.

I approach my topic from a non-reductive perspective of culture, what Peter Burke called an "open social history."[12] It is "open" because it looks at the *interconnections* among levels in society, rather than reduce one level to another. It does not follow classical Marxism in reducing ideas to the material basis of class division. Nor does it do the opposite of Marxism: produce a "history of the spirit" by focusing on artistic intentions and great ideas without sufficient attention to material conditions.[13] I will use any rigorous method that sheds light on a subject. I do not have a method fetish. I prefer discussions that seek a broad view of phenomena, even though they may not arrive at strict definitions or final conceptions.

12 Burke, *The Italian Renaissance*, 4.

13 This approach can be seen in Jacob Burckhardt's otherwise great work in the nineteenth century, *The Civilization of the Renaissance in Italy*.

The book has three parts. In the first, I define the notions of rationality and irrationality, and I explain how, in history, forms of rationality and irrationality have been in an almost continual pendulum motion. Associated mentalities (e.g., a preference for order and authority versus a preference for liberties) have also swung on a cultural pendulum.

In the second part, I analyze eras when irrational groups erupted, such as the Crusades, the Inquisition, modern fascism, Stalinist Russia, irrational artistic modernity, and today's cults.

In the third part, I use evolutionary theory and archeology to explain the origin of rational and irrational traits in human prehistory – the evolution of our hard and soft traits, our altruism, and our tribalism. What responses people have to current events – whether they are tolerant or intolerant, rational or irrational – depends on what triggers in the culture prompt our nicer or nastier selves, from the news media to the fierce rhetoric of demagogues. Psychologically, social irrationality occurs when people adopt what I call the "enemy stance," which treats others as foe or a threat.

I conclude with an epilogue that discusses the sorts of measures we need to take to protect our democracies from irrational and extreme groups.

I am a philosopher, an ethicist, and a journalist who is deeply committed to accessible public writing on major issues. Thus I have written a popular philosophy of irrational groups, which means a book any educated citizen can understand. Also, I believe the book is academically strong and should be of use to scholars and their students in a range of disciplines. I have sought to do what pragmatist John Dewey encouraged: to use the ideas of philosophy and the sciences to help people think about the major issues.

In sum, this is a book of philosophy on what we know about the eruptions of irrational publics. It is not a scientific book or a book in a specific discipline such as psychology or ethics. It is a book that offers a philosophical perspective based on the best available theories and facts.

One of my motivations in writing this book is to alert moderate and tolerant citizens to the growth of social irrationality, of dangerous psychological and communication patterns right under their noses. If not checked, these patterns grow like cancer in the body politic. As a war reporter I have seen what irrational intolerance can do to communities in the Balkans and elsewhere. So, I have long wondered about the dark side of humans.

SECTION 2: MAPPING IRRATIONALITY

Naturalized Mind

How should we approach the study of the mind, rational or irrational, from the perspective of naturalism?

I define naturalism as a philosophical commitment to explain the world as a complex, evolving natural entity. There is no appeal to non-natural processes. Theories posit no deities, no spirits or demons, and no metaphysical entities beyond experience. When it comes to humans, theories posit only natural things such as chemical interactions, brain states and anatomy, mental capacities and representations, and adaptations to natural and social environments.

I think of rationality and irrationality as *natural* – as psychological capacities and tendencies that exist in a natural organism (the human species) that acts in a natural and social environment. Rationality and irrationality have a natural, *existential* root: our need to distinguish the rational and irrational originates in the needs of existence, such as in the need to predict what will happen next, and to develop new means to better ends. I treat the rational and irrational realistically, by studying actual events and social contexts. This book is not a study of rationality in the logic classroom; nor is it a study of irrationality among patients in a clinic. It is a study of how the ideas of rationality and irrationality operate in the real world.

Naturalism treats cultural phenomena – actions, practices, worldviews, artistic works – as symbolic expressions. They contain interpretations of life rich with meaning – what Paul Ricoeur calls a "surplus of meaning."[14] There is no one, uniquely right interpretation. There is no digging below all interpretation to find something pure or without interpretation. We cannot pole vault our way out of embedded existence to see things as perhaps God might see them: absolutely and objectively. We can only compare ideas as we sail on Neurath's ship of inquiry.[15] All

14 See Ricoeur, *Interpretation Theory: Discourse and the Surplus of Meaning*. For a clear exposition of this concept, see Christians, *Media Ethics and Global Justice in the Digital Age*, 179–82.

15 On situated inquiry, see my *Objectively Engaged Journalism*, chapters 5 and 6. The metaphor of inquiry as a sailing ship was used by the logical positivist Otto Neurath and popularized by the neo-pragmatist Willard V.O. Quine. See Quine, *Word and Object*, 11.

that is human is interpreted. Moreover, symbolic acts are often political. They express specific purposes, amid rival purposes. In any act of language, painting, or philosophizing some things are stressed while other things are ignored or repressed. Some perspective is advanced; some other perspective is not. Hence, it is always good to ask of anything cultural and symbolic: What is *not* being represented?

By "mind" I do not mean the classic picture of the mind, found in early empiricists like Locke and Hume. In these writers, the mind is depicted as an inner theatre where the mind's eye reviews a parade of impressions and ideas caused by external objects. It combines ideas into judgments of cause and effect, and so on.[16] Nor do I think of mind as a Cartesian mental substance completely different from physical substance or matter.

By "mind" I mean a natural property of a species that has developed through evolution. Like a Russian doll, mental evolution is embedded in brain evolution, which is embedded in human evolution, which is embedded in the evolution of life on a planet that is part of the evolution of the cosmos. "Mind" is a composite term. It refers to a set of psychological capacities that allow us to understand reality. It includes cognition, consciousness, reasoning and reflection, perceiving, forming habits and mindsets, valuing, deciding, feeling, and having emotions. Psychology is the study of this natural mind. The mind is a tool kit for an organism that needs to understand, predict, and function in the natural and social world.[17]

How is the mind anchored in this natural world? It cannot float free, a mysterious, independent, mental substance. Our mind is embodied, intertwined with the matter of our brains and our bodies. As Merleau-Ponty says, the mind is incarnate in the body.[18] The human brain, which realizes our mental capacities, is enormously complicated, some 10 billion neurons, one of nature's finest designs, created over eons.

The best study of the mind adopts a holism of inquiry and method. Multiple factors are at work in almost any psychological phenomenon. So, we need a multi-levelled, multi-disciplinary approach. One understands any item – biases, emotions, patterns of thinking – by

16 Hume, *A Treatise of Human Nature*, book 1, section VI, 253.

17 Damasio says our mind is not embedded only in a brain but in a complete organism. The mind is the "body-minded brain." Damasio, *Descartes' Error*, 222–44, 245.

18 Merleau-Ponty, *Phenomenology of Perception*, part 1, 67–205.

showing how it fits into a larger genetic, social, and environmental context. Holism rejects reductionist explanations of psychological phenomena, the "nothing but" approach which asserts, for example, that aggression is nothing but high levels of the hormone testosterone. Given the complexity of humans, a multi-levelled approach has become dominant of late in the sciences of the brain and mind.[19]

Rationality is a natural capacity of human nature due to evolution. Rationality is a much wider phenomenon than what philosophers call Reason – a presumed inward source of necessary truths. Moreover, rationality includes but is not reducible to logic, the ability to organize propositions into argument. Rather, rationality is a psychological faculty that connects ideas for practical action. It serves our practical engagement with the world, intersecting with emotions, hopes, and goals. Rationality serves an agent that *needs to decide* how to act.

What are the rational capacities? They include our capacity to think logically and carefully by way of concepts, categories, propositions, abstract properties, and relations; to recognize universals in experience; to restrain our actions by principle; to debate and deliberate with others; to think mathematically and to construct formal systems; to think through language and other symbolic media; to do science, abiding by complex methods; to link means to ends.

What are the irrational capacities?[20] They include the capacity for sentiment and emotion; the capacity for overwhelming feelings of hatred, wrath, and jealousy but also feelings of great sublimity and awe; the capacity to will; the capacity to love from the heart; the capacity to imagine and fantasize; the capacity to have visions; the capacity for hallucinations; the capacity for fanaticism; the capacity to have "special" intuitions about reality; the capacity to dream; the power of instincts and impulses; the capacity to construct gods and cults and engage in ecstatic ceremonies; the will to believe despite reality.

Rationality is sometimes portrayed as a disengaged power of thought. In fact, rationality, as employed daily, is associated with our will, our motivational side. Our willingness to commit ourselves to rational methods is as important as knowing the methods of rational thought. Without a willingness to be rational and to reach truth, the methods go unused.

19 See Passingham, *Cognitive Neuroscience.*

20 Here I am using irrationality in the first of three senses, explained above.

Irrationality is also a natural capacity, and it too is related to will and motivation. At its worst, irrationality is against rationality. It makes rationality a slave to other faculties or needs. Irrational individuals lack the desire, capacity, or will to adopt the discipline of the rational stance, although they may simulate it with fake rationality. Irrationality subverts the function for which rationality was biologically intended: to provide correct cognitions of the world for action.

Finding the Ratio

The meaning of rationality derives from "ratio," which refers to some order in what exists, what we think, and what we do. Things make sense when we find some reason in them. They exhibit some pattern, some cause, some proportion, or some regularity. Similarly, our thinking is rational when we think carefully, putting our ideas in order. We act rationally when we link means to ends in a coherent fashion. Our actions display reason and order.

Why seek order? Because discovering the reason in things makes objects knowable and controllable. They acquire meaning. How someone makes music on a guitar makes sense when I understand the ratio of tones expressed by the strings. Discovering that certain types of bodies, e.g., atoms, obey physical laws is discovering a ratio in nature. Sometimes, we just need an ordinary reason to figure things out. We understand the furtive behaviour of a friend at a party when we realize he is trying to avoid speaking to his former wife.

The distinction between what is rational and irrational is one of the oldest distinctions in humanity's philosophical vocabulary. The two terms are conceptually inseparable. We understand rationality in contrast to irrationality and vice versa. There are four main kinds of rationality and, correspondingly, four main kinds of irrationality.

Ontological rationality: Ontological rationality is the order that appears to exist in the world. Ontological rationality seeks beliefs that describe this order. We want to be *reality informed*, i.e., to be open to what reality tells us. This is the primary assumption of philosophical realism – that true beliefs correspond to the way things are. Reality speaks to us via observations, the consequences of acting, facts, successful theorizing, failed predictions, and the perspectives of other people. The opposite of being reality informed is being *reality averse* – to avoid reality cognitively and/or emotionally. One is reality averse if one prefers conspiracy theories or wishful thinking. To be reality averse is to be ontologically irrational. It is to fail to perceive, or to misperceive, an order in the world.

What does it mean to look for order in reality? Imagine that you read a scientific work on the mathematical and physical laws that govern the planets. It inspires awe. You think of outer space as a rational order that does not depend on the human mind. Then, you turn on your television to watch a video of a nuclear weapon exploding over a major city. You say to yourself, "The world has gone mad." The wanton destruction makes no sense.

Reacting to the world as rational or irrational, to the degree it exhibits order, goes back to the beginning of civilization. The same nature that brought humans the order of the four seasons and provided water to drink and plants to eat, also brought the disorder of floods and pestilence, deadly disease, and uncontrollable storms. In ancient Greece, what was rational was the "logos" or the "word" of the world – things that could be explained by words and rational argument.

Today, ontological rationality tends to express itself *negatively* in philosophy and art, as a lack of order: Some existentialists, such as Sartre and Camus, experience the world as absurd. We have no reason to be here.[21]

Epistemic rationality: Epistemic rationality is order in the mind; thinking in an ordered, appropriate way. It is about rigorous method and logical ways of justifying beliefs. Its central value is the critical, independent mind.

The rise of humanism and a scientific spirit in the early modern era encouraged an epistemic sense of rationality. The Reformation encouraged scepticism about traditional sources of knowledge while a new scientific methodology revolutionized our views about how to use the mind. Rationality became psychological, individualized, and methodological. In science, what was rational in the world was what the individual mind could prove by mathematics and justify by empirical experiment. Rationality started from within the mind and moved outward to explain the world. Both Descartes and Bacon, the founding fathers of modern rationalism and empiricism, respectively, thought the untutored or undisciplined mind was full of bias and error. Descartes

21 Albert Camus reflected on the lack of ontological rationality in the world. Should we go on living in a world-order that is not responsive to our desires? Camus, *The Myth of Sisyphus*, 11.

proposed rules for Reason, Bacon an empirical method for science. Yet, epistemic rationality did not detach from the ancient project of discovering order in the world. Instead, scientific method, in the hands of Newton and Galileo, led to the notion of an ordered world under scientific law. But, now, epistemic rationality grounded ontological rationality.

Epistemic irrationality, then, is disorder in the mind, the failure to apply proper methods and forms of reasoning. Irrational people come up short when they aspire to be a critical, independent mind. Bacon blamed the "idols" of the mind for such irrationality, such as the pressure of other people's beliefs. Subsequent psychological study has provided a long list of cognitive biases in the mind.

Social rationality: Social rationality is order in individual and group conduct. It is practical rationality or prudence, where reason serves our interests. It is a form of reasoning prominent in economics, ethics, and politics. In this view, we, as persons or societies, are rational if we prudently pursue goals with appropriate means, while avoiding undue harm. To seek an end that does not exist or is actually harmful, or to seek it with means that are wildly inefficient, is to be socially irrational.

An enormous amount has been written on practical reasoning, going back to Aristotle. Its modern form was provided by psychological explanations of human understanding from Locke and Hume to Bentham and beyond. The starting point are individuals who seek to fulfil their desires and utilities. Contract theorists, from Hobbes to Locke to Rousseau, argued that it was in the self-interest of individuals to agree to live in a rule-ordered society.

In recent years, economists, political scientists, and philosophers have sought to explain how economic and social decisions are the result of the preferences and prudential decisions of individuals. One prominent view is "rational choice theory." Individuals are treated as highly rational agents who take into account available information, the probabilities of events, and the costs and benefits.[22] Groups also seek to act prudentially. How can societies make "cogent aggregate judgments" about the welfare of its citizens?[23] How to avoid decisions that are arbitrary or foolish? This issue is studied, for example, by proponents of "social

22 The idealized assumptions of rational choice theory have many critics. See Green and Shapiro, *Pathologies of Rational Choice Theory*.

23 Sen, "The Possibility of Social Choice," 66.

choice theory," especially as developed in the mid-1900s by economist Kenneth Arrow.[24] Social choice theory is a determined attempt to avoid social irrationality.

Social rationality has an important sub-species, what I call moral rationality. Moral rationality is the attempt to act on the morally best beliefs possible, as individuals or as groups. "Best" means promoting moral ends and abiding by moral principles. Given the plurality of moral systems, "morally best" can be interpreted in varying ways. But, in all forms of moral rationality, moral considerations enter into our social rationality. They urge us to go beyond self-interested prudence by impartially considering the good of all affected parties, and by pursuing the common human good. We are morally rational (and objective) when we seek just and impartial decisions in society. Otherwise, we are morally irrational. Moral rationality looms large in public debates where government policies are assessed. It influences the procedures of social institutions and officials, such as when they hire employees, award contracts, or judge court cases. People insist that officials make decisions based on objective criteria in line with the moral aims of equality and fairness. People distinguish between objective reasons, such as hiring on the basis of merit, and subjective reasons, such as hiring on the basis of nepotism or racial prejudice.

Public rationality: Public rationality is a species of social irrationality. It is a way of thinking, feeling, and acting in the public sphere, where groups discuss, negotiate, and approve measures – laws, policies, reforms – on matters that have serious impact on citizens. Many countries do not have publics, defined as citizens able to participate in meaningful political discourse and decision making. A country may be a dictatorship. But in most democracies, we can speak about publics attempting to come together to pursue the common good.[25] Public rationality is moderate, informed, deliberation among citizens seeking the common good. Public irrationality is immoderate, reality averse verbal attacks by groups against other groups. Public irrationality as forms of thinking, acting, and communicating that weaken, or make impossible, democratic processes and practices, mainly in the political sphere. I call public irrationality communicative violence.

24 See Arrow, *Social Choice and Individual Values.*

25 On the definition of publics and kinds of publics (and democracies), see chapter 4 of my *Ethical Journalism in a Populist Age.*

These forms of rationality and irrationality have been interpreted in varying ways by different philosophies, cultures, and historical eras. In a changing world, the task for a culture is to decide which conception of rationality and irrationality it wishes to embrace.

All So Human

Humans have distinct forms of rationality and irrationality, given our advanced capabilities for thinking, language, and nuanced emotion. There is no great divide in mental powers in the animal kingdom. Instead, the differences tend to be matters of degree concerning some capacity. Some species have better visual or auditory perception than others; other species have better memory or a better capacity to plan and think. Nonetheless, the differences in degree are important and can distinguish a species from other species.

Such is the case with human rationality. To see why human rationality is distinct, consider John Searle's discussion of why apes have rationality but it is different from human rationality. He considers an experiment with chimpanzees during the First World War conducted by the famous animal psychologist Wolfgang Kohler.[26] He put an ape in an environment containing a box, a stick, and a bunch of bananas high up out of reach. The ape figured out how to get the bananas. He moved the box under the bananas, got the stick, climbed onto the box, reached up with the stick, and brought down the bananas. Searle says the ape displayed a type of rationality that humans display. But, he adds, there are many other types of rationality available to humans in which the ape cannot engage. *Reasoning about future events*: the ape cannot figure out how to organize conduct and available time to achieve a goal in the distant future. Many human decisions are based on long-term reasoning: decisions about our career, what kind of family to have, and whom to marry. Humans think about how to allocate their time prior to death or over a lifetime. *Conflicting reasons*: humans make decisions among conflicting means and goals, and they make sophisticated calculations about them. The ape does not. *A gap between desires and reasons*: humans, unlike apes, have reasons not dependent on their desires. We have desire-independent reasons, based on duties, promises,

26 Searle, *Rationality in Action*, 1–4. See also Kohler, *The Mentality of Apes.*

social roles, and contracts. For example, we have a reason to pay a debt, even if we do not desire to do so; a defence attorney has a duty to defend a notorious criminal even if she does not desire to do so. *Rationality is linked to selfhood*: the ape has a limited conception of himself as an agent capable of assuming responsibility for decisions in the past.

Humans display distinct forms of irrationality and madness. Shakespeare's Othello commits an envy-driven, rash murder of his wife, Desdemona, based on Iago's slender, manipulated evidence of her unfaithfulness. After the murder, upon learning of his wife's innocence, Othello says he should be remembered as one who "loved not wisely but too well" and kills himself. I agree with the "not wisely" but dissent from the "too well." I would substitute "too irrationally." One misunderstands this play of envy, betrayal, jealousy, power-seeking, and racism if one thinks Othello's consuming irrationality is simply some overwhelming passion. Othello's irrationality is possible only because he is (otherwise) rational. He is able to think, represent the world, imagine scenarios, put thoughts into language, and adhere to social norms, such as spousal faithfulness. Similarly, Hamlet is a multi-levelled tale of madness combined with rational cunning, fuelled by agonizing thoughts of the betrayal of one's father. A non-human animal could not experience such forms of psychological drama and irrationality.

SECTION 3: IRRATIONALITY BY DEGREE

From Trivial to Debilitating

The four kinds of rationality and irrationality are logical categories that help us traverse the terrain of irrationality. But it is not enough. The categories are too static to give us a true feel for the dynamic of irrationality. Irrationality, typically, is not a static, binary condition: either you are completely irrational or not. Irrationality comes in degrees, ranging from an insignificant bias to debilitating psychosis. Our irrationalities vary in length, frequency, and intensity. Almost everyone displays irrational or unwise conduct from time to time. Many people live with some phobia or some small obsession. Are people who erupt into road rage on the highway temporarily irrational? It appears so. Irrationality exhibits degrees of intensity, from the irritating narcissist at social gatherings who talks only of herself and the political ideologue who won't listen to facts, to the anxious world of the neurotic. If we are psychopaths, we are social predators who are irrational not because we cannot reason or plan but because we lack basic human feelings, like empathy for others.[27] Rationality depends not only on the ability to reason abstractly. It also depends on the capacity to have a wide range of human experiences, from empathy to the voice of conscience.

As our irrationality becomes more intense, our thinking loses its robust connections to reality. We become detached from what Dewey called intelligent interaction with the environment.[28] The mind begins to operate under its own imperious impulses and imaginings. Increasingly, we are ontologically irrational. Also, we misapply norms of rational thought or let subjective impulses warp judgment. We are epistemically irrational.

We can place forms of irrationality on a continuum from insignificant to significant. On the insignificant pole, there are *occasional/inconsequential irrationalities.* Examples are superstitions to improve sports performance – the hockey goaltender who carries a lucky charm – or a minor obsession, e.g., following football teams online. Or, a minor delusion – believing that Mary thinks I am sexy. Next along the continuum are *persistent/significant irrationalities*: Examples include ignoring contradictions in one's beliefs. On Sunday, a businessman holds to a pious Christian belief of kindness to others but, on Monday, when he returns to the office, he treats employees with disrespect and meanness.

The next stop on the continuum is *pathological/systematic irrationalities.* These irrationalities are deep and harmful. They are pathological because they impair or disable the person, or cause serious harm to others. Among them are paranoia, narcissism, delusional mindsets, and so on. These pathologies can prompt an unreasonable enmity to strangers.

Finally, we reach extreme forms of irrationality or *psychotic irrationalities.* Psychosis may be regarded as a severe and unusual mental disturbance of individuals secluded in institutions. This view ignores, in history, the many psychotic actions of leaders and groups in society against innocent persons. What are we to call Stalin's paranoid murder of up to forty million people or today's terrorist beheadings of journalists, other than psychotic irrationalities?

27 Hare, *Without Conscience: The Disturbing World of the Psychopaths Among Us*, xi.
28 Dewey, *Experience and Nature*, 358.

Grey Zones

Between rationality and irrationality, there is a large grey zone where we refrain from calling things rational or irrational, or we are not sure what to call them.

Ordinary errors are not cases of irrationality. To err is human, not irrational, where mistakes are routine and without serious consequence. We make mistakes in working with data, e.g., we misread a road map or add up numbers incorrectly. I also rule out eccentric conduct. When I lived in Vancouver, a man would walk by my home every day singing arias in full voice. Such conduct is eccentric but not irrational.

I exclude from this book discussions about individuals born with serious mental incapacities or individuals whose mind is impaired by dementia or Alzheimer's disease. Also, I am not interested in analyzing irrationalities caused by brain damage. Recall, for example, neurologist Oliver Sacks's case of a brain-damaged man who mistook his wife for a hat.[29] Brain injuries blur the line between rational and irrational. For example, Damasio analyzed the case of Phineas Gage, a foreman who suffered severe brain damage due to an explosion when Gage was laying down railway track in Vermont during the mid-nineteenth century. After the accident, Gage appeared rational. He was able to hold conversations, ask questions, and recall his actions prior to the explosion. But his character dramatically changed. He cared little for social conventions, cursed in front of others, cared little about planning, and consistently made decisions to his disadvantage.[30] Was Gage rational or irrational or a bit of both?

Prejudgment and Prejudice

Irrational intolerance has many names. Sometimes it is called prejudice. Other times it is dismissed as a stereotype. Gordon Allport, in *The Nature of Prejudice*, said prejudice is a form of categorical thinking, i.e., placing something into a category. Categorization is the "basis for prejudgment" upon which orderly living depends.[31] This muddies the water, logically. Prejudice is *not* just any type of categorization or prejudgment.

29 Sacks, *The Man Who Mistook His Wife for a Hat*, 8–22.

30 See Damasio, *Descartes' Error*, chapters 1 and 2.

31 Allport, *The Nature of Prejudice*, 6.

Let us start over.

Prejudgment is the primary concept. Prejudice, stereotypes, and intolerant attitudes are kinds of prejudgment. To prejudge is to put objects into categories before one obtains all relevant data. It can also include ignoring counterdata and accepting questionable data.

Sometimes, prejudgment is necessary and useful; sometimes, it is not necessary and harmful. When driving my car to the airport, my perceptual system is constantly and quickly recognizing objects and categorizing them – as a stop light, a pedestrian in the crosswalk, an on-coming truck, and so on. I do not have time to wait for the arrival of all relevant data. I do not stop the car and examine every object to conclusively verify that they are as they appear. I need to make judgments based on partial data. This is necessary and useful prejudgment.

In contrast, a racial prejudice or a social stereotype is an unnecessary swift and harmful prejudgment. I conclude that a person is of a certain type, an Irishman, and conclude immediately and falsely that he has certain qualities, like being a drunk. The judgment is made based on limited evidence or attention to individual differences. The problems with racial and cultural stereotypes are manifold. There is, in most cases, no dire need to quickly judge people racially or ethnically or religiously. Since these judgments may harm others, we should refrain from quick judgment. Another problem is the stereotype's rigidity. Good prejudgment at least seeks as many facts as time allows, but people who judge someone prejudicially lack a concern for facts, even when they are available. And no amount of facts will change their view.

Prejudice is more than a negative opinion of someone. Prejudice is bias and hostility towards the other. Prejudice is "a pattern of hostility in interpersonal relations which is directed against an entire group, or against its individual members; it fulfills a specific irrational function for its bearer."[32] What irrational function? It fulfills some irrational desire, unreasonable fear, or delusional goal. Or, it makes insecure people feel superior. Its rigidity is due to the fact that the prejudice is *rooted in* irrational parts of our human nature and hence can't easily be

32 Ackerman and Jahoda, *Anti-Semitism and Emotional Disorder*, 4.

altered by logical, rational thought. Therefore, we have a responsibility to critique our social categories.[33]

Tolerance is from the Latin *tolerans*, which means to forbear and endure. Tolerance can endure in two ways: (a) a person accepts the other's ethnic origins, views, or practices without dislike, dismay, or protest or (b) a person dislikes and disapproves of the other's origins, views, or practices but "puts up with it." To be intolerant is to "not put up" with the other. It is to seek censorship or discriminatory policies against people of certain groups. The decision to be tolerant or intolerant should be based on reason. There are many things, e.g., someone's expression of their viewpoint on an issue, that are rational (and good) to tolerate. Other things, e.g., sexual abuse of children, are horrendous, and it would be irrational to tolerate. The irrationality of prejudicial intolerance, e.g., hating someone for the colour of their skin, makes it objectionable.

Rosnow said prejudice is "any unreasonable attitude that is unusually resistant to rational influences."[34] Allport defined prejudice as a "feeling, favorable or unfavorable, toward a person or thing, prior to, or not based on, actual experience."[35] Is not being "resistant to rational influences" and believing things "not based on experience" – where persistent – a feature of irrationality? Indeed, it is. There is an important link between intolerance and irrationality.

SECTION 4: IRRATIONALITY AND CULTURE

Promoters of extreme irrationality do not occur in a vacuum. They emerge at a specific time in a specific culture, surrounded by citizens anxious about the future. This air of anxiety is the psychological basis without which extremism would never grow. The promoters twist existing ideas about society into extreme forms.

Extremism inherits *ways of making* the rational and irrational distinction. Every culture is a zone of contending ratios about the proper order

33 The need to critique our categories is shown by the influence of culture on even allegedly objective scientists. For example, the first psychological research into prejudice, in the 1920s, sought to prove the correctness of white supremacy – the mental superiority of the white race. See Garth, "A Review of Race Psychology."

34 Rosnow, "Poultry and Prejudice," 54.

35 Allport, *The Nature of Prejudice*, 6.

in life and society. Many of these ratios are troublesome, even irrational, infected with prejudices or utopian thinking divorced from reality. They parade as a matter of common sense, espousing a simple solution to complex problems.

Culture provides the raw material for extreme philosophies.

It is important, therefore, to look at how cultures make the distinction between rationality and irrationality and how they use it to justify wars, crusades, pogroms, social reform, or conservative crack-downs on progressives.

Rhetoric of Irrationality

When we use the terms "rationality" and "irrationality" to discuss public figures or social issues, what type of language do we use?

Typically, it is not the strict language of logic. Nor is it the voice of a neutral observer. It is the pragmatic language of rhetoric, the language of an agent seeking goals. It is the language of persuasion. The rhetoric uses metaphors, analogies, dramatic examples, and narratives that seek to affect people emotionally, causing fear, disgust, or hope. The more intense the debate and the higher the stakes, the more heated the language.[36]

Citizens, as rhetoricians, paint rationality and irrationality in attractive or unattractive colours. They borrow terms from other areas – morality, aesthetics, or religion. They *use* basic distinctions to make things happen. For instance, we call a leader irrational in the hope that others will call on him to step down, or we call a solution to a social problem irrational in the hope that people will oppose it. To call something rational or irrational becomes a social act.

The social history of the rational–irrational distinction is a history of how people have used the distinction to maintain their social position, to support a hierarchy, to protect a way of thinking or a system of belief, or to justify a way of government. Therefore, at any given time, we need to ask why *this* conception of rationality or irrationality is dominant in *that* society and note how the conception is used to characterize groups

36 Rhetoric, in my view, does not equate with falsehood or manipulative language. Rhetoric is an important form of social communication and can be used well or poorly.

and practices. We also ask about the relationship between ideas and power. Consider, for example, strong versions of conservatism. The view that rationality is order in the world is extended to society: People should support leaders, hierarchies, and forms of government that maintain order in society. This may legitimate an unjust status quo, e.g., it justifies the oppression of rebellious "irrational" lower classes. It may be asserted that to create disorder is to go against an order established by God or nature.

Over the centuries, established power, whether the Medici in Florence or the capitalist monopolies of modern society, identify rationality with methods that channel or repress sources of chaos and dissent. For centuries, leaders have stayed alert to the chaos outside their walls, whether they lived in the gilded corridors of the Vatican, walked the rationally ordered gardens of the Palace of Versailles, or strode confidently down Wall Street.

Swings and Ruptures

Rivalry among social classes, or some other clash of interests, swings the pendulum as groups assert their own view of what is rational.

There have been four major swings of the rational–irrational pendulum in Western history: (1) the rise of rationalism in classical Greece and then the return of the irrational;[37] (2) the eclipse of Greek rationalism by faith during medieval Christianity; (3) the ascendency of scientific rationality in the early modern era and the Enlightenment, and its critique by romanticism and reactionary conservatism; and (4) the rejection of modernity and its technological rationality by decadent or alienated writers, artists, and composers.

Each swing contains component swings and tensions which spread across the social spectrum – swings in art, in popular movements, in provocative new theories, and new social practices. Tangential questions are raised, from the nature of knowledge, mind, and God to the possibility of immortality. Political questions are raised about legitimate authority. The debate stirs up a swirling cloud of disagreements. Like a dust storm, the disturbance covers all in its path.

37 I explore this swing in chapter 2.

When the pendulum swings in a culture, there is rupture. Rupture in ideology, values, and practices. Ruptures give life to rebellion. In return, adherents of prevailing ideologies resist and, like the Catholics of the counter-Reformation, launch a counterrevolt. Fragmentation ensues. Unhappiness with the status quo can cause rupture. It can repel people backward in time in search of a better (or golden) age. In art, the Pre-Raphaelites in nineteenth-century England had a taste for medieval art and sought a return to the detail, intense colours, and complex compositions of quattrocento Italian art – before Raphael. Imitation of nature was revived as a central purpose of art.[38]

Rupture, where substantial, is not only a conflict among the intelligentsia. The rupture of the French Revolution was a dispute over ideas concerning society. But it was also a *red hot* political dispute over power forged in the caldron of class conflict, inflamed by aristocratic privilege and unequal social hierarchies. When the Catholic Church unleashed the Inquisition on Galileo, power and prestige were at stake.

Promiscuous Ideas

How do people construct arguments for notions of rationality and irrationality?

One technique is to associate rationality and irrationality with other terms. What is called irrational is decried as unnatural, diseased, wicked, lacking harmony or proportion, dark, chaotic, or ugly. What is called rational is praised as natural, healthy, virtuous or good, proportionate, and full of light. People embellish their arguments with a halo of fine-sounding terms or to a brooding set of worrisome terms. The terms come from ethics, art, design, and religion.[39]

Why do people do this? Is it simply because they lack discipline of thought? No. It is because our ideas are eager to mingle. Humans use analogies among different areas of life.

38 See Hilton, *The Pre-Raphaelites.*

39 This interconnectedness of terms occurs in science and epistemology. Scientific theories are evaluated not only empirically but also by such criteria as elegance, economy in assumptions, the coherence of propositions, and conservatism, i.e., accord with existing theories. See Thagard's *Conceptual Revolutions.*

Note what is happening, rhetorically: categories from different parts of life are being mixed, in the hope that their emotional charge will rub off on each other. If I call your proposal wicked or unnatural, I hope that the negative connotation of those terms sticks to your ideas. This does not have to be a cynical strategy. I may think that your proposal *is* wicked.

Western theologians, philosophers, artists, and political thinkers have mixed concepts from at least five different areas:

Ideas of the natural or unnatural: *x* is regarded as rational or irrational because *x* reflects what we think is natural or part of nature. *X* could be a form of gardening, a musical composition, a painting, or a form of human association (e.g., a commune close to nature). What is natural includes the Aristotelian idea of objects seeking their ideal natural form (do not acorns seek to be grand oak trees?). Natural may also reflect ideas from modern biology, such as what enhances the fitness of a species.

It follows that something is irrational because it is unnatural. For example, in medieval times, what was stunted in growth, such as a dwarf, was considered ugly and unnatural. Hence, irrational. Irrational and ugly things lack the components of a whole and integrated object (e.g., beggars with missing teeth, the handicapped with withered limbs). Or, the unnatural object has an uncommon or exaggerated feature like a protruding brow. Ancient and medieval writers used the uncommon feature to discuss the ugliness of monkeys or foreign peoples. Meanwhile, what was irrational, socially, offended some conception of what was natural, e.g., women doing work "naturally" done by men.

Ideas of the healthy or diseased: Some people claim that *x* is rational or irrational because it is healthy or diseased. For centuries, medical notions have provided metaphors for philosophical arguments about health and disease in the mind and in society. What is unhealthy shows signs of decline and degeneration. What is diseased threatens the healthy with infection and contamination. For example, the Nazis claimed that the healthy "Aryan" population was being contaminated by the Jews, while German art was becoming degenerate. Hence, the German leaders argued, it was natural and rational to eliminate the Jews as a social disease, the way a doctor cuts out a tumour from the body.

Ideas of the morally good or bad: Philosophers have argued that rationality and virtuous character go together. Plato argued that the rational soul was the good soul, where reason controls the passions and seeks the highest things.[40] Aristotle, following Plato, talked about a harmony of reason, emotion, and passion.[41] Theories of the virtuous soul, such as the Sage, depict the morally good person as radiating rationality, light, and wisdom. In religion, the good soul rejects Satan's irrational and evil temptations.

Ideas of the aesthetically good or bad: What is rational has been influenced by aesthetic notions such as being beautiful, graceful, or elegant in movement and form. A Greek sculpture, the life of a saint, a mathematical equation, a classical ballet, or a theory of planetary motion can be said to be beautiful or aesthetically pleasing. Also, using ideas from design and architecture, humans have associated rationality with the symmetrical and the simple. In contrast, the irrational has been portrayed as a jumble, heavy and ungainly, out-of-proportion, and ugly.

Ideas about the order, or disorder, of nature: Metaphysical and religious worldviews claim the world is ordered according to some ratio, such as God's plan for us, or around some other source of cosmological order. Medieval philosophy depicted the world as ordered according to a fixed chain of being from the highest being (rationally, metaphysically, morally, and aesthetically) to lesser forms of being.[42] The chain extended from God to the angels, from kings to aristocrats and clergy, from the higher social classes to the lowly peasants, from Satan to lesser demons, and finally to brute matter. Rationality is acting according to this scheme by recognizing what was "high" or "low." What is irrational is what violates this order.

Ideas of conformity or originality: Rationality has been defined as conformity with existing laws. For example, classicism asserts that works of art should conform to the laws of beauty, such as clarity of structure. In music, composers follow the laws of harmony (e.g., they avoid dissonance). To imitate natural law-like forms is to reflect the rationality of the world.

However, at least since the Renaissance, there has been an enthusiasm for non-conformity, i.e., a romantic enthusiasm for originality produced by individuals. Ideas should excite and reveal, and stimulate. The producer of such works is not an anonymous craftsman but a strong and nonconforming individual. Think of Michelangelo, Beethoven, or

40 Plato, *Republic*, 441c–448e, 1072–7.
41 Aristotle, *Nicomachean Ethics*, 1119b4–18, 141.
42 Lovejoy, *The Great Chain of Being*.

Picasso. To follow existing rules is to be less than rational or human; it is to be a machine.

These five categories do not form a tidy system of evaluation. Concepts are mixed in multitudinous ways, crossing conceptual and disciplinary boundaries. As we will see, this mixing can generate specious argument. But it would be a mistake to dismiss entirely this messy mental process. We have in such patterns of thought a wonderful "theoretical indiscipline"[43] that refuses to draw hard lines between how we respond to the world – epistemically, morally, and aesthetically. In modern terms, it is a form of cross-modal thinking, where the mind uses concepts from different sense organs. From the mixing of ideas comes much of the power of the mind. The mind is rejuvenated by new ideas and by finding analogies with things strange or different. This is the true power of experience. Experience enriches not when it is reduced to hard fact but just the opposite: when we allow ourselves the freedom to range over categories of thought and to probe the testimony (and skill) of others who inhabit different "worlds." At some point, firm method and careful verification must enter into our thinking. But until then, and even after, we should learn from this riot of unruly experiences called human life.

In summary, the mind is promiscuous. It loves to mingle ideas. Theories that incorporate rich realms of experience can be intellectually attractive and voluptuous.

SECTION 5: IRRATIONALITY AND WORLDVIEWS

Where do these sets of concepts come from? They come from worldviews, sets of beliefs about the world and what is true, rational, and good.[44]

Sovereignty of the Good

The entanglement of rationality with worldviews can be seen when social patterns or proposals for social change conflict with our moral intuitions about what is good for humans.

43 I take this term from Attali, *Noise: The Political Economy of Music*, 5.

44 Cornford pointed to the importance of identifying unstated assumptions in philosophical writings. Cornford, *The Unwritten Philosophy and Other Essays*, chapters 1 and 3.

Take, for example, how people react to the dystopian society depicted in George Orwell's famous novel, *1984*. Recall that the main character, Brian Winston, lives in the state of Oceania, which is constantly at war with the two other world powers, Eurasia and Eastasia. In Oceania, where the Party is in power, the "thought police" punish all forms of thinking and acts of dissent outside the dogmas of Groupthink. Big Brother is always watching. People are kept "happy" by taking the drug soma. Their capacity to think critically is weakened by repeating contradictory slogans such as "War is Peace."

Why does the novel make us uneasy? Democrats dislike the society's politics: its authoritarian cast. Libertarians are repelled by the lack of freedom of thought. However, I think the root of the unease runs deeper. Oceania violates a deep moral sense of what it is to be human or what it means for humans to live fully. The type of society being promoted and the type of happiness being promoted – drug-induced passivity – insults our notion of the human good. It runs up against our conviction that humans flourish when they are active, critical, and self-aware agents, where happiness is not reduced to physical pleasure or the lack of disturbing thoughts. The rationality and happiness promoted in *1984* violates our moral vision of a good life. This is the "sovereignty of the good."[45] Thinking from within our worldviews, we define and judge what is rational not only by logic or fact but also by using moral notions. And in many cases, moral notions are primary. We use substantive moral and psychological beliefs about humans and their good to object to a form of life as irrational and not worthy of humans. As Putnam says, the mental life of humans in Oceania does not fit our idea of "human cognitive flourishing."[46]

Judgments of what is rational or irrational are not context free. They are not stand-alone cognitions disconnected from our belief systems. To say that *x* is rational or irrational is to say that x is rational or irrational *relative* to a background set of beliefs and norms from logic, science, morality, and other domains. We tap into substantive beliefs about what the world is like and into substantial value judgments absorbed from our culture.

45 See Murdoch, *The Sovereignty of Good*, chapter 3.

46 Putnam, *Reason, Truth and History*, 134.

Therefore, in this book, I have not hesitated to ground my claims of what is rationality and irrationality on substantive moral and other beliefs. I talk about the irrationality of causing great harm, not just the immorality of causing great harm. I appeal to substantive beliefs which, in my estimation, most reasonable people hold. I appeal to beliefs shared by many intellectual and moral traditions.

If someone has a better set of background beliefs, bring them forward.

Perfectionism and Imperfectionism

A good example of how worldviews and cultural beliefs shape judgments of rationality and irrationality is the centuries-long influence of perfectionism.[47]

Perfectionism is a view about how the world is rationally ordered. We have already mentioned one type of perfectionism: the medieval view of nature's chain of being. Perfectionism began as the perspective of ancient Greek rationalism which sought perfect knowledge of a higher realm. Then, Christian theologians gave this pagan perfectionism a Christian interpretation, a seeking of God, as the source of perfection. It was not until relatively late in the Middle Ages that the perfectionist view of the ratio of things began to be seriously challenged by an imperfectionist movement in philosophy, art, and politics. This set in motion a swing toward the imperfect, which perfectionists declared irrational.

Perfectionism, like imperfectionism, is a general philosophy. Perfectionism is a way of seeing life and the world, even if its principles are not explicit. Simply stated, perfectionism is a love of the perfect – love of perfect objects, perfect performances, perfect forms, perfect physical shapes, perfect moral principles, or perfect (and higher) spiritual beings. The realm of the perfect is contrasted with the imperfect realm of our daily lives and the material world around us. This love of the perfect shapes our lives, our judgments, what we consider rational and a matter of knowledge, and what we consider worthy of pursuit.

47 I introduced the distinction between perfectionism and imperfectionism in *The Invention of Journalism Ethics*, 29–30.

Intellectually, perfectionism produces models of the perfect. The model could be an ideal other world, such as Heaven. If you want to experience religious perfectionism, walk into any magnificent basilica. You will not only see the architectural influence of perfectionism but feel, in its music and ceremonies, how the promise of transcendence to a perfect world still shapes the hopes of modern people.

Perfectionism does not have to be religious. It can be defined as the cognitive tendency to understand and evaluate any object by reference to some presumed perfect form of that object. A work of art may be compared to revered masterpieces of that genre. A sculpture may be compared to Michelangelo's *Moses.* One's moral character may be shaped by imitating a perfect guru. A baseball player's skills may be compared to the skills of the greatest players of the game – the gods of baseball. Perfectionism takes the common tendency to posit ideals and turns it into a metaphysics or theology. In matters of knowledge, perfectionists want knowledge to be perfect, i.e., absolute.

On the everyday level, perfectionism produces people with personalities familiar to us. Perfectionists relentlessly strive for greater improvement. They are driven to come closer and closer to perfection in some domain, often at a cost to other concerns in life. Perfectionists may be difficult to live with because they expect perfection from others. In public life, where disagreement flares, they refuse compromise on their ideal standards. The perfectionist has little tolerance for a gap between ideals and actual behaviour. There is the sports coach who will accept nothing but perfection from his team, and the parent who demands perfection from their child, never satisfied with anything they do. Perfectionists can be tyrants.

In contrast, imperfectionism – the view I hold – sees value in the imperfect object, practice, or institution even if it does not achieve the perfection of an ideal model. The imperfectionist sees beauty in the eyes of a finite human being, in their struggle or death, even if there is no Heaven. The imperfectionist believes that inquiry is rarely perfect by reaching unchallengeable findings. The complexity of the world resists perfect results. The imperfectionist is tolerant of, and sometimes positively cheerful, about living in an imperfect world.

Imperfectionists want to improve imperfect, concrete communities, not achieve utopia. They listen to ordinary people. They learn from public discourse that is not scholarly and less than perfectly rational, yet still reasonable and persuasive. Imperfectionists believe the sphere of morality is no less important because it is an imperfect human invention. Psychologically, imperfectionism is acutely aware of the good and bad sides of humans. In art, imperfectionists express what is not captured by perfectionist concepts. They do not heed the siren of perfect beauty. Imperfectionists ponder the problem of evil and suffering without false consolation from perfectionist philosophy or theology. It sees significance in the obscene and comic, the lewd and the homily. Nothing human is below its consideration. All is part of existence. There is a nobility to rude life, when left unpolished by perfectionism.

At the centre of imperfectionism is a decision to know, love, and create within the limitations of human life.

The Trinity

Perfectionism in Greco-Christian philosophy and theology stressed how life on earth is temporary, chaotic, and imperfect. Earthly objects are poor copies of idealized objects. For Plato, worldly justice is a faint copy of justice in itself, the pure form of justice. For Augustine, we are earth-bound beings racked by irrational or sinful desires.

The perfect world lacks irrationality, evil agents, cruel passions, sin, and madness. Rather, it contains angels, gods, and perfect forms. We see this world in the loving, perfect Madonna of Christian art. In Greek art, the Olympic gods are models of beauty, far above the imperfect bodies of humans. The human sphere is a second-rate world. Why that is so depends on your religion or metaphysics. But second-rate it is.

If this is true, then it seems clear what humans should do: imitate the perfect beings and seek their support by sacrifice, prayer, ecstatic communication, and other means. Artists should paint edifying and beautiful depictions of the perfect realm. This supplication of the divine is portrayed by major Western museums in their religious collections of art. The paintings on the ceilings and on the walls depict humans with eyes looking upward to the gods or angels, begging for assistance or forgiveness.

In what, exactly, does the perfection of the perfect consist?

A philosophically popular answer in Greco-Christian times was that perfection is the convergence of three perfections – perfect (or ultimate) reality, perfect goodness, and perfect beauty – in one and the same object or realm. I call this the trinity conception of perfectionism.

In Greek antiquity, the idea that beauty, goodness, and truth were related came first from Greek culture, then Plato. The idea of perfection was commonly called *kalokagathia,* which brings together *kalos* (literally translated as beautiful) and *agathos,* which means good but includes many things such as military skill and virtuous character. The person who exhibits *kalokagathia* is a person who unites into their personality different features such as courage, a largeness of spirit, persuasive speech, and physical beauty. Moral, aesthetic, and physical beauty intertwine. The human form comes close to instantiating the trinity of perfection and such people are like the gods.

For Christians, God is perfection. God is the highest reality, the most wise and all-knowing, and, hence, the most rational. God is also the perfection of moral and aesthetic goodness. Lower beings have value, rationality, and goodness relative to this absolute standard. This is Christianity's conception of ontological rationality. God is the source of ratio, or order, in the world. The Christian view mingles what is real with what is good and beautiful. In Genesis, when God rested on the seventh day, did he not judge his creation to be good and beautiful?[48]

Consider the mingling of the concepts of order, form and goodness in Augustine:

> The more things are according to measure, form, and order, the more they are surely good; but the less they are according to measure, form and order, the less good they are. Therefore, let us consider these three aspects: measure, form, and order, not to mention countless others that can be traced back to these three; well, it is precisely these three aspects – measure, form and order – that are like a general good in God's reality, both in the spirit and in the body.[49]

For centuries, this grand perfectionist cosmology would be expressed in the dualisms of perfection and imperfection: of spirit and matter, soul and body, rationality and irrationality, beautiful and ugly, light and dark, high and low. It would dominate the Western way of looking at the world. It was no mere philosophy in the abstract. It gave objective

48 I am not sure if this trinity was in the mind of John Keats when he wrote at the end of "Ode on a Grecian Urn," "Beauty is truth, truth beauty – that is all / Ye know on earth, and all ye need to know."

49 Augustine, cited in Eco, *On Ugliness,* 48.

meaning to life. It defeated death and imperfection down here on earth and offered immortality. Moreover, the perfectionist worldview provided a basis for evaluating almost anything in the world. All things find a niche in the scale from high to low.

In modern times, philosophers questioned this trinity. Empiricists such as Hume, for example, separated what "is" from what "ought" to be. Modern positivists divided facts from value. But, as we will see, it would be a large-scale cultural movement starting in late medieval times, a movement towards imperfectionism, that would do the most damage to the worldview of perfectionism.

World without Meaning

Today, the search for ratio occurs in a postmodern world where the presumption that there is some overall objective meaning or purpose to life is doubted. Like never before, we can give scientific accounts of phenomena and describe how nature works in all of its complex mechanisms and material laws. This is the great intellectual achievement of modern times. Yet it also seems that in developing a materialist worldview, disenchanted of spiritual agencies, that much has been lost. The world does not respond to the human need for meaning.

To understand this paradox, we need to distinguish between factual meaning and purpose-driven meaning. Factual meaning is a product of empirical rationality which studies the nature of objects, their properties, and the material laws that explain their behaviour. Science is an international enterprise dedicated to discovering factual meaning.

Purpose-driven meaning arises when we explain an object by appealing to conscious intention and prior design by an external mind or spiritual agency. In the creation or design of the object, there is implanted in the object some objective purpose which it naturally aims at or which fulfills its being most completely. This type of explanation has dominated Western religion and culture, often in terms of a God who creates humans within a purposeful universe. Life has objective meaning. Purposes exist in nature, objectively. Truth begins with an apprehension of that objective plan, and virtue begins with the wisdom to follow the plan.

The rise of alternate scientific explanations of nature, especially the emergence of Darwinian theory, has led to what evolutionary philosopher Michael Ruse has called the "unraveling" of belief in a purpose-driven world.[50] The whole point of Darwinian natural selection is that design in evolution is not caused by a prior, conscious designer. Design is the unintentional product of genes, species, and interactions with changing environments. There is no world designer. There is *no* objective meaning to the life of humans, no reassuring existence of a merciful God and life after death. The search for ratio is restricted to more modest inquiries into factual meaning, plus human-made cultural meanings.

Ruse pointedly summarizes the meaning of life as suggested by a Darwinian perspective:

> You are born. Then you die. It's terrifying … We came from an eternity of oblivion. We return to an eternity of oblivion. In between? We try to make sense of it all and to lead worthwhile lives. In the end, you know truly that it doesn't mean a thing.[51]

For some people, life without objective meaning and purpose is meaningless. So, it is *not* rational. That conclusion is unacceptable so they seek answers elsewhere. Given the human desire for meaning, belief in objective meaning will probably never fade away. But for Ruse and others, intellectual honesty requires that we accept the death of objective meaning in life. Their comments sound much like Zarathustra when he asked, "Have people not heard that God is dead?"[52] What Ruse can offer humans is a limited meaning created during their brief lives on earth. To many people, today, this is not enough.

50 Ruse, *A Meaning to Life*, chapter 1.
51 Ibid., 1.
52 Nietzsche, *Thus Spake Zarathustra*, 6.

2

The Revenge of the Imperfect

For I see the true state of all us that live. We are dim shapes, no more, and weightless shadows.

Odysseus[1]

The best things we have come from madness, when it is given as a gift of the god.

Socrates[2]

THIS CHAPTER EXAMINES FOUR SWINGS in the rational–irrational pendulum:

First, the swing from ancient Greek rationalism to the return of the irrational in the post-classical Hellenic world. Perfectionist Greek philosophy gives way to the dark forces of irrational cults, black magic, occult properties of objects, and pseudo-scientific teachers who promise salvation from the world.

Second, the swing within medieval times from Christian otherworldly perfectionism to a more secular, worldly imperfectionism. It begins to appear in the twelfth century and it gathers momentum by the late Middle Ages. For Christian perfectionism, nature is rationally and perfectly ordered by God and this order grounds the authority of the pope, the king and fixed social hierarchies. By the late medieval era, writers like Rabelais and others were questioning the rationality of the existing social order while celebrating the imperfect in life: our irrational capacities, the lowly, and the ugly. It was the revenge of the imperfect.

Third, the swing in religion from reliance on the sacraments and priests of an external church – an external source of authority and rationality – to a reliance on internal, individual experience, reflection, and

1 Sophocles's *Ajax*, 15.

2 Plato, *Phaedrus*, 244a, 522.

personal faith, which are the defining features of the Reformation. This spiritual movement inward encountered our irrational capacities as powerful impulses that corrupt us and cause sin. The pilgrim's progress is a struggle. One must constantly monitor one's thoughts and desires, while controlling one's wicked and irrational self. The self-monitoring is evident in the personal insecurities of Luther and Calvin. The Reformation made irrationality personal and a threat to salvation. Ironically, this notion of inner wickedness, a revival of the doctrine of original sin, was employed by leaders of the Catholic counter-Reformation to justify obedience to the pope. Sinful man needs obedience to authority – the central premise of the Catholic apologists such as Joseph de Maistre. Modern conservativism begins in this climate of fear of the irrational self.

Fourth, the swing, in the Renaissance and early modern era, from an idealistic view of politics and art to a secular, empirical approach that takes life as it is, not what it is supposed to be. It prefigures the modern secular age. With Machiavelli in politics, Caravaggio in art, and Rabelais in literature, we have examples not only of an imperfectionist perspective but also the emergence of proto-modern thinking. They take us up to the doorstep of the early modern period where a new form of rationality is emerging – the rationality of science.

RATIONALISM AND IRRATIONALISM IN CULTURE

Our rational and irrational faculties weave a tapestry of experiences. The excitement of rationally grasping a new idea, for example. Or, to be overwhelmed by an erotic desire for someone. Or, to be struck suddenly by the answer to a nagging problem as one walks a beach. Or, to experience a dream, which paints surrealistic landscapes in our minds through which we wander, lost. Only to awake, perspiring.

We experience the capacities of cooperating and competing. I study the history and musical score of an opera to enhance my understanding and emotional experience in the theatre. Or, my compulsive tendency to seek revenge conflicts with my rationality to stay calm and seek legal remedies to the offence.

This is rationality and irrationality "within." It is the phenomenology of rationality and irrationality. It is how individuals experience the activity of our faculties.

Rationality and irrationality can also be group experiences. We join in the irrational passions of a lynching mob, or we slum with struggling artists who share a passion for counterculture works that are deliberately strange and irrational. Or, we experience the values of scientific rationality by being enculturated into the rational priesthood of science – we achieve a PhD in biology and go to work in a science lab.

We can experience rationality and irrationality as "without." We experience irrationality as a feature of external objects and social structures. For instance, we may come to think of our entire society, or major parts of it, as rational or irrational in spirit. We may feel that our society is too rational in thinking that science and technology have all the answers and too cold and logical in how we interact with others. We complain that modern society has no place for the emotions and passions, for genuine warmth and fellow-feeling. Or, we may be discouraged by the fact that, although society is now scientific, people still act against rationality, listening to fake preachers, fake facts, and messages designed to manipulate our irrational side. Our society may attract or alienate us.

From these experiences, we develop views about the worth of the rational and irrational components of our human nature. Sometimes, those views are implicit. People have not formulated their theory of rationalism or irrationalism. Instead, a belief in rationalism or irrationalism are implied in their judgments and actions. Historically, theorists have constructed explicit philosophies about rationality and irrationality and have favoured rationalism or irrationalism as the path to knowledge or to live happy lives. Rationalism includes philosophical rationalism from Plato to the modern rationalism of Descartes, Spinoza, Leibniz, and others. Philosophical rationalism includes metaphysical views, such as Hegel's sweeping claim that the evolution of the world is an evolution towards greater states of rationality.

These varying views, implicit or explicit, can be placed into two very large categories: rationalism and irrationalism. We can study how these views have played a part in developing or criticizing cultural trends and movements. Throughout this book we will observe, within cultural history, how views that subscribe to rationalism or irrationalism come into opposition, such as the conflict between Enlightenment reason and romanticism. We will also see how, at times, rationalism and irrationalism become entangled, as the worldviews of individuals or movements contain elements of both rationalism and irrationalism.

In simple terms, rationalism and irrationalism can be defined as asserting contradictory theses. Rationalists think the rational capacities are dominant or influential powers, shaping human nature, inquiry, and the lives of most people – and that influence is a good thing, overall. Irrationalists think the opposite: the irrational capacities are dominant or influential powers, shaping human nature, inquiry, and the lives of most people – and that influence is a good thing, overall. Rationalism and irrationalism can also be understood as opposite normative claims: even if rationality (or irrationality) is not a significant or dominant force in life or in society, it *ought* to be. For the rationalist, knowledge and truth are best approached through the deliberate, methodical use of reason, i.e., epistemic rationality. Without a significant commitment to rationality, people and groups tend to act unwisely or intolerably. For the irrationalist, the repression or exclusion of irrational capacities leads to arid thinking and frustrated individuals. Our irrational capacities are sources of energy, imagination, and inspiration.

This characterization of rationalism and irrationalism may seem too simplistic. We can all think of proper and improper uses of our rational and irrational capacities. Also, why can't rational and irrational capacities be judiciously combined, rather than insist on one set of capacities as dominant and perhaps exclusive of the other?[3]

The first step toward improving the rationalism–irrationalism distinction is to build into their definitions the good and bad uses of these capacities. I do this by distinguishing between dark and creative rationalism, and dark and creative irrationalism. Dark rationalism is the use of rational capacities for dark, dubious, or immoral ends. For example, dark rationalism supports rational and technological utopias (in history or in science fiction) that would lead to inhumane societies. I consider B.F. Skinner's behaviourist utopia, in his 1948 novel *Walden Two*, a dark and hyperrational society. Orwell's *1984* is a dystopia created by extreme, and troublesome, uses of rationality, e.g., through wall-to-wall propaganda, to create irrationally obedient citizens. The novel is about dark irrationality: the use of rationally derived techniques to *destroy* other people's rationality. Perhaps, a better example is Arthur Koestler's classic on the ideology and immorality of Soviet communism, *Darkness*

3 I discuss the holism of our psychological capacities later in the book.

at Noon. Rationality and ideology combine to produce not just a revolution but Stalinist atrocities.[4] One is left with a scepticism about the value of rationality and a heightened awareness of how our rational capacities can be misused.

Creative rationalism is the proper and moral use of rational capacities to guide knowledge seeking, social planning, problem solving, and professional work. Rationality should be put to creative, positive, use.

Dark irrationalism is the use of irrational capacities for dark, dubious, or immoral ends. The dark forces of selfishness, envy, hatred, anger, and the desire to cruelly dominate constantly threaten the attempts of individuals and of societies to live in peace and concord. These dark impulses, within me and others, are to be controlled and channelled. Dark irrationalists, such as cult leaders, can employ irrational methods to further their interests or control others. In contrast, there is creative irrationalism. Here, the more positive irrational capacities, such as intuition, insight, and empathy, are praised as the basis for creativity, originality, or for getting us in touch with ourselves and nature. It is the irrational in humans that creates great individuals and societies.

I warn readers not to think that philosophies or trends can always be clearly divided into belonging to rationalism or irrationalism. As we will see, most major terms for movements or eras, e.g., "the age of reason," "romanticism," and "modernism," are so loosely defined that one can always question their application in real-world cases.[5] The categories of rationalism and irrationalism are introduced as an aid to conceptualizing the swings of the pendulum. They should not be treated as clear and unbridgeable dualisms. The rationalism–irrationalism distinction is, in some cases, clear; but, in other cases, it is blurred as individuals (or groups) use both reason and unreason to make their arguments, or to develop their art. The intersection of the rational and the irrational is as interesting as their opposition. Often, the rationalism–irrationalism distinction is a tangle of ideas, or, to shift the metaphor, a site of cultural

4 On Koestler's novel and the rationalism of Soviet communism, which "justified" Stalin's Great Purge of 1936–38, see Kirsch's "Assassin's Creed."

5 The lack of precision is not due to a lack of mental capacity among thinkers who use these categories. The cause is the nature of social reality, which itself lacks precision. The categories attempt to capture complex cultural phenomenon which display different, inconsistent, and contradictory features.

contention. All of this means that the swings of the pendulum are more complex and often more perplexing than indicated by any set of categories. It should come as no surprise that what is clear to logic is not always clear in the real world.

SECTION 1: RETURN OF THE GREEK IRRATIONAL

Where shall I turn for refuge? All that I was has perished … and I am abused by a fool's dream.

Ajax[6]

Dionysus and Apollo

The ancient Greeks, although known for developing reason as a tool of philosophy and science, needed no instruction in the importance of the irrational in life.

Yet this fact is lost on many. Except among experts in antiquity, there is today a lack of appreciation of how rationalism and irrationalism, in a variety of cultural forms, arose together, co-existed, borrowed ideas from each other, and then competed for public support.

Cultural expressions of Greek rationalism and irrationalism were different, to be sure, but they were not static opposites. Grasping the Greek rationalists' view of the irrational is a subtle affair. Not even the prototypical Greek rationalists such as Socrates, Plato, or Aristotle are rationalist in the narrow, modern sense of thinking that only reason counts in life. Aristotle studied the effects of music and instruments on the passions.[7] Plato was heavily influenced by religious and mystical ideas about the immortal soul. Socrates claimed to listen to an inner daemon, and may have participated in the rituals of irrational cults that induce mania and divine possession.[8]

In Plato's *Symposium*, Socrates describes the great importance of Eros in the cosmos. Eros is not just a sexual impulse. Nor is Eros a chubby,

6 Sophocles's *Ajax*, 25.

7 Aristotle, *Politics*, Chapter 7, 1341b–2b, 235–8.

8 Socrates talks about the rituals of the Corybantic cults in a way that suggests he observed or participated in such events. See Plato, *Euthydemus*, 277d–e, 714–15.

cute Cupid.[9] The Greeks viewed Eros as a powerful force that must be treated with some care because it can take over a person. Socrates agrees and makes Eros an erotic force of attraction, a sort of daemon, that runs through all areas of life, including the love of philosophy.

Nor did Plato and Aristotle dismiss the madness of people when participating in manic religious cults. Instead, they sought to explain it. They recognized the social usefulness – or cathartic function – of people expressing anxieties and emotions through irrational ceremonies. In Plato's *Phaedrus*, Socrates states that "the best things we have come from madness, when it is given as a gift of the god." He distinguishes four divine types of madness, as distinguished from madness caused by disease or illness. The blessings of madness come from the gods in four ways: a prophetic madness whose patron is Apollo, a ritual madness whose patron is Dionysus, a poetic madness inspired by the Muses, and an erotic madness inspired by Aphrodite and Eros.[10]

In retrospect, we see that it was impossible for philosophy, at its birth, to *not* bear the imprint of the rich Greek culture along the Aegean Sea. Greek antiquity was redolent with orgiastic cults, Orphic mysteries, Homeric myths, magic, a love of madness, oracles to divine the future, secret rites, plus meddlesome gods above and horrific underworld spirits below.

The Greeks had gods of rationality and irrationality, of order and discord.[11] There was Apollo, the god of reason, of order and light, and the prophetic deity of the Delphic Oracle. There was Dionysus, the god of irrationality, of wine and fertility, of ritual madness.

Nietzsche identified the origin of Greek tragedy in the intertwining of reason, represented by Apollo, and the irrational, represented by Dionysus.[12] The Greek theatrical tradition contains some of the greatest plays ever written about madness. There is Sophocles's *Ajax*, a hero of the Trojan War who ends with a dishonouring insanity, a delusional slaughter of animals, and a heroic suicide. There is Euripides's *Medea*, portrayed as the dark murderer of her own children to avenge the unfaithful Jason of the Argonauts.

9 The Romans turned Eros into Cupid.

10 Plato, *Phaedrus*, 244a–5b; 265a–b, 522–3; 542–3.

11 The Greek god of discord is Eris, who helped to start the Trojan War. The god of order is Harmonia or Harmony.

12 Nietzsche, *The Birth of Tragedy and the Case of Wagner*, 33.

We tend to think about Greek culture as the classical tradition that created the beautiful white marble statues of Athena and Apollo, that produced the symmetry – created by rational calculation – of the Temple of Athena on the Acropolis in Athens. We fail to recall that turbulent political struggles, class conflict, and blood-letting were the background from which these masterpieces of rational sculpture and architecture arose.

Nor is classical mythology a realm of perfect beings. It is an evil and cruel realm. Saturn devoured his own children. There are the satyrs, those woodland gods associated with Dionysus. Their animal features symbolize their irrational passions. Consider the strange creatures in the Greek underworld, or consider the ugly and wicked monsters like Medusa, with her hair composed of snakes, who could turn observers into stone. Also, there is the dangerous siren, half woman and half bird, who coaxed men, against their reason, to listen to their songs and die in shipwreck. To make matters worse, the gods fight among themselves constantly. A number of them kill, dismember, boil, and then eat the children of opponents. They make other gods go mad so they will mistakenly kill their own children.[13]

The Greeks viewed irrational impulses as literally awesome and difficult to understand. They were experienced as an external force that takes possession of the mind. Hence the tendency to blame the gods. Aristotle says people overtaken by passion are like people who are "asleep, mad, or drunk."[14]

If you want to fully appreciate the complex interplay of unreason and reason in ancient Greece literature, look no further than the Orphic legend of Dionysus or the taming of the Furies.

Dionysus was born the son of Zeus through the latter's incestuous relationship with his daughter Persephone. At the direction of Hera, the infant Dionysus was torn to pieces, cooked, and eaten by the evil Titans. But his heart was saved by Athena, and he was resurrected by Zeus. Zeus struck the Titans with lightning, and they were consumed by fire. From their ashes came the first humans, who had the evil nature of the Titans and the divine nature of the gods. Men, therefore, are

13 See Graves, *The Greek Myths*.

14 Aristotle, *Nicomachean Ethics*, 1147a, 1041.

partly good and partly bad. Among philosophers, this myth of man's dual nature came to correspond to the dualism of an impure body and our immortal soul (or reason).

Now turn to the end of Aeschylus's trilogy of tragedies *Oresteia*[15] where the Furies, the three goddesses of revenge and unbridled anger, come under the control of society. In the play, Athena introduces legal institutions to end the endless cycle of vengeance among quarreling citizens. Blood guilt will now be replaced by rational law. The Furies experience a remarkable transformation. At the beginning of the third drama, the Furies are disgusting creatures that exist to do evil. They are creatures of the irrational. Athena persuades them to be members of the city of Athens. Further, they are given a special place in the underworld. The moral: the forces of rationality and irrational must combine to create an ordered society.[16]

The shift to rational philosophy was gradual. From fragments of writings, we discern that ancient Greek philosophy was a mixture of reason and proto-science with rhetoric, myth, mysticism, and literary style. Xenophanes, for example, wrote in hexameters, the style of Greek epic poetry.[17] In the *Timaeus*, Plato explains the origin of the world with the assistance of a grand cosmological myth. The limits of reason were acknowledged. Heraclitus is known for saying we cannot step into the same river twice, because it is in flux. Yet he also notes that the river maintains its identity; it "gathers" itself and it persists amid change.[18] Such complexity was a challenge for reason, with its static categories of thought. Philosophers also transformed ideas from religion. Pythagoras, influenced by purification religions, held that the human soul needed purification through contemplation to escape the cycle of reincarnation.[19]

15 The *Oresteia* is a trilogy of tragedies by Aeschylus in the fifth century BC. It contains the murder of Agamemnon by Clytemnestra, the murder of Clytemnestra by Orestes, the trial of Orestes, the end of the curse on the House of Atreus, and the taming of the Furies.

16 For a perspective on this transformation, see Nussbaum, *Anger and Forgiveness*, 1–5.

17 Kirk and Raven, *The Pre-Socratic Philosophers*, 169.

18 Ibid., 196.

19 We have no writings of Pythagoras, only what his followers and contemporaries said about him. On Pythagoras, see Gottlieb, *The Dream of Reason*, 25–6.

Yet, amid irrationalism, the presumption that reality had a rational structure could be held with great emotion. For example, the Pythagoreans of sixth century BC were shocked by the discovery of irrational numbers, such as the square root of 2. Why shocked? Because the Pythagoreans believed that nature had a rational, mathematical basis.[20] Everything from the order of the planets to musical harmonies could be explained by whole rational numbers and their ratios. Then it was discovered that the length of the diagonal of a square with each side 1 unit in length was the square root of 2. But the square root of 2 cannot be represented as a whole number or a ratio of a whole number. The square root of 2 is not 1 × 1. Hence it is an irrational number. Tradition has it that distraught Pythagoreans had Hippasus of Metapontum, the discoverer of this irrational number, murdered at sea so his discovery would die with him.

The Greek Enlightenment

Rational inquiry first appears during the Ionian Enlightenment[21] of the seventh and sixth centuries BC as Greece transitioned from archaic times to the classical period. The enlightenment was led by the first natural philosophers such as Thales, Heraclitus, and Anaximander. The movement began on the Ionian coast of western Anatolia in Miletus and Samos.[22] Thales, one of the Seven Sages of Greece, appears to have sparked the movement by predicting a solar eclipse that actually occurred. Physicians, historians, and natural philosophers constructed naturalistic explanations of a lawful nature. The natural philosophies were joined by rational theories in mathematics, logic, and geometry and, in time, by the philosophical systems of Plato and Aristotle. These rational constructions departed from religion and myth, which based their stories on revelations, myth, oracles, and the weight of tradition.[23]

20 Kitto, *The Greeks*, 192.

21 See Freely, *Flame of Miletus.*

22 Stimulated by contact with Egypt, Persia, and Babylon, these philosophers were freethinkers who had no emperor to placate or sacred book to defend. See Boardman, Griffin, and Murray, *The Oxford History of Greece and the Hellenistic World*, 126–41.

23 The poet Pindar explained the annual flooding of the Nile as the result of a god moving his feet. Herodotus considered natural causes, including the melting of snow on distant mountains.

Natural philosophers postulated non-divine causes for phenomena. These causes explained the ratio of things. The causes were intelligible to the mind but not evident to the senses. It was a deeper reality. One had to identify the fundamental natural elements that combined to create the world as it appears. Anaximander's *On Nature* gave explanations of the origin of the universe and of life. The basic stuff for Anaximenes was air; for Empedocles, the four elements of water, fire, air, and earth.

The fifth century produced a second stage in rationalism, the Fifth Century Enlightenment.[24] It occurred as Greek cities, especially Athens, enjoyed a golden age of empire and of outstanding artistic and philosophical creation.[25] Philosophy turned towards society and the nature of humans. Socrates stressed care of the soul. Plato established his academy in 383 BC. This set the stage for an intellectual confrontation. On one side were the sophists, those itinerant teachers who espoused the relativism of social norms and taught rhetoric and other public skills. On the other side were rationalists such as Plato who sought a non-relative knowledge of man and the universe.[26] Sophists said society was a rational, self-interested, compact among men. Its rules were conventional. Nature, however, was governed by universal laws.

The development of critical rationalism created a gap between the beliefs of the elites and the beliefs of ordinary Greeks. This gap would play a role in the reaction against rationalism. The philosophical theories, whether it be a world of atoms circulating in a void or a Platonic world of abstract forms, were not attractive to many common people. The latter continued to worship the gods and to follow custom. The rationalists' critical methods sounded arrogant and threatening to the polis, as young people flocked to hear the charismatic sophists. There was a growing resentment toward the debunking proofs of the philosophers.

24 See Guthrie, *The Fifth Century Enlightenment.*

25 The golden age of Athens began in 478 BC after the defeat of the Persian invasion. It led to the Athenian empire whose wealth could afford Pericles's (495–429 BC) development of the Acropolis. Athens, which was able to afford half its population on the public payroll, was the dominant naval power in the Greek world. Playwrights Aeschylus, Sophocles, and Euripides lived in fifth-century BC Athens, as did the historians Herodotus and Thucydides, the physician Hippocrates, and the philosophers Plato and Socrates.

26 Guthrie argues that this early relativism was sparked by the fifth-century Enlightenment when regular contact with other cultures showed the plurality of human beliefs. Guthrie, *The Fifth Century Enlightenment.*

Philosophers tended to be an aristocratic class separate from the ordinary people, despite the gregarious Socrates. One of the things that strikes you when you read about the first philosophers, such as Parmenides in Italy or Empedocles in Sicily, is that they were wealthy and "nearly all leading men in their cities."[27] The sophists aspired to be considered elite professionals. Socrates (470–399 BC), born of a midwife and whose wife was a vegetable seller, seems to be the exception. When Plato, born to a prominent family, set up his academy, philosophy became institutionalized, an education for upper-class students.

The distance between the philosopher and the people was expressed by the disdaining Epicurus: "The things which I know, the multitude disapproves, and of what the multitude approves, I know nothing."[28] Protagoras, in Plato's *Protagoras,* objects to Socrates asking about the opinions of ordinary people because they "will say whatever occurs to them."[29] Even Socrates, who believes in helping people seek wisdom, complains that the feelings of anger, pleasure, love, and fear hinder the knowledge of ordinary people. Their knowledge is a slave "utterly dragged about" by unreason.[30] It did not help that rationalists made fun of the beliefs of fellow citizens.[31] Xenophanes attacked the myths in Homer and Hesiod as immoral and denied the validity of divination, omens, and oracles. Xenophanes underlined the relativity of religious belief by observing that if horses and cattle could draw, "horses would draw the forms of the gods like horses, and cattle like cattle."[32] Heraclitus declared that "character is destiny." In one phrase he placed in doubt the traditional belief that actions were dictated by gods, fate, or luck.

In the heyday of classical Athens, rationalist philosophy became overly optimistic and intellectualist. For elites, the golden age was not a lost paradise, as stated in Hesiod. It was just ahead. This optimism would come crashing down during the city's disastrous thirty-one-year Peloponnesian War (431–400 BC) with Sparta and its allies. In the end,

27 Hamlyn, *Being a Philosopher,* 8.

28 Cited in Dodds, *The Greeks and the Irrational,* 241.

29 Plato, *Protagoras,* 353a, 782.

30 Ibid., 352b–c, 782.

31 On the rationalists' criticism of myth and magic, see Lloyd, *Magic, Reason and Experience,* chapter 1.

32 Kirk and Raven, *The Pre-Socratic Philosophers,* 169.

Athens became subject to Sparta and was ruled by tyrants. Meanwhile, philosophers such as Socrates and Protagoras, and later the stoics, affirmed the intellectualist dicta that "virtue is knowledge" – that humans could never act against what they *knew* was true or right. Immoral acts were a mistake in judgment or perception. The mistakes could be corrected by habit and training, according to the sophists, or corrected by philosophy, according to Socrates.[33] This was a departure from the usual good sense of the Greeks to take the irrational seriously.

Philosophers made the intellect divine or immortal, the defining part of humans. Aristotle, in the *Nicomachean Ethics*, identifies the intellect as the divine in man. He urges humans to not settle for the mortal and mediocre but to "make ourselves immortal" and to "strain every nerve to live in accordance with the best thing in us."[34] Zeno, founder of stoicism, claimed that our intellect was part of the divine substance. This intellectualism would continue after the classical period in the practical philosophies of the epicureans, sceptics, and stoics, which claimed to know the key to a happy life. Epicurus held that to maintain a constant meditation on philosophical truths is to "live like a God among men."[35] Happiness or mental tranquility was achieved by an exercise of reason. Reason and meditation could exclude troublesome emotions and beliefs, such as the fear of death, which were due to an error in judgment.

Perfectionist Rationality

A central strand in Greek rationalism was its inclination towards perfectionism. There was the mathematical perfectionism of Pythagoras, the perfectionism of abstract forms in Plato, the perfectionism of a unified or one reality in Parmenides, and the mystic perfectionism of the universe according to the last great philosopher of antiquity, Plotinus.

33 Socrates believed that this knowledge was achieved through a long, inward reflection on what was truly valuable in life, a process that led to wisdom. On Socrates's ideal of individual enlightenment, see Cornford, *The Unwritten Philosophy and Other Essays*, 59–60.

34 Aristotle, *Nicomachean Ethics*, 1177b–8a, 1105.

35 Cited in Dodds, *The Greeks and the Irrational*, 238.

Greek perfectionism is evident in aesthetics. Greek sculptors sought to depict an ideal or perfect beauty. Beauty was rational: it consisted of objects that had a correct proportion and harmony (or symmetry) among their parts. Then they set out to provide mathematical accounts of how to create proportionate works. In the fifth century BC, Polykleitos was instrumental in creating the Greek style in sculpture. Polykleitos literally wrote the canon of beauty in sculpture. He wrote a treatise called the Kanon and then created a statue of a male nude known as Kanon. The statue, which no longer exists, is said to have embodied the rules of ideal proportion. The treatise stressed how a statue should be composed of parts related to one another according to a system of mathematical proportions – a mathematics of sculpture.

Marcus Vitruvius Pollio, known as Vitruvius, was a Roman architect and civil engineer of the first century BC. He adapted the Greek ideal of rational form and proportion to architecture. In his *On Architecture*, Vitruvius became famous for his triad of ideal features for architecture: utility, strength, and beauty. The book also contained an influential discussion of perfect proportion in architecture and in the human body. The book had enormous influence on Renaissance writers when the text – the only surviving text of ancient Greek architecture – was discovered in the fifteenth century in an abbey. It prompted Leonardo Da Vinci, about 1490, to create the famous drawing of *Vitruvian Man*.[36] The drawing depicts a man in two superimposed positions with his arms and legs apart and inscribed in a circle and square. The drawing and text are sometimes called the Canon of Proportions.

These same values were applied to morality. Virtuous actions were proportionate and wise responses. They made humans admirable and beautiful. Aristotle explained the virtues as a middle road between irrational extremes, a golden mean.[37]

In Greek philosophy, perfectionism led to the search for absolute knowledge, not relative to human perspective or interest, contra the sophists. Philosophers arrived at abstract truths, proofs, and ideal models about society and human nature. The truths were claimed to be universal and known with certainty. They also developed a form for expressing this higher knowledge – the deductive argument, as in

36 Chisholm, "Vitruvius."

37 Aristotle, *Nicomachean Ethics*, book II, chapter 6, 1106a20–7a25, 957–9.

Euclidean geometry where theorems are deduced, with necessity, from self-evident principles.

Parmenides, in the early fifth century BC, was a perfectionist who followed "the way of truth." In a poem, *On Nature*, Parmenides provides what may be the first sustained argument in the history of philosophy. He writes that, while on a search for knowledge, a goddess taught him the difference between absolute truth and the beliefs of ordinary people. Truth lies far "from the beaten track of men." The opinions of mortals are false yet they have the "semblance of being."[38] The way of seeming is what happens to be the case, while the way of truth is knowledge held fast by "necessity" such that "no judgement of mortals may outstrip you."

With Plato, in the *Republic*, the search for knowledge is a rigorous, austere path from the beliefs of experience to mathematical ideas and finally to philosophical truths. Plato postulated a perfect reality of forms of justice, goodness, beauty, and equality which the soul strives to know and exemplify. Plato's psychology of the soul makes beauty the opposite of the ugly. Beauty is order in the soul, a matter of harmony and proportion. The just soul is directed by reason which controls the emotions and the passions. Plato uses the promiscuity of ideas to link morality and aesthetics: "The absence of grace, rhythm, harmony is nearly allied to baseness of thought and expression and baseness of character; whereas their presence goes without that moral excellence and self-mastery of which they are the embodiment."[39]

Plato's rational perfectionism is on display in the allegory of the soul in his *Phaedrus*.[40] The soul is a chariot where reason – the charioteer – controls two winged horses, one noble and potentially moral, and another base and usually against reason. The latter represents desires and impulses. Driving the chariot is difficult amid the quarrels between the horses. Reason's task is to firmly control the base horse, enlist the support of the noble horse, and direct the chariot upward toward truth.

For what sort of knowledge does Plato search? Listen to this passage from his *Phaedrus*, where the immortal soul and the minds of gods are nourished in heaven by pure knowledge of justice, self-control, and

38 Kirk and Raven, *The Presocratic Philosophers*, 267.

39 Plato, *Republic*, Trans. Francis Cornford, book III, chapter III, 400a–1a, 89–90.

40 Plato, *Phaedrus*, 246a–54e, 524–53, 506–56.

other things, as they really exist. They see the real: "Knowledge – not the knowledge that is close to change; that becomes different as it knows the different things which we consider real down here. No, it is the knowledge of what really is what it is."[41] This is perfectionist rationalism.

Plotinus, living in Rome during the third century AD, wrote *The Enneads* to entrench Platonic perfectionism in the philosophy and religion of his day.[42] Like Parmenides, he taught, in mystical fashion, that there is a supreme, totally transcendent One from which there emanates Intellect and Soul. The latter creates the world according to Plato's perfect forms. Plotinus adopts the trinity of perfectionism. He identifies this One, or ultimate reality, with the ultimate Good and the ultimate Beauty.

Plotinus defines human nature relative to this metaphysical perfectionism. A person's true essence lies within himself, in their rational soul, which, through mediation and purification, can come into union with the rational One. The human journey is pre-given by our nature. We "journey to the Good" which is the primal reality.[43] Happiness is a being that lives fully, by possessing "the Supreme Good."[44] The wise person "will give to the body all that he sees to be useful and possible, but he himself remains a member of another order."[45] Plotinus pulls out all the stops on his intellectual organ when he describes the morally evil soul:

> Let us then suppose an ugly soul, dissolute, unrighteous, teeming with all the lusts; torn by internal discord and the envies of its pettiness ... perverse in all its impulses, the friend of unclean pleasures, living the life of abandonment to bodily sensation and delighting in its deformity ... dragged ever as it is towards the outer, the lower, the dark ... So, we may justly say, a Soul becomes ugly – by something foisted upon it, by sinking itself into the alien, by a fall, a descent into body, into Matter.[46]

41 Ibid., 247d–e, 525.

42 Plotinus is called a "neo-Platonist," a term invented by nineteenth-century scholars of antiquity.

43 Plotinus, *The Enneads*, 24.

44 Ibid., 33.

45 Ibid., 44.

46 Ibid., 50–1.

I can hardly think of a classical passage which better embodies, fiercely, the ideas of perfectionism, the trinity of concepts, and the promiscuity of ideas – complete with reference to disease, the unclean, the wanton, the dark, the lower, and the contaminated.

The Irrational Redux

At this point, one might think that the swing towards perfectionist rationalism was an unstoppable cultural force. Surely, it would continue to banish the irrational from Greek society.

All the signs were good. From the fifth century BC to the end of the third century BC, Greek science was transformed from a collection of isolated observations, mixed with a priori speculations, into a system of disciplines. Greek thought establishes the first, organized, approaches to the sciences of physics, botany, biology, zoology, geography, and logic, not to mention the history of language, and the politics of human society. In astronomy and mathematics, intellectual thought reached a level not attained again until at least the sixteenth century.

Yet, the pendulum is fickle.

Just as rationalism appeared triumphant, the pendulum started to swing back towards irrationality, i.e., toward customs and rituals that rely on something other than reason. The reaction against rationalism was already underway in the fifth century and it grows in the fourth and third centuries BC, and onward, as the Greek world becomes dominated by empires.

What caused the return of the irrational? There are many theories. Some suggestions are not helpful, such as saying that the Greeks had become decadent. But, why? Others point to an internal breakdown within rationalism, which was running out of intellectual steam. It "wasted away as a fire burns itself out for lack of fuel," stated Nilsson.[47] But *why* did it run out of fuel? Another explanation is political. The collapse of the power of Athens dented the prestige and optimism of the golden age rationalists. Reason prospers in better times. This seems insufficient to explain the long and complex drift towards the irrational.

47 Nilsson, *Greek Piety*, 140.

Other explanations look to psychological and cultural factors. They are more helpful. Erwin Rohde, the nineteenth-century Greek scholar, claimed that the origin of the cults and the Greek belief in the soul's immortality was a desire to escape the limits of ordinary existence by participating in religious mysteries.[48] This same escapism encouraged a turning away from rational philosophy. Dodds explained the decline as an escape from freedom, "the unconscious flight from the heavy burden of individual choice which an open society lays upon its members."[49] Dodds says the ordinary Greek "bolted from the horrified prospect"[50] of freedom and found comfort in the determinism of astrology and in a conservativism described by Plato's *Laws.*

My view is not far from these psychological ruminations. Humans crave meaning, reassuring sameness, and a sense of security as much as they do freedom and originality. This was a time when the individual was beginning to emerge as an autonomous entity. In philosophy and in drama, humans were being told to question themselves. Socrates insisted that the unexamined life was not worth living. Yet, old ideas die hard. Even in the late fifth century, Jason, at the end of Euripides's *Medea,* explains his wife's murders as the act of a meddlesome god. However, at the same time, Euripides, across his plays, was portraying evil as part of human nature. Medea's depravity, was no mere error in judgment. It was part of her nature. People saw the impotence of reason on stage, at the very time philosophers were insisting on a life of reason, beyond the security of tradition. Confused, people returned to the old protection of the gods while intellectuals withdrew into their own world. Irrational practices and teachings made a comeback. They filled a cultural vacuum.

The sad truth is the old truth that humans can only take so much reality. Psychologically, people ran from these disturbing raw truths of human responsibility to the arms of magic and magic men. And, while they ran from a world stripped naked spiritually, they struck out at the philosophers. Thus began the prosecution of intellectuals on religious

48 Rohde, *Psyche,* vol. 2, 258.

49 Dodds, *The Greeks and the Irrational,* 252. Dodds cites Erich Fromm's *Escape from Freedom,* published in 1941, which explains authoritarianism as an escape from modern life.

50 Dodds, *The Greeks and the Irrational,* 246.

grounds in Athens in the second half of the fifth century. In Athens, from 432 BC onward, to doubt the gods and to question astrology was a criminal act. Charges were laid against Anaxagoras, Diagoras of Melos, Protagoras, and Euripides. Banishments and other penalties were applied. The populace turned on Socrates in 399 BC, a year after the end of the Peloponnesian War, when Socrates was seventy years old. The intolerance was the beginning of the return of the irrational.[51]

What forms of irrationality would mark the decades and centuries ahead?

The first sign of degeneration was an increased demand for magical healing. It transformed Asclepius from a minor figure to a major god. It made his temple as famous as Lourdes, in France, is today.[52] The surge in his popularity began with the Plague of Athens in 430 BC. It prompted people to look to magic for protection. Ironically, they did so as scientific Hippocratic treatises on medicine were being published. A second sign was the interest in foreign cults, such as from Thrace, of a highly emotional and orgiastic kind. These groups developed quickly during and after the Peloponnesian War. There was also a revival of Pythagorism as a cult. Another sign was the popularity of using magic to attack your enemies. People inscribed a curse from an underworld power on a tablet and placed it in a dead man's grave. Then something bad would allegedly happen to a living person. This black magic worried Greek officials.

By the second century BC, we see the emergence of pseudo-scientific literature on life, health, and nature by anonymous authors claiming access to divine revelation. The ideas were dressed up to look like the rational philosophy and science of the past.[53] Astrology became widely popular in Greece for the first time and practical manuals appeared. In addition, the second century BC saw the development of an irrational doctrine that would influence late antiquity and the Middle Ages: the theory of occult properties or forces in certain animals, plants, and precious stones. Even the mainstream schools of Greek philosophy became not just practical, but "dealers in salvation."[54] Marcus Aurelias

51 Ibid., 244.

52 Asclepius is a Greek mythological god of medicine, a son of Apollo. He is usually depicted with his holy snake.

53 Dodds, *The Greeks and the Irrational*, 245.

54 Ibid., 248.

defined the stoic man in religious-sounding terms as "a kind of priest and minister of the gods."[55]

There was no greater sign of the return of the irrational than the reaction of the father of Western rationalism, Plato. As he grew old, Plato came to see the limits of his idea that humans should construct an ideal republic ruled by philosopher kings. He developed a deep appreciation for the power of the irrational in society. In his *Laws*, Plato opts for a right-wing state where laws repress people's passions and self-interests. He proposed laws to make doubting religious beliefs a crime, despite his formative experience, as a young man, of the death of Socrates. Plato imagined a theocratic government based on the union of religion and state. It anticipated the theocracies of the Middle Ages.

Cornford summarizes Plato's final views:

> If the ideal State of the *Laws* had ever become a living reality, we might imagine … Socrates arraigned for a second trial before the Nocturnal Council; and confronted by Plato in the president's chair. Socrates had held out the same gift of unlimited freedom and self-rule; and Plato had foreseen that mankind would not be able to bear it.[56]

These examples can be seen as a return to the past. But they can also be seen as pointing to the future. Greece was entering not an Age of Reason but a period of slow intellectual decline. For centuries, the Hellenic world would produce no poet as good as Theocritus, no scientist as good as Eratosthenes, no mathematician as good as Euclid or Archimedes, and no philosopher who could rival Plato or Aristotle. This is not to dismiss Hellenistic thought and art entirely. There were interesting and high-quality writings and art in that long period. But the mountain peaks of the classical era were often much higher than the peaks of Hellenistic times.

The return of the irrational would make possible the triumph of Christianity based on faith in revelation and an authoritarian church.

55 Aurelius, *Meditations*, book 3, section 4, 56.
56 Cornford, *The Unwritten Philosophy*, 67.

SECTION 2: DARK IRRATIONALISM

Dark irrationalism believes that life and nature is not rational and orderly; rather it is conflictual, violent, extreme in passion, and prone to aggression. The world is "red in tooth and claw" not only among tigers in the jungle but among humans in society. The bloody, crazed people who kill each other at the end of Shakespeare's *Hamlet* is a more realistic depiction of human nature than Rousseau's depiction of humans as naturally virtuous in a state of nature.

The dark irrationalist stresses anxieties and fears and is sometimes fascinated by the destructive potential of irrational forces, such as out-of-control wrath, fierce jealousy, and the desire to dominate others. The dark irrationalist, historically, has leaned toward authoritarian views of society and hierarchical religion to restrain the dark forces.

With the advent of Christianity, the tension of rationalism and irrationalism would be given a religious interpretation. Christian philosophy would interpret the world as originating in a metaphysical battle between God and Satan for the loyalty of humans, a battle between good and evil. The devil would be director-general of the forces of dark irrationalism. Yet irrationalism was not *entirely* set against man's hopes for salvation. Humans could also seek support in other irrational faculties, such as the capacity to have ecstatic, erotic visions of Christ and his realm.[57]

Christianity in the Middle Ages was a counter-rationalist movement to distinguish Christian practice from Greek confidence in reason and the Roman love of worldly things. What mattered was strength of will, discipline over one's body, and obedience to scripture, not reason or the pursuit of world power. What mattered was a pragmatic commitment to *being* a Christian. Christian philosophy was faith supplemented

57 Recall the religious passion of St Theresa (1515–1582). Theresa was a Spanish, Carmelite nun and mystic whose work played a part in the counter-Reformation. In her autobiography, she described the ecstasy of her encounter with an angel carrying a spear on fire. "He appeared to me to be thrusting it at times into my heart … and to leave me all on fire with a great love of God. The pain was so great, that it made me moan; and yet so surpassing was the sweetness of this excessive pain, that I could not wish to be rid of it … It is a caressing of love so sweet which now takes place between the soul and God." *The Autobiography of St Theresa*, 17. Bernini immortalized the experience in his sculpture, *The Ecstasy of Saint Teresa*. See a copy at https://en.wikipedia.org/wiki/Ecstasy_of_Saint_Teresa#/media/File:Ecstasy_of_Saint_Teresa_September_2015-2a.jpg.

by reason. Augustine was thoroughly conversant with Greek philosophy. Aquinas used Aristotelian concepts to create his synthetic theology. But even here, the use of rationality was instrumental, for higher religious purposes.

In the seventeenth and eighteenth centuries, Catholics launched a counter-Reformation against both the Protestantism and the Enlightenment in France.[58] Anti-Enlightenment conservatives argued that rationalism was naïve because it ignored our dark side. Consequently, for every Enlightenment group, like the Bavarian Illuminati,[59] there was a counterbalancing group, such as the Jesuits. For every liberal Voltaire, there was a conservative Joseph de Maistre. For every movement toward liberty of thought, there was a conservative movement to control thought, such as the Inquisition. Even Enlightenment thinkers clashed. In England, Edmund Burke attacked Rousseau and the French revolutionaries for causing a Reign of Terror. Their error was excessive rationalism: trying to use reason alone to construct a new society from scratch.[60]

Dark Night of the Yearning Soul

Given Christian psychology, many Christians endured dark nights of the yearning soul. This high anxiety was felt not only by ordinary pilgrims. It marked the psychology of Christianity's greatest leaders, from Augustine in the fifth century to Martin Luther and John Calvin during the Reformation.

No one can read Augustine's *Confessions*, especially his conversion to Christianity in book 8, without being struck by the great divisions in his psyche, his intense, debilitating anxiety and, at times, his irrationality. His was a tormented mind. In these passages, we find a source for the dualisms of Christianity for centuries forward – body versus soul, flesh

58 "Counter-Enlightenment" is a term of relatively recent coinage, probably invented by Nietzsche in "Nachgelassene Fragmente" in 1877. But it was Berlin who established the term in the history of ideas, beginning with "The Counter Enlightenment" published in 1973. See Nietzsche, "Nachgelassene Fragmente," 478.

59 Historically, the name usually refers to the Bavarian Illuminati, an Enlightenment-era secret society founded in 1776. The society's goals were to oppose superstition, obscurantism, religious influence over public life, and abuses of state power.

60 Burke, *Reflections on the Revolution in France*, 274.

versus spirit, scripture versus reason, the will to purify the body versus the will for tainting pleasures. Augustine blames his own sinful youth, his "carnal habit," on man's sinful nature going back to Adam.[61] Augustine says he sinned not so much for the pleasure but for the pleasure of being wicked. Sinning was motivated by self-destructive urges. Augustine refers to bodily impulses as "filth" and "shameful." He concludes: "So my two wills, one old, one new, one carnal, one spiritual, were in conflict, and they wasted my soul by their discord … *the flesh lusteth against the Spirit and the spirit against the flesh.*"[62] In a garden under a fig tree, Augustine's dark night of the soul ends with overwhelming tears and the embracement of God.

Centuries later, Luther and Calvin would articulate a dark, Augustinian view of human nature and would experience anxieties and struggles that visited Augustine in his garden of conversion. For Luther, since humans are corrupt, fear and discipline must rule. Every inner thought requires scrutiny, and every sin needs absolution. Luther's anxiety about his sinfulness reached almost absurd proportions as a young friar at the Augustinian monastery in Wittenberg. To ward off the devil, he confessed frequently, often daily, and for as long as six hours on one occasion. Luther biographer Roland Bainton commented on Luther's obsessive confessional mania: "the soul must be searched and the memory ransacked and the motives probed," running through lists of deadly sins in case he forgot one. His superiors sought in vain to persuade him that this worrying was the "scruples of a sick soul."[63]

It would be helpful if Christians could use reason alone to perfect their souls, as Pythagoras and others believed. But that option was not available. Luther declared that "reason is a whore." Reason could be used for any purpose. Moreover, reason was not a guide to salvation. "Since God is true and one, he is utterly incomprehensible and inaccessible to human reason," said Luther.[64] What Luther needed, above all, was certainty. He found it in faith, in a direct relationship with God,

61 Augustine, *The Confessions*, 178.

62 Ibid., 168. Italics in original text.

63 Bainton, *Here I Stand*, 54.

64 This was not a new idea. Logician William of Ockham (1285–1349) contended that one cannot demonstrate, by reason, God's existence. It can be known only by faith.

a "surer reality."[65] Bainton observed, perhaps controversially, that Luther's religion had elements of a "very primitive character, which hark back to the childhood of the race" such as a "savage's fear of a malevolent deity."[66]

Luther increased the insecurity of the individual Christian by asserting that not even a life devoted to good works secured salvation. One must always be anxious of one's progress to God. Outside the confessional, Luther was stirred by frightening insecurities which resemble paranoia. He panicked at unexpected events, he feared nightmares, such as waking at dusk to look into the eyes of someone who had come to take his life. Fiends were ever-present. Luther's anxiety led him to an explanation: Man's nature is corrupt. The entire man needs forgiveness.

The same psychology characterized John Calvin. In a chapter called "Calvin's Anxiety," William Bouwsma analyzed the reformer's anxious soul. Calvin had an almost pathological fear of disorder – disorder in thinking, in categories of objects, and in society. Sin is frightening because it gives rise to chaos in world. "All human desires are evil," Calvin declared, "and we charge them with sin, not as they are natural but because they are disordered; and we affirm that they are inordinate because nothing pure or sincere can proceed from a corrupted and polluted nature."[67] Calvin saw nature as a turbulent sphere where natural events are discrete and even miraculous. Generalizations about the world were limited. He attacked the "madness" of "philosophers who understood nature as an intelligible order."[68]

For Calvin, God could, at any time, change the face of the earth, sending thunderstorms or creating violent seas. Such events impressed and frightened Calvin. It was God wanting to "shake the world." Both the integrity of the universe and the survival of mankind were constantly dependant on God's will. He approved of clear boundaries around nations, peoples, and social hierarchies. For example, he disliked men who acted in an effeminate manner or women who took up the manners or dress of men. Boundaries maintain order. The result was that Calvin was a conservative social thinker and a dualistic thinker in philosophy, dividing things into darkness or light, black or white. Another

65 Haille, *Luther: An Experiment in Bibliography*, 124–6.
66 Bainton, *Here I Stand*, 41.
67 Bouwsma, *John Calvin*, 22.
68 Cited in Bouwsma, *John Calvin*, 33.

dualism was "we and they," between the faithful and unfaithful, the righteous and the unrighteous (such as heretics), compatriots and aliens – a tendency that helps to explain his antisemitic sentiments.[69]

Calvin was anxious about impurity and pollution. Sins resemble "filth" and make us "loathsome in the sight of God." At times, his pollution anxiety reached extremes: "We take nothing from the womb but pure filth," he wrote. "The seething spring of sin is so deep and abundant that vices are always bubbling up from it to bespatter and stain what is otherwise pure." We have not one sin but are "buried by innumerable impurities ... all human works, if judged according to their own worth, are nothing but filth and defilement ... it is certain that there is no one who is not covered with infinite filth." Sinners, he said, make the whole earth "stink" and the doctrines of Rome were "stinking excrement."[70] However, Calvin recognized that anxiety had its uses. It made Christianity attractive to souls fearful of death and God's judgment on their sins.

Joseph de Maistre: Blood and Obedience

A biographical note on Joseph-Marie, Comte de Maistre (1753–1821), might say this: The French arch-conservative philosopher, diplomat, and lawyer was a dominant, intellectual voice of the counter-Enlightenment. Before and after the French revolution, de Maistre constructed arguments for monarchy, the supremacy of the church (ultramontanism), and strong authoritarian government to guide a violent and sinful humanity. In calling for the restoration of the House of Bourbon to the throne of France, he claimed that rationalism and liberalism were responsible for the Reign of Terror.

This note leaves the reader with little appreciation for how the intellectual force and inner hatred of all things liberal combined in this co-founder of modern conservatism, with Englishman Edmund Burke. Compared with de Maistre, the conservativism of Burke is tame, although better known. Today, de Maistre is regarded as a somewhat obscure and not-that-interesting figure, the voice of a fading aristocratic order seeking to stop the march of history. But this dismissive portrait misses his importance. De Maistre is, as Isaiah Berlin has argued in a vivid sketch

69 Bouwsma, *John Calvin*, 33–6.
70 Cited in Bouwsma, *John Calvin*, 36.

of the man's ideas, an unstinting dark irrationalist, fascinated by power and blood. His writings are a precursor of totalitarian thought.[71] De Maistre bluntly raises problems for liberalism, such as the source of legitimate authority in non-monarchial states. He makes assertions that were unpalatable to his liberal opponents, e.g., their view of man as rational and perfectible is a myth. To know the blind spots of liberalism, examine de Maistre.

De Maistre was not a lone voice in the wilderness. He belonged to the counter-Enlightenment, stirred to life by the French Revolution. Educated by Jesuits, he was influenced, early on, by the French mystic Louis-Claude de Saint Martin who rejected materialism. De Maistre shared the views of fideists who saw little role for reason in religion. His views were similar to other Catholic reactionaries and antisemites, such as Louis de Bonald and Charles Maurras. De Maistre began what Stern calls a "conservative revolt" in politics,[72] a severe conservatism that ranges from reactionary Catholic groups in the eighteenth century and antisemitic fronts in France during the nineteenth century to modern fascist parties in Germany and on to today's extreme, intolerant populism. Enlightenment liberals, who believed ardently in the progress of reason and science, did not see this nationalist, conservative revolt coming. They mis-diagnosed its manifestations and underestimated its attraction for the masses.

Although he shared their interest in the irrational, de Maistre was no romanticist. He would have no truck with idealizations of peasants or the freedom of the individual. He detested romantics almost as much as he hated the liberals who had undermined what he regarded as a social order established by God. De Maistre yearned for Christian unity. He rejected equality and described tolerance as a "stupid indifference." His irrationalism was expressed by a love of esoteric and occult ideas in the Bible.

De Maistre's fame was established by his political books such as *On the Pope, Essay on the Generative Principle of Political Constitutions and other Human Institutions* and *Considerations on France.* He argued that the royalist and papist traditions were superior to rational social constructions precisely because the former were *irrational,* i.e., they did not try to

71 See Berlin, "Joseph de Maistre and the Origins of Fascism."

72 Stern, *The Politics of Cultural Despair,* xx–xxii.

provide an answer to liberal questions about their validity. He claimed that constitutions are not products of reason but come from God. Attempts to rationally justify government only leads to disagreement on the legitimacy of the existing government and to violence and chaos. The legitimacy of government must be based on religious grounds – the authority of an all-powerful God who approves of leaders capable of firm action. Citizens must not be allowed to question this God-based social order.[73] Submission and obedience is the role of the good citizen. Not surprisingly, de Maistre, in a late work, argued for a theodicy, written in the form of a dialogue. It takes its inspiration from Plato's *Laws*.[74]

Against the "satanic" forces of atheistic liberalism, de Maistre would give no quarter. Men were not rational, sociable, and peace-loving. Men were moved by instinct, prejudice, and blind faith. Humans were irrational and cruel – with a love for violence and war. Life was, by divine design, a realm of conflict and suffering, "sin and retribution, bloodshed and war" – the natural condition of fallen man, cursed by original sin. He decried the wickedness and stupidity of men left to themselves, without God. As a total believer and violent hater, he resembled in psychology, but not in belief, the revolutionary anti-royalist Jacobins of France under the dangerous Maximillian Robespierre. Like many of the Jacobins, de Maistre had a fascination for blood, death, and the public executioner.

So, there was an enemy to be opposed. Who was the enemy? De Maistre had a long list: liberals, atheists, Protestants, Jansenists, freemasons, Jews, democrats, utilitarians, journalists, and more. They work constantly and secretly to undermine the old social order. They are "la sect" which must be stopped at all costs. De Maistre exhibits a paranoid view of society shared by future totalitarian leaders and apocalyptic cults. Berlin summarizes de Maistre's view of society as "a network of sinful, helpless human beings, torn by contradictory desires, driven hither and thither by forces too violent for their control, too destructive to be justified by a comfortable rationalist formula."[75] Humans can only achieve anything under the stern guidance of God, the pope, and the king.

De Maistre has been praised and condemned. The *Catholic Encyclopedia* of 1910 praised his learning, dialectic, and "strong, lively" style. However,

73 On these political arguments, see Bradley, *A Modern Maistre.*

74 See Kochin, "How Joseph de Maistre Read Plato's Laws."

75 Berlin, "Joseph de Maistre and the Origins of Fascism," 174.

French author Emile Faguet called him "a fierce absolutist ... apostle of the murderous trinity composed of Pope, King, and Hangman."[76] No doubt, many of us find it difficult to relate to his philosophy since de Maistre starts from different premises, such as the existence of God and original sin, the divine right of kings, and the infallibility of the church. He provided a necessary correction of optimistic liberalism by stressing conflict in life. Yet many people rightly refuse to follow him to his right-wing political conclusions. Also, while his arguments are learned, his dogmatism is disturbing. He will allow no objection, no dissent. He uses every scrap of logic and fact to support a pre-given worldview that is incapable of error or alteration. Nonetheless, there is a grave irony in the oft-heard criticism of de Maistre that he was looking backwards to a time that was passing. In looking backward, de Maistre described the future. The authoritarian societies of the past would become the totalitarian societies of the future. Regrettably, he was more visionary than many of his critics. He was, Berlin concludes, a "terrifying prophet of our day."[77]

SECTION 3: REVENGE OF THE IMPERFECT

Gargantua and Pantagruel

In 1532, a book called *Pantagruel of the Dipsodes* appeared in France written under the pseudonym Alcofribas Nasier. It caused a stir. So did four other novels that formed the series, *The Life of Gargantua and Pantagruel.*

The series was by Francois Rabelais (1483–1553), friar, priest, physician, bawdy sceptic, laughing philosopher, deeply learned Greek scholar, friend and advisor to bishops and aristocracy, and yet one of the "heretics of the first class."[78] Plus one more accolade: one of France's greatest and boldest writers.

76 Cited in Berlin, "Joseph de Maistre and the Origins of Fascism," 94.

77 Berlin, "Joseph de Maistre and the Origins of Fascism," 174.

78 Rabelais's authorship of the fifth book, published after his death, is disputed. In 1564, the Council of Trent of the Catholic Church declared Rabelais to be one of the "heretics of the first class" and his writings to be placed on the list of prohibited works.

Unsmiling officials and preachers disliked and feared him. Others – many in the upper classes who were at the pointed end of his barbs – could not help but enjoy his raucous tales.

Calvin preached against him. Stodgy theologians at the Sorbonne sought to ban his books. Yet kings Francois I and Henry II, and several powerful cardinals, gave him protection. Rabelais never lost his common touch, always aware of how the ordinary people lived. Many of his ideas came from popular literature. Yet he was not an easy, popular writer to read at the beach. His writings swirled with deep ideas and demanded much from readers. He is one of the foremost proponents of philosophical comedy, making deep points without dry logic. He preached pantagruelism – a "smiling, charitable, and tolerant wisdom which accepts and surmounts misfortune."[79] As a devout Christian, his novels frequently underline the idea that what we do with God's grace is important. We should not waste it. Even the bawdiness had its serious point. The earthy acknowledgment of our physical nature, of sex and gluttony, is an amusing entry into a wider reflection of what humans are.

Published between 1532 and 1564, the books were grotesque and rowdy tales of two knock-about aristocratic giants. As a doctor, Rabelais wrote a lot about the body and what it ingests and excretes. The giants discourse such lewd matters as farting and the best type of arse-wipe. But this was not just slapstick or grossness for its own sake. Readers were presented with characters whose lives were free from mendacious officials and redolent with wine-induced good spirits. Beneath the robust humour was a searing, rollicking criticism of the social and political order, educational schemes, and religious authority. Hell was depicted as not such a bad place after all, although the souls there worked at poorly paid jobs. Judges were ridiculed. The church's wealth was criticized.

In the first book, *Pantagruel*, Pantagruel becomes friends with Panurge, who loves to party.[80] Together with some friends, they intoxicate an army of invading giants, burn their camp, and drown the survivors in urine. Epistemon, a friend, is decapitated in the battle. Panurge sews his head back on to his body.[81]Absurdism is a frequent device. For

79 Rabelais, *Gargantua and Pantagruel*, xiv.

80 Ibid., 50.

81 Ibid., 145.

example, in the first book, the height of the two giants is not specified but their size varies from chapter to chapter. In one chapter, Pantagruel can fit inside a courtroom to argue his case. But in another chapter, the giant is much larger. The narrator resides in Pantagruel's mouth for six months and discovers an entire nation living among his teeth.

In the second book, *Gargantuan*, Gargantua is born in a strange manner, after an eleven-month pregnancy.[82] The labour is so great that his mother threatens to castrate his father, Lord Grandgousier. Gargantua comes into the world through his mother's left ear and 17,913 cows are employed to provide his daily milk. His huge penis delights the nurses. After an education at home, Pantagruel travels to Paris where the crowds bother him so much that he drowns thousands of them in a flood of urine. Gargantua helps to build the abbey of Theleme, which is unlike any monastery. It is an "anti-church" open to monks and nuns. There are no clocks in sight. The men and women live in Renaissance luxury. The Thelemites abide by one rule: "Do what thou wilt."[83] The text is a critique of educational practices and a call for free schooling.

Over time, the criticism grows more biting and the philosophizing more prevalent. The third book is largely a philosophical dialogue between Pantagruel and Panurge. The *Fourth Book of Pantagruel* was published at a time when Rabelais had substantial protection from the upper classes and could dare to be even more critical and outspoken. To settle whether Pantagruel should marry, he and Panurge take a long sea voyage to consult the Oracle of Bacbuc (Divine Bottle). Amid the hilarity, Rabelais criticizes the arrogance and wealth of the Roman Catholic Church. He ridicules political leaders and popular superstitions.

Rabelais's novels have sparked different responses from readers, literary critics, and conservative social institutions. The *Catholic Encyclopedia* of 1913 chastised Rabelais as a "pagan" attacking "all the past." His writing "has the charm of the rabble" and as a whole "exercises a baneful influence."[84] Today, Rabelais is considered to be the father of the

82 Ibid., 215.
83 Ibid., 373.
84 Bertrin, "Francois Rabelais," 131.

modern novel and one of France's greatest writers.[85] I have no doubt that he is a master of the French language and an inspired satirist. Yet I understand why the significance of his work may be puzzling. How can these tales amount to great literature, to something important?

To explain Rabelais's stature, his biographers call him a Christian humanist[86] and an Erasmian.[87] Such characterizations are accurate, but I feel the terms are too weak and academic to capture why he attracts, as well as repels, ordinary people and the critic.

The answer was inadvertently provided by the aforementioned *Catholic Encyclopedia* of 1913: Rabelais appeals not just to free-thinking aristocrats but to the rabble. Precisely. Rabelais struck fear into a good number of members of the upper classes and the church. Public attraction to a skilled satirist made officials nervous because the novels appeared at the beginning of the Reformation, the religious wars in France, and the counterreformation. What the Roman Catholic Church did *not* need at this time was a powerful critic popular with the masses. Politics, class resentments, and a growing desire for a new social order are at the heart of Rabelais's work. It is fitting, then, that Rabelais found the allegory of the giants in the popular literature of his day – the folklore legend of a giant Gargantua sold as an inexpensive pamphlet or chapbook at the fairs of Lyon.[88]

For centuries, writers had satirized the lower classes as ignorant and foolish. But now it was time to turn the tables and apply the satire to the excesses and arbitrary power of the ruling classes. Rabelais makes possible the revenge of the imperfect, the lowly. The ugly. Rabelais's ethic of revolt through satire was incendiary. He made attractive the things that religious perfectionists labelled as irrational and unworthy. Rabelais was at the head of the parade of the ordinary, articulating a bold, even militant, imperfectionism that would turn the world upside down in the decades ahead and would express itself in art, architecture, and politics.

85 Jean-Marie Gustave Le Clezio, in his 2008 Nobel Prize Lecture "In the Forest of Paradoxes," on 7 December 2008, called Rabelais "the greatest writer in the French language."

86 Bowen, *Enter Rabelais, Laughing*, 5.

87 See Screech, *Rabelais*.

88 Rabelais, *Gargantua and Pantagruel*, xxvi.

This proto-modern imperfectionism was not careful and obsequious. It was increasingly willing to celebrate the body and material existence. Given these trends, it is little wonder that, in his life, Rabelais was denounced by the Sorbonne in 1543 and then the Roman Catholic Church. The French parliament suspended the sale of his fourth book in 1552. In their work, many academics were disinclined to mention his books.

Rabelais would have been convicted of heresy, and perhaps burnt at the stake, if it was not for the popularity of the works, his powerful supporters, and the fact that he lived in – and sometimes fled to – cities like Lyon, the capital of the French Renaissance, and Metz, then an imperial German free city and a republic.

The Grotesque Aesthetic

Rabelais represented a new aesthetic which, if you scratched its surface, revealed a worldview. The aesthetic was imperfectionism: art is more than what is beautiful, well-formed, pleasing, or pretty – a tranquilizer for the busy mind. It includes what is ugly, base, disproportionate, instinctual, and grotesque, even if disgusting. The glory of Rabelais's two giants was their ridiculous lack of proportion and deformity. Rabelais's *Gargantua and Pantagruel* was the "proud assertion of the rights of the body" in all of its grotesque or offensive qualities.[89]

The aesthetic of the grotesque appeals to people who find what is real in the dark and the imperfect, before a perfectionist theologian tries to put lipstick and powder on the harsh face of life. Russian literary critic Michael Bakhtin, in his analysis of Rabelais, described the emergence of a grotesque realism, a valuing of what is bodily, basic, and not beautiful – what the upper classes would call degradation.[90] I think this realism can be understood as consisting of two theses: First, a reductionist impulse which thinks that all that is abstract, spiritual, and ideal originates in the material level. For example, grand philosophies are ideologies for material power. Second, an aesthetic perspective that what was once considered lowly is an essential part of being human.

89 Bakhtin, *Rabelais and His World*, 102.
90 See Bakhtin, *Rabelais and His World*.

Whence this grotesque realism? It was not due simply to Rabelais's novels. It was a broader cultural movement. There were at least two primary sources: the growing art of the imperfect and social events such as the carnival which indulged degradation and gave free rein to the irrational.

Art of the Imperfect

Ironically, it was the medieval Christian church, despite its perfectionism, that encouraged an art of the imperfect and the lowly. Beginning in the twelfth century, this art would become, over the long term, an independent force, challenging perfectionist ideas.

Until the High Middle Ages, Christian art tended to be iconic, uninterested in natural portrayal, and hence lacking in realism. Moreover, what should be depicted in early or "paleo-Christian" art and literature was limited and controversial.[91] The crucifixion was not a suitable topic. Detailed depictions of Christ on the cross, or of the devil, were not encouraged.[92] The crucifixion was evoked through the abstract symbol of the cross. One restriction was that the Greek concept of perfect beauty could not be applied to Christ on the cross. Another restriction was the view that images and sculptures encouraged the heathen worship of idols.[93] Also, Christian art in the Byzantine Empire favoured an abstract aesthetic of icons and mosaics. The purpose of art was to express a religious meaning, not provide accurate portraits. The story of Christianity was mainly told by icons, abstract symbols, formal portraits of the Madonna, and standardized images from the life of Christ.

Eco notes how it is only in the High and late Middle Ages that paintings begin to realistically portray Christ on the cross, in a non-ideal manner.[94] He is shown as a man, bloodied and suffering on the cross,

91 "Early Christianity" extends from its origins to the first council of Nicaea (325 AD). Early Christian art extends from the earliest period of Christianity to sometime between 260 and 525, depending on one's definition of Christian art.

92 The only place in the Bible where the devil is described in detail is in the book of Revelation.

93 For example, the church's Synod of Elviram, circa 306, declared in Canon 36: "Pictures are not to be placed in churches, so that they do not become objects of worship and adoration." This canon was debated by Catholic and Protestant scholars after the Protestant Reformation.

94 Eco, *On Ugliness*, 49.

deformed by pain. They show him humiliated, mocked, and whipped as he endured the Passion. An emotive genre formed around the mourning of Christ – how Mary and friends mourned Jesus after he was taken down from the cross. In Giotto's *The Mourning of Christ*, painted about 1305, the crucified Christ is cradled in the arms of his mother.[95] Everyone, including the angels, is weeping. Or, look at Mathias Grunewald's *Crucifixion*, about 1515.[96] It was painted for the Monastery of St Anthony in Isenheim, near Colmar, Alsace. The monks cared for sufferers of the plague and skin diseases. The image of Christ is pitted with plague-like sores. The ordinary person could identify with this art because it showed the saviour as a real man suffering in the real world, like the rest of mankind. Patients at the Monastery of St Anthony saw that Christ understood their diseases.

The church increasingly needed emotional, striking paintings and sculpture to appeal to the masses. Theological and philosophical treaties would not stir the people, especially in an era of wide illiteracy. The art also served the political purpose of identifying the enemies of the church. A primary target were the Jews, depicted as hideous creatures who smiled as they tormented Christ in the Passion.[97] As Hegel wrote, "the enemies are presented to us as inwardly evil and this evil shows itself in depictions of their barbaric and ugly faces ... there enters here as a necessary feature what is unbeautiful in comparison with the beauty of Greek art."[98]

The depiction of the disfigured Christ on the cross and the dramatic scenes from his life opened the door to other forms of the art of the imperfect. The masses could be moved by negative, frightening images of what happens to people who sin and reject the church. Artists depicted the wicked, horrific, and ugly. A new genre called the "triumph of death" consisted of paintings, writings, and sculptures that reminded people that death was imminent – a reality anyone living in the Middle

95 The painting by Giotto di Bondone is now in the Scrovegni Chapel, in Padua, Italy. See a copy at https://en.wikipedia.org/wiki/Lamentation_of_Christ#/media/File:Giotto_-_Scrovegni_-_-36-_-_Lamentation_(The_Mourning_of_Christ)_adj.jpg.

96 Grunewald painted it for the Isenheim Altarpiece about 1515. It now hangs in the Museum Unterlinden, Colmar, Alsace, France.

97 For an example, see *The Arrest of Christ* attributed to Hieronymus Bosch or a follower: https://commons.wikimedia.org/wiki/File:Bosch_follower_The_arrest_of_Christ_c._1530-1550.jpg.

98 Hegel, *Aesthetics: Lectures on Fine Art*, vol. 1, part 2, section III, chapter 1c, 536.

Ages could appreciate.[99] Images of skeletons, devils, the Last Judgment, and the horrors of hell were less-than-subtle *memento mori.*[100] In the twelfth century, Helinand de Froidmong writes, "In one hour Death undoes all. What price beauty, what price riches."[101] Petrarch (1304–1374), in his poem *The Triumph of Death*, wrote, "Wretched is he who hopes in worldly things."[102] Writers provided putrid descriptions of what happens to the human body after death. Sebastian Pauli (1684–1751) described the corpse's "nauseating pallor," the blackening of the body from head to toe, and the swelling of a "foetid, greasy mould" on the swelling stomach.[103]

Christian medieval society was enthralled with depictions of fascinating yet frightful armies of imperfect creatures. Dante's *Inferno* is the *locus classicus* of such battalions, a text overflowing with all manner of devils, beasts, and horrible tortures. Lucifer himself has three faces and six huge bat wings. Irrational and ugly creatures seemed to outnumber saints and angels. At the same time, people were on the alert for portents and marvels in nature that foretold of disaster or apocalypse. Marvels included blood raining down from the sky, visions of the New Jerusalem on the horizon, babies born with male and female sex organs, and a pig born with human hands. The Gutenberg printing press created a news press whose revenues were enhanced by reporting on marvels.[104]

Hieronymus Bosch (circa 1450–1516) developed an uncanny capacity to portray strange creatures as hybrids of parts. But the parts do not seem to belong to known animals. Where do these nightmarish creatures

99 See Pieter Bruegel the Elder's *The Triumph of Death*, 1562, in the Prado Museum in Madrid: https://en.wikipedia.org/wiki/The_Triumph_of_Death#/media/File:The_Triumph_of_Death_by_Pieter_Bruegel_the_Elder.jpg.

100 During the European plague of the fourteenth century, the dance macabre was performed in holy places and cemeteries.

101 Helinand de Froidmont, *Verses on Death*, circa 1197. Cited in Eco, *On Ugliness*, 64.

102 See Petrarch's "The Triumph of Death" in *The Sonnets, Triumphs, and Other Poems of Petrarch.*

103 Cited in Eco, *On Ugliness*, 65.

104 On marvels in the early press, see my *The Invention of Journalism Ethics*, chapter 4.

come from? In Bosch's *The Triptych of the Temptation of Saint Anthony,*[105] about 1500 AD, the creatures that torment the hermit are not traditional demons. They look more like carnival characters or something dredged up from the unconscious, a prelude to surrealism.

The fascination with the marvellous led to an unprecedented effort to name and interpret the meaning of these many beasts. Dozens of multi-volume compendiums and encyclopedias, redolent with drawings, catalogued this imaginary universe. Books called "bestiaries" gave every animal or plant an ethical or theological meaning. For example, the lion by legend wipes out his track with its tail to elude hunters. This becomes a symbol for Christ who wipes out the sins of man.[106]

The world may be God's creation but it was teeming with the ugly, the irregular, the diabolical, and the irrational.

Let Us Carnival

The power of the grotesque was evident in the popular practice of carnival, or the "feast of fools," in medieval culture, going back at least to 1200 AD.[107] It is a period of over-indolence in worldly things before Lent arrives to purify the body for Easter. Today, carnival lasts about forty days and is practised around the world. Millions participate in cities such as Rio, Venice, and New Orleans. But in medieval times, carnival could take up the entire length of time from Christmas to Lent.

It was not just a medieval party. It was a social catharsis.

The elements of the medieval carnival are well known. There are the masks and elaborate costumes, the music and dancing, the orgies, the populist street plays, parades, and masquerade balls. Overindulgence in almost every bodily and sexual pleasure occurs, breaking all the rules of propriety and proportion. Sin is sanctioned, officially. There is much mocking of the social order, especially the authorities. Yet, this was not

105 Bosch's *Temptation of St. Anthony* is in the National Museum of Ancient Art in Lisbon: https://en.wikipedia.org/wiki/Triptych_of_the_Temptation_of_St._Anthony#/media/File:Jeroen_Bosch_(ca._1450-1516)_-_De_verzoeking_van_de_heilige_Antonius_(ca.1500)_-_Lissabon_Museu_Nacional_de_Arte_Antiga_19-10-2010_16-21-31.jpg.

106 Eco, *On Ugliness,* 114.

107 See Bossy, *Christianity in the West,* 42–4. Some scholars suspect the carnival had a pre-Christian origin but the thesis lacks sufficient evidence.

a real social or political revolution. Rather, for a *temporary* period, people were allowed to turn the social order upside down in the sure knowledge, that after carnival, things would return to normal.

The carnival marked regularities or ratio in the cosmos: the passage from winter to spring, the return of light from dark winter days, the replanting of the fields. Psychologically, carnival affirmed the primal physical forces of life over spiritual forces. The true power in life comes not from heaven but from the body: the stomach, the sex organs, and the instincts.

The aesthetic of the grotesque made carnival possible. The whole idea was to subvert conventional ideas of what was rational, right, and higher by focusing on what was irrational, wrong, and lower. Carnival degrades the higher functions of thought, speech, and the soul by making them serve the grotesque and pleasurable. Subversion was accomplished through satire and laughter, mockery, wild dancing and music, and gross rituals that could abuse animals, such as hanging them from the roofs of buildings. There were carnal parades featuring the carnal sins along with dancing skeletons and reminders of the folly of life. Masks and costumes accentuated and exaggerated gross parts of the body, such as the nose or genitalia. People ate in a grotesque manner, forcing into their mouth huge amounts of food, while washing it down with excessive amounts of alcohol. Social satire used grotesque props such as excrement and urine.

Freedom from social rules unite to give the carnival crowds a heightened sense of unity. The medieval populace participates in Bacchus-like rituals, and their mindset resembles the mania cults of ancient Greece.

In Rabelais's time, the elements needed for a new and a more dangerous social criticism were in place: a society-wide interest in the imperfect, depicted in an art that created a society constantly alert to the irrational, and social events like carnival that directly contradicted the spirit of perfectionism but were thought to be cathartic.

That a tension between classes was growing in the late Middle Ages is perceptible in Pieter Bruegel the Elder's *The Battle of Carnival and Lent*, painted in 1559.[108] A contemporary of Rabelais, Bruegel (1526–1569) painted the coarseness of peasant life. In this painting,

108 The painting is in the Kunsthistorisches Museum in Vienna, Austria: https://en.wikipedia.org/wiki/The_Fight_Between_Carnival_and_Lent#/media/File:Pieter_Bruegel_d._%C3%84._066.jpg.

he depicts the clash of the lower and upper classes as Lent arrives in the Southern Netherlands. It reminds us that not all members of medieval society embraced the sobering demands of Lent but wanted to carry on with their worldly ways. Two sides of life are represented: an inn on the left side stands for unrestrained pleasure and enjoyment; the church on the right side for restrained religious piety. The higher classes celebrate Lent with reverence and the lower classes seek the pleasures of the carnival, while playing musical instruments. Obedient children stand near the church; a beer-drinking party occurs near the inn. The two groups come together, awkwardly, at a well in the centre of the painting.

Rabelais no doubt felt these tensions and sided with the carnival lovers and the beer-drinking classes.

With Rabelais, we sense the swinging of the pendulum away from a Catholic perfectionist conception of society. Rabelais's role was to unmask this ideology and its perpetrators. In a manner of speaking, to laugh it out of court. And in laughing to make possible a dialogue, which is impossible within the utter seriousness of religious or political authoritarianism. As Bakhtin observes, Rabelais's goal was "to destroy the official picture of events ... from the laughing chorus of the marketplace." To speak "in the tongue of popular comic images. While breaking up false seriousness ... he prepared the soil for a new seriousness."[109]

SECTION 4: THE POLITICAL IMPERFECT

With Rabelais we get both a summing up and a pointing forward. He brings together diverse complaints and criticisms of society into works of literature. His writings point forward to the further deconstruction of medieval perfectionism.

Arguably, the greatest changes in the decades ahead would be economic and political. Across the late Middle Ages and into the Renaissance, society would be redesigned by the death of feudalism, the emergence of capitalism, and the establishment of independent city states.

109 Bakhtin, *Rabelais and His World*, 439.

Das Kapital

The economic changes can be summed up in one simple, and undeniable fact: society was increasingly secular in activity and in value. No amount of preaching piety from the pulpit or enumerating the terrors of hell could reverse the emerging juggernaut of capitalism in the late Middle Ages and in the Renaissance, a society of burghers and bourgeoisie.

Religion did not die. Citizens continued to call themselves Christian. The pope retained influence in the Vatican and the Holy Roman Emperor continued to exist for a remarkably long time. But the once all-powerful religious ethos was in decline. Citizens became capitalists. They became agents of enterprise within mercantile republics that traded with the world. By the Renaissance, Europe was divided between states controlled by monarchs and a landed elite, mostly in northern Europe, and states controlled by a commercial elite, such as the republics in Italy.[110] In northern Italy, one of the first regions to fully embrace the marriage of capitalism and politics, the secular impulse in life began with the rise of independent republics in the eleventh and twelfth centuries. It survived their devolution into non-democratic states run by despots, princes, *signori*, and patrician merchant families like the Medici.[111]

The cathedrals of capitalism – from ornate guild houses and imposing banks to the palaces of the nouveau riche – stood beside basilicas where priests still counselled the vanity of all things in this world. As Jacob Burckhardt has said, a "new fact appears in history – the State as the outcome of reflection and calculation, the State as a work of art."[112] Urbanization and trade created the active, worldly involved "educated layman."[113]

110 However, independent city states and republics, including "free" imperial cities, did exist in France and then Switzerland. In northern Europe, there was the Hanseatic League.

111 Among the earliest independent city-states of Italy was the Duchy of Naples by 661 AD. The Republic of Venice followed in 742. By the end of the twelfth century, almost all Italian city states were republics who recognized neither the authority of the pope nor the authority of the Holy Roman Emperor. However, by the early 1300s, most of the states were no longer republics.

112 Burckhardt. *The Civilization of the Renaissance in Italy*, part I, 1–86.

113 Burke, *The Italian Renaissance*, 67.

The ascendence of money, supported by international financial institutions and a rising middle class, ended medieval society. As time went on, the voyages of discovery, and the search for colonies to exploit, shattered the parochial, inward- and upward-looking medieval world. Now, men looked outward to the world. They scanned its horizons for new prospects. Activities once thought to be sinful or unseemly – the headlong pursuit of riches and power, the charging of interest – were components of a world that was forming, as Rabelais was laid in his grave.

Secular Politics on Display

The new worldly attitude found expression in art. A good example are three frescos in the heart of Sienna, one of Tuscany's many walled communes at the top of a hill.

By the late thirteenth century, Sienna was a notoriously unstable state, due to constant fighting among factions. Regimes arose and fell frequently. But there were exceptions. One was the "Rule of the Nine Governors." They were an oligarchy of nine wealthy merchants and bankers elected by the middle and upper classes to make executive decisions.[114] They ruled during a time of prosperity and peace from 1285 to about 1355. In 1338, the governors commissioned Sienese painter Ambrogio Lorenzetti (1290–1348) to paint giant frescoes on three walls of a large chamber within the Palazzo Pubblico, where the Nine met to conduct business.

Lorenzetti approached his task with passion. He mixed allegory, moral symbolism, myth, and panoramic landscapes, to create an early work of secular, political art that embraced republicanism, not monarchy. The frescos are called the Allegory of Good and Bad Government.[115] The aim was to communicate ideology: to legitimate the Nine by showing how they provide peace, stability, and a robust communal life. Idealization is inherent in the frescos. But now it is man-made government that is being idealized.

114 See Bowsky, *A Medieval Italian Commune; Siena Under the Nine.*

115 To view the three frescos: https://en.wikipedia.org/wiki/The_Allegory_of_Good_and_Bad_Government#/media/File:Sala_amb_frescos_d'Ambrogio_Lorenzetti,_Palazzo_Pubblico_de_Siena.JPG.

The fresco that portrays good government includes personifications of concord, justice, peace, strength, prudence, temperance, and magnanimity. There is a reference to the Last Judgment to underline the fact that the Nine were following the wishes of divine authority. On an adjacent wall is the much different allegory of bad government where tyranny is flanked by the terrible human vices that support tyranny: cruelty, treason, fraud, division, and war.

Lorenzetti saved the best for the last: a third fresco that provides a vista of fourteenth-century Sienna, with its famous cathedral dome in the background. It shows a free and vigorous community life in shops, schools, and taverns. The streets are full of activity, while outside the city walls, there are wondrously green fields of agriculture.

These frescos affirm in a creative manner an emerging political ethic: that cities need to be run by responsible representatives of the people, as in the ancient Roman republic. In this case, the representatives were merchants and bankers, not emperors or popes. It is an allegorical ode to mercantile republicanism.

Machiavelli the Proto-Modern

The swing of the pendulum towards the imperfect is found not only in literature. Or in painting. It is also found in political tracts. A good example are the writings of Niccolò Machiavelli (1469–1527), diplomat and official for the Renaissance Republic of Florence, and then its controversial political philosopher. If Rabelais summed up currents in sixteenth-century France, Machiavelli brings together the political practices of Florence into a frank assessment.

Machiavelli was born in 1469 in his father's house near the Pecchio Bridge which leads into central Florence. His father was an attorney with property who could claim descent from minor nobility. Despite this bourgeois standing, the letters of Machiavelli display a sense of vulnerability, of living on the margins of respectability, and worries about becoming poor. This sense of insecurity no doubt fuelled his ambitions to rise in stature in the great mercantile city.[116]

116 Unger, *Machiavelli*, 15.

Some thirty-five years before Machiavelli was born, Cosimo de' Medici took de facto control of the city and launched the Italian Renaissance. Throughout Machiavelli's life, republican forces and the Medici fought for control of Florence, with power swinging back and forth. Florentine politics was a dangerous and brutal blood sport. Yet it strongly attracted Machiavelli.

Machiavelli's Florence displayed the capitalistic and secular trends sweeping across the Italian peninsula and the rest of Europe. The Republic of Florence began in 1115 as a commune ruled by a signoria (a council). The city grew rich on trade in wool and banking. The economy reached its zenith in the latter half of the thirteenth century, which was reflected in new buildings such as the famous Palazzo della Signoria. Cosimo de' Medici's governance began in 1434. The Medici maintained control until 1494 when Florence once again became a republic. However, Giovanni de' Medici overthrew the republic in 1512 and Machiavelli would suffer.

Machiavelli received a humanist education, but he considered it useless for what he really loved: participation in the politics of his beloved Florence. He studied politics not from a book but from experience, as a diplomat for Florence at the Vatican and in the French and Spanish courts. In 1503, Machiavelli became responsible for the Florentine militia. He rejected mercenaries. Instead, he filled the militia with loyal citizens. At first, the policy went well, including a victory over Pisa. But in August 1512, the Medici, backed by Pope Julius II, used Spanish troops to defeat the Florentines at Prato. Many members of Florence's militia ran away from battle. The Florentine republic was dissolved. The Medici banned Machiavelli from politics and spent some time torturing him in a prison. Upon release, Machiavelli retired to his property near San Casciano, Tuscany. From his rooms, he could see Florence's famous duomo. He longed to return to public life.

The Fox and the Lion

The return would never happen. In the meantime, Machiavelli had time to ponder his life and write about politics. He wrote serious works on republicanism, looking back to the Roman republic. But it was a slim volume called *The Prince* – a practical guide for new princes – that would make him notorious for centuries.

The Prince was in the traditional medieval genre of "Mirror for Princes." Writers would hold a mirror to the prince to see if he satisfied the dictates of Christian morality. But this mirror was radically different. Machiavelli's advice to a new prince was to maintain power by acting with cunning and not to shrink from brute force or deception to foil opponents. The ruler should be both a fox and a lion. A fox notices traps that lie ahead, and a lion can frighten the wolves at his door.[117] Machiavelli also counsels the prince to give his word but, in fact, he should feel free to break his word. "Since men are a contemptible lot and will not keep their promises to you, you likewise need not keep yours to them," he writes, provocatively.[118] The prince should appear to have all the virtues of being merciful, faithful, trustworthy, and religious, but he should be ready to divert from those virtues as needed.[119] It sounded like Machiavelli was advising the ruler to act against Christian morality and virtues and that the ends justify any means.

He wrote *The Prince* in 1513 and, surprisingly, dedicated it to the Medici ruler, Lorenzo the Magnificent. True, he wanted to get back into politics by gaining the favour of the Medici. But there was another reason. He saw a golden opportunity for the Medici to unify much of Italy against foreign armies. The ruler of Florence, Lorenzo, and the pope, Pope Leo X, were both from the Medici family.[120] A united Italy under Tuscany and the Papal States would stop France, Spain, and the Holy Roman Emperor from interfering in Italian affairs.[121] Machiavelli was willing to swallow his pride because he saw a unique historical opportunity to strengthen Florence and central Italy. His friends thought his "making nice" with the Medici was shameful. Yet his attitude was not unusual. It was the sort of pragmatism that he had practised all his life for the sake of Florence. As fate would have it, the book was not published until after his death. This is because the historic opportunity came and went with the death of Pope Leo X in 1516. Therefore, his *The Art of War* and *Discourses on Livy* appeared before *The Prince*, the latter published in 1532.

117 Machiavelli, *The Prince*, 58.
118 Ibid., 59.
119 Ibid.
120 The pope was Giovanni de' Medici, the son of Lorenzo.
121 Machiavelli, *The Prince*, ix.

"Old Nick"

Today, it is difficult to recover the importance and seriousness of Machiavelli's political philosophy because of a centuries-long attack on *The Prince.* His substantial contribution to the history and nature of republicanism, as found in *Discourses on Livy,* was recognized by Enlightenment figures, such as Hume and Montesquieu, who hailed him as a writer that exposed the nature of political tyranny. John Adams, a founding father of the American republic, used his works to argue for a mixed government. Francis Bacon saw in Machiavelli an empiricism in political thought that reflected his new empiricism of facts. He praised Machiavelli for describing "what men do and not what they ought to do."[122] Today, Machiavelli is said to be the father of realism in political thought.

But such praise was drowned out by Machiavelli detractors. For every Hume during the Enlightenment, there was a Voltaire. Voltaire prompted Frederic II of Prussia to assail Machiavelli's immorality.[123] In Machiavelli's own era, moralists were dismayed by the advice he had for princes. They portrayed the book as cynical maxims for evil tyrants. Clergy called it the work of an atheist. In northern Europe, he was considered a menace to Christian society. The book was placed on the index of prohibited books of the Catholic Church in 1559. In England, Machiavelli's first name was associated with the popular term for the devil: Old Nick. His last name became the basis for a derogatory term, "Machiavellian," to signify manipulative people.

What to make of this sound and fury?

First, we should recognize that Machiavelli was partly to blame for the reaction. He knew full well that his advice would be controversial yet he made little or no effort to write more systematically or to explain himself at key points to avoid the worst misunderstandings. To the contrary, he wrote it quickly to catch the moment.

However, there is no excuse for us, centuries later, to recycle gross mistranslations of his ideas. Let us start by stressing that he *never* said "the ends justify any means" in political decision making. Instead, he talks about acting in exceptional ways under exceptional circumstances. He never said, and I believe he never imagined, that *any* sort of political

122 Bacon, *Of the Advancement of Learning,* book II, section 21, 9.
123 Machiavelli, *The Prince,* xii.

action is justified. To the contrary, he condemns politicians whose only aim is power, who kill their citizens, betray their friends, and lack mercy. Machiavelli says that by these means you can "acquire power but not glory." Might is not right and the merely powerful are set aside from praiseworthy princes by the ends they pursue.

The highest political goal – a goal that warrants the cunning of a fox or the fierceness of a lion – is establishing and maintaining an independent, self-sufficient, and stable free state. Where the body politic is endangered by evil factions and treacherous opponents, Machiavelli thinks the prince may act in ways judged violent or immoral by Christian standards. Otherwise, the prince should defend his state with an army of free citizens and he should derive his power from the love of his subjects. As he writes in *The Prince*, "As long as possible, he should not stray from the good, but he should know how to enter into evil when necessity commands."[124] This exceptionalism may be questioned. But it is, at least, an interesting principle for political morality, worthy of debate. It is not a cynical maxim of Old Nick.

We can now see Machiavelli's thinking in a better light.

He did not deny that there was an ethical component to political life. To the contrary, he promotes a republican political ideal: an independent republic, free of tyranny. The protection of this ideal, during extraordinary times, may not be compatible with Christian morality.

Once we have gotten beyond the charge of lacking any morality, we then need to define what he meant by republican virtues since these ideas shape his political morality.

For Machiavelli, political actions depended on three forces which he called virtue, fortune, and necessity. Machiavelli gives his own meaning to these old terms. Virtue is *not* a Christian term. It refers to the "strength and vigor needed to construct a politically successful society."[125] Fortune refers to the contingencies and unexpected events of life, some of which offer rulers a unique opportunity to consolidate their power or to weaken an opponent. Necessity is a psychological term: the firmness of the will of the ruler to do what is necessary to take advantage of fortune, even if it should be cruel or underhanded.

Political life is a constant struggle against fortune by taking advantage of opportunities. This was what spurred him to write *The Prince.*

124 Ibid., 60.

125 Koenigsberger, Mosse, and Bowler, *Europe in the 16th Century*, 156.

Machiavelli's proto-modern cast of thought maintains a distance from the religious perfectionism of his day. There is little evidence he was religiously devout. He regards religion as something created by humans and it contributes to social order, although moral rules may have to be ignored if state security requires it. There is a pervasive secular naturalism in his thinking, which corresponds to the secular humanism and capitalism that was arising in Europe. His virtues are Roman, pagan, and political. What life gives us comes not from God and his grace but from fortune and our capacity to respond. Also, Machiavelli is among the first to draw the is/ought dualism, stressing the blunt reality of "is," a division that has shaped modern moral theory. He is proto-modern in theorizing about the state as a work of humans, a view developed by social contract theory in Hobbes, Rousseau, and others.

Although he may not have realized it, Machiavelli is close to Aristotle in making life in a well-ordered polis the most meaningful of all human experiences.[126] Machiavelli is not trying to lead humans back to Christ or Christian piety or to an ideal Christian community. He wants to lead humans back to the worldly republican virtues of Rome.

SECTION 5: PUNK GENIUS

With the rise of Rabelaisian satire and Machiavellian politics, imperfectionism is ascendant. We are on the verge of the early modern era. But not yet. One more step was taken in late Renaissance culture: the recognition of decadence – as personal decline – as part of human nature. One of its first uses in art was in the early 1600s.

Rome's Decadent Painter

Long before the Marquis de Sade, Nietzsche, or Freud, a volatile but brilliant painter from Milan was introducing the sub-conscious, decadence, and the irrational impulse into his shocking, often gruesome paintings.

Using chiaroscuro, he made his figures – whether they were holy, suffering, or evil – appear dramatically out of the darkness of the

126 Machiavelli infrequently quotes Aristotle. He appears to disapprove of his political thinking.

painting, illuminated by bold shards of light. With perfect timing, the painter catches the character at the height of dramatic tension, e.g., just as John the Baptist is beheaded or the exact moment when a boy recoils from being bitten by a lizard. The action is brought forward and condensed in the foreground, close to the viewer. His style is called psychological realism but that hardly does justice. This painter seeks to grab the viewer by the collar and bring him closer to scenes of great emotion, violence, or depravity. The impact is immediate, direct, personal, in-your-face, and sensational – and therefore suited to the modern taste.

This is a painter of genius. He troubles us. But we can't look away.

He is Michelangelo Merisi da Caravaggio (1571–1610), the punk genius of Christian art and by 1600 the most famous painter in Rome. Supported by Catholic cardinals seeking to attract the masses with emotive art, Caravaggio's sacred scenes contain visceral, imperfect, secular humanity – from the grimy feet and tired flesh of its characters to the love of the erotic and the cruel. The church could not have found a more unpredictable and iconoclastic artist.[127]

Caravaggio's works would define Baroque painting, undermine mannerism, and influence Rubens and Rembrandt. As art historian Andre Berne-Joffroy said, "What begins in the work of Caravaggio is, quite simply, modern painting."[128]

Caravaggio has had many biographers. They dilate on his violent temper and swagger, his scuffles with police, his excessive drinking and dissipated lifestyle, his megalomania, and his fateful murder of a young man in Rome in 1606. They describe how he became a fugitive on the run and how he would continue to paint as he took refuge in Naples, Sicily, and then Malta. They debate the true causes of his death at the age of thirty-nine, as he returns to Rome expecting a papal pardon. At times, Caravaggio's life draws attention away from his art.[129]

127 Caravaggio moved to Rome in 1592. In 1595, Cardinal Francesco Maria del Monte, a patron of the arts, offered him lodging and a pension after seeing Caravaggio's *The Card Sharks* in a shop. Caravaggio stayed for six years.

128 Cited in Lambert, *Caravaggio*, 8.

129 One recent biographer, Robb, argues that many of the official records on Caravaggio's "wickedness" are unreliable, revengeful, or forced statements. Caravaggio, he believes, was a victim of powerful interests. Robb, "A Note to Readers," in *M: The Man Who Became Caravaggio.*

I will not add to these biographies. Instead, I discuss briefly one aspect of his art: the use of decadence. I select a few paintings to make my point: that Caravaggio is one of the first Western painters to take decadence seriously and to skillfully use it in his paintings. He is proto-modern in art, the same way that Machiavelli was proto-modern in political thought.

Rotten Grapes and Dirty Fingers

Consider two early paintings, *Boy Bitten by a Lizard*[130] and *Sick Bacchus*,[131] from 1554 and 1553 respectfully, as Caravaggio arrived in Rome. *Boy Bitten by a Lizard* is an effort by Caravaggio to paint extreme emotions such as fear or grief, a trend in early seventeenth-century painting. But it is also a reflection on his decadent lifestyle and attraction to young men.

In *Boy Bitten by a Lizard*, a young man recoils as he is bitten by a lizard. The painting shows an artist who knew what he was doing, with technical skill. The detail in a water bowl is dazzling and reflects the painter's studio. Such detail is impressive given that Caravaggio painted direct to canvas, without drawings. And, as usual, he uses a friend as a model, apparently Mario Minniti. Some regard the painting as a self-portrait due to the reflection of the studio and the fact, as Michael Fried has pointed out, that the subject's hands – one stretched out, the other raised up – are similar to how a painter holds a palette while painting.[132]

The lizard, in Caravaggio's hands, is a phallic symbol and a symbol of what was then considered decadent sexual desire, love among young men. As any Roman street person in Caravaggio's time would tell you, "lizard" was a nickname for the penis.

The painting uses, with great skill, the signs of decadence. There is the tired, effeminate look of the boy, his curly dark hair and pursed lips. His skin is a pale colour. A flower is tucked behind his ear and his

130 See a copy at https://en.wikipedia.org/wiki/Boy_Bitten_by_a_Lizard#/media/File:Caravaggio_-_Boy_Bitten_by_a_Lizard.jpg.

131 See a copy at https://en.wikipedia.org/wiki/Young_Sick_Bacchus#/media/File:Sick_young_Bacchus_by_Caravaggio.jpg.

132 Fried, *The Moment of Caravaggio*, chapter 1.

shirt is erotically lowered over his shoulder. The boy looks too worldly, too jaded, and too decadent for his age.

Sick Bacchus is considered a self-portrait, likely used by Caravaggio to market himself, demonstrating his ability to paint still-life, portraits, and figures from mythology. Bacchus's sickly look is sometimes attributed to the fact that Caravaggio was recovering from a stay in hospital due to a serious illness.[133] But that does not explain the painting. Caravaggio, with his skill, could have painted a more flattering image of himself. Rather he takes advantage of his appearance to paint a decadent Bacchus.

Sick Bacchus was an outrageous challenge to the conventional depiction of Bacchus as young, healthy, and beautiful. Caravaggio seems to mock the Greek god of excess. His lips are grey; the eyes leering, the skin sallow. Bacchus, with filthy nails, offers us a bunch of grapes that have gone to rot. Bacchus, says Schama, looks like an overdressed "party animal" the morning after.[134] Caravaggio could have taken an ordinary model and, using the illusions of art, make him into a beautiful god. Instead, Bacchus is a jaded mortal looking worn down by his lifestyle. This is not the painting of an immortal god; it is the painting of decay and decline. Schama notes that the painting is "a revolutionary statement of intent."[135] The purpose of art, according to Renaissance theorists, was the idealization of nature. Caravaggio announces that he will naturalize the ideal.

Now, fast-forward to the final years of Caravaggio's turbulent life. How will he see himself as he approaches death? How will his early life of decadence, street fights, and libertine sexuality play itself out? Look at his masterpiece, *David with the Head of Goliath*,[136] painted in 1605 or perhaps a few years later.

David, the Biblical symbol of goodness, independence, and courage holds the head of the Philistine giant Goliath in his hand, dripping with

133 A 2009 article in the American medical publication *Clinical Infectious Diseases* claimed that Bacchus (or Caravaggio) was recovering from malaria and perhaps other ailments.

134 Schama, *The Power of Art*, 27.

135 Ibid., 28.

136 See a copy at https://en.wikipedia.org/wiki/David_with_the_Head_of_Goliath_(Caravaggio,_Rome)#/media/File:David_with_the_Head_of_Goliath-Caravaggio_(1610).jpg.

blood. But it is the face of Caravaggio. That this is a painting with a personal moral lesson is beyond doubt. David carries a sword with the inscription HASOS which has been interpreted as an abbreviation of *humilitas occidit superbiam* (humility kills pride). David's sword points towards his groin, apparently referring to Caravaggio's murder in Rome, where he injured his enemy in the groin area. A wonderfully depicted soft cloth is gathered over David's belt into the shape of a penis.

David seems emotionally affected by, even sympathetic to, the plight of Goliath. Is David the young Caravaggio, before he became decadent? Or does David stand for the young men who controlled the great painter through their erotic power?

Caravaggio's expression is of horror and a silent scream. It is the face of what Caravaggio has become. Once a proud, strutting painter and street fighter, Caravaggio is an ugly, pathetic, old ogre. His face is a "grotesque mask of sin."[137]

Caravaggio incriminates himself without mercy.

Conclusion: When Beauty Became Ugly

In 2017, Charlie Fox of the *New York Times* wrote an article called "The Beauty of Ugly Painting."[138] The premise of the piece was that, today, the art world has embraced an "age of ugliness" as a new generation of "transgressive artists" produce ugly, dark, or offensive art, mixing cartoons, kitsch, and traditional images. They reject "accepted notions of aesthetic beauty."

The article notes that the embrace of the non-beautiful can be found among the Dadists of the 1920s, such as painter Francis Picabia (1879–1953). The article says ugly and daring forms of art hark back to Tristan Tzara (1896–1963), Dada's chief theorist, who in 1918 rejected beauty as "a sort of boring perfection, a stagnant idea of a golden swamp."

Not so.

The revenge of the ugly, and the daringly ugly, was long in the making.

137 Schama, *The Power of Art*, 16.

138 Charlie Fox, "The Beauty of Ugly Painting," *New York Times*, 4 September 2017, https://www.nytimes.com/2017/09/04/t-magazine/art/ugly-painting-laura-owens-karen-kilimnik-sam-mckinniss.html.

3

The Tangle of Modernity

Built into the mortal soul are "terrible and necessary disturbances."

Plato[1]

Art is the cry of distress by those who experience at first hand the fate of mankind.

Arnold Schoenberg[2]

IN THE NINETEENTH CENTURY, the modern world began in earnest. "Modern" means a society that was capitalistic, industrial, pragmatic, mercantile, and increasingly bourgeoisie. The middle classes would rise in great numbers, creating mass society, mass art, and emerging mass democracies, weakening aristocratic society. Yet modernity in the nineteenth century was hardly egalitarian. Its prime economic feature was exploitive capitalism, sparking class warfare.

Modernity, or the new modern life, was praised and despised. Enthusiasts declared they were "modernists," i.e., they supported modern ideas and methods. They considered capitalistic modernity to be rational and that opposition to it was irrational. Liberal artists decried modernity as irrational, ugly, and dehumanizing. Traditionalists complained that it arrogantly set aside classicism and the past. The avant-garde would organize to oppose crass modernity. By the end of the century, modernity's ideology of optimism – ever greater progress – would show signs of wear and tear. Disillusioned citizens looked elsewhere – to the past or to the future – for new ideas, new ideals, and new artistic values. In the early twentieth century, extreme forms of music and art – such as atonal compositions and surrealistic art – were developed and considered by many to be irrational or incomprehensible.

1 Plato, "The Timeus," 69c, 1271.

2 Schoenberg, "Aphorismen."

The new art and music were a desperate attempt to escape the deadening clutches of bourgeoisie, mass modernity.

How does this history connect with our concerns?

Modernity redefined (and narrowed) rationality to what I call industrial, techno-rationality: a positivism of hard facts, technology, and science accompanied by a utilitarianism of results, as a public philosophy. At the same time, romantics promoted the virtues of irrationalism – passion, will, spontaneity, individualism – and the glory of autonomous art – creativity without the necessity of concrete results. This would be a counterweight to narrow rationality. Therefore, we encounter in modernity a new and important example of the tension of rationalism and irrationalism in culture. We encounter attempts to move the pendulum toward rationalism or irrationalism. It would shape modern thinking.

The debate over modernity made debates over rationalism and irrationalism concrete and important. This was not an academic dust-up. People justified social ideas, trends, and movements on their apparent rationality. With modern forces completely changing cities and lifestyles, the philosophical question, "But is this rational and good?" could not be evaded. And such questions begged another query: *Which* notion of rationality are we talking about? Such questions remain with us today.

A cultural history of the rationality–irrational distinction must come to grips with the clashes over modernity from the nineteenth century onward. The task is made difficult by the fact that rationalism and irrationalism became entangled, as movements appealed to both rational and irrational capacities, or they used rationality to question rationality.

In this chapter, we examine these tangles.

SECTION 1: MODERNITY AND ITS ENEMIES

Meanings of the Modern[3]

As a first step, we need a better understanding of the key terms.

"Modern," according to the *Shorter Oxford Dictionary*, means "of or pertaining to recent times." "Modernism" is "a usage, mode of expression,

3 For a detailed analysis of modernity as a term, see Marino, *Modern, Modernism, Modernitate.*

peculiarity of style or mode of thought or techniques that is characteristic of modern times." A modernist, then, is someone with an affinity for what is modern, a supporter of modern ways or methods.

Modern or modernity was largely absent from antiquity. By the second century AD, the Romans had "classic" for ancient and revered writers. But "classic" was not contrasted with modern. Instead, it was contrasted with "vulgar." The classic writers were people high in the social hierarchy, the "first class" of Roman citizens, who did not write for the vulgar or ordinary people. But as time went on, there was a need to distinguish the present from the past and, by the late fifth century, the Latin term *modernus* appears, coined from the adverb *modo* meaning recently or just now. The term was widely used in medieval Latin. After the tenth century, other terms like *modernitas* (modern times) and *moderni* (men of today) became popular.

To say that modern means recent times is not very informative because everything today is modern. However, modern had a specific meaning when it was used in historical and literary circles. Modern was at the centre of Western cultural disputes. For example, modern was contrasted with ancient. By the High Middle Ages, scholars were arguing over which era had the best poetry, paintings, or sculpture. Renaissance humanists, like Petrarch, looked back, disparagingly, at what they called the "Dark Ages." In seventeenth-century France, there was the "Quarrel of the Moderns and Ancients" among literary scholars.[4] What appear to be merely academic quarrels were in fact serious disagreements on knowledge, the way forward for civilization, and the future of science. The learned debates cloaked tensions between social hierarchies and sources of authority.[5]

Writers used rival metaphors to explain the relationship of the new to the old. The most famous metaphor, from the twelfth century, was that moderns are "dwarfs" standing on the shoulders of ancient "giants," thus the dwarfs can see further. The use of the term dwarf usually suggested that the writer's sympathy was with the ancients. Isaac Newton eliminated dwarfs and famously said, in a letter to Robert Hook, that

4 Swift satirized the quarrel as the "Battle of the Books." On the origins of "modern" and "modernity" and the battles between the moderns and ancients see Calinescu, *Five Faces of Modernity*, chapters 1 and 2.

5 Calinescu, *Five Faces of Modernity*, 23, 27.

"if I have seen farther, it is by standing on the shoulders of giants."[6] Francis Bacon turned the comparison around to favour modern science by comparing the historical development of knowledge to that of the growth of a child into manhood. The wisdom of ancient Greeks represents the "boyhood of knowledge" with lots of talk and barren controversies because there was no method to factually verify claims.[7]

The term modernity took longer to develop than modern. In the English language, the *Oxford English Dictionary* records its first occurrence in 1627. In France, *modernitié* was not used before the middle of the nineteenth century. The word appears in Francois-Rene Chateaubriand's (1768–1848) diary notes of 1833 during a trip from Paris to Prague. The word reoccurs in his *Memoires d'outre-tombe* (*Memoirs from Beyond the Grave*) in 1849. Chateaubriand used *modernitié* to refer to the meanness and banality of everyday modern life. One of the first major discussions of modernity and painting is in Charles Baudelaire's analysis of Constantin Guys work, *The Painter of Modern Life,* written in 1859 and published in 1863.

Two Modernities

The literature on modernity talks about two modernities.[8] First, the actual historical era and its features, i.e., the conditions of human life in the modern era. Second, an "aesthetic modernity" which refers to a negative artistic reaction to historical modernity. Not all artists deplored modernity but, overall, especially in major Western cities like Paris, the reaction was overwhelmingly scathing and rebellious.

I begin with modernity as a historical era.

Modernity, as an era, is an elastic term. Some scholars focus on the emergence of new ways of thinking, such as notions of time or nature that anticipated current ideas. As a result, they stretch modernity as far back as to the Renaissance. Others divide modernity into three eras from (a) early modern science in the seventeenth century to (b) the eighteenth-century Enlightenment and (c) to the scientific-technological

6 More, *Isaac Newton,* 176–7.

7 Calinescu, *Five Faces of Modernity,* 24.

8 Ibid., 41.

era of our time.[9] For the purposes of this book, modernity extends, roughly, from 1800 to the end of the early decades of the twentieth century, say up to the Second World War. I regard the period from 1950 to the present as marked by the continuing development and intensification of modernity, alongside the birth of the postmodern.[10]

At the turn of the nineteenth century, something new was occurring, a new era. A new modern. Modernity was, and is, a fundamental shift in society away from the past, a break with medieval culture, and a break with the restrictions and privileges of a hierarchical, religion-dominated Western culture. Of course, this new age did not appear over night. Modernity was built upon numerous developments from prior centuries: In economics, the small-state capitalism of the Renaissance; in politics, the rise of modern republicanism; in the sphere of ideas, the birth of experimental science and the rationalism of Descartes. At the dawn of the nineteenth century, the powerful cultural trajectory of rationalist Enlightenment converged with the powerful economic system of industrial capitalism to create a new, secular, and temporal society which literally erased much of what had been deemed by prior generations as important.

Therefore, to talk about modernity is to gesture towards our modern life, the conditions of existence under which most Western humans have lived since the nineteenth century.

What were the most important of those new conditions?

Massive social change. Modernity refers to an unprecedented rise of technological, economic, and social change that began to be visible in the early 1800s. Modernity was characterized by the rise of large-scale, industrial, monopolistic capitalism; factory production and the international search for resources and trade; population growth; urban growth; the mass immigration of people into cities; the weakening of old social hierarchies and elite control of culture; and new technologies such as trains, airplanes, electricity, and the telephone. What strikes one about modernity – and is still remarked upon today – is the *persistence* of change and the increasing *speed* of change.

9 For an example of this "plural era" approach see Marshall Berman's *All That Is Solid Melts into Air*.

10 Credit for coining the term "postmodern age" is given to historian Arnold J. Toynbee, who first used it in 1939: "Our own Post-Modern Age has been inaugurated by the general war of 1914–1918." Toynbee, *A Study of History*, 43.

Emergence of mass society: Modernity altered the fabric of society. Mass society was created, characterized by large populations in alienating cities; the weakening of smaller centres with communal feeling and common traditions. Large parts of cities were razed to build dirty, polluting factories where thousands of workers trudged to work.

Emergence of mass politics: Gradually, the masses became central to politics, as democratic representation in parliaments became important. Mass democracy undermined aristocratic liberalism and conservatism. The common man called for greater liberties, the end to monarchies, or other reforms. Elites began losing control over politics, the arts, and other important dimensions of life. Mass politics also included political movements that threatened the status quo, from radical liberals and anarchists to communists. Modernity was marked by the questioning of tradition and an emphasis on individualism, freedom, and equality.[11]

New mass media: Modernity saw the advent of new, international forms of media, from massive commercial newspapers and global wire services to the cinema, photography, radio, music halls, and the emergence of popular culture – all of it supported by greater public education and literacy.

Spread of capitalistic, material values: The economic system of modernity was industrial capitalism supported by global financial systems and internationalism colonialism. While aristocracies still had influence, power and wealth was increasingly centralized in the hands of a minority of large corporations and industrialists, over and against the proletariat, the small land owner, and the bourgeoise shop-keeper. Nineteenth-century capitalism created its own value system: the values of profit-maximizing, commercial success, material wealth and status, efficiency, the capacity to quantify and measure, and the mechanical. It sought the standardization of mass production resulting in the reduction of craftsmanship to jobs of routine, habitual procedures. Capitalism's power, in part, came from its capacity to produce efficiently and routinely those commodities popular with the masses.

An aesthetics of pleasure and popularity: Modernity changed the aesthetic values of the general populace – what the masses desired, took pleasure in, and found interesting. In other words, what ordinary people would

11 Foucault, *Discipline and Punish: The Birth of the Prison.*

consume and be prepared to purchase. The capitalist control of consumption seeped into almost every corner of modern life, including the industrialization and commodification of music, writing, and art. Higher values, such as providing artistic insight into life, for its own sake, were seen as superfluous. Art should be useful and popular. By the second half of the 1800s, there was, especially in American and European cities such as New York and Paris, an aesthetics of plenty. Both ordinary people and leading artists were drawn toward a hedonistic enjoyment of the new material and popular culture and all it had to offer: movies, radio shows, jazz music, and goods of all kinds sold in large and opulent department stores.

Metaphysics of Modernity

This dramatic deconstruction of old elitist society and its reconstruction under the flag of mass modernity changed how people saw the world. It changed what people believed and pursued. The name for this set of beliefs is called modernism, the affirmation of the modern.

Modernism had a metaphysics: What was real was not what was eternal and perfect, transcending the ordinary world. That view belonged to the medieval past. What was real was change, not stasis. Time marches forward, linearly, and all actions are evaluated as to how they adjust individuals or societies to the future. Those who do not stay with the incessant, all-demanding march of time and do not progress, get left behind.

What was real was not Platonic forms in another realm but ordinary life as it was perceived and modified by human action. What was real was not the ethereal and the philosophical. What was real was worldly, empirical, and pragmatic. What worked or had results, in ways evident to our senses and practical interests, was the test of what was real and significant. One *created* the future, through intelligent action in the world. Modernism was an extension of imperfectionism. But modernism's imperfectionism was distinct in its overwhelming interest in the novel. Modernism asserted "the superiority of the present over the past (and by implication, of the future over the present), with all that implies in terms of optimism and faith in progress."[12]

12 Taruskin, *Music in the Early Twentieth Century*, 1.

Progress, for modernity, was the almost unstoppable motor of society, and the old ways should make way for whatever progress required, such as tearing down sections of cities for a more rational system of roads and buildings. The pressure for constant innovation and ever new techniques rubbed off on social attitudes and even artists. Despite many artists' dislike of industrial modernity, composers sought to create ever new music – to progress – rather than imitate past masters. Repetition, imitation, or the respectful copying of past artistic works were anathema to the modernist. The aim of modernism was captured by American poet Ezra Pound's catchphrase: "Make it new."[13]

Modernity developed a philosophy of rationality, knowledge, and value that suited its metaphysics of the new. The theory of rationality was, as noted, industrial, techno-rationality. Modern rationality, embodied in the many new empirical sciences or in the shops of inventors, was industrial. One of its tasks was to assist the progress of industry and to work with governments dependant on the growth of capitalism. Industrial rationalism developed new methods for increasing (and testing) the efficiency of production or of statistically studying some social problem. Government, it was thought, should be operated with the same efficiency as the new Ford car factories. This rationality was techno because it was based on, and gave birth to, technology. Techno-rationality served progress; metaphysics and the arts did not.

The philosophy of knowledge and value was positivism and utilitarianism, both stars in the intellectual firmament by the mid-1800s. Positivism, led by John Stuart Mill in England and Auguste Comte in France, declared knowledge to be reducible to (or constructible from) empirical facts of observation and generalization upon the facts. Positivism justified the claims of the rising empirical sciences to be the future. They were positivistic sciences, using facts to create progress-enhancing technology.

Techno-rationality was not entirely new. The usefulness of fact-based knowledge was one of the attractive features of modern science as it emerged in the sixteenth and seventeenth centuries. Scientific rationality was not a scholastic deduction from theological principle. It was secular and pragmatic, seeking *new* empirical truths, not learned commentaries on past systems of thought. Knowledge was power.

13 Pound, *Make It New.*

However, early modern science maintained an appreciation for the intrinsic worth of deep theorizing about nature, such as Newton's new physics. With industrial, techno-rationality the balance between instrumental and non-instrumental rationality shifted towards the former. Aligning nicely with techno-rationality was utilitarianism, as led by Jeremy Bentham and John Stuart Mill. Utilitarianism benefitted from the veneration for instrumental rationality and calculation. Bentham, for example, claimed to have an objective, reliable method by which one could rationally calculate the relative utilities of different policies or proposed actions, rather than depend on tradition, intuition, or guesswork. One calculated the expected utilities (expected pleasures and pains) and then determined which action would most improve the welfare of the greatest number of people.

Utilitarianism in the hands of philosophers such as Mill was a nuanced ethical system, and its philosophical proponents today are equally sophisticated in thought. But too often, in the hands of government officials, industrialists, and other pragmatic people, nineteenth-century utilitarianism was a crude pragmatism which narrowly defined utility as what could be materially measured: profits, results, pleasures. It prompted social satire.[14]

Therefore, by the mid-1800s, rationality was narrowed to industrial rationality – the creation of ever more efficient means of production and social engineering based on the new sciences, statistics, machines, and measurements. One does not have to be a sage to see, in retrospect, that Western societies, following the techno-rationality of modernity, were moving towards the First World War. The race was on to determine which society could adapt most successfully to modernity. Who would be the new techno-power? Who could produce the most robust and modern industrial sector? Who could design the best airplanes, the best bombs? Development of new military weapons was heavily subsidized by nations because the ability to change now entailed national survival. The breathless race to the new locked nations into a trajectory toward war.

14 Perhaps the classic satire of the cold-blooded rational utilitarian is Thomas Gradgrind, the school board superintendent in Charles Dickens's novel *Hard Times*. Gradgrind treats all things, including interactions with his children, in terms of numbers, facts, and expected utility.

Modernity both liberated and imprisoned human potential. On the negative side of the ledger, there were the disruptions of massive urbanization and factory-based manufacturing due to the industrial revolution. There was the creation of mass society – thousands gathered into large and isolating cities which were the home to a new class, the exploited proletariat as slaves of expanding capitalism. Yet, on the positive side, there was the impressive rise of scientific knowledge that cast much former medieval thinking into the category of superstition. Politically, modernity, despite the exploited proletariat, encouraged a gradual levelling of hierarchies and the rise of democratic politics. Also, there were the new technologies, plus better treatment for illnesses.

Good or bad, there was no looking back, was there? Only looking forward to the novel, to the future.

Not quite.

The history of the nineteenth century and early twentieth century is, in large part, a history of opposition to modernity.

SECTION 2: MODERNITY AND THE ROMANTICS

Romanticism as a Movement

Romanticism began as a form of creative irrationalism. It was a view of literature, the arts, and human nature that stressed the positive contribution of the irrational or non-rational capacities. Romanticism, in the late eighteenth century, was an alternative to the rationalism of Enlightenment. Romanticism was defined as a period of time or a style of art. Then, in the first half of the nineteenth century, romanticism became more than a style. It became a militant rejection of modernity, leading to the avant-garde.

We are familiar with romanticism's many features as a style of art: an emphasis on turbulent emotion, passion, and vision; idealization of humble forms of life close to nature; tormented individuals seeking self-realization; the romantic hero or genius who creates art spontaneously through flashes of insight; the importance of will, imagination, and creativity over reason; the rebel who rejects social rules. Philosophically, the romantic mindset rejected the tradition of natural law, universal truths, objective values, and the control of passion.

Romanticism stressed plurality, difference, and uniqueness.[15] The world is a "battle of perpetually new and ceaseless conflicting wills, individual or collective."[16]

The history of romanticism is a twisting narrative.

"Romantic" comes from the Old French *romanz*, the vernacular "romance" languages that developed from Latin, such as French and Spanish. In medieval times a romance was a tale of chivalry written in a romance language, usually in verse, and typically involving a quest.[17] Our popular idea of the romantic as passionate and quixotic stems from these medieval tales. By the middle of the eighteenth century romantic in English and *romantique* in French were commonly used as praise for natural phenomena such as grand views and sunsets. The application of the term to literature and the arts began in Germany, especially by the literary critics and brothers August and Friedrich Schlegel. They began to speak of *romantische poesie* (romantic poetry) in the 1790s, contrasting it with classical poetry in terms of spirit and style. Friedrich Schlegel wrote in his *Dialogue on Poetry* of 1800, "I seek and find the romantic among the older moderns, in Shakespeare, in Cervantes, in Italian poetry, in that age of chivalry, love and fable, from which the phenomenon and the word itself are derived."[18] Yet, still, the term did not spread rapidly, catching on in England later in the nineteenth century. It is only from the 1820s onward that romanticism knew its name. A sign that the term had come into its own appeared in 1824 when the Académie Française in France condemned it as literature.

Historically, romanticism was anticipated by the mannerism of El Greco and Michelangelo which expressed the manner or personality of the painter, rejecting the classicism of Raphael. In the baroque period, Caravaggio revealed the strength of impulse and worldly ambition in his dramatic paintings. Francisco de Goya (1746–1828), court painter to Charles IV in Madrid, produced Gothic images of nightmarish

15 For historical studies of romanticism, see Berlin's *Political Ideas in the Romantic Age* and *The Crooked Timber of Humanity*.

16 Berlin, "The Decline of Utopian Ideas in the West," 44.

17 Heath and Boreham, *Introducing Romanticism*, 3.

18 Ferber, *Romanticism*, 6–7.

intensity especially in *The Disasters of War* (1810–14) and then in his "Black Paintings" where reason is absent from an anarchic universe.[19]

Rousseau's notion of the natural man as good and happy, because he is not corrupted by reason and civilization, was a major philosophical statement of the romantic attitude. The romantic approach would also be developed by Herder, Goethe, Schiller, Blake, Wordsworth, Byron, and many others. Romanticism is usually said to end in the mid-1800s. But the influence of romanticism extended beyond the mid-1800s. It shaped the work of Brahms, Liszt, Wagner, and Nietzsche. Traces of romantic psychology can be found in the arch-modern composers and writers of the early twentieth century.[20]

In the first half of the nineteenth century, romantics had to come to terms with ground-shaking political and social events: the French Revolution and its bloody failure, the rise of Napoleon, and then the restoration of the old order in Europe. In many respects, the revolution was propelled by romantic notions of striving and individualism, and a quixotic quest to create a republic of liberty, equality, and fraternity. The Reign of Terror that sank the French Revolution showed that humans were moved by deep irrational forces. Romantics turned inward and examined this conflicted self. William Wordsworth thought that romantic poetry would not only provide pleasure but purify the affections. It would constitute a revolution through words, now that the physical French Revolution had failed.[21]

Romanticism would first become a cultural movement in Germany. German romanticism, in general, disliked French Enlightenment ideas. Part of this was due to envy of the accomplishments of the French Enlightenment. Anything considered "French," such as the superiority of reason or the universal laws of human nature, was to be opposed. Rather than seek the universal, the romantics studied the particular:

19 The Black Paintings are fourteen works, between 1819 and 1823, whose haunting images speak to his fear of insanity and his negative view of the future of humanity.

20 On romanticism in music, see Plantinga, *Romantic Music.*

21 In 1798, Wordsworth and Samuel Taylor Coleridge published *Lyrical Ballads*, one of the first works of romantic English poetry, on events from "common life" in the "real language of men." In his preface, Wordsworth says poetry is "the simultaneous overflow of powerful feelings" worked over by an "organic sensibility" and modified by deep thought. Byron despised this tranquil romanticism. Coleridge was often not tranquil. He probed the "demonic" within, sometimes with the help of drugs, such as in *Kubla Khan.*

the inner self which makes individuals distinct and the languages and cultures which make nations distinct. For Johann Gottfried Herder (1744–1803), the natural unit for human society is *das Volk*, the people. The volk of each nation are unique in its land and customs.

German writers created the first stirrings of romanticism in the 1770s with *Sturm und Drang* (storm and stress), a movement featuring major and popular works by Johann Wolfgang Goethe (1749–1832) and Friedrich Schiller (1759–1805). It was followed by two more phases of romanticism. One in Jena (1798–1804) and then in Heidelberg beginning in 1806. The latter featured writers such as Ludwig Tieck (1773–1853), poet and literary critic Friedrich Schlegel (1772–1829), philosopher Johann Christoph Friedrich von Schelling (1775–1854) and the poet Novalis (1772–1801).

For romantics, one problem of the Enlightenment was the celebration of reason. English artist William Blake (1757–1827) decried Newton's rational "mechanical" universe. "I will not Reason and Compare: my business is to Create," wrote Blake. "Nature is imagination."[22] The universalism of Enlightenment reason was another issue. For many romantics, like the Greek sophists, there were no universal laws of society and no universal human nature. There was, instead, the parochialism of one's experience and one's volk. For Schlegel and Novalis, laws and values are not objectively given or fixed, they are generated by humans. The romantics embraced a deep relativity. Historian Isaiah Berlin described German romanticism as "a new and restless spirit, seeking violently to burst through old and cramping forms, a nervous preoccupation with perpetually changing inner states of consciousness, a longing for the unbounded and the indefinable, for perpetual movement and change, an effort to return to the forgotten sources of life, a passionate effort at self-assertion both individual and collective, a search after means of expressing an unappeasable yearning for unattainable goals."[23]

Romanticism worshipped self-realization, the striving, free self which is full of passion and spontaneity as it breaks with convention and creates new ideas. What is valued is the originality of the artist, writer, or

22 Ackroyd, *Blake*, 217.

23 Berlin, *The Crooked Timber of Humanity*, 92.

military commander.[24] The goals have cosmological significance. For Schelling, creativity in humans reflects the creativity of the divine; self-realization reflects organic growth in nature.

Romantics created the idea of the hero or genius outside of society – the free artists, outlaws, or Byronic outcasts. The romantic hero is a modern Prometheus liberating humankind. In pursuing liberation, the romantic comes close to the goals of the Enlightenment – but by different means. Freedom and self-realization are the goals; intuition and artistic vision are the means. The classic romantic genius is, of course, Ludwig van Beethoven. "The poor, dishevelled genius in the garret, diseased, unhappy, and violent, a rebel against all convention, incapable and unwilling to adjust himself to any of the normal requirements of polite society, the sacred dervish, a man chosen, and dedicated to the fulfillment of a holy mission – was something very new in the consciousness of Western mankind."[25]

Another image is of the tormented young man, as in Goethe's incredibly popular but controversial *The Sorrows of Young Werther* in 1774. Werther is enchanted by peasants in a small, fictional village. He has a passionate, conflicted nature that prompts suicide because he has lost the love of his life. Also, Schiller created the Sturm und Drang outlaw in another scandalous success, his play *The Robbers* of 1781. It features a charismatic Karl Moor, a violent, criminal outlaw, living dangerously by rejecting society's conventions, a free man who cannot submit to others. Preceding the French Revolution by eight years, the play raised doubts about putting radical ideas, infused with darkness, into practice.

Romantics did not deny dark irrationalism. The romantic self struggles with inner demons and is driven from one idea or passion to another. Goethe mentioned many times his personal struggle to reconcile opposite ideas and passions. In these depths, many a romantic found dark things, like Augustine and Luther. Schiller, reflecting on how tragic art stimulates our emotions, considers the darker emotions. He says that the sad, the terrible, and the horrendous hold an "irresistible attraction for us." We are both repelled and attracted by scenes of

24 Napoleon was initially seen by romantics as a great individual, a commander genius.

25 Berlin, "Two Concepts of Freedom," 195.

horror and pain. Neither the desire for revenge nor the desire for justice explains the public's desire to witness executions and "listen to the expression of his suffering." This dark desire is embedded in human nature.[26] Meanwhile, Gotthold Ephraim Lessing (1729–1781) in *Laocoon* writes the first systematic aesthetic treatment of ugliness. Striking a non-classical, modern note, he ponders the difficulty of representing the disgusting.

Romanticism is often associated with the sublime. The eighteenth century's preoccupation with the sublime is frequently misunderstood as something serene and pleasant – looking up to the stars on a cloudless night or admiring a painting of soft, ethereal beauty. This is a popular misconception. The romantic conception of the sublime is an experience of great emotion and disturbed feelings, a sense of being both threatened and awed by a great object. We sense a lack of symmetry between finite humans and infinite nature, as when we confront a menacing storm. Romantics sought out these extreme experiences.

The difference between the rationalist and romantic sense of the sublime is evident if we compare Kant's view with the romantics. Kant talks about the mathematically sublime, e.g., where we comprehend the infinity of the universe, and the dynamically sublime, e.g., where we confront a large object that frightens us. In both cases, the sublime is the feeling that we, through reason, can comprehend the object or, through reason, protect ourselves from the threat. Sublimity is a feeling of the superiority of our power of reason, as a faculty distinct from physical nature. Sublimity resides in the mind, not in nature, in so far as we can "become conscious that we are superior to nature within."[27] Edmund Burke, no Kantian idealist, dropped the reference to reason's superiority and explained the sublime as the enjoyment of strong emotions when we feel awe or horror for things that shrink our stature – sea storms, cliffs, abysses, boundless tracts of land – but do not harm us.[28] Schopenhauer comes closest to the truth when he says that the sublime is an encounter that shows us our "frail wills" as individuals, compared with nature. Sublimity is a state of personal elevation achieved when,

26 Schiller, "On the Art of Tragedy," 55.

27 Kant, *Critique of Judgment*, 104.

28 See Burke, *Philosophical Inquiry into the Origin of our Ideas of the Sublime and Beautiful.*

faced with a threatening nature, we overcome our fear and do not run away. Instead, we contemplate "those very objects that are terrible to the will."[29] This is not a triumph of reason.

Militant Romanticism

In the first decades of the 1800s, romanticism became caught up in the response to modernity. Previously, authors and artists like Chateaubriand had defined romanticism "mildly" as a period of time or an important artistic style. Chateaubriand portrayed romanticism as part of the "genius" of Christianity, a religion that he thought was the most receptive to art.

But the mood turned militant in France with the theories of Marie-Henri Beyle, better known as Stendhal (1783–1842), and Charles Baudelaire (1821–1867). Stendhal was one of the first major European writers to term himself a romantic in the sense of being an aesthetic modern. He defined romanticism as "an awareness of contemporary life, of *modernity* in its immediate sense." Romanticism is the sense of the present conveyed artistically. He was one of the first to define romanticism relative to time periods and in clear opposition to classicism. In *Racine and Shakespeare,* he says Sophocles and Euripides were romantic in their day, as was Jean Racine in his faithfulness to the taste of the court of Louis XIV. Romantics, he said, regard taste as "the ability of pleasing today." Even if the public is not pleased by a writer in his time (as happened to Stendhal), the writer is a fighter who hopes his work will please a future generation.

Stendhal's full aesthetic comes into view as he adds further qualities to the personality of the true romantic. A romantic should have the courage to shock the public, if its taste has been corrupted by art academicism. Freedom and originality are indispensable to art. A genuine artist follows his own individuality, rejecting the temptation to imitate, or to reduce art to a set of rules. In *Racine and Shakespeare,* Stendhal promoted the romantic aesthetic by unfavourably comparing the rules and strictures of Racine's classicism to the freer verse and settings of Shakespeare.[30]

29 Schopenhauer, *The World as Will and Idea,* vol. 1, book. III, 227, 229.
30 Stendhal, *Racine and Shakespeare,* 11–21.

In his *Salon of 1846*, Baudelaire follows Stendhal in saying romanticism is "the most contemporary expression of beauty." More radically, Baudelaire rejects modernity as a period of time and identifies it with romantic art characterized by such features as intimacy, inventiveness, and creative imagination. Like Stendhal, he defines romanticism relative to its era. What counts as an expression of beauty in the present depends on what present is in question. What is unique to current modern art is its stress on what is novel, particular, and transitory. Baudelaire thinks that all forms of beauty contain "an element of the eternal and an element of the transitory," a combining of the absolute and the particular. Absolute beauty does not exist. Our emotions determine what particularities attract us, and this leads us to our own sense of beauty, a beauty specific to individuals and their era.

In *The Painter of Modern Life*, Baudelaire says that today's art is enthralled by immediacy: the sensuous grasping of a present thing, grasped in its transitoriness, and depicted by our own imagination apart from any tradition. The proper form of modern imagination is a "forgetful immersion in the now," which is the real source of originality. This means that the painter seeks worldly forms of beauty, not the transcendent beauty of the past. The modern artist explores the realms of the ordinary, ugly, and evil. With Baudelaire, the classical ideal of beauty has declined to the point where artists can appreciate the new beauty of transitoriness. Baudelaire writes, "Modernity is the ephemeral, the fugitive, the contingent, the half of art whose other half is the eternal and immutable."[31]

Both Stendhal and Baudelaire see the romantic artist as cut off from the past. The alienation of the modern artist begins with romanticism. History is a succession of modernities, each unique. So, no link or comparison between them is possible. Past models only hinder our imaginative encounter with present. Being a modern artist is not about accepting existing conditions; it is not about imitating the past or nature. Baudelaire rejects all forms of realism. Being modern is to "heroically" challenge those conditions and recapture the present in art using only your imagination.

31 Baudelaire, *The Painter of Modern Life*, 15.

Among the avant-garde, this romantic alienation was given a positive description: the artist is autonomous and follows the slogan "art for art's sake." The autonomy expressed itself in subversive art forms, in decadent lifestyles, and in political ferment. Kant had defended autonomous art in his *Critique of Judgment* of 1790. Beauty was a disinterested pleasure in the beauty of an object. But, for romantic moderns in the mid-1800s, such as writer Theophile Gauthier in France, autonomy was not just an aesthetic theory of beauty. It was also a rallying cry – politically, socially, and aesthetically – against bourgeoisie mercantilism and utilitarianism.[32]

As the nineteenth century progressed, the theoretical idea of autonomy would become a Hegelian doctrine. Not only did art exist for its own sake but, also, art was following a necessary (or inevitable) historical path to a completely free art. It would be master of its own domain, far from grubby utilitarian demands that art show the public that it was useful.

The "Great" Immoral Individual?

For romanticism, self-expression – pure, independent, and non-compromising – is all. One burns within with passion. Away with obstacles. One must remain pure of worldly influence in a way Luther and Calvin never envisaged. One is pure not by repressing desire but the opposite: by giving vent to the desires and feelings within oneself, unrestrained by propriety. Socially, the romantic should appear to be different and novel. One adopts a persona or nonconforming style that draws notice. This ideal of the expressive self was mimicked by the public across Europe in Goethe's time. Like Werther, young men started wearing blue coats and yellow breeches, and they committed suicide.[33] Fifty years later, in the 1820s, "Byronism" – copying the outcast style of Lord Byron – swept across Europe.

This romantic psychology contains a worrisome moral component.

Freedom for the self leaves open the question freedom for what? If freedom and self-expression are absolute, what is prohibited? Maybe

32 Calinescu, *Five Faces of Modernity*, 45.

33 Heath and Boreham, *Introducing Romanticism*, 38.

the free spirit will use violence or reject social mores against robbery and murder. What if the romantic vigilante, beloved of today's action films, decides to "go bad," killing and robbing for private gain? Is he not expressing himself? Can mass murders, powerful leaders, or immoral groups, say the mafia, use the romantic ideal to justify their "spontaneous" and "authentic" actions? Is there not a strong dose of romantic psychology in the sympathetic portrayal of the murderous gangster family in the movie, *The Godfather*?

Or, go back to the admiration of Byron among romantics in the nineteenth century. Now, list the qualities of Byron or the Byronic individual. On your list should be intellectual and artistic virtues such as being intelligent, self-sufficient, creative, courageous, and willing to challenge the status quo. But what about his other qualities? Byron's life is redolent with uncaring, erratic, often immoral actions, causing a former lover, Lady Caroline Lamb, to call him "mad, bad, and dangerous to know."[34] What do we say about Byron's moral vices of being cunning, ruthless, and arrogant?[35] Does a commitment to romanticism excuse these vices? Surely not. Should the Byron myth not make us wary of naïve enthusiasm for passionate, powerful, and romantic-like individuals? Rather than get caught up in the cult of personality, should we not rationally critique the *goals* and *consequences* of such people and their projects?

The admiration of Byron in his time initiated the cult of the great, if immoral, individual. But here is the really frightening part for us today: What if individuals, feeling lost in their romantic universe, decide to join a collective effort, say the construction of a great totalitarian state, run by a superman (a political hero or genius). Freedom is now defined as losing oneself in a marching army of patriots avenging alleged historical grievances. Was this irrationalism not anticipated by the philosopher of German nationalism Fichte when he made the bald, and false, assertion that "I am wholly my own creation"?[36] Then Fichte contends that this individual, self-creating ego can only be fully realized by devotion

34 See Hayle, *Lord Byron and Lady Caroline Lamb: Mad, Bad and Dangerous to Know.*

35 On Byron's strange private life, including repeated attempts to starve himself and his defence of his actions in the name of spiritual freedom, see Peattie, *The Private Life of Lord Byron.*

36 Fichte, *The Vocation of Man*, 91.

to the "fatherland." Nationalistic romanticism emerges from individual romanticism. We arrive at a paradox: freedom of the individual by submersion into the freedom of the general will.

To their credit, many romantic writers did realize, quite quickly, the limits of romantic psychology. Goethe left the romantic movement, disowning Wertherism and adopting classicism as he became both a senior government official and revered artist in Weimar. He was followed by Schiller. Yet Goethe remained a romantic at heart.[37]

The inability of romanticism to deal with the demands of morality is clear in Goethe's great poetic drama *Faust.* Its overarching theme is that of human striving, then straying, and then finding salvation in that straying. Another theme is the fascination we have with dark irrationality. Why are we so entranced by Faust and the scheming Mephistopheles if not because we recognize the same dark irrationalism within ourselves? From an ethical view, *Faust* is an immoral tale. Bargaining with the devil is, of course, not to be recommended, ethically. It is a metaphor for self-corruption. By the end of the play, Faust has the lives of at least seven people on his hands. In league with Mephistopheles, Faust wipes out an entire family (Margarete, her child, mother, and brother) and acquiesces in the murder of the elderly, peaceful couple, Baucis and Philemon. Yet, in the end, Faust escapes judgment and, with a cleansing of his soul, is borne on high to the blessed. Goethe makes the romantic need for striving an absolute value, overriding ethics. Great actions matter the most. In the play, the Lord of the Prologue in Heaven says that striving man is bound to "err." But is "err" the right word for murder?[38]

Meanwhile, the gifted romantic poet Percy Bysshe Shelley (1792–1822) published *Prometheus Unbound* in 1820. He was a self-confident atheist with anarchist leanings. All forms of authority were wicked. Mary Shelley (1797–1851) must have known a thing or two about unbounded ego. She was married to Percy Shelley. Mary Shelley wrote *Frankenstein, or the Modern Prometheus* – the tale of scientist Victor Frankenstein who creates a hideous creature. It is a clear warning against unbounded

37 Goethe never completely distanced himself from romantic motifs. Goethe substantially reworked the *Sorrows* for a 1787 edition, despite his complaints about Wertherism. Also, Goethe's second novel, *Wilhelm Meister's Apprenticeship* (1795) has the hero undergo a journey of self-realization to escape the life of a bourgeois businessman.

38 On the ethic behind *Faust*, see the translator's note, xxv.

egos – self-proclaimed geniuses whose projects transgress moral limits. Her works argue that cooperation and sympathy, particularly as practised by women in the family, were the ways to reform civil society. This view challenged the individualistic romantic ethos promoted by Percy Shelley and the Enlightenment political theories of her father, William Godwin.

It is hard not to see this ethic of romantic striving, this worship of the ego or the will, as an eerie foreshadow of the atrocities to come under fascism and its collective, unbounded will. To be fair, the romantics did not foresee fascism. But their ideas were used to weaken moral boundaries just when they were needed. In 1898, the young novelist Herman Hesse (1877–1962), enthused by his study of German romantics such as Novalis, told his parents that morality was replaced by aesthetics. The world would live to regret this aesthetic revolution in morals.

Ever since romanticism, popular culture has degraded the ideal of great individuals or geniuses. Romanticism is not popular in today's high culture. Yet popular culture, especially in the United States, produces a steady stream of money-making, superficial portraits of romantic individuals. In 1955, James Dean, template for the young American rebel, acted in the movie *Rebel without a Cause.* In the 1960s, an era of freedom, drugs, and rock and roll led to movies such as *Easy Rider,* where rebellious young men drive Harley-Davidson bikes and live on the road. Bob Dylan changed his public persona so often – from protest singer to genial Nashville cowboy – that popular magazines kept asking who the real Dylan was. The ideal was recycled to produce avenging cowboys and vigilante cops who were stopping an apocalypse or getting even. Actor Clint Eastwood made the rugged, violent individual a stock figure in his cowboy movies, such as *The Good, the Bad and the Ugly.* Eastwood's cowboy pictures fit the romantic myth that the history of the American West is one of strong individuals who, often by themselves, overcame adversity and dispensed justice. The *Die Hard* movie series updated the Eastwood genre. It featured John McClane (portrayed by Bruce Willis), a police detective who continually finds himself in the middle of a violent crisis where he is the only hope against disaster.

To take one more example, romanticism's interest in gothic culture is transformed by today's trendy "goths" whose persona of dark clothes and hair (and love of dark and morbid rock lyrics) seeks recognition as different while scoffing at conventional society.

SECTION 3: THE AVANT-GARDE ADVANCES

As Western modernity gathered force by the mid-1800s, a major reaction was the development of a class of artists who called themselves the avant-garde of art and, by extension, of society.[39] The avant-garde reached its zenith in the early decades of the twentieth century, as an international art movement. The avant-garde was incubated in Paris, that incredible nineteenth century centre of cultural movements and avid capitalism, of fierce conservatives and simmering revolutionaries, of stiff social hierarchies and bohemian gatherings on the edge of respectability. Paris was where modernity was invented, distilled, tested, and exported abroad.

The avant-garde tended to be critics of capitalistic modernity, especially as applied to art. Many of the avant-garde saw modernity as social irrationality, in a negative sense. It was an irrationality "without": crowded cities turned brown with coal pollution with a mass culture that ignored the fine arts.

The development of the avant-garde can be divided into two stages. The first stage extended from the late 1880s to its apex from 1910 to 1914, before the First World War. The war put an abrupt end to the movement. The second stage was the interim war years, from 1919 to the rise of the fascism in the early 1930s. I deal only with the first stage in this chapter.

A Scout for Society

Today, avant-garde is still popular but its original meaning has been watered down. Often, current usage means no more than that a consumer product or work of popular culture is new and different. Marketers use the images of famous avant-guarde artists, such as Picasso, to polish their corporation's public image, or they use avant-garde work to enhance commercial brands, such as using Jackson Pollock paintings as background at a fashion shoot for *Vogue* magazine.[40] Today, it is a genuine question whether a true avant-garde can exist in a

39 Pioneering works on the avant-garde include Poggioli's *Theory of the Avant-Garde*.

40 Cottington, *The Avant-Garde*, 90–1.

hypercommercial world that co-opts any and all images. The stance of being anti-commercial is a selling point for pop artists.

The concept of avant-garde has an important history.

The term came from the French military. The avant-garde were soldiers who scouted ahead of the main army. We should not be surprised that the term originated in France or among soldiers. The French Revolution showed how humans had the power to make fundamental changes to society. The term acquired a political sense as early as 1794 amid the revolutionary wars. A revolutionary military newspaper called itself *L'Avant-garde de l'armée des Pyrénées orientales* (The vanguard of the Eastern Pyrenees Army)[41] in support of the Jacobin Terror of 1793. On its banner was the image of a sword with the words "Liberty or Death."[42]

During the first half of the nineteenth century, avant-garde acquired additional meanings, most of which were aesthetic, i.e., referring to the role of the artist in society. Yet the political meaning did not dissipate. With the restoration of the French monarchy in 1815, groups sought ways to improve the restoration. One influential left-wing group was led by Henri de Saint-Simon. Just before his death, he described a society where artists would be the avant-garde or an advance lookout. Society would be led by an elite trio of artists, scientists, and industrialists. Among other things, artists would create art that supported the Saint-Simon socialist–technocratic conception of society.

Ideas on the social role of poets were expressed by Percy Shelley who was born in the middle of the revolutionary years and supported revolutionary aspirations. In 1821, he wrote *Defence of Poetry*. Shelley did not use the term avant-garde, but he did call artists "heralds" and "mirrors of futurity," and he used the famous phrase that poets were the "unacknowledged legislators of the world."[43] Shelley argued that poets introduce moral and legal ideas, which society codifies. In Shelley's worldview, great imaginative poets replace the great rational philosophers that were to direct Plato's ideal republic.

41 The Army of the Eastern Pyrenees was one of the French Revolutionary armies, active from 30 April 1793 to 12 October 1795. The army fought against the Kingdom of Spain during the War of the Pyrenees.

42 Cottington, *The Avant-Garde*, 22.

43 *Defence of Poetry* was first published posthumously in 1840 in *Essays, Letters from Abroad, Translations and Fragments* by Shelley's wife Mary Shelley.

However, there was a major difference between the views of the Saint-Simons and Shelley. The Saint-Simons, including the socialist leaders that would follow them, wanted artists to support *specific* political programs. The Saint-Simon view was an authoritarian approach to art as socially useful. Shelley, a romantic liberal, had no political program for artists. He wanted artists to be free to use their imagination as they pleased.[44]

Karl Marx and Friedrich Engels in *The Communist Manifesto* critiqued the "critical utopian socialism" of Saint-Simon for ignoring the proletariat. The Saint-Simons sought to bring about utopian social improvements for all, peacefully. Marx and Engels complain that the Saint-Simons reject "all political and especially all revolutionary action," to bring it about.[45] Neither Marx nor the communist leaders that came later dispensed with the notion of an avant-garde. As Lenin argued in his 1902 political pamphlet *What is to be Done?*, the proletariat movement should be led from above by a vanguard of revolutionary forces – their most energetic and committed members. There was no room for a Shelley-like elite of free artists. Writers and artists were to serve the Communist Party. Lenin declared that he was a philistine who did not understand and did not derive any pleasure from modern art. Art should start with the "beautiful" as portrayed by masters of old. "Why must we bow low in front of the new, as if it were God, only because it is new?"[46]

For Lenin and other Bolsheviks, the difference between the communist and non-communist avant-garde was that the communist leaders were *part* of the proletariat. The illusionary nature of this claim became clear not long after the Russian revolution, when the masses were led by a powerful and tyrannical Communist Party bureaucracy which used ideology, like the bourgeoisie they criticized, to justify their elite privileges. This leadership was *not* part of the proletariat.

From the mid-1800s, a new aesthetic meaning of the avant-garde was developing. Originally, the Saint-Simons and others saw all of art as avant-garde. But now the notion arose that only a select group of artists constituted the avant-garde. They were the most advanced, progressive, historically important, and artistically autonomous. Avant-garde came

44 On the difference between Shelley's romantic view of the artist and the authoritarian view, see Calinescu, *Five Faces of Modernity*, 105.

45 Marx and Engels, *The Communist Manifesto*, 35.

46 Zetkin, *Reminiscences of Lenin*, 14.

to refer to artists outside the margins of French establishment culture. The avant-garde claimed to be autonomous from the advancing bourgeoise culture of modernity and its decadent artistic forms. They would embrace radical and oppositional aesthetic principles and practices.

To belong to the avant-garde, one must, first and foremost, experiment in new artistic topics, formats, and techniques. This made the avant-garde modernists in art. Experiment encouraged abstractionist, absurdist, and cubist methods. In music, composers stretched tonality. Some artists, such as dadaists Marcel Duchamp (1887–1968) and Jean Arp (1886–1966), introduced methods of chance to select notes, the next line of poetry, or the next brush stroke (e.g., shuffling a deck of cards with notes associated with each card).[47] Surrealist Joan Miró's (1893–1983) artistic imagination could be triggered by a chance element – a random patch of colour or texture from which a painting would emerge. Therefore, artistic works could be strange or shocking. Avant-garde works were more than new. Their newness was radical.

Many of the nineteenth-century artists and thinkers were *both* modernists and members of the avant-garde. Picasso, by the early 1900s, was quintessentially modernist and avant-garde. Modernism in art is a psychological reaction to modern life resulting in artistic works, while the avant-garde is a sociological concept, referring to groups of artists that shared aesthetic practices and positioned themselves against other art philosophies. By the early 1900s, the convergence of modernism and the avant-garde created an "alternate professionalism" in art.[48]

Yet the terms "modernism" and "avant-garde" were not co-extensive. There were artists who did not belong to avant-garde groups.[49] And, modernism did not *necessarily* mean the use of new forms. For example, a composer could use traditional materials, such as folk music, in novel ways. This trend appeared in the works of composers Béla Bartok and Ralph Vaughn Williams and in the poetry of William Butler Yeats. However, in the main, a modernist work was created within an avant-garde group or with an awareness of avant-garde concerns.[50]

47 Cottington, *The Avant-Garde*, 32–3.

48 Ibid., 17.

49 For example, Henri Rousseau in Paris from 1900 to 1910 and Alfred Wallis in Cornwall, England about 1930.

50 Cottington, *The Avant-Garde*, 13.

Rejecting Mainstream Values

What sparked the first stage of the avant-garde?

I have already alluded to one major factor: the infiltration of capitalism into the art market. Paris experienced a phenomenal growth of artists and works of popular art between the 1830s and the 1880s. Art production was commercialized and industrialized. Between 1860 and 1880, the number of writers in Paris doubled. The number of published novels, volumes of poetry, and plays published increased by 50 per cent by the mid-1880s.[51] The growth of a mass art market was due, in part, to increased literacy and a need for entertainment outside the factory gates. This increase in artists and artistic production provided the resources for a popular culture where commercial success and popularity ruled. Popular culture wanted paintings in different sizes and on a broader set of topics than favoured by high art. Art became decorative, as something to embellish one's private rooms and to impress visitors. *More and more* artworks were needed to satisfy demand. Art was part of the new capitalistic mode of life, of commodification and consumption. Anything could be sold, and everything had a price. Nonetheless, aristocratic French institutions of high art did not collapse or retreat. Despite the influx of artists, conservative art institutions continued to favour a minority who followed the rules of classicism. This blocked attempts by new artists to display their non-classical works.

Therefore, the avant-garde became a two-fold dissent: a dissent against capitalistic art and a dissent against traditional art culture. The avant-garde set out to create their own art, to find their own art dealers and patrons, to produce their own magazines, and to find places to display their work. Their quest was assisted by a new media. The government relaxed the press laws and printers began to use the new rotary web press. This paved the way for an alternate press of small magazines each representing some political or aesthetic point of view.

Just as the new medium of newspapers fuelled the French Revolution in the previous century, the new medium of alternate small magazines in nineteenth-century Paris fuelled the avant-garde revolution. Artists' sense of autonomy was enhanced by the fact that they could publish manifestos and ideas in their own magazines. Artistic ideas spread

51 Ibid., 15.

quickly such as the rejection of metre by symbolist poets; the Fauvism rejection of classical pictorial representation; and the discovery of non-Western art, such as Miró's attraction to pre-historic cave art and Japanese calligraphy, Paul Gauguin's inclusion of Tahitian motifs in paintings, and the "negro art" that influenced a young Picasso.[52]

By 1914, a pan-European network of avant-garde artists existed with their own art sellers, critics, publishers, and markets. The term avant-garde was now a proud badge of artistic non-conformity – saving art from decadent forces. Yet beneath the solemn art manifestos were ambitious creative artists seeking to promote their own interests and fame.

SECTION 4: MODERNITY AND DECADENCE

Paris Renovates

In 1853, a public works project to change the face of central Paris began under the direction of the prefect of the Seine,[53] Georges-Eugène Haussmann, commissioned by Emperor Napoleon III.[54] The project would continue until 1927, long after Napoleon III dismissed Haussmann due to opposition to his plan. Today, the centre of Paris is the result of Haussmann's renovation.

The renewal was justified on grounds of population growth, increased traffic, and the need for better sanitation. The industrial revolution had brought people from the countryside into the city. From 1825 to 1850, Paris's population grew from 855,000 to 1,314,000. It was the most heavily populated European city, after London.

The plan was a child of modernism. The idea was to make the centre of Paris modern and more rational. What did rational mean? It meant techno-rationality applied to the aesthetics of city planning. This aesthetic had no patience for chaotic neighbourhoods with small, dark,

52 Finlay, *Picasso's Life*, 61.

53 The Seine, created in 1790, was the French department that overlooked the Paris area. Its prefect had direct authority over the city of Paris. The department was abolished in 1968.

54 He was Charles Louis-Napoleon Bonaparte, nephew of the famous first emperor. Elected president of the Second Republic in 1848, Louis-Napoleon organized a coup toward the end of his first term. He dissolved the legislature, changed the constitution, and named himself Emperor Napoleon III. During the Franco-Prussian War, Napoleon III was captured by the Germans, and the empire was overthrown.

and winding streets. Tourists today find such areas quaint but officials in 1850 saw them as signs of medieval backwardness. This chaotic jumble of idiosyncratic areas must be organized into a clear, efficient, and lawful order. Central streets must be wide, paved, clean, and well lit. Streets were to be organized according to geometrical grids of avenues, running perfectly straight in a north–south and east–west direction. If streets turn, they are graceful arcs. Given this layout, the heart of the city becomes more accessible to the democratic masses, or so it was argued. In fact, Haussmann's plan exiled the poor to the margins of the city. The city centre would be solidly middle and upper class. The centre would speak of bourgeois progress.[55]

Haussmann's plan became a battle over the virtues and vices of making things modern, a debate over modernity. When political pressure mounted in 1870, the emperor dismissed Haussmann, who initially refused to resign. Haussmann's successors completed his plan.

Two of France's greatest writers despised the renovation: Gustave Flaubert (1821–1880) and Charles Baudelaire. Both shared "a horror of progress and a hatred of modern life"[56] and adopted a decadent stance. In his *Salammbô*, Flaubert combined an anti-modern sensibility with a relish for extreme acts of sadism, images of gruesome decay and a dense, opaque style where it is difficult to follow the narrative. By the time Baudelaire died in 1867, about 25,000 buildings had been destroyed, including the house and the street where he was born.

Decadence as Decay

Originally, decadence was a term of limited application, a term of historical studies referring to certain historical periods, e.g., the decline of Greek democracy. With the seventeenth and eighteenth centuries, the application of decadence widens. It begins to be used to portray certain tendencies in human nature, to analyze social relations, and to

55 An earlier effort to instantiate the values of modernity was the redesign of Washington, DC, by French engineer Pierre D'Enfant, commissioned by President Washington. Once again, grids and graceful curving avenues took priority while a democratic note would be struck by the openness of the National Mall. Interestingly, London also underwent a facelift but avoided massive grids. Officials restated medieval styles, such as the neo-Gothic parliament buildings.

56 Weir, *Decadence*, 32.

critique culture. Some people were decadent in personality; some societies were declining because they were in a decadent phase; some art was decadent, falling short of a better art in the past.

By the nineteenth and twentieth centuries, decadence referred to a lifestyle in the artistic and bohemian circles of Paris, London, Vienna, Berlin, and elsewhere. Decadence became a rebellion against modernity.

The literal meaning of decadence is simple. It means decay. Decay of something thought strong, robust, healthy, growing, or natural. Apples decay and flowers wilt, and people's external appearances can become sickly or pale, their energy replaced by ennui. These observable features are used in paintings and novels to symbolize decay in life. Also, decay can be thought of as abnormal behaviour or someone sinking into moral depravity. It can be a scepticism of what is higher. As we saw with the aesthetic of the grotesque, humans can reduce all that is intellectual, spiritual, or higher to bodily impulses.

By the 1880s, the term was used in discussions of art and life, such as in the novel *À rebours* (Against the grain) in 1884 by French writer Joris-Karl Huysmans wherein the artist-hero is a sickly aristocrat with esoteric, exacting taste. The novel influenced Oscar Wilde. Nietzsche here and there refers to himself as a decadent.[57] Towards the end of his life, he wrote that "nothing has preoccupied me more profoundly than the problem of decadence" whether it is the decadence lurking beneath morality or embodied in Wagner's "corrupt" music.[58] A few decades later, Freud defined psychological decadence as degrading oneself or others sexually or in other ways. The desire to degrade is attributed to a death instinct, one of two primary instincts in the libido.

Types of decadence include (1) political decadence, e.g., the decline of an empire, the loss of power or vigor in a nation, or the corruption of a political scheme; (2) personal or individual decadence, e.g., someone adopts an unhealthy libertine lifestyle. Decadence is usually associated with what is excessive and harmful. Moral and sexual mores draw lines between the normal and abnormal, the healthy and the decadent. For

57 Nietzsche has many meanings for decadence, but a primary meaning is the incapacity or unwillingness to affirm life lived vigorously, to live according to our will to power. This meaning was placed in opposition to Christian morality as non-affirming of life. It also was placed against Schopenhauer's pessimism that life is full of struggles caused by our will and that the best response is to deny one's will.

58 Nietzsche, *The Birth of Tragedy and the Case of Wagner*, 155.

example, sadomasochistic desires may be considered moral decadence. Moreover, decadence may be associated with bizarre behaviour or the onset of madness. For example, the soldiers in the film *Apocalypse Now,* tottering on the edge of madness due to a barbaric Vietnam war, display a decadence in their worldview and actions. (3) Decadence may also include cultural decadence, such as a decline in a culture's art, philosophy, science, and public life.

Historians have used the decline of the Roman Empire to discuss the three kinds of decadence: the political decline of a once formidable empire, the personal decadence and excessive lifestyles of emperors such as Nero and Caligula, and the cultural decline in writing and the arts during this period. The same claims are made about contemporary life. Writers worry about the decline of the American political system or worry about the cultural decadence of democracies where the public are submerged in hypercommercial popular media.

What we consider to be decadent and whether we think decadence is good or evil depends on our conceptions of the good life, of what is healthy or socially valuable. If you believe that ancient Greek rationality was a progressive development, then you are likely to regard the return of the irrational as a sign of cultural decadence. Claims of decadence can be controversial, and what is thought decadent can change. Lesbianism was once considered abnormal and decadent. So much so that writers in the nineteenth and early twentieth century used it to shock conservative moral opinion. Today, many people think it is normal and not decadent. In the nineteenth century, Oscar Wilde and other artistic decadents challenged conventional thinking by favouring the writings of the decaying Roman Empire, thereby displaying the "fascination of corruption."[59] Unfortunately, the philosophy of decadence can itself deteriorate. It becomes nothing more than a chic attitude, e.g., an attempt by popular artists to appear different. The attempt to shock becomes wearisome. Trite.

59 Weir, *Decadence*, 62.

Baudelaire's Protest

Artists grasped the meaning of modernity and its decadence long before social scientists, through laborious studies, defined it features.[60]

Decadence in Paris was expressed in the irrational literary style of Baudelaire, Paul Verlaine (1844–1896), and others. It was irrational for several reasons. One, and typically, the text did little to help the reader understand the work in a traditional, rational way. There is no logically unfolding narrative and no unifying meaning behind the events. There was, instead, a lack of unity and a "lack of reason."[61] Decadent writing did not aspire, like classical literature, to speak great moral truths about life and human grandeur. To the contrary, the removal of morality was a hallmark. The style does not try to be orderly. There was an attention to detail that took attention away from any overall message; there are unexpected combinations of ideas and a moving back and forth between emotions and moods.[62] Decadent writers seem to have no moral to tell because, one suspects, they do not think the world is morally or rationally ordered.

Further, readers or viewers are confronted with objects and people who are contradictory and paradoxical. Take, for example, Édouard Manet (1832–1883), who was not a decadent but a modernist, one of the first to paint modern life. In 1859, Manet painted *The Absinthe Drinker.*[63] *The Absinthe Drinker* is a full-length portrait, in dark tones, of an alcoholic rag-picker named Collardet near the Louvre in Paris. The painting could be called Baudelairean because of how it treats the derelict, i.e., as dignified and sordid at the same time. When Baudelaire writes about prostitutes, they too are given a sort of nobility "even in the mire."[64] Both men give different aspects of the modern world, the

60 I am reminded of Freud's astonishment that Arthur Schnitzler (1862–1931) had come to the same conclusions about the human psyche in his plays and stories that Freud had reached through laborious clinical work. See Weir, *Decadence*, 90.

61 Weir, *Decadence*, 35.

62 Nietzsche identified this attention to detail – details that obscure a larger perspective – as a mark of "literary decadence." Nietzsche, *The Case of Wagner*, 170.

63 See the painting at https://en.wikipedia.org/wiki/The_Absinthe_Drinker_(Manet_painting)#/media/File:Edouard_Manet_-_The_Absinthe_Drinker_-_Google_Art_Project.jpg.

64 Weir, *Decadence*, 38.

low and the high, the bourgeoise and the destitute, equal billing. They deserved equal attention and respect.

In Baudelaire, we have a founder of modern poetry and one of the chief theorists of aesthetic modernity. How do we even begin to describe Baudelaire, with all of his psychological and artistic complexity?

We begin with his life and how it altered the image of the creative person. Baudelaire spent his life fleeing creditors, hanging out with prostitutes, tramping through poor and sometimes dangerous parts of Paris, sleeping in cheap hotel rooms, and trying to sell articles to journals. With Baudelaire and Verlaine, and other poets of the street, the social image of the writer and the artist shifts from that of a higher philosophical seer to that of a social misfit who is ridiculed and ostracized. The artist joins the ranks of the down and out. These artistic misfits give us a new language for understanding life, and they provide a different view of life: from the bottom up, not the top down. T.S. Eliot said Baudelaire achieved a "complete renovation" not only of poetic language but of our attitude towards life.[65]

What are the elements of that renovation?

First, Baudelaire brings the prosaic and the disgusting into verse. Baudelaire continues the imperfectionist tradition. But he *intensifies* the portrayal of the imperfect in art. His verbal images, like dissonant music, clash and give us the central theme of modern psychology: that humans are deeply conflicted beings, with a psyche of competing capacities. If modernity means anything, psychologically, it means that there is a lack of unity and order in individuals and in society. We are disassociated from our selves and from others. The bits and pieces of the modern psyche do not go together well. Baudelaire's poetry expresses, in an uncompromising manner, modern experience as inchoate. The chaos felt within reflects the disorder without. It is an irrationality induced from the ambient world and culture. This not just alienation, a feeling of being separate from society. It is a visceral sense that we ourselves lack integrity. Modernity as psychology threatens us with incoherence and nihilism.

Second, Baudelaire is one of the first poets of the modern city with its many levels, from the opera house to the subterranean labyrinths of the underground, where low-life figures look more ghostly than real.

65 Baudelaire, *The Flowers of Evil*, xxv.

Poetry, or any serious intellectual work, faces the task of somehow speaking about and understanding this reality, which is far from classical Greek perfectionism. As he says in the *Salon of 1846*, the artist's "heroic" duty is to observe the spectacle of fashionable life and thousands of roaming existences – criminals and "kept" women – drifting in the underground of a great city. "The life of the city is rich in poetic and marvelous subjects ... but we do not notice it."

Within aesthetic modernity, there arises a secular mystery about life that replaces the theological mysteries of the medieval era. It is the mystery of why there is irrationality and imperfection. In the bowels of Paris, Baudelaire sees seven old men emerge from the dark streets and is "struck by the mystery, this absurdity."[66] This is no sugary romanticism about the imperfect. Victor Hugo (1802–1885) had written poems of the city, its workers, and prostitutes. But, unlike Baudelaire, Hugo maintained a romanticism and sentimentalism. Prostitutes had hearts of gold and criminals had a conscience. Baudelaire will not allow us even this illusion. To be modern is to live without old comforts.

Third, Baudelaire's writing displays the irony that comes with modern hyper self-consciousness. Self-consciousness becomes a trademark of contemporary writers and theatrical characters, as they remark on their circumstances before the audience. Baudelaire seems to live with a *constant awareness* of himself, a self-scrutiny that seems more unrelenting than Luther's religious scanning of his sinful soul. What comes from such scrutiny? An internal voice that "gnaws on me and shakes me hard ... her poison in all my veins."[67] The poetic imagination is a source of self-torture, which then becomes, in true Baudelairean form, a perverse satisfaction.

Ironically, Baudelaire's modernist rebellion is fuelled by traditional, ancient ideas.

He explained his conflicted world by using ideas from religious conservativism while he was nostalgic for aristocratic culture. Democracy was a tyranny of liberty and the bad taste of the majority.

From religion, he uses the role of the devil. In his note to the reader at the beginning of *The Flowers of Evil*, Baudelaire states that the devil moves us like puppets on a string. Humans pretend to be good and

66 Ibid., 181.
67 Ibid., 157.

offer "vows of faith" but we love sin more than anything and we "turn back gladly to the path of filth." The only reason we have yet to indulge in "slaughter ... arson, poison, rape" is that our spirit "lacks the nerve."[68] This is modern dark irrationalism from medieval times. It is the doctrine of original sin. It is the brutal acknowledgment that human nature has an inescapable dark side and we secretly love that side of ourselves.

Lurking Nihilism

Baudelaire's analysis of capitalistic modernity was correct in the main. His poetry, in an uncompromising and courageous manner, opened up artists to the reality of the modern world.

Yet his thought raises difficult questions and tangles. There are seeming inconsistencies. Also, his portrayal of modernity, for all of its rich and poetic astuteness, leaves one with a feeling of incompleteness, of things not said. Or worse, a whiff of nihilism.

Is he not inconsistent in his declaration that the modern artist is cut off from the past and must be radical, yet it is permissible to employ ancient ideas of aristocracy and of the devil? If, as he says, ideas and traditions from the past weaken our capacity to respond originally to the present, does this not apply to conceptual schemes of the past?

Further, members of the nineteenth-century avant-grade, such as Baudelaire, needed to explain, more carefully, their use of key terms such as "decadent." They called themselves decadent and that was, apparently, a good thing, or a term of approval. But when they applied it to capitalistic modernity, it was a fiercely negative term. So, which is it: is decadence positive or negative? Logically, you can't have it both ways. Or, you *can* have it both ways as long as you carefully explain how you are using the term with different meanings in different contexts.

One can wonder about the completeness of Baudelaire's assertions about human life and his social philosophy. For example, is there any sign of hope for ordinary people in modernity? To be sure, artists can capture such humans living in modernity in all of their particularity and discordant experience, but what about the people themselves? Psychologically, is it possible for such people to establish some tolerable level of integration in their person? Or is this a naïve wish?

68 Ibid., 5–7.

Politically, does Baudelaire have any new and positive ideas about how humans can regain control of their society? Democracy is ruled out. What is left? Aesthetic protests from artists who have removed themselves from the mainstream? Art alone cannot save the world, so what else needs to be done? Does Baudelaire provide an adequate perspective or agenda for dealing with capitalistic modernity? The answer, I think, is no.

Supporters of Baudelaire will protest that writing psychological or political theory is not the role of a poet. His worth is found in his poetic writings and visions. I agree with this objection. It would be absurd to ask Baudelaire for extended philosophical treatises. But it is not absurd to ask him to provide a more complete explanation of his view of society than he provides in a relatively small number of highly polemical articles. A poet of his influence should not step into the public sphere, provide a searing critique of modernity, and then not stay around to engage others in a protracted philosophical give-and-take. Baudelaire the militant voluntarily stepped into the zone of philosophical thought about humans using non-poetic language. Once he does so, he opens himself up to a dialogue, in non-poetic terms, about his philosophical conceptions. That dialogue does not occur. Or, is the point of Baudelaire's work that such attempts to spell out an alternate course of action or to hope for something positive are pointless?

For an example of why great poets cannot avoid discursive reflection, take Baudelaire's double take on morality. He denigrates conventional morality yet he also helps himself to moral terms to condemn capitalistic modernity and democracy. He calls on artists to heroically challenge capitalistic philistines. But why? Why not give up the struggle and dive into the distractions and forgetfulness of modern life?

Here, Baudelaire needs a serious, detailed, discursive *moral argument,* not poetry, on what one *ought* to do and how society *ought* to be. He simply cannot assert his view and not engage other critical perspectives. He needs to articulate a plausible moral philosophy, if he wants to participate credibly in this public zone of debate. But if morality is conventional and, by implication, arbitrary or relative, how to construct a moral viewpoint to defend one's values? Why are Baudelaire's moral assertions not simply conventional, also? As ancient philosophers warned, moral relativism is a self-refuting position.

Baudelaire described himself as a helmsman trying to steer a boat in a storm "through a monstrous, shoreless sea." He believed that artists had a *responsibility* – to depict modern life as it is. Responsibility is a moral notion. Given his dark conception of humans and modern life, we must ask Baudelaire, why take on this responsibility? Why bother?

Baudelaire's case underlines the predicament of modern thought. If one pushes decadence and relativity to its logical extent, one ends up with a thin morality that cannot support one's favoured values. Also, one ends up with a lurking nihilism.

Does Baudelaire's view lead to hopelessness, or does it provide an excuse for inaction? For, if many modern humans are as Baudelaire depicts them – conflicted, attracted to mass society, driven by Satan, corrupt in nature, and keen to conform to empty values – what terrible things can we expect of this human? Truly, there is nothing we can do, is there?

This is a council of despair. It should cause fear. What will these Baudelairean humans do as they run from their intolerable nothingness, the way that ordinary Greeks ran from news that their gods were dead?

We already know the answer. Less that fifty years after Baudelaire died, we moderns would start the first of two world wars.

CONCLUSION: THE GREAT SPLIT

This chapter has examined how, at some point near the middle of the nineteenth century, an "irreversible split"[69] occurred within Western civilization, a split between capitalistic modernity, as a state of society, and aesthetic modernity, as artistic values opposed to capitalistic modernity.

In the end, what did all of this protesting mean for Western art and culture? Can it be dismissed as artists acting badly or arrogantly? Was it a local flare up now in the past?

No. It was not local and not just about art. The problems remain today.

The split was deep and of great portent. It signalled that ancient tensions in the Western world were rising and threatening civilization. Things were reaching a cultural climax.

69 Calinescu, *Five Faces of Modernity*, 41.

Ideologically, ancient dualisms remained unresolved, placing different views of society at odds. The dualisms were reason versus passion, logic versus romanticism, ideas versus praxis, the eternal world versus the earthly world; perfectionism versus imperfectionism, eternal beauty versus contingent beauty; absolute authoritarianism and relativistic liberalism.

Socially, competitive capitalism, class warfare, and then severe nationalism would place these ideologically divided people at each other's throat. The tensions could not be resolved. Nor could they be safely contained within academia. The frustrations, hatreds, and conflicts would erupt into mass movements, fascism, and world war.

The artistic revolt was a sign of the terrible trouble brewing in the belly of Western society. In 1914, the Western world would fall apart amid war, and its pretense of being a higher civilization would be shattered, like Humpty Dumpty after his great fall. What is worse, no one to this day has known how to put Humpty Dumpty back together again, despite two world wars, and millions killed.

The world still follows the direction set by modernity as it arose in the nineteenth century. It still chases after ever new technology and the delusion of technological fixes to deep cultural problems. Global capitalism still seeks resources and wealth at the expense of equality. Leaders still seek great power. Nations still divide along tired ideological lines and, amid the chaos, authoritarianism once again looks attractive. But now, twenty-first century modernism faces the additional threats of nuclear or climatic disaster – *real,* not mythical, apocalyptic dangers.

4

Makers of Other Worlds

Art is dangerous: yes, it can never be chaste, if it's chaste, it's not art.

Pablo Picasso[1]

Art is the cry of distress by those who experience at first hand the fate of mankind.

Arnold Schoenberg[2]

BY THE MID-1800S, modernity's attempt to redefine the balance between rationalism and irrationalism ended in a tangle and then a split. This first swing of the pendulum in modern times split culture into two modernities: a capitalistic modernity promoting a new industrial techno-rationalism and an aesthetic modernity promoting romantic irrationalism. The values, attitudes and aims of the two modernities were opposites. Aesthetic modernity created a hostile avant-garde whose members could be attracted to decadence as an attitude or lifestyle.

SECTION 1: MAKING WORLDS

Desperate Creation

In the next two chapters, I jump ahead about fifty years to the turn of the twentieth century and look at a second swing that was no less a tangle: the emergence of what I call the *hypermodern* mindset. Modernity sought to save itself through intense and at times desperate attempts to create new ideas as optimism declined and the world, confused, fell back on authoritarianism and mad war. Many artists took to creating

1 Cited in Schama, *The Power of Art*, 1.

2 Schoenberg, "Aphorismen," in 1910.

new worlds of art, music, and philosophy that were radically unlike the world as ordinarily experienced.

World making is the capacity of the human mind to radically re-conceptualize reality or some domain of reality. Humans *make* theories and express visions of alternate or other worlds. These other worlds are works of art, philosophical worldviews, new forms of music, or exotic worlds in novels. These worlds of imagination and unbounded intellect are first experienced as beyond what we understand as rational. Hence, initially, they tend to be rejected as impossible portrayals of the world, the way we first react to Escher's "impossible" drawings.[3]

By entering into these worlds through imagination, careful listening, and deep thinking we take in new forms of rationality and irrationality. Through our ears, we take in music that seems to make no sense or confronts us with a new universe of tones. Through our eyes, we see strange objects appear on a painter's canvas. When we read novels, we encounter puzzling narratives as in Kafka's *Metamorphosis*, where Gregor Samsa finds himself changed into an insect. Through abstract cognition, our minds may grasp a new rationality in the form of an "alternate logic."[4]

In world making, we encounter the boundaries of the rational and irrational. Such controversial creations of the mind, whether plausible or implausible, are motors of intellectual, artistic, and social development. I think of these makers of other worlds as creators of irrealist art. Irrealism is the view that humans literally create versions of worlds when they engage in philosophy, art, and other forms of creative thinking.[5]

I am interested in twentieth-century makers of these austere, strange, ridiculous, dangerous, confounding, or ravishing other worlds. I regard these world makings as hypermodern responses to increasing despair over the direction of modernity. These makers have largely defined the modern consciousness.

In this chapter, I reflect on the creators of the new irrational music in the early twentieth century in the West, particularly in Austria and

3 See Seckel, *Masters of Deception: Escher, Dalí & the Artists of Optical Illusion.*

4 Alternate logics are another creation of modernity that initially was considered irrational because it rejected classical logic's stress on bivalence (sentences are either true or false). Many-valued or fuzzy logics apply to thinking where assertions are other than true and false. See Haack, *Philosophies of Logics.*

5 Goodman, *Ways of Worldmaking*, chapter 1.

Germany. This music is often called atonal music. It refers to composers who departed from the rules and tonality of classical music, especially the Austrian composer Arnold Schoenberg.

In the next chapter, I will look at makers of worlds in art and philosophy. I discuss the paintings of surrealists, with their irrational melting clocks and impossible landscapes. Then I look at an example of the opposite: the ultra-rationalism of logical positivists in the early 1900s, with their dream of constructing the world – a new world – through pure logic and pure facts. Even where constructions have failed, they advanced human thought and experience. With atonality and surrealism, the pendulum swings toward the irrational; with the positivists, the pendulum swings toward rationalism.

Before turning to music, I sketch some features of modernity and modern music from the mid-1800s and into the 1900s. This is necessary because trends during this period prompted the hypermodern.

Exhaustion and Extremism

As the second half of the nineteenth century progressed, there grew a sense that Western society was declining and its energy becoming exhausted. Mixed with the perception of decline was dissatisfaction, disappointment, and frustration. Later, in the twentieth century, analysts of the period would coin a term to describe the malaise, *fin-de-siècle*. Many books would be written on world weariness in centres such as Vienna, Berlin, Paris, and London.

The perception of exhaustion prompted the offering of stronger and stronger solutions. Somehow, it was urged, the downward spiral needed to be stopped. People thought of society as a sick person who needs strong medicine. Society also needed to be awakened to apparent threats and hidden causes of the decline. This opened the door to extremism of all kinds, including racial intolerance, scape goats, tribalism, and militarism. This transition to extremism happened in Western Europe, dragging the rest of the world into the first of two world wars.

The dissatisfaction was wider than the prior romantic critique of modernity. There was dissatisfaction with *both* capitalistic and aesthetic modernity. Capitalism and the alternative of romanticism lost their allure, their vitality.

One source of scepticism had to do with nineteenth-century politics. People began to question the promise of freedom and equality under nineteenth-century liberalism, the successor to the French Revolution. Liberal society was good for the bourgeoisie and the capitalists but not so much for the poor or minorities such as the Jews.

Countries also encountered their own demoralizing events, such as the humbling French defeat in the Franco-Prussian war. Arch-conservativism re-emerged. In Vienna, for example, liberalism went into decline in the 1890s as the Austro-Hungarian empire decayed. Liberalism seemed in the past when the city elected Karl Lueger, an antisemitic Christian Socialist, as mayor. In Germany, as we will see, the *volk* movement despised liberalism and democracy and blamed the country's problems on capitalistic modernity, liberalism, and the Jews.

By the 1880s, romanticism was another ism or trend, along with nationalism and a revived realism in art. Romanticism's constant stress on great emotion was tiring and eventually tiresome. For example, new romantic music had to be bigger, more emotional, and grander. The trend ended with Richard Wagner's mammoth productions and Mahler's aspiration to write a symphony "so great that the whole world is actually reflected therein."[6] As Ezra Pound complained, "the whole flaw of 'emotional music'" was that it acted like a drug, so you must have more drug because the drug's effect "is constantly weaker and weaker."[7]

At the same time, socialists, syndicalists, anarchists, ultra-conservatives, and Marxists began to offer more extreme answers to social problems articulated in bombastic manifestos. In the late 1800s and into the 1900s, there was an *intensification* and *polarization* in society. This included the European avant-garde. Artistic positions were also more extreme. Artists would follow the political radicals with their own manifestos.

Collectivism: Saving the World through Art?

The avant-garde was at its height before the First World War. Powerful, modernist movements, such as expressionism, fauvism, and cubism, took the art world by storm, its radicalness shocking the bourgeoisie.[8]

6 Gustave Mahler to Anna von Mildenburg, 18 July 1896 (on his Third Symphony), *Selected Letters of Gustave Mahler*, ed. Knud Martner, 190.

7 Pound, "Arnold Dolmetsch," 434.

8 The term "fauves" was coined by French critic Louise Vauxcelles to described the outrage and dismay at Matisse's (and others) boldly coloured and distorted compositions. Hamilton, *Painting and Sculpture in Europe, 1880 to 1940*, 100.

After the First World War, avant-garde artists picked up the pieces of their movement. But the world had changed. The overwhelming issue for the avant-garde, like many other groups, was how and why civilization had imploded. Artists rejected the causes and values that resulted in the war. But there was no consensus on what those causes and values were. This avant-garde still saw itself as a social scout but its component groups were intensely caught up in politics and separated on liberal and conservative lines. What they had in common was a stress on *collective* social action, directed by some political philosophy. Some groups were conservative and scientific. Other groups were left-wing, as before, but now the left-wing groups were more radical, with dadaists supporting anarchism and surrealists supporting communism. Others were excited by the Russian revolution and worked to promote the proletariat movement.

During the First World War and after, a conservative call for order swept through France and other countries. French conservatism had, of course, existed in the late 1800s, as evidenced by the prosecution for treason of Captain Alfred Drefus, a Jew. Now, after a bloody world war, conservatives called for a return to traditions that made France "true" and great, a return to classicism in art, and an antipathy to foreigners and Jews. The conservatives portrayed France as a nation steeped in ancient Latin traditions and aristocratic, civilizing values – which flew in the face of modernism. This patriotic ideology was supported by a chauvinistic press. Thus, out of the disorder of war there was another swing of the pendulum, this time to the right.

Conservatives blamed pre-war individualism, liberalism, and forms of art like cubism, for the war and for social decline. The answer, they said, was collectivism and a scientific, orderly approach to all things. Collectivism was embraced so seriously by conservatives in France that they called for national standards in cuisine, nutrition, and fashion, which ran against France's legendary, and individualistic, approach to creating great food and high fashion. There was even a proposal that all citizens wear a French national shoe to support the economy.[9]

9 Worries about nutrition led to the creation of a "Scientific Society for Nutritional Science and the Rational Nourishment of Man."

Many conservatives saw the future in terms of capitalism, industrial rationality, and the machine. They took scientific methods of manufacturing as a model for re-establishing order in society. They argued that social processes, from manufacture to art, should be based on scientific theories and mechanical processes. The machine was idealized as precise and useful. Its usefulness was quantifiable. This kind of thinking found its bible in Frederick Taylor's *The Principles of Scientific Management* of 1911. The American mechanical engineer was called "the father of the efficiency movement."

The years between the two world wars show that authoritarianism and fascism were part of the "anti-democratic legacy of modernism."[10] Many traditionalists saw fascism as the best way to prevent the spread of communism and to preserve aristocratic traditions.

In mid-November 1918, less than a week after the war ended, a French manifesto of art appeared called *After Cubism*. It was published by painter Amédé Ozenfant (1886–1966) and the architect Charles-Édouard Jeanneret (1888–1965), who called himself Le Corbusier. The manifesto celebrated the "modern spirit" as exhibited by the stylessness of industrial machinery, the practical efficiency of engineering projects such as dams and the functionalism of buildings such as silos. Ozenfant and Jeanneret created the movement of purism in art, influential between 1918 and 1925. Purism would be a purer cubism, producing paintings of severe abstraction and formal lines. Purism was based on the belief that humans had a fundamental need for order and, therefore, were attracted to art expressed in orderly, intellectual terms. Rationality was manifested by geometric designs and the orderly work of machines. Moreover, a pure art would be "immune from personal interpretation," thereby reducing the possibility of contrary opinion. Purism was a conservative attempt to return to the simple in a time of complexity and chaos.[11]

The attraction of machines and "art with a social purpose" was international. In Russia, an art movement called "constructivism," beginning in 1913 with Vladimir Tatlin, rejected the Parisian avant-garde's ideal of autonomous art. Communist artists, such as Aleksandr Rodchenko and Vladamir Mayakovsky, insisted that artists should be useful to

10 Taruskin, "The Dark Side of Modern Music," 34.

11 See Ball, *Ozenfant and Purism: The Evolution of a Style 1915–1930*. Also, Hamilton, *Painting and Sculpture in Europe*, 170.

socialist society. Artists should not settle for creating baubles for the bourgeoise. Machine-like design and thinking would construct a new modern society for proletariat Russia.[12] Constructivist artists showed their usefulness to the Russian revolution in many ways. Some created propaganda poster art; others produced stage sets for plays that promoted the revolution. This movement laid the ground work for the Stalinist doctrine of socialist realism, of useful communist art.

Other collective efforts for a new society included the Bauhaus school of design in Germany and, in the Netherlands, the De Stijl movement from 1917 to 1932. De Stijl was a group of Dutch abstract artists who employed a rigorous geometry of horizontal and vertical lines. Theo van Doesburg (1883–1931), a central figure in De Stijl, talked about creating art from universal "logical principles of style."[13]

Meanwhile, authoritarianism and fascism found support among avant-garde movements. In London, the short-lived vorticist group came together in the summer of 1914 around painter-writer Wyndham Lewis, poet Ezra Pound, and sculptor Henri Gaudier-Brzeska.[14] It espoused a patriotic British jingoism at variance with the international spirit of the avant-garde. Artistically, as outlined in their magazine *Blast* (which blasted artists that Lewis disliked), the vorticists rejected landscapes and nudes in favour of a geometric style tending towards abstraction.[15] Politically, Lewis and Pound were admirers of Hitler and Mussolini. After a visit to Berlin, Lewis published his book *Hitler* in 1931. The book portrayed the aspiring dictator as a "man of peace" whose party members were threatened by communist street violence. Pound, angered by the bloodshed of the First World War, turned against Great Britain and blamed the war on usury and international capitalism. Pound moved

12 Hamilton, *Painting and Sculpture in Europe*, 201.

13 See Fabre and Hotte, *Van Doesburg & the International Avant-Garde: Constructing a New World.* De Stijl was utopian. It dreamed of a universal art style that could be applied to almost every aspect of modern like, from architecture to painting. The "logical principles" phrase appeared in the manifesto of the De Stijl movement written by Van Doesburg, published in the first issue of a monthly magazine of the same name in October 1917. The theme of construction from primary materials (e.g., principles) reoccurred in logical positivism.

14 The name of the group originates in the idea of a vortex or a great amount of energy.

15 See Antliff and Green, *The Vorticists.*

to Italy in 1924 and throughout the 1930s and 1940s favoured Mussolini's fascism, expressed support for Adolf Hitler, and wrote for publications owned by the British fascist Sir Oswald Mosley. During the Second World War he was paid by the Italian government for hundreds of radio broadcasts criticizing the United States, Franklin D. Roosevelt, and Jews.[16]

Perhaps the most famous case of avant-garde fascism was the leader of futurism, Italian poet Filippo Tommaso Marinetti. Futurism was born on 20 February 1909, when Marinetti published a manifesto on the front page of the prestigious Paris daily *Le Figaro*. Bombastically, Marinetti called for the obliteration of past Italian culture and the creation of a new art and new society based on speed. Speed was the essential feature of modern life, as seen in the speed of a racing automobile, which, "like a machine gun," was more beautiful than a great painting. He supported a political program of extreme nationalism and colonial expansion. Perhaps a war with Austria was needed to wake up the Italian public to the realities of modern times.[17] He wrote, "Art, in fact, can be nothing but violence, cruelty, and injustice." He advised futurists to "destroy the museums, the libraries, every type of academy." Together, "We will glorify war – the world's only hygiene – militarism, patriotism, the destructive gesture of freedom-bringers, beautiful ideas worth dying for, and scorn for woman." Later, in 1923, Marinetti declared that fascism and futurism were part of the same revolutionary movement.

Although futurism would last only seven years, until 1916, its impact on modern art goes much further than the quantity or quality of its actual artistic achievements. Cells of futurists popped up all over Europe and beyond. They reacted not so much to Marinetti's militaristic sentiments but to his declaration of war on the art establishment, to revive culture as a whole. Futurists shared an enthusiasm for modernity and modernism, a movement ably directed by Marinetti. The futurists adopted the entrepreneurial spirit of capitalism and sought the support of the masses through manifestos, exhibitions, music-hall performances, and other methods. Using hyperbole and provocation, the futurists exploited the era's "rage for novelty."[18]

16 See Antliff, *Avant-Garde Fascism.*

17 Hamilton, *Painting and Sculpture in Europe*, 177.

18 Cottington, *The Avant-Garde*, 52.

SECTION 2: RATIONAL MUSIC, IRRATIONAL MUSIC

Between noise and silence is music, with its patterns of tones and rhythms. What we hear, musically, can strike us as having meaning and making sense or as being absurd and irrational. What societies think is rational or irrational music changes, swinging on the pendulum.

Music is linked to the social and the political and changes therein.

So much of music displays the social order, from lavish concert halls and the hierarchy of musicians in orchestras to the social classes that favour one form of music over another. Even the way we listen to classical music concerts – silently, like in church, and dominated not by a preacher but by the conductor – evolved over time.

Politically, certain types of music have been seen as supporting the status quo or suggesting revolution. Plato banned certain forms of music and images in the ideal republic because he considered them decadent to our nature. In medieval times, certain kinds of musical dissonance were considered the work of the devil. Later, monarchs in France, from the Sun King, Louis XIV, in the seventeenth century to Louis XVI in the eighteenth century, did their best to discourage Italian opera to protect French culture but also because Italian opera was *too* popular with the masses. Its stories subverted the social order, making heroes of middle-class (and lower) characters. It could be violent and disorderly.[19] Meanwhile, the classical period of Mozart saw courts and high society favour rational and perfectionist attitudes toward music. In our own time, dictators have been musical tyrants. Hitler branded modern art and music as degenerate.

Why do I call the new, atonal music of the early 1900s irrational? First, because many people, used to the classical and romantic traditions, *heard* the new music as irrational. It lacked meaning in the sense of lacking a ratio and proportion. It was heard as noise, a cacophonous rumble piercing to the ear. Second, the new operas and other staged compositions were experienced as irrational and immoral. In Strauss's *Salome* of 1906, Schoenberg's melodrama *Pierre lunaire* of 1912, and Stravinsky's *Rite of Spring* of 1913, the music seemed to spring from the

19 McClary, "Afterword," 155.

composer's irrational capacities and subjective experiences: from dreams, unconscious stirrings, and erotic impulses to personal and professional struggles, and from reading mystical texts. Clashing chords accompanied extreme emotions; ambiguous chords supported dream sequences. There was graphic violence, mythical tales, biblical stories reworked to emphasize incest and necrophilia. There was naked, ritual dancing of "primitive" people. In the *Rite of Spring*, there were no melodies. Unusual rhythms took over from melody.

What was played shocked traditionalists. It was meant to shock.

I do not have the expertise to discuss the technical complexities of the music of this period. Rather, as a philosopher, I seek epistemological ideas and social meaning in the clash of musical aesthetics. The pendulum swung from rational, ordered, and centred compositions – which were rational from the perspective of the status quo – to irrational, less-ordered and decentred compositions. The rebellion was a musical avant-garde adjusting to modernity.

Yet, this narrative has a surprise ending.

We will see that musical composition can be both rational and irrational, and musical aesthetics can contain ideas from rationalism and irrationalism. The rational–irrational distinction in music is not an absolute dualism. In the complex compositional work of Schoenberg, his aesthetic stressed how great composing sprung from the irrational or unconscious, but the structure of those musical ideas should be subjected to what may be called pure reason, i.e., a strictly, rational method to make sure the musical idea had order.

Sticking to the Root

To understand rationalism in music, we go back to the origins of modern music theory, from the Italian Gioseffo Zarlino (1517–1590) to Jean-Philippe Rameau in France (1683–1764).

The theorizing centred around the harmonies produced by music triads – three-note structures that we call chords. A triad consists of a root or tonic, say the note C, and two more notes above it, say the third and fifth intervals, e.g., E and G. This gives you the triad or chord of C–E–G. The root becomes the name of the chord and it is the key in which the music is played. Melodies and harmonies have to fit the key and its sequence of chords. This is called tonal music because it organizes the music around basic tones. Tonality dominates today's popular music.[20] Folks songs today often have a simple chord progression which resolves or returns to the root at the end of the song. Rock groups build songs on a thundering sequence of chords. In the blues, a regimented sequence of chords defines the genre.

At the beginning of the fifteenth century, the triad began to be imported into continental music from England. Triad-based tonality was gradually becoming the dominant mode of music in Italy, France, and other countries. Western music was changing from a horizontal contrapuntal style of interwoven melody lines to melodies carried along by a progression of triads.[21] People looked at musical structure vertically by stacking intervals on top of one dominant note.

Zarlino was one of the most famous music theorists between Rameau and Aristoxenus (360–300 BC), a student of Aristotle. Zarlino wrote a four-volume work in 1558, called *Le Istitutioni harmoniche* (Principles of Harmony). It codified the rules of triadic music. He was the first to explicitly promote the triad as the "perfect harmony."[22] Zarlino also argued that music was now a science whose structure could be known by reason rather than the senses. Music had achieved perfection, an *ars perfecta.* "All was known" musically speaking, and now the task was to codify the rules of harmony so it could never be lost or forgotten. Music in the sixteenth century was beginning an age of classicism, of "conformity with established excellence."[23] What made the music perfect, according to Zarlino and others? For the same reasons that people accepted the philosophical worldview of perfectionism, discussed earlier: proportion, balance, and reason. The proportions of triadic music were so perfect that they could be expressed in mathematical terms.[24]

Rameau was one of France's great composers. He wrote masterpieces for harpsichord, a high point in baroque chamber music. In 1733, his opera *Hippolyte et Aricie* appears to be the first work of music to be called "baroque" but as an insult.[25] Nonetheless, Rameau was praised for his

20 See Tagg, "Harmony."
21 See Hyer, "Tonality."
22 Taruskin, *Music from the Earliest Notations to the Sixteenth Century*, 586–7.
23 Ibid., 586.
24 Ibid.
25 Ibid., 797.

operatic works. A friend of Voltaire and an enemy of Rousseau,[26] Rameau created beautiful compositions that define rational music. They are proportionate, clear in structure, yet with moments of creativity and invention, and even a dash of dissonance.[27]

Yet what Rameau really wanted to be was a great theorist of music. To this end, he wrote the *Treatise on Harmony* in 1722, which, despite its opaque writing and confusing array of mathematical symbols, became a basis for teaching music theory for centuries. Echoing Descartes, Rameau declared that he had arrived at a clear and distinct idea of the basis of all music. He came to it through reason, not experience, i.e., not by listening to music. Echoing Newton, he claimed that all major features of music could be deduced by reason from several universal principles with the "aid of mathematics." The theory of music could be a deductive science, like physics or geometry.[28] With Rameau, Enlightenment rationalism is applied to the sensuous, emotive experience of music.

What was Rameau's wonderous idea?

The triad. All musical harmonies, all of tonal music, could be expressed as different kinds of triads and mathematical variations on them. Rameau's *Treatise* uses mathematical operations, such as expressing the relation between notes as a ratio. Some ratios are heard as pleasant, i.e., as consonant, and others are heard as unpleasant, i.e., dissonant. Rameau believed the consonant harmonies of classical music express a natural and perfect order. They made the music of his day superior to the "Ancients."[29]

Yet, a number of these notions had already been expressed by Zarlino. Surprisingly, Rameau does not mention Zarlino's ideas in his *Treatise on Harmony*. What we can say about this matter is that Rameau did not discover these basic ideas, but he did elaborate on them, providing extensive, practical rules for composing tonal music.

26 Rousseau in his *Confessions*, especially book VII, details his disagreements with Rameau. Rousseau wanted to be taken seriously as a composer. Rousseau and Rameau were also on the opposite sides of a pamphlet war in the 1750s which pitted Rameau and supporters of French opera against Rousseau and supporters of Italian opera.

27 Rameau recognized that dissonance could be used to excite the passions and to create certain moods, such as despair. But it should be used with "great discretion." Rameau, *Treatise on Harmony*, 155.

28 Rameau, *Treatise on Harmony*, xxxiii–xxxv.

29 Ibid., xxxiii, xivi.

Some contemporary musicologists lament that Rameau's *Treatise* has had a negative impact on the teaching and performance of classical music. Susan McClary, for example, criticizes Rameau's stress on the triad as a static way of looking at music. We get precision by reducing music to tirades and ratios, but we miss the fluidity and emotion of the music. McClary says the rationalistic approach has taught generations of students that music has no meaning other than its formal structure. We believe that music has always been "pretty, orderly sound."[30]

Behind Rameau's aesthetic is an ideology. It favours the rational, the objective, the hierarchical, the perfect, the clear, and the orderly. It disapproves of the irrational, the subjective, the non-hierarchical, the imperfect, the unclear, and the disorderly. This preference is not limited to music. The analogue between musical rationalism and political rationalism, understood as firm hierarchy and order, is evident.

Modernity's Music

This rule-bound rationalism would provide a firm structure for classical music in the eighteenth century, exemplified and perfected by Bach, Haydn, and Mozart. Romantic music would both draw ideas from and attempt to move beyond classicism, starting with Beethoven, who would be an inspirational source for almost every major romantic composer.

What part of the aesthetic of romantic music would influence Schoenberg and others? It began with the fundamental romantic concept, discussed in chapter 3, of the great individual as a genius. Great musical composers, for the romantics, were geniuses who were outside the normal rules of conventional society and its musical tastes. The source of their greatness was not their ability to follow the rules of classicism or to imitate the masters. Their greatness resided in their free creativity and imagination, as Baudelaire had stressed for poets and painters. This creativity manifested itself, musically, in new styles, new techniques of composition, new forms of music, and the solution of musical problems inherited from the past. Every great work of music, and every great musical composer, must show progress through invention and originality.

Progress for what? Progress in music's capacity to represent human emotions and existential situations, to express the strivings of mankind,

30 McClary, *Afterword*, 151–2.

to produce a sense of sublimity or grandeur, to seek transcendence from the ordinary, banal world and to express a spirituality or higher reality. To reach these aims, music had to be autonomous, disconnected from the restraints of everyday life and seeking its Hegelian final stage, where music is complete and free.

Romantic music was popular with the public. Great melodies, engaging operettas, sweet harmonies that resolve an earlier dissonance, music that spoke of courage or military victory, songs that expressed love, passion, sorrow, and many other emotions – who would not pay to listen? Sitting in the opera house, the bourgeoisie could flatter themselves as cultured.

Yet there was, from the start, a desire in aesthetic modernity to keep a distance from the public. Many members of the avant-garde despised mass culture. There was also the doctrine of autonomous art. By Schoenberg's time, this arms-length approach to the public would become a badge of artistic integrity. Capitalist modernity's concern with pleasing the masses, and supporting their bad taste, was of no concern to the great musician or composer. The public's views on music were irrelevant. Modern music was what philosopher Jose Ortega y Gasset said about abstract painting. It was an aristocratic aesthetic for people with "finer senses." It was "art for artists."[31]

Romantic music, from the 1850s onward, also had a flattering theory to prove it was special, historically. This was the view, a form of perfectionism, that art is necessarily steadily making "progress toward a state of ever more perfect autonomy." This view was developed chiefly by music historian Franz Brendel for the New German School of music led by the likes of Franz Liszt and Richard Wagner.[32] This separated art history from world history, i.e., from the history of capitalistic modernity and the musical preferences of the public. What mattered were stylistic advances and technical changes *within* musical composition. There was no need for musicologists to reference external events or social forces.[33]

31 Ortega y Gasset, *The Dehumanization of Art*, 6, 12.

32 Taruskin, *Music in the Nineteenth Century*, 411.

33 This view of music and musicology was articulated by Guido Adler (1855–1941) in Vienna, in 1885, in his paper, "Scope, Methods and Aim of Musicology." It would become the dominate theory of music.

Although romantic music often sought to portray the spiritual and the grand, running across the music are barely disguised social biases and repressed sexuality. Misogyny is seen in the mad and dangerous women of operas by Straus and Wagner. There are also the workings of the erotic absolute and erotic sublime – the stimulating and erotic effects of sublime music, paintings, and sculpture, and the erotic charge that is felt when one surrenders to the authority of an absolute leader.[34] The erotic sublime expressed itself, for example, in daring gothic clothing for female opera stars and erotic acts on stage were justified by mythic tales. The performance was depicting people that dressed and acted differently – to the erotic delight of the audience.[35]

This repressed eroticism can also be seen in the aesthetic theory of philosopher Arthur Schopenhauer in the nineteenth century. He refused to recognize what he called the "stimulating" or "charming" – what we might call the seductive – as part of any aesthetic experience, especially of the sublime. The goal of aesthetic experience was to separate oneself from the influence of one's will and desires, not indulge them with erotic paintings, sculpture, or music.[36] Schopenhauer's theory entails that an arousing display of nude sculptures prevents aesthetic contemplation because it inevitably excites lust and thus runs counter to the proper goals of art. As one commentator says, "Schopenhauer may have room in his aesthetic theory for erotic art, but this is not a topic which he explicitly addresses."[37] Indeed, he does not. Neither did many romantic artists and composers. Lurking beneath the aesthetic logic and euphemisms like "the stimulating" is the influence of the erotic[38] combined with nineteenth-century repression of any candid recognition (or discussion) of that power.

34 Later, I will explore the role of the erotic absolute in politics and mass irrational movements.

35 For an example of the erotic sublime at work in literature, see MacDonald, "The Erotic Sublime: The Marvellous in The Monk."

36 Schopenhauer, *The World as Will and Representation*, 232.

37 From Sandra Shapshay, "Schopenhauer's Aesthetics," *The Stanford Encyclopedia of Philosophy* (summer 2018 edition), section 4.2, Edward N. Zalta (ed.), https://plato.stanford.edu/archives/sum2018/entries/schopenhauer-aesthetics.

38 For a critique of Schopenhauer's eros-banning aesthetic, see Maes and Levinson, *Art and Pornography*.

These are some of the general features of the romantic musical aesthetic as handed down to the composers of the early 1900s. But, as a list of properties, they don't give concrete insight into romantic music, as an actual, breathing entity. A few additional points may help.

First, late nineteenth-century romantic music scrambled the original meaning of modernism. Originally, modernism, in art or elsewhere, was associated with progress towards a better future through new methods. But, as we saw with the conservative avant-garde in art, the musical avant-garde could turn this forward-looking modernism into a conservative reverence for the past. Richard Wagner is perhaps the best example of this scrambling. To do so one has to distinguish methods from aims. In methods, Wagner is rightly regarded as an innovative composer. In method, he was modernist. But, in aims, he was not a friend of modernity. To the contrary, the social philosophy that motivated his creative methods and approaches was the hope for a "restored premodern harmony." By the time he completed his gargantuan *The Ring of the Nibelung*, Wagner was not a futurist but the opposite: a "nostalgic … reactionary one."[39] For Wagner, the dreaded symbol of modernity was the emancipated, assimilated, urbanized Jew – people like Mahler, Heine, and, later, Schoenberg.[40]

As romanticism tried to maintain its commitment to modernity – to ever new invention and progress – it became overreaching and, in a sense, too big. The ends of music remained the same. But late nineteenth-century romantics maximized or intensified their methods and means. They turned musical works into "awe-inspiring mountains" by extending their length, increasing the size of orchestras (thereby amplifying the music's volume), and complicating the structure of music and the stories told. They introduced a higher level of acceptable dissonance and a longer postponement of its resolution, which increased both the emotional tension and the listener's involvement with the music. At its peak, fin-de-siècle music created what German music historian Rudolf Stephan called *Weltanschuungsmusik*, i.e., a "philosophy-music" or "music expressive of a world outlook."[41]

39 Taruskin, *Music in the Early Twentieth Century*, 3.

40 Katz, *The Darker Side of Genius*, 15.

41 Taruskin, *Music in the Early Twentieth Century*, 6.

Both Schoenberg and French composers in the early twentieth century would reject this overly dramatic approach and sought a simpler, less rhetorical music. French composers such as Ravel, Satie, and Debussy aimed not at encompassing the world or history or at achieving transcendence. Instead, they tended to create well-crafted, restrained music that caused pleasure and, because of its very restraint, affected people as emotionally as grand scores.

The transition from a romantic to a steelier, less effusive, modern music in the twentieth century was a complicated affair, as all cultural movements are. On the one hand, by the end of the nineteenth century there was a growing division between disillusioned (and established) romantic composers, such as Mahler, and younger moderns who wanted to start fresh.[42] An exhausted romanticism would be replaced by a hypermodern aesthetic. On the other hand, as we will see, the new composers carried forward, in their personalities, a number of romantic ideals including the idea of the great individual and the importance of irrational capacities in musical invention.

Egos Unbound

The romantic ideal of the great individual not only carried on. It took on ironic dimensions. Everyone was a genius, or so it sometimes seemed. While Marxists sought a collective revolution in politics, writers and composers at the turn of the twentieth century sought an aesthetic revolution that stemmed from *them* as great, creative individuals.

Encouraging this egotistical individualism was the growing importance of art in people's worldviews. Art was becoming more and more central to people's lives. As religious authority weakened and as tradition was rejected, art was a word that referred not just to paintings hanging in a museum. Art was the way you lived a life, a worldview gathered from aesthetics, not the Bible. Also, aesthetics melded with political views. People looked to composers and artists for new expressions of modern life. Art was something pure for a tarnished era, something cleansing and surpassing the dreary duties of bourgeois life. Art as experience, as Dewey termed it,[43] became "almost a religion,

42 Ibid., 1–2.

43 Dewey, *Art as Experience.*

a source of meaning and the food of the soul."[44] Hence, disagreement with new music at concerts was hot. It resulted in cat-calls, derisive laughter, and fist fights.

All over fin-de-siècle Europe, young men took up the romantic pose of the suffering artist who cannot stand the society which makes his art possible. In 1904, Thomas Mann wrote a portrait of these aesthetic megalomaniacs in his "At the Prophet's." The text drips with irony.

> Pale young geniuses work under roofs and sit and brood: and then on to cheap studios with solitary and rebellious artists, inwardly consumed, hungry and proud, wrestle ... with devastating ultimate ideals. Here is the end: ice, chastity, null. Here is valid no compromise, no concession, no half-way, no consideration of values ... Here reign defiance and iron consistency, the ego supreme amid despair; here freedom, madness, and death hold sway.[45]

Mann expressed the psychology of the great individual in his last novel, *Doctor Faustus*, first published in 1947. It is a reworking of the Faustian legend on a political level – Nazi Germany sells its soul to the devil for greatness. On an individual level, it is the story of composer Adrian Leverkuhn who sells his soul to the devil for greatness. He is offered years of incredible creativity on the condition that he expunge from his soul the ability to love his fellow man. "You may not love," commands the devil.[46] The desire for greatness ends in nihilism in Nazi Germany and nihilism in the composer who eventually suffers terrible illness and death.

In the pivotal chapter 25, the devil appears to Leverkuhn to make his patient, clever pitch.[47] The devil does not take umbrage at the arrogant Leverkuhn's insults. Gradually, the devil ropes in his quarry by dangling the desires of romantic psychology: fame for eternity, unparalleled creativity, and the rejection of safe, bourgeoise values – what the devil calls "lame prudence, and the deadly reins of reason."[48] There is perhaps no better presentation of the dangerous attraction of the idea of the great individual.

44 Schorske, *Fin-de-siècle Vienna*, 27.
45 Mann, *Stories of Three Decades*, 283.
46 Mann, *Doctor Faustus*, 264.
47 Ibid., 237–65.
48 Ibid., 252.

Typically, individualism embraced an elitist view of art. The public (or "the masses") was unimportant since they were unable to appreciate true art.[49] Ordinary folk were fooled by kitsch, and they preferred commercially successful works.

Debussy assumed an anti-populist stance in the years before 1900. Stephané Mallarmé (1842–1898) defined poetry as a hermetic practice that should wrap itself in mystery to protect its truths from the hoi polloi. Debussy agreed. In 1893, he wrote that music ought to be a hermetical science "enshrined in texts so hard and laborious to decipher as to discourage the herd of people who treat it as casually as they do a handkerchief." Debussy proposed that, instead of spreading music among the people, he should start a Society of Musical Esotericism.[50] When Ravel was offered the Legion of Honour medal in 1920, he refused the decoration because he considered popularity an offence.

Tone Deaf

The term "atonal" is used to described the new music of Schoenberg and others in the early 1900s. But it is not a happy word. There is a cost to adopting this label. First, as Schoenberg complained, the term suggests, ridiculously, that the new music was *against* the use of tones, or had no tones at all, as a-rational means to lack anything rational.[51] Schoenberg preferred "pantonal" and suggested that the only reason we find music today atonal is that we have yet to understand its unique mode of tonality.[52] Second, and more importantly, the label is incapable of capturing the many-faceted revolt of Schoenberg and non-traditional composers. The new music cannot be reduced to one quality: its

49 This standard avant-garde theme stemmed in large part from a disdain for the bourgeoisie. See Cottington, *The Avant-Garde*, 100.

50 Debussy, *Debussy Letters*, 52.

51 The word "atonal" occurs only twice in Schoenberg's influential *Theory of Harmony*. The first usage is on p. 128 where, discussing tonality, Schoenberg argues that it is not always necessary to return to an original tone. In a footnote later in the book, Schoenberg says he must "disassociate himself" from current atonalists because he is a musician who must perforce deal with tones. Moreover, he clarifies the definition of "tonal" so that its reference is wider than music that returns to the root. He defines tonality as "everything implied by a series of tones" whether it is constructed by reference to a root or not. Schoenberg, *A Theory of Harmony*, 432.

52 Schoenberg, *Theory of Harmony*, 312–13.

increasing tolerance and exploration of dissonance or atonality. The music, produced by Schoenberg, his students such as Anton von Webern, the early Stravinsky and Straus, and others had other features: dramatic departures from melody-based composing. The music had new rhythms, new and rich chord structures, and risky subject matter. This was the music of modernity, so it emphasized progress through new styles, and new composing techniques. Therefore, when I refer to atonal music, these qualifications must be borne in mind.

Why not drop the term? Unfortunately, since Austrian composer Joseph Marx (1882–1964) introduced the term in 1907, atonal has taken on a life of its own. So, we need a rudimentary grasp of atonality before proceeding.

Tonal music is typically considered to be music with a home.[53] It is centred around central tones and consonant harmonies. Atonality is music that lacks a home. It has no tonal centre to which one returns. Atonality is marked by dissonance. To understand dissonance, walk over to a piano and strike the middle C key. Then move up 3.5 keys and hit the black key designated as F#. Strike the two notes at the same time. There you have it. Dissonance.[54] According to the ears of many in our culture, the two notes clash.[55] It is stressful to hear. In early classical music, the dissonance was always resolved by moving on to play notes that were consonant. The resolution brought relief. Atonality also lacks clear-cut chords in the major and minor scale, such as A major or D minor. The music employs what might be called ambiguous, sprawling, augmented chords, or diminished sevenths. Or, new chords are invented.

53 The term "tonality" was introduced in 1810 by French musicologist Alexandre Choron to describe triad-based music. Choron said the beginning of modern tonality is found in the music of Claudio Monteverdi (1567–1653), a founder of opera. This modern tonality was different from the plainchant of church music.

54 In the Middle Ages, this dissonance was condemned as the "devil's chord" or the "diabolus in musica" because it created a mood of foreboding. The use of the devil's chord (and other dissonances) was revived by heavy metal bands such as Black Sabbath in the 1980s.

55 How we hear music depends on the framework of music that was part of our education. To someone brought up in a different musical culture, say in India, what sounds musically unpleasant to us is not dissonant.

In the early 1900s, tonality was in difficulty. The era of high romanticism, dominated by such prodigious figures as Gustave Mahler, was coming to an end. The new music was increasingly atonal and less structured around accepted patterns of music.[56] By the late 1910s, the Rameau approach was increasingly irrelevant as a guide to composing.[57]

The new music did not happen overnight, say, with the premiere of *Rite of Spring*. At the turn of the twentieth century, music, like the rest of the world, was on the edge of a traumatic revolution.[58] Mahler would die in 1911 taking the romantic age with him; Puccini's *Turandot*, unfinished at his death in 1924, would end an era of melodic Italian opera that began in the 1600s.[59] Atonality had been growing in influence since at least the 1880s. Franz Listz's (1811–1886) *Bagatelle sans tonalité* of 1885 lacked a tonal centre. It was a startling change from the romanticism of his *Hungarian Rhapsodies*, a series of piano pieces he was completing as *Bagatelle* was constructed.[60]

For composers seeking a new path in music, occult writings and mysticism were more attractive than the rational tracts of logicians and philosophers. Erik Satie (1866–1925), lover of the occult, wrote his six-note Rosicrucian chords for *Le Fils des Etoiles* (The son of the stars) of 1891 – a music score for a poetic drama of the same name.[61] Both Arnold Schoenberg in Vienna and Alexander Scriabin in Moscow were influenced by theosophist spirituality. Scriabin devised a harmonic language around a "mystic chord" of six notes. In the United States,

56 Forte, *The Structure of Atonal Music*, 1.

57 Meyer, *Music, the Arts and Ideas*, 241.

58 See Eksteins, *Rites of Spring: The Great War and the Birth of the Modern Age.*

59 Recent scholarship has modified the story of the birth of opera, usually attributed to seventeenth-century Florence. Florence's experiments were one strand in a century of musical experimentation in many Italian centres. See Abbate and Parker, *A History of Opera*, 39. Other scholarship asks whether the first opera actually goes back to 1283 when a troupe of players put on a "play with music" before the king of Naples. The play was written by Adam de la Halle, and its combination of dialogue and dance-songs resembles a comic opera. Taruskin, *Music from the Earliest Notations to the Sixteenth Century*, 127.

60 The *Hungarian Rhapsodies* are nineteen piano pieces based on Hungarian folk themes, composed during 1846–53 and later in 1882 and 1885.

61 Mystical Rosicrucianism emerged in Europe in the early seventeenth century after several texts claimed the existence of ancient books with hidden truths about nature. Rosicrucian manifestos predicted "a universal reformation of mankind" through a science being kept secret until the world was ready to receive it.

composer Charles Ives was an advocate of the philosophy of transcendentalism, initiated and led by Ralph Waldo Emerson.[62] Ives wrote music in several keys at one time or no key at all. In Paris, Claude Debussy (1862–1918) was an avid reader of decadent poet Paul Verlaine and of occult lore.[63] He came close to embracing atonality with his use of the whole-tone scale.

SECTION 3: SCHOENBERG'S TANGLED RATIONALISM

No composer exemplifies better the tensions between the romantic and the post-romantic music aesthetic than Arnold Schoenberg (1874–1951). The composer is a study in the tangle of rationalism and irrationalism, of autonomous art and socially useful creation. Schoenberg was an audacious maker of other musical worlds. For his daringness, he earned the enmity of lovers of the status quo – tonal, melodic, romantic music.

The Revolutionary Juncture

It was Schoenberg who adopted atonality holus-bolus.

Schoenberg recognized his own radicalness, saying, as he took his fateful step into atonal music, that he had broken through "the limits of a bygone aesthetic." This decision to leap into the atonal came a decade after his well-known, tonal *Transfigured Night* and after much soul-searching. Further evidence of Schoenberg's radical self-consciousness was his view of the twelve-tone technique for atonal composing, which avoids being in a key. In 1922, during a walk with his student Josef Rufer, Schoenberg said it guaranteed "the supremacy of German music for the next hundred years."[64]

Schoenberg's psychology is complex and frustrating. There is so much to admire musically; yet also much to find disconcerting in his authoritarianism.

62 On Emerson, see Albrecht, *Reconstructing Individualism*, 53–124.

63 Ross, *The Rest Is Noise*, 44–5.

64 Stuckenschmidt, *Arnold Schoenberg*, 66, 82.

His passion for creating radically new art co-existed with his conservative impulse to carry on what is best in the German musical tradition. His fierce individualism led to a rejection of the mediocrity of bourgeoise music and values. Yet he was a solid member of the bourgeoisie. Politically, his nationalism, when provoked, could flare up as authoritarianism. While he sought deliverance of the Jews from the force of arms, he was, in personality, a militarist with a fighting spirit. Schoenberg's self-confidence is balanced by his merciless criticism of his works. Yet he was not gracious about external criticism. Schoenberg regarded composers who disliked his music, such as Richard Strauss, as his "enemies."[65]

These attitudes originate in his early days. Schoenberg was scarred psychologically by the antisemitism he endured as a young person, and his struggles to be accepted by antisemitic music leaders. Bitterness and a sense of isolation mark large stretches of his life. There are times when his reaction reveals a touch of paranoia and megalomania – encouraged by biblical tales of prophets who suffered and prevailed. Looking back in 1947, four years before death, what Schoenberg saw was not his achievements but the fact that he never gave up, always swimming against the tide.[66]

Schoenberg's work forms an opus of about fifty pieces, ranging from 1896 to 1950. His journey through the austere geography of atonality began in earnest during a crisis in his marriage in 1908 when Schoenberg caught his wife in a compromising position with another man. Thoughts of suicide arise. Instead, he channels his disturbed emotions into music, resulting in an impressive period of composition that leads up to the First World War. The early works include atonal sections of the fifteen-song *The Book of Hanging Gardens*, based on poems by the aristocratic

65 In 1945, Strauss's financial assets were seized by American forces. Strauss and his wife left Germany for Switzerland where they settled in a hotel just outside Zürich, supported by Swiss music critic Willi Schuh. In 1946, Schoenberg said he regretted Strauss's current situation, yet he was no friend of the composer. He did not admire all of Strauss's work, but Strauss would go down in history as an outstanding figure, and some of his work would not perish. However, because Strauss changed his attitude towards him – was critical of his music – Schoenberg wrote that "in this respect I show him no mercy: I consider such people as enemies." Like a paranoid, Schoenberg's world was full of enemies.

66 Stuckenschmidt, *Schoenberg: His Life, World and Work*, 546.

Stefan George (1868–1933).[67] Also in 1908, he completes his *String Quartet #2*, wherein the first two movements use traditional key signatures but the final two movements, using poetry by George, wander from traditional tonality. The piece also incorporates a soprano voice, breaking with string-quartet practice. In 1909, he enters into a period of creativity that would see him embrace atonality in such pieces as *Three Pieces for Piano* and *Anticipation.* By 1912 he completed the influential *Pierre Lunaire,* twenty-one songs set to German translations of poems by Belgian poet Albert Giraud. A vocalist speaks the lyrics in a melodramatic fashion and is joined by an ensemble of five musicians. His early successes, such as *Anticipation,* took up decadent or risky themes and used poems by Vienna's leading decadent, Richard Dehmel.

However, by 1912 his style was changing rapidly. He began repudiating his former musical successes as not representative of his expressionism. He refused to recognize the public's applause after a performance. His works were too public or too public-appealing. This uncompromising stance made him a hero to his students and admirers and became the new music's paradigm of austerity and separation from the public. Decades later, a few years before his death, Schoenberg retained this stance. "If it is art, it is not for all, and if it is for all, it is not art," he famously wrote.[68] He doubted that his music had a public. He noted that there are composers such as Johann Strauss and George Gershwin whose ideas "actually coincide" with the "average man on the street." They are not being decadent. No composer should depart from his best ideas and lower his style just to "flatter the masses."[69]

At this crucial juncture in his life, in the pre-war years, Schoenberg is a formidable musical rebel. After the First World War, Schoenberg's Second Viennese School made a systematic effort to compose without tonality.[70] He was determined to break with existing musical patterns and was highly confident in his musical intuitions and capacities.

67 George wished to create a new, noble German culture, a new kingdom that would be governed by intellectual and artistic elites, united behind a leader. National Socialists adopted some of his concepts but he came to detest the Nazi ideology, especially its idea of the Nordic superman.

68 Schoenberg, *Style and Idea,* 124.

69 Ibid., 97, 124.

70 The Second Viennese School consisted of Schoenberg and his pupils and close associates in early twentieth-century Vienna, where he lived and taught, sporadically, between 1903 and 1925. The first "school" were the great classical composers such as Mozart and Haydn.

A Convocation of Cats

Schoenberg anticipated the storm of protest that would greet his works.[71] "I feel the heat of rebellion rising in even the slightest souls," he wrote in a program note in 1910, "and I suspect that even those who have believed in me until now will not want to accept the necessity of this development."[72]

In February 1907, his contrapuntal but not yet atonal *First String Quartet* was greeted by laughter and whistles. Mahler, in the audience, tried to defend Schoenberg. Mahler almost got into a fistfight with a detractor.[73] Three days later, Schoenberg's *First Chamber Symphony* caused seat-rattling and walkouts. When the *Second Quartet* premiered in December 1908, the critic Ludwig Karpath shouted out, "Stop it! Enough!" A Vienna newspaper review conjectured, sarcastically, that Schoenberg was "tone deaf." The piece sounded like "a convocation of cats."[74] Editors, for added emphasis, placed the searing review in its crime column.

Nor were leading composer's comments about atonality much kinder. When Richard Wagner heard Listz's *Bagatelle,* Wagner told his wife, Cosima, that his old friend was showing signs of "budding insanity."[75] Richard Strauss thought Schoenberg had lost his mind. Strauss wrote to Alma Mahler that Schoenberg "would be better off shovelling snow than scribbling on music paper."[76]

Not all responses to the new music were negative. When Strauss conducted *Salome,* on 16 May 1906 in the Austrian city of Gratz – with much public anticipation – Giacomo Puccini complained that he would attend to hear that "terribly cacophonous thing." Yet, at the end of the performance, the crowd roared its approval. On the train back to Vienna, Mahler was bewildered: Why did the people like it?[77]

71 Schoenberg wrote several tonal works later in his life.

72 Schoenberg-Nono, *Schoenberg and Nono,* 70.

73 La Grange, *Mahler,* vol. 3, 608–9.

74 Cited in MacDonald, *Schoenberg,* 1.

75 Wagner, *Diaries,* vol. II, 963.

76 Ross, *The Rest Is Noise,* 58.

77 Ibid., 10.

This hostile reaction only deepened Schoenberg's sense of being an outsider, and the misunderstood genius. Like his music, his life in Vienna would be austere and simple, interrupted only by teaching and an adoring group of students. That he was a genius, Schoenberg rightly introspected. Remarkably, he was self-taught in music. He learned basic classic composition techniques by reading an encyclopedia.

Irrational Inspiration

Schoenberg's aesthetic of music in these heydays of atonal experimentation can be summarized by three concepts: autonomy, inwardness, and inspiration. Both Mahler and Schoenberg were modern in seeking a pure music that was free from tradition and external pressures, although Schoenberg's modernism had a harder edge. It was a fierce aesthetics of autonomy. In 1926, Schoenberg proclaimed the "emancipation of dissonance" and the emancipation of music from service to political ends.[78] Schoenberg would have nothing to do with Bartok's notion that music should have social validation, a sense of social mission, since that would interfere with music's free evolution, internally.[79] The artist is a romantic hero, fighting for freedom in art and in life.

Autonomy was wedded to the idea of inspiration. The free artist does not work according to reason but according to inspiration. The task is to express, as directly as possible, the feelings and ideas from the unconscious or from one's creative instincts.[80] At times, the artist experiences the process as beyond rational control or as the voice of an inner power.

This inspiration was an intense, inward experience. Schoenberg described the process as the experience of closing one's eyes and paying strict attention to what happens within. "The world revolves within – inside them," he writes. "What bursts out is merely the echo – the world of art." In these reflections, Schoenberg is moving back to an earlier, individual romanticism, not the often public and gaudy romanticism of his time. It is the romantic attitude associated with Beethoven and Schubert. The ultimate aim of art is to express a unique individuality. Only through artistic creation does one become a person. This required

78 Schoenberg, *Style and Idea*, 260.

79 Taruskin, *Music in the Early Twentieth Century*, 380.

80 Later, we will see how the idea of expressing the unconscious influenced the surrealists.

a uniquely personal music expressing inner freedom and autonomy. It required the rejection of convention and past styles.[81] This was progress, within. For Schoenberg, primitive art is just imitation of the outer or nature. Romanticism too often is the result of a composer's attempt to stimulate and manipulate emotions that are too common, experienced by everyone. The most advanced art is "exclusively concerned with the representation of inner nature."[82]

Inspiration is the source of creativity and this inspiration is instinctive. Emotional intensity is crucial. "I write what I feel in my heart," he said. "And what finally comes on paper is what first coursed through every fibre of my body." Consciousness does not have a great influence on this process. In his *Theory of Harmony*, Schoenberg rejected rationalism and formalism. Beauty or creativity cannot be defined by "eternal laws" of music.[83] He would, in time, return to rationalism.

Schoenberg quotes approvingly the German philosopher Arthur Schopenhauer, who admired music. He cites Schopenhauer's famous statement, "The composer reveals the innermost nature of the world, and expresses the profoundest wisdom in a language that his reasoning faculty does not understand."[84] This "innermost nature" for Schopenhauer was the raw energy of the will, which moves all things. People can only reach tranquility and knowledge of a world of timeless Platonic ideas by restraining or negating their restless wills – the cause of constant suffering. The grasping of Platonic ideas is an aesthetic experience characterized by disinterestedness in the ordinary world of striving and conflict. The mind passively mirrors the world. This is true objectivity. The mind is totally immersed in the object, the way that Dutch masters were immersed in capturing ordinary objects in the still life. In such experiences, the person forgets about their self.[85] Art expresses this other-worldly knowledge when it is provided by the mind of an artistic genius. Schoenberg saw himself as that disciplined and austere genius who seeks to overcome the gap between "the musical

81 Taruskin, *Music in the Early Twentieth Century*, 306.

82 Schoenberg, *Theory of Harmony*, 18.

83 Ibid., 8–9.

84 Schopenhauer, *The World as Will and Idea*, vol. I, book III, 288.

85 Schopenhauer, *The World as Will and Representation*, xv.

idea" – the idea that unifies a piece in its entirety – and its realization.[86] He wrote that the composer loses himself when he tries to translate musical visions into a language which reason "does not understand."[87]

In private conversations and letters, Schoenberg expressed the need for liberation from existing norms and the need to delve into his irrational capacities. In a letter to Italian composer Ferruccio Busoni in 1909, Schoenberg writes that he strives for "complete liberation from all forms, from all symbols of cohesion and of logic."[88] In 1911, in a letter to Wassily Kandinsky (1866–1944), Russian painter and friend, Schoenberg used a phrase reminiscent of Schopenhauer's negation of the will. Schoenberg says that what Kandinsky calls the "unlogical" he calls the "elimination of the conscious will in art." He continues, "Art belongs to the *unconscious*! … Express oneself *directly*." One must not express one's upbringing, education, or skill.[89]

Schoenberg's reference to the unconscious is no accident. He was well aware of Freud's psychoanalytic movement which sprung up in his own city of Vienna. Yet both Freud and Schoenberg faced the same epistemic question: how can one know the unknowable or the unconscious. Dreams and intense internal introspection were possible methods. In a program note to the premiere of *Five Orchestral Pieces* in 1912 in London, he wrote that "the music seeks to express all that swells in us subconsciously like a dream."[90]

Yet liberation stems, paradoxically, from an inner necessity. Schoenberg says his composing expresses the "force of an inner compulsion," something he just *had* to do. "I am the slave of an internal power more powerful than my education," he wrote.[91] For Schoenberg, this inner force is God

86 Schoenberg wrote extensively on the "idea" in music, with writings extending from 1923 to 1949. He contrasted it with "style" or a particular way of expressing (or making popular) an idea. A composer must believe in art for art's sake and not let anything interfere "with the real idea." Auner, *A Schoenberg Reader*, 176, 329.

87 Schoenberg, "The Relationship to the Text," 142.

88 Busoni, *Busoni Letters*, 389.

89 Auner, *A Schoenberg Reader*, 89. Italics in original text.

90 Slonimsky, *Music Since 1900*, 207.

91 The idea of an inner necessity or calling was a fundamental notion of Kandinsky's philosophy of creative activity. Kandinsky began correspondence with Schoenberg in 1911. He spent the summer of 1927 with Schoenberg and his wife at Lake Worth in Austria, when Kandinsky was a teacher of painting at the Bauhaus in Dessau, Germany. Duchting, *Kandinsky*, 7, 94–5.

speaking through him. At times, he was depressed that his mortal ears were not up to the task of properly conveying such messages.

There are interesting parallels between the personalities of Schoenberg and Kandinsky. Both had no tolerance for people who did not agree with them. Both sought relief from the grubby world of mass society in a higher reality – religious abstractionism for Kandinsky and Schoenberg's other-worldly atonal works with their rigorous twelve-tone scales. Both arrogantly looked down their noses at ordinary people and politics, yet both were affected by politics. Both were attracted, at least initially, to fascist ideas and leaders. Despite their arrogance, Kandinsky and Schoenberg both accepted the protection, or "protected isolation," of mass society in France and America, respectively.[92] Yet while Kandinsky was an enthusiast for modernity and technology, Schoenberg was not an enthusiast and preferred an aristocratic order in society and music.

William Benjamin has argued that, prior to the First World War, Schoenberg had a Nietzschean view of life and art. Schoenberg's view of inspiration is comparable to Nietzsche's notion that irrational Dionysus forces[93] are the sources of great art.[94] Schoenberg is said to share a number of other Nietzschean notions: that life (and art) seeks to express a unity of the rational and irrational, the ugly and the beautiful, the consonant and the dissonant. This analysis is correct in the main. Schoenberg had read Nietzsche, as shown by the fact that he entitled a piece he wrote in 1905 after an essay by Nietzsche, "The Wanderer." However, we should not forget the things that Schoenberg and Nietzsche did not share, such as a belief in God, not to mention Schoenberg's German nationalism and authoritarianism.

The stress on Schoenberg's irrational aesthetics can blind us to the fact that there were other important aims to his music. One was the romantic aspiration to express the sublime and the spiritual and, of course, Schoenberg's God. He looked at his music as an "ascent to a higher and better order,"[95] a higher music space which integrated many

92 Buenger and Holz, "Antifascism or Autonomous Art?," 72.

93 See Nietzsche, *The Birth of Tragedy*.

94 Benjamin, "Abstract Polyphonies: The Music of Schoenberg's Nietzschean Moment," 1–6.

95 Schoenberg to Nicholas Slonimsky, 3 June 1937, in Slonimsky, *Music since 1900*, 1316.

elements, not just dissonance. Like Mahler, his music was a form of *Weltanschauungsmusik*, music with a spiritual worldview. This ascent drew him towards books on the occult and special forms of knowing the higher reality. He was interested in representing spiritual transcendence. But how could his focus on the inner be coherent with this focus on the external and transcendent? By thinking of the inner occurrences as emanations or messages from a spiritual source.

In his correspondence with Kandinsky, who also saw art from a spiritual perspective, Schoenberg expressed his spiritual side.[96] In a 1912 letter to Kandinsky, Schoenberg asserted that his artistic ideal was "*a unity of musical space demanding an absolute and unitary perception*."[97] He identified this aim with a book that he and Kandinsky adored, Honoré de Balzac's *Séraphita* of 1835. Schoenberg called it "perhaps the most glorious work in existence." In the main chapter of the book, Balzac provides a fanciful description of the teachings of occult philosopher Emanuel Swedenborg (1688–1772): Wilfred, thirty, and Minna, seventeen, both love an ethereal creature who in the last chapter ascends to heaven and becomes an angel. Wilfred and Minna witness the assumption and are promised a place in heaven. Heaven is an infinite space where everything is integrated. For example, light gave birth to melody and melody to light. Colours were both light and melody. This vision of integration inspired Schoenberg's vision of an integrated musical space. For instance, Schoenberg concludes his *Theory of Harmony* with excited speculation about the possibility of creating "tone color melodies" where timbre would play the role of pitch. Such melodies, he gushes, would enhance music and our lives.[98]

Nomos and Order

For a man who loved order and authority, Schoenberg, at least by the 1920s, began to feel uncomfortable with his heavy stress on emotions, intuitions, unconscious forces, and spontaneous impressions. Schoenberg worried about his irrationalism. One of the psychological factors at work was Schoenberg's misogyny. The composer admired the outrageously

96 In 1912, Kandinsky had published his *On the Spiritual in Art*.

97 The italics are in Schoenberg's letter.

98 Schoenberg, *Theory of Harmony*, 421–2.

misogynistic writings of philosopher Otto Weininger, for whom intuition was regarded as something feminine, a weakness. Schoenberg cited Weininger in *Theory of Harmony* as an example of someone who had "thought earnestly."[99]

But there were other factors at work.

Schoenberg's discomfort arose from two different spheres, music and politics. In music, he wanted to compose in an expressionist manner, but he also wanted his pieces to have a unity that satisfied musical standards set by himself and past masters. In music, there should be nomos, i.e., law and order. He seemed to fear his former emancipation. The other area was a discomfort with the lack of discipline and order in political life, especially in democracies. He wanted order in society, ideally established by authoritarian methods. In both areas, Schoenberg was swinging on the pendulum towards rationalism. The return of the rational and neo-classicism.

In music, he developed the view that what could unify the inner occurrences was not so much a theme as a strict method that operated on its own principles, not on convention, routines, or public taste. It had to be a rational method that transcended – or disciplined – impulse and emotion. What could that be? It would be Schoenberg's famous twelve-tone method of composition. The method was severely organized and demanding, e.g., each tone of the scale had to sound before a note could be repeated. Moreover, he developed various mathematical ways of using the method to create musical forms. Schoenberg and the twelve-tone composers went further than any neo-classicist in their devotion to abstract or generic forms. Their rationalism subjugated content to form. At the same time, they constructed a "cult of difficulty" around music to keep "the hostile crowd at bay."[100] Even Schoenberg struggled to describe concisely the twelve-tone method.

Building walls around music was an old Schoenberg strategy. In 1918, Schoenberg, along with his student Alban Berg acted on their alienation from society rather than just write about it. They formed the Society for Private Musical Performances where everything was monitored and regulated. Schoenberg ruled over the society like a dictator. Subsidized

99 I discuss Weininger in chapter 7.

100 Taruskin, *Music in the Early Twentieth Century*, 738.

mainly by subscriptions, the concerts were not advertised in the papers, and critics were never invited. Anyone seeking to buy a ticket was regarded with suspicion. Attendees promised to not write about the event in publications. Subscribers were not told about the programs in advance. Applause, disapproval, and even saying thanks were forbidden. Performers were told not to engage in virtuosity. Their only role was to make the composer's music intelligible.[101] Schoenberg and his supporters, when they spoke of this period, make their efforts appear heroic. They were saving embattled high art.

As we will see, talk of rational order and veneration for lawful musical structures would mesh with the right-wing thinking of the 1920s and 1930s. In *Doctor Faustus*, Thomas Mann compared the mentality of the twelve-tone method to the authoritarian mindset of the Nazis.

Theodore Adorno recognized early this absolute rationalism in Schoenberg's personality and work. Adorno talks about a severe rationality at work, which puts enormous emphasis on method and how one constructs music from basic and purified elements. Adorno portrays Schoenberg's works, especially his "iron-clad" twelve-tone compositions, as the enforcement of a rational pattern on the material of music, such as tones, harmonies, and sentiments. Interestingly, Adorno says the sheer force of this rationality – a music of "cognition" – is an irrationality. Rationality, played out to its extreme, becomes an irrational, dominant force.[102]

Autonomy Questioned

The path that Schoenberg would take from the 1930s onward could not have been predicted. His view of autonomous art would be challenged by one of the most terrible events in history: the Jewish holocaust during the Second World War. In the vortex of these times, art for its own sake was questioned. How could art be apolitical or detached from events when the lives of millions of people were in jeopardy? With an approaching holocaust, this detachment collapsed as a sufficient ethic for art. Despite his love of artistic autonomy, Schoenberg would become

101 Slonimsky, *Music Since 1900*, 1307–8.

102 Adorno, *Philosophy of Modern Music*, 117–24.

a major activist for a Jewish homeland; he would write music in service of the survival of the Jews. His music remained an inspirational art from God, but now it was a more communal, engaged art. This worldliness was expressed in pieces such as *A Survivor in Warsaw,* his testament to the Warsaw Jewish uprising during the Second World War.

There is a myth that Schoenberg was always apolitical. His presumed neutrality led to criticisms, e.g., Marxists who claimed he betrayed the proletariat, although he was quintessentially bourgeoisie and anything but a socialist.[103] The existence of the myth is, to some extent, understandable. Schoenberg *did* state in letters, writings, and speeches that he was apolitical and artists should not attempt to be politicians. Also, Schoenberg's early biographers did not say much about his political activity. Further, most of his political writings and the papers that document his Zionist activism remained unpublished in his lifetime. After death, his writings and copious letters were published gradually. A full picture of his views and activities came into view slowly. In the meantime, his political thoughts remained buried in his unpublished corpus of writings as manuscripts, letters to artists and public figures, drafts of potential speeches or publications, and notes that sought to clarify his ideas.[104]

To make matters more complicated, it is difficult to provide a simple, coherent explanation of his claims to be apolitical despite his political actions. In 1928, just before the Nazis came to power, he would say, "I have nothing to do with politics" and that he kept his "irreverent private opinions to myself." Those who think the arts influence politics – such as those who call for a "peace hymn" – are fooling themselves.[105] This claim to be apolitical was increasingly inaccurate as Schoenberg became involved in opposing antisemitic fascism across the 1920s and 1930s, in Europe and again in the United States. As early as 1923, he was complaining that professors at the Bauhaus school of design in Berlin were antisemitic. At about the same time, Schoenberg gave up on hopes that Jews might assimilate. He had, in 1898, converted to Protestant Christianity in an attempt to assimilate. He came under social

103 Ringer, *Arnold Schoenberg and the Politics of Jewish Survival*, 12.

104 I am grateful to the Arnold Schoenberg Center in Vienna for providing me with materials on Schoenberg's political views on the future of Jewry.

105 Schoenberg, "Does the World Lack a Peace-Hymn?," 500.

pressure to conform to non-Jewish bourgeoisie culture. Also, conversion to Lutherism was a defence against rising antisemitism. This pressure to assimilate was a major feature of German and Austrian political life during the late 1800s – the early, formative years of Schoenberg's life.[106] But he grew dissatisfied and was never "convinced by Protestantism."[107] His last hopes for assimilation died in the late 1920s when he learned that Jews could no longer vacation in the Austrian resort of their choice, causing him to write his Zionist political play, *The Biblical Way*. He returned to his Jewish faith in 1933.[108]

In the 1930s, his political activity increased substantially. Schoenberg sensed the growing danger of a holocaust earlier and more clearly than many Jews. Schoenberg spent countless hours prodding fellow Jews, criticizing Jewish organizations, writing for support from Jewish artists, attending Jewish conferences, and considering whether he should lead a United Jewish Party to save Jewry. He rejected the futility of half-measures such as an economic boycott of German goods. He was an isolationist: If the Jews were to be survive, they would have to do it on their own, not trust the hesitant altruism of European nations. His plans included measures to raise money for the purchase of a homeland, a multi-media campaign of propaganda in which he would arouse Jews around the world, and the idea of leading a Jewish extra-territorial government.[109] Despite his earlier dismissal of the public, Schoenberg now *needed* an audience to get his word out on the holocaust. He had important things to say but what if no one took notice?[110] Compositions such as *Kol Nidre*, his foray into Jewish sacred music and intended for use in synagogues, and *A Survivor in Warsaw* required the largest possible audience.

Schoenberg became a Jewish prophet in the Old Testament sense. He was already a prophet in music, leading culture toward new musical landscapes. Now he would become a prophet for Jews in the wilderness

106 On the growing antisemitism in Germany during the late 1800s and controversies over Jewish assimilation, see Katz, *The Darker Side of Genius*.

107 Feisst, *Schoenberg's New World*, 90.

108 MacDonald, *Schoenberg*, 93.

109 For details on his many pro-Jewish activities in the 1930s in Europe and then in America, see Feisst, *Schoenberg's New World*, 85–90.

110 Daub, "Introduction," *The Doctor Faustus Dossier*, 14.

of fascist Europe. The romantic artist as hero was replaced by the artist as political martyr.[111]

Prior to leaving for America in 1933, Schoenberg explained his decision to dive into politics in a letter to his student, Anton von Webern. He wrote that, having officially returned to the Jewish religion, it was his intention to "do nothing in the future but work for the Jewish national cause." Schoenberg said he was now considering a tour of America and perhaps a world tour to "persuade people to help the Jews in Germany." If necessary, large projects, such as his opera *Moses and Aron*, would be shelved.[112] Leaving Austria, his first stop was Paris. There he began an extensive letter writing campaign to Jewish leaders about his plans for a United Jewish Party that was "nationalist-chauvinistic to the highest degree, in the religious sense, based on the notion of the chosen people, militant, aggressive, against all pacifism."[113]

SECTION 4: A CALIFORNIA SUNSET

Suffering Hero?

His American years, from 1933 to death in 1951, is a contentious topic among Schoenberg scholars. His early biographers, such as Hans Stuckenschmidt and Willi Reich, were Europeans. As former students or admirers of Schoenberg, they portrayed his time in the new world of southern California as a terrible period.[114] He was depicted as an isolated, financially strapped, figure who never accommodated himself to Los Angeles. Americans received him badly. His new music was ignored or, for some critics, they were compromises to the hypercommercial capitalism of America. Stuckenschmidt, for example, describes Schoenberg as arriving in America feeling "not only homeless but

111 The notion of martyrdom was important to Schoenberg, since the notion is central to the Bible. Schoenberg saw his enduring of the hostile response to his music as a form of musical sacrifice or martyrdom. In the first edition of *Theory of Harmony* in 1911, Schoenberg dedicated the book to Mahler, who had just died. Schoenberg described him as a "martyr, this saint" who forwent many pleasures for his art.

112 Ringer, *Arnold Schoenberg and the Politics of Jewish Survival*, 11–12.

113 Ibid., 25.

114 See Stuckenschmidt, *Schoenberg: His Life, World and Work*, 365–524; and Reich, *Arnold Schoenberg*.

speechless" (due to his lack of English).[115] That view was adopted by American historian Kevin Star and British music writer Malcolm MacDonald. For MacDonald, Schoenberg in America was "in the wilderness."[116] In Europe, he was the great musical prophet. In America, he was a suffering hero. But many of these early biographers were left-wing writers who disliked capitalism and portrayed Schoenberg as engulfed in American philistinism.

More recently, scholars have begun to balance this portrait of Schoenberg in America. Feisst goes to considerable length to undermine these negative myths of Schoenberg's America years.[117] She admits that the early years were tough but eventually Schoenberg acculturated himself. He was *not* an isolated figure, and he improved his English. He was politically active. He was financially comfortable and lived in a lovely house. He was productive, writing new works to his death, and he was musically influential as a composer and teacher. He had extensive social networks, hosted many parties, came to like American movies, and even took up American ways of dressing. He enjoyed playing tennis with his neighbour George Gershwin. In the Los Angeles area, Schoenberg was not without fellow émigrés. Up to 20,000 central European emigrants would make their home in Los Angeles by 1945, about 70 per cent of them Jewish.[118] The Austrian-German group was called "Weimar on the Pacific." Mann, Adorno, and Schoenberg lived relatively close to each other.

However, this increased analysis of his American life has also raised tough questions about his attitudes and actions. Critics have attacked his authoritarian attitude and his lack of enthusiasm for democracy. Some have suggested that he sympathized with fascism or fascistic ideas on governance.[119]

One bone of contention is his claim to be apolitical. For example, in the early 1930s, when he was never more active in Zionism, Schoenberg gave talks to American Jewish groups, wherein he expressed a desire to stay away from politics. He made no mention of his turn to Zionism and his political plans. In 1934, Schoenberg gave a public speech in

115 Stuckenschmidt, *Schoenberg: His Life, World and Work*, 393.

116 See Starr, *The Dream Endures*, 382–3, 363; and Malcolm, *Schoenberg*, 43–51.

117 See Feisst, *Schoenberg's New World*, especially chapters 1 and 3.

118 Daub, "Introduction," *The Doctor Faustus Dossier*, 7.

119 See, for example, Taruskin, "The Darker Side of Modern Music."

Hollywood, California. He began by saying he would disappoint the audience by refusing to tell "nightmarish tales" about Jewish persecution "which cause an agreeable kind of shuddering." Neither nightmarish tales nor fighting against Germany, e.g., by mounting an economic boycott, would help world Jewry. "I want to abstain from politics ... I did not come to this marvellous country to speak about terrors – but to forget them. Let us leave them!"[120] How different is this rejection of the horrors from the approach of another Jew, Marc Chagall, who in 1941 fled to America as the Nazis approached Paris. Chagall's war experience prompted him to paint poignant and searing images of the persecution of Jews, beginning with *White Crucifixion* in 1938.[121]

How to reconcile Schoenberg's comments on avoiding politics with his advocacy for a Jewish state? Maybe he meant that speaking about terrors or fighting Germany economically was not what Jews should be doing. They should be responding differently? Perhaps, as Ringer suggests, Schoenberg "never even thought" of his many proposals, speeches, and letters as political activity but as a holy mission. God made him the "one chosen" to help the Jews.[122] I find this explanation unsatisfactory. Schoenberg knew very well that taking up the Zionist cause was political activity, no matter how you define political. He was not being completely truthful.

A more candid explanation is that he liked to portray himself as apolitical when it was in his interest to do so. Otherwise, he acted politically. For example, in 1939, with antisemitism rising, he worried that President Roosevelt might let Americans decide democratically the fate of German and Jewish emigrants, such as internment or deportation. He acted politically. In 1942, he wrote the *Ode to Napoleon*, with a text by Byron that was interpreted as anti-fascist, a tribute to Roosevelt. Schoenberg hoped that the president would use his *Ode* as wartime propaganda.

In the 1940s, Schoenberg began to reduce his political activities. At the end of the Second World War, as the Cold War inflamed anti-communist fears in the United States, Schoenberg revived his claims to be an apolitical musician. To be fair, the threat to his status in the United States was real. While the FBI did not create a special file on Schoenberg,

120 Schoenberg, "Two Speeches on the Jewish Situation," 501–5.

121 Affron, "Constructing a New Jewish Identity," 114.

122 Ringer, *Arnold Schoenberg and the Politics of Jewish Survival*, 13.

his name was cross-listed in the files of other people. Also, the FBI visited his house and found German books in his library (one author's last name was, unfortunately, Marx). Schoenberg had to explain that these were musical books. In 1943, FBI chief J. Edgar Hoover classified him and other Jews as "thoroughly disreputable Communist Zionists" for supporting an independent Jewish army unit to fight in the Second World War – the Jewish Army of Stateless and Palestinian Jews.[123]

Martin Jay states that such political caution was common, a "progressive deradicalization" among the European émigrés. Jay says it was clear to those who arrived in wartime America with strong political allegiances, from Marxists in the Frankfurt School to Hannah Arendt and leadings members of the Bauhaus, that "they would have to modify their positions or keep them hidden from public view." The McCarthy witch hunt also had a chilling effect. Jay argues that it was only in the 1960s, during the Vietnam era, that "voices with thick German accents," e.g., Arendt, Erik Erikson, and Herbert Marcuse, felt comfortable enough to challenge mainstream American thought and government policy.[124]

In 1947, Schoenberg's former student, composer Hanns Eisler, was questioned by the US House Un-American Activities Committee. He was one of the first artists placed on the Hollywood blacklist by film studio owners. During two interrogations by the House Committee, the composer was accused of being "the Karl Marx of music" and the chief Soviet agent in Hollywood. Eisler's supporters included his friend Charlie Chaplin, folksinger Woody Guthrie, and the composers Igor Stravinsky, Aaron Copland, and Leonard Bernstein. Schoenberg was not among his public supporters. Perhaps, Schoenberg disagreed with his student's socialist views, or Eisler had become another of his musical enemies. Eisler agreed with Adorno that much of Schoenberg's new American music was written for a "false society." Eisler thought that Schoenberg had fallen "prey" to the delusions that accompany capitalist culture.[125]

123 Hoover's comment was made as Jewish groups took out full-page ads in the *New York Times* and the *Los Angeles Times* demanding the right of Jews to fight in their own unit, as news of the holocaust was emerging. Schoenberg's name was among the signatories in the ads. Feisst, *Schoenberg's New World*, 87.

124 Jay, "The German Migration," 329–31.

125 On music for a false society, see Adorno, *Philosophy of Modern Music*, 121. On falling prey, see Eisler, cited in Heilbut, *Exiled*, 157. Ironically, it would be Eisler who made artistic compromises to the American market as a film composer in Hollywood from 1942 to 1948, Feisst, *Schoenberg's New World*, 258.

In 1948, Eisler was extradited to Europe. In a 1948 letter to his student in Josef Rufer, Schoenberg reiterated his idea of apolitical art: "We who live in music have no place in politics … We are apolitical and the most that we can do is endeavor to stay quietly in the background."[126]

Then, in 1950, as a retired professor, Schoenberg was caught up in the controversial demand by the University of California's board of regents that all university employees sign a loyalty oath to not take part in communist activities. Many professors refused to sign, on grounds that the oath was an unnecessary intrusion into their civil right to hold personal beliefs and it violated tenure. Schoenberg thought the oath requirement was "tactless" but agreed to it, stating that he never was a communist and he promised to be a "reliable citizen" and to live strictly according to the law.[127] Several teachers resigned in protest or lost their positions. Among those who left were the psychologist Erik Erikson and the classical scholar Ludwig Edelstein, both of them Jewish refugees from Nazi Germany. In August 1950, the regents fired thirty-one faculty.[128]

Later in 1950, in his essay "My Attitude Toward Politics," Schoenberg sought to explain his views, once again stressing his apolitical nature. He wrote that, as a young, developing composer, he had to spend time developing musical, not political, skills. He recalled being introduced to socialist theories when young, and he remembered the enthusiasm for such theories among the choruses that he directed. But, he says, "I was never a communist."[129] Schoenberg said that he was a monarchist. He fought proudly as a soldier in the First World War because he was a "true believer in the house of Habsburg." He preferred the Habsburg monarchy because it had 800 years of wisdom in the art of government. Schoenberg says that, when he moved to America, monarchist ideas were obviously superfluous, and, in any case, as a refugee he had no right to participate in American politics.[130]

126 Schoenberg to Rufer, 25 May 1948. In the Arnold Schoenberg Center in Vienna.

127 Feisst, *Schoenberg's New World*, 157.

128 Those who were terminated sued. By 1952, they had been rehired, after the university declined to pursue its case against them in court.

129 Schoenberg, "My Attitude Toward Politics," 505–6.

130 Ibid.

Ringer has called Schoenberg's "My Attitude Toward Politics" an "admittedly somewhat pathetic disclaimer."[131] Critics might say the truth is somewhat stronger. His failure to note his Zionist activity was a lie of omission. His failure to regard the oath issue as an urgent issue of freedom of speech (not tactfulness) – a freedom that allowed him to work in the United States – is disappointing. How could he ignore the parallel between Nazi censorship and right-wing American censorship? His lukewarm support for democratic principles offers no excuse for his timidity. However, defenders of Schoenberg might reply that all of us, as emigrants, would feel nervous about having the FBI investigate one's life. Moreover, Schoenberg, in 1950, was old, and the thought of being deported must have struck him with fear.

Authoritarian Prophet

Finally, there were his political projects, with their extreme ideas and authoritarian cast.

To grasp Schoenberg's political viewpoint, one needs to read Schoenberg's political magnum opus,[132] "A Four-Point Program for Jewry."[133] In 1938, after revisions since the early 1930s, Schoenberg completed the plan. It was vintage Schoenberg: intellectually sharp, committed to difficult truths, and peppered with controversial ideas.

His "Four-Point Program" sets out to explain what Jewish leaders should do to avert a humanitarian catastrophe. The essay astutely predicts that up to 700,000 Jews will be forced to flee from Nazi Germany and Austria. But where will they go, given that Western nations can be antisemitic and they have other axes to grind? He writes, "Is there room in the world for almost 7,000,000 people? Are they condemned to doom? Will they become extinct? Famished? Butchered?" What should Jewish leaders do?

Jewish leaders, he says, must do four things: (1) Stop trying to fight antisemitism because non-Jews will always hate the "arrogant Jew" who thinks he is special, part of God's Chosen People. Antisemitism is natural and cannot be fought. (2) Since Jews are distinct by religion, assimilation is not an option. Instead, leaders must find land for an independent

131 Ringer, *Arnold Schoenberg and the Politics of Jewish Survival*, 12.

132 Ibid., 38.

133 Schoenberg, "A Four-Point Program for Jewry."

Jewish state. (3) A united Jewish party must be created that (4) enforces unanimity of opinion by all (legal) means. Contrary views should not be tolerated. This party should begin with an elite group of Jewish leaders who do not make decisions based on democratic debate or majority vote.

Schoenberg justified this elite conception of the party as necessary to achieve an urgent goal: to find a safe homeland. Democracy is too long and messy a process to save the Jews. "Unanimity is very seldom a thing in the life of a nation at which a people arrive voluntarily," Schoenberg writes. Jewish leaders of his new party, on crucial issues concerning unity, should "never enter into discussion."[134]

That Schoenberg would adopt an elitist structure for his imagined party is not surprising, given that he grew up under monarchy. He harboured a life-long scepticism about democracy and the masses – a common view among European intellectuals of his time. Also, he had seen how democracy in the Weimar Republic had not protected Jews, and, ironically, the republic was overthrown by people using democratic institutions. His notion that great art was created by great individuals translated easily into political authoritarianism.

Schoenberg's strong nationalism and militarism were evident early in his life. Caught up in the war mania of 1914, he denounced the music of Ravel, Stravinsky, and Bizet. He characterized Germany's assault on France as comparable to his assault on decadent bourgeoise artistic values: "Now comes the reckoning! Now we will throw these mediocre kitschmongers into slavery, and teach them to venerate the German spirit and to worship the German God."[135]

Schoenberg saw value in democracy historically, especially in its support for human rights. But this acknowledgment was out-weighed by his multiple criticisms of democracy: democracy is unstable, democracy meant inconclusive debate, and the masses would always be moved by leaders who flattered them. Schoenberg speaks derisively of democracy as mindless and a corruption of the individual. The will of the majority is "accidental" – it is, actually, the will of certain groups. Ideas should arise, naturally, from one brain with its merits and faults. But democracy works on ideas that "no one has had" and have arisen from

134 Ibid., 59.

135 Cited in Ross, *The Rest Is Noise*, 72. From 28 August 1914 letter, in the Mahler-Werfel Papers, University of Pennsylvania.

"no single brain." The will of the whole is achieved only through "compromises" and "in striving to belong to a majority the individual corrupts his own will."[136]

Schoenberg's comments on freedom of speech are no less critical and troublesome. In a letter to Thomas Mann in 1939, as the Western world was fighting to maintain democracy and basic freedoms, Schoenberg writes that he is no leftist, which means that "I would in no way grant to everyone the right of freedom of expression, only to those who actually possessed an opinion worthy of expressing." He then calls himself a "progressive conservative" who wants to develop and preserve "things worthy of preserving."[137] But who decides who has an opinion worthy of expression, and who decides what voices should be censored? This is a central problem for elitist political philosophies. Schoenberg says he recognizes the trouble with fascism. It puts great power into the wrong hands. But the same abuse of power arises when we give to a chosen few the power to decide which opinions can be voiced publicly.

Schoenberg exaggerates the inability of democracy to meet emergencies, and his anti-democratic conclusions, e.g., to enforce unanimity, are too sweeping. It struck people that the Nazis had the same attitude toward politics. Schoenberg was right that there are conditions where action is needed and cannot wait for democratic agreement. But this does not rule out some overarching democratic structure. Moreover, what about *after* the crisis? There is little indication from Schoenberg that the government of a Jewish homeland would be democratic in any robust manner. By the time he completed his plan, it was too late for implementation. This was not due to democracy. It was due to the murderous Nazis and the immoral hesitancy of Western leaders.

A number of music scholars and historians have gone further than to talk about Schoenberg's authoritarian personality. They claim, or at least suggest, that Schoenberg had fascist tendencies or what I will call a fascist mind. This caused him to feel closer to right-wing and aristocratic attitudes than mass democratic attitudes. For example, Bluma Goldstein has questioned Schoenberg's model for Moses in *Moses and Aron*. Moses, she writes, is a great, authoritarian leader. She wonders

136 Auner, *A Schoenberg Reader*, 246.

137 Arnold Schoenberg to Thomas Mann, 15 January 1939. In Feisst, *Schoenberg's New World*, 115.

why Schoenberg would write such an opera at a time when Hitler was "putting into practice" his idea of a "leader with absolute power."[138] Others have noted his caution in criticizing Hitler, although this may have been done to protect family and friends trapped in Nazi Europe.

Music historian Richard Taruskin claims that Schoenberg, along with major composers such as Stravinsky, saw fascism as an attractive ideal since it appeared to support their conservative, aristocratic view of society. Fascists like Mussolini would protect society from both a communist revolution and a corruption of values by mass democracy. Artistically, this fascist attitude supports a steely, well-ordered, neoclassicism against the romanticism of the masses. As English critic Thomas Hulme (1883–1917) said about these times, if you knew whether a person admired the classics or the romantics, "you could deduce from that what his politics were."[139]

Taruskin notes that, in the 1920s, Schoenberg, with his "German supremist" views, joined the postwar reaction against modernity. Schoenberg "made common cause with the blue blood against the masses, and sought its protection."[140] Taruskin quotes from Schoenberg's 1924 letter of acceptance of an invitation by Prince Max Egon to conduct one of his twelve-tone compositions at the prestigious Donaueschingen festival in southern Germany. Schoenberg was delighted and reminded the prince of bygone days when princes protected the artist, "showing the rabble that art, a matter for princes, is beyond the judgment of common people." True art showed the distinction between people who were "born what they are" and those common people who have "merely worked their way up." Taruskin states, Schoenberg's personality was as "absolute and despotic as any dictator's."[141]

I think Schoenberg *was* strongly authoritarian and aristocratic but he did not approve of fascism as an actual form of government, not to mention the pogroms of fascist leaders. Despite his reputation as the radical atonalist and modernist, Schoenberg never lost his conservative distrust of the masses when it came to art or politics, although such

138 Goldstein, "Schoenberg's *Moses and Aron*," 188.
139 Taruskin, "The Dark Side of Modern Music," 32.
140 Ibid.
141 Ibid., 33.

antipathy was softened by his years in America. Perhaps, we might think of him as an anti-modernist, if modernism is associated with liberal and romantic viewpoints.

Schoenberg, in the "Four-Point Program," seemed oblivious to the fact that his ideas, had they been published, could have been used (and twisted) by fascists. Schoenberg's sceptical remarks about democracy doubted the very system that stood against the Nazis and ensured Schoenberg's own safety. He criticized Jewish intellectualism as a diversion from practical, social reform.[142] This criticism, coming from a prominent Jew, could have been used by the Nazis to support their propaganda about the weak mind and culture of the Jews. Saying there was no use fighting antisemitism would have been welcomed by Nazi propagandists. Then there are moments in the "Program" where his overwhelming stress on the "chosen people" thesis seems to sound like a Jewish "superior race" thesis.

Further, I suspect that there was a deep psychological reason for his scepticism of democracy: a megalomaniac desire to control and a view of oneself as a genius. In a note from September 1933, Schoenberg states, "To me democracy has always meant an environment in which *I* shall *never succeed in making my will known, let alone enforce it* … Democracy will never permit the ideas of the truly great to prevail."[143] His "will"? "The truly great"? There is here a worrying tone of the emerging authoritarian tyrant, the megalomaniac, frustrated by restrictions.

In a 1933 note called "My Plans," an eerie, almost paranoid voice is expressed: "You want to know what I am planning?" he asks, apparently to no one in particular. "I do not have the intention of telling you that. Only he can win my trust whom I can use for a specific assignment." He says only his most intimate friends will know as much as it is "useful for them."[144] Later, we will see that this attitude characterizes authoritarian and cult leaders.

142 By Jewish intellectualism, Schoenberg meant the Jewish facility for developing ideas and theories. He thought this was an "enslavement" to non-Jewish culture based on the delusion that intellectual prowess would lead to greater cultural acceptance of the Jew.

143 Ringer, *Arnold Schoenberg and the Politics of Jewish Survival*, 41. Italics in original text. Also in Auner, *A Schoenberg Reader*, 245.

144 Auner, *A Schoenberg Reader*, 246.

The "Four-Point Program" provides a revealing insight into his authoritarian personality. He gives a telling example from his own life. As head of the Society for Private Musical Performances in Vienna, he became, he says, "a kind of dictator." If he encountered opposition within the group, he did what he said would otherwise be illegal:

> I dissolved the whole society, built a new one, accepted only such members who were in perfect agreement with my artistic principles and excluded the entire opposition. There were some sentimentalists who considered it wrong, but it was the only healthful means of avoiding the encroachment of non-artistic principles upon artistic ones. Right or wrong – these principles were my country.[145]

Schoenberg's political authoritarianism was an expression of his overall elite conservatism, especially in art. Writing to Thomas Mann in 1936 on the twenty-fifth anniversary of Mahler's death, Schoenberg says he is the last of the "old guard" who were "hotly striving to fortify the borders of the artistically–morally acceptable to the most severe and impenetrable degree," while others "flirted with folklore, popularity … and suitability for use." The old guard – Mahler, Adolf Loos, Alban Berg, and others – were aristocratic in attitude towards folklore. They did not think of adapting themselves to it. They did not expect their music to be popular, any more than Kant expected his philosophy to be popular. The old guard sought to lead lives fitting for "national heroes" with "purity of motives, incorruptibility of conviction, strength of character, selflessness in attack, chivalrousness in defence." They sought to preserve the past by going beyond it because "what does not grow dies."[146]

Schoenberg's comments are a powerful example of the promiscuity of ideas, discussed in previous chapters. Musical trends and ideas are treated like military or political forces in combat, fortifying the borders. Schoenberg also wanted to "emancipate" atonality. Musical choices are treated as moral choices, a matter of character and courage. The danger with this mixture of individualism and conservatism in art is its implication that, in the political realm, strong national heroes with uncompromising ideologies should run the country.

145 Schoenberg, "A Four-Point Program for Jewry," 55.
146 Ibid., 279–80.

In December 1938, Schoenberg sent another letter to Mann, both men now in the United States. Schoenberg mentions the "Four-Point Program" and complains that he has tried to get it published, without success. After reading the essay, Mann agreed with the goal of helping the Jews, but he disagreed with Schoenberg's anti-democratic tactics, telling Schoenberg in a letter that the piece had a "fascistic bent" and a "will to terrorism."[147] This may have been the moment when Mann decided to make Schoenberg the model of the composer in his novel *Doctor Faustus* with Theodore Adorno apparently providing Mann with details about Schoenberg's life. The novel created a bitter dispute between the three German emigrants in Southern California.[148]

Why, exactly, was the "Four-Point Program" not published at the time?[149] It is hard to believe that if Schoenberg, as a composer of great renown, sent an open letter to major newspapers and broadcasters in the Western world, outlining his plan, that it would have remained unpublished. Schoenberg indicates that he initially sought publication in several (unspecified) venues. His decision to not publish may have been due to Mann's hostile reaction. Or, Schoenberg may have given up trying to get it published. Did he have second thoughts about the wisdom of publishing these ideas at this time? We do not know. The "Program" remained a thirty-seven-page typed document among his writings for four decades.

In retrospect, Schoenberg's intent to become a prophet and party leader was ill-starred from the beginning. The brutal fact is that he lacked the personality and social skills to carry it off in an age of mass media and mass democracy. He was not a warm, gregarious, person who loved the public spotlight; certainly, he was no populist. He was spiritualistic, uncompromising, intellectually arrogant, and he lived quietly. It is hard to imagine Schoenberg stirring the masses at a political rally with passionate words and media sound bites. Nor was his personality, which took almost anything as a personal slight, and held bitter grudges, suited to the knock-about world of politics.

147 Correspondence of Mann to Schoenberg, 9 January 1939. In the Arnold Schoenberg Center, Vienna. Also cited in Daub, "Introduction," *The Doctor Faustus Dossier*, 15.

148 For a full record of the famous and much discussed Schoenberg–Mann dispute over *Doctor Faustus*, see E. Randol Schoenberg's *The Doctor Faustus Dossier*.

149 It was published in 1979 by the *Journal of the Arnold Schoenberg Institute*.

Moreover, other leading Jews thought his plan for Jewry, described in letters and discussed in conversations, was extreme. Or, they had their own, and differing, ideas on what ought to be done. A significant number of his letters to Jewish leaders, asking for political support, went unanswered. Albert Einstein and other liberal Jews disagreed with his Jewish isolationism and militarism. Also, Schoenberg's faith did not fit easily into any of the main branches of Judaism. It was highly personal, idiosyncratic in belief, and not communal – he did not attend a synagogue. His wife would bring up the Schoenberg family of three children under Catholicism. Judaism was not something that shaped family affairs.

Schoenberg's reality-averse thinking in politics was evident as early as his letter to Webern in 1933. Schonberg announced that he had managed to cut himself off "from all that tied me to the Occident" and he would take up national Zionism.[150] Later, he endorsed the idea that what form of government existed in a country was not essential. Jews might do well under democracy, fascism, or monarchy, depending on circumstances. These forms of government belonged to the culture of the gentiles. Given the political reality of Jews in Europe, the idea that they could, solely by themselves, find the money, means, and unanimity to create a homeland within a few years was sadly utopian. Jews lived *within* Occident countries as minorities, within governments that were democratic, socialist, or fascist. The idea that they could go it alone and simply purchase the land (from where?) was fantastical.

Also, the view that the form of government did not matter was illusional. As history showed, Jews had much more reason to fear authoritarian and fascist regimes than democracies.

In the end, those Western democracies that Schoenberg viewed with distrust finally would be prompted, after the war, to help the Jews realize the dream of a homeland.

150 Ringer, *Arnold Schoenberg and the Politics of Jewish Survival.*

5

Surreal Worlds, Logical Worlds

I look for the noise hidden in silence, the movement in immobility, life in inanimate things, the infinite in the finite, forms in a void, and myself in anonymity.

Joan Miró[1]

THE HYPERMODERN MINDSET produced music of great originality, rocking the musical status quo. Yet during the early 1900s, other world makers were at work. In this chapter we examine two examples, both between the world wars: the creation of surreal worlds by painters and the attempt to construct a new logical world by virtue of scientific philosophy.

SECTION 1: IRREALIST ART

In the early 1920s, in Paris, a distinct form of irrationalism arose in art. It depicted a strange world. Yet the artists did not describe their paintings as unreal or purely imaginary. They presented their creations as a window into another, deeper reality, the Freudian unconscious. They were the surrealists, the creators of "sur-real" or supra-real objects.

The surrealists were irrealists and irrationalists. At its best, surrealism was a creative irrationalism, using irrational capacities to create new and striking art, and to reform culture. Their works confounded traditionalists among the bourgeoisie, just as the new music had done. Surrealism would share with the earlier fauves (wild beasts), such as Matisse, and then the cubists, the primary premises of modern art at the start of the twentieth century: radicalness, subjectivity, and a rejection of naïve objectivity. Radicalness meant a search for a new art with a new means

1 Interview, 15 February 1959. In Rowell, *Joan Miró: Selected Writings and Interviews*, 253.

of expression that dares all. Subjectivity meant that the artists distrust authority and rely instead on themselves and the truth of their own experiences. Overcoming naïve objectivity meant that, as with the early cubists, the work of art no longer had to imitate or be faithful to objects as ordinarily perceived or understood by common sense.[2] For Pablo Picasso (1881–1973) and Georges Braque (1882–1963), founders of cubism, new art meant not just new forms, at odds with normal perception, but the creation of a new space in which they occurred. The idea that works of art may have little direct relation to the phenomenal look of objects preceded Picasso. Painters in the nineteenth century had already begun to consider the form of a painting as existing independently from its colour and actual subject matter.

Everyone Loves a Parade?

Evidence that surrealistic themes preceded Dadaists and surrealists comes from the remarkable modernist ballet *Parade* of 1917.[3] The ballet is about a publicity parade in which three groups of circus artists try to attract an audience to an indoor performance. The ballet premiered on 18 May at the Théâtre du Châtelet in Paris, performed by the prestigious Ballet Russes. Profits from the play were to go towards helping French soldiers at the front.

The ballet showed the interdisciplinary nature of the avant-garde. The work was a collaboration of giants. Music was by Erik Satie. A one-act scenario was written by Jean Cocteau, while Léonide Massine oversaw the choreography. Pablo Picasso, in his cubist mode, created outrageous sets and costumes. The theme of the circus and its characters haunts the paintings of Picasso during this period. Some of Picasso's costumes were in solid cardboard, making it difficult for dancers to move. It has been claimed that this was the first time that Picasso's cubism "had to face the crowd."[4] *Parade* also consolidated the Ballet Russes's avant-garde credentials. In writing on the play, poet Guillaume Apollinaire, a close friend of Picasso's, described *Parade* as "a kind of surrealism," coining the word several years before surrealism emerged in Paris.

2 Hamilton, *Painting and Sculpture in Europe, 1880 to 1940*, 101.
3 See the ballet performed at https://www.youtube.com/watch?v=YejpJ4kMH_o.
4 Steegmuller, *Cocteau: A Biography*, 176.

Parade was novel and scandalous, intentionally. Ballets Russes impresario Segei Diaghilev told a young Cocteau to write a script that would astonish him.[5] Cocteau did not disappoint. The ballet included popular forms of music only heard at Parisian music halls and during American silent films, such as ragtime music. It used noise instruments such as a siren, a roulette wheel, a typewriter, and the sounding of a loud gun. These experiments were in the spirit of futurist painter Luigi Russolo's manifesto in 1913, which called for a "MUSIC OF NOISE."

Reaction to *Parade* was, not surprisingly, divided. Critics praised or damned the ballet. Some complained that this was a shameful attempt by the collaborating artists to draw attention to themselves when soldiers were dying at the war front. One part of the audience booed and hissed. Many detractors were upset at Picasso's cubist designs, which were met with cries that the painter had gone "too far." They shouted out "foreigners" and insinuated that the play was the work of the "huns." They almost caused a riot, before they were drowned out by wild applause.

Dadaists and Surrealists

Dadaism amid the First World War was a disruptive protest against the values and institutions of Western civilization – military, government, and artistic establishment. The Dadaists opposed the many forces that had caused the slaughter of the First World War. It was as much a political attitude as it was an artistic style.[6] While it resulted in artworks, Dadaism was defined by anger, agitation, and social action. Dadaists created meaningless poetry and absurdist street performances to ridicule rational Western civilization. Dadaism was anti-art, i.e., against the traditions of established art. It attacked the cultural symbols of what it saw as a corrupt culture. "Dada" was said to signify nothing, a word picked out from a dictionary. Not surprisingly, the first manifestations of anti-war Dadaism during the war years were in two neutral cities, Zurich and New York. It is customary to trace the origin of Dadaism back to 1916 in Zurich when German poet Hugo Ball (1886–1927) opened the Cabaret Voltaire to "remind the world" that there are independent men

5 Findlay, *Picasso's Life*, 94.

6 Romanian poet Tristan Tzara, one of Dadaism's founders, said Dadaism was a "state of mind."

who live for "other ideals" than war and nationalism.[7] At the cabaret, artists and other disaffected individuals began meeting in an old quarter of Zurich to create a new art and a new movement.

Dadaism spread to Cologne, Hanover, Paris, Berlin, and other cities. Dadaists were more militant in social protest, and less influenced by Freud, than the surrealists that would soon appear in Paris. Dada used nonsense to set aside bourgeoisie reason and logic. They leaned toward anarchism, politically, while surrealists tended to favour the Bolsheviks. Many surrealists joined the French Communist Party and elaborated a program for both psychic and social revolution.[8] Surrealists and Dadaists agreed at least on one thing: a new start was needed amid the shipwreck of civilization. The world needed a tradition-smashing, shocking art.

In 1926, Jean Arp, co-founder of Dadaism, explained what the First World War meant to Dada artists in Zurich:

> Revolted by the butchery of the 1914 World War, we in Zurich devoted ourselves to the arts. While guns rumbled in the distance, we sang, painted, made collages and wrote poems with all our might. We were seeking an art based on fundamentals, to cure the madness of the age, and find a new order of things that would restore the balance between heaven and hell. We had a dim premonition that power-mad gangsters would one day use art itself as a way of deadening men's minds.[9]

The Dadaist goal of challenging mainstream and traditional values was transformed into a new artistic reality, surrealism. In Paris, Andre Breton (1896–1966) in the early 1920s joined Dadaists in their activities. But it soon became clear he wanted to lead the artistic parade himself. He called on Dadaists (and other artists) to organize an international congress to "establish directives for the modern spirit." The thought of Dadaists channelling their anger into congress-organizing committees and writing up official directives was ridiculous, and it stirred internal dissent within Dadaism. By 1922, the movement was dead, and Breton was the leader of the Paris avant-garde.[10] Meanwhile, a number

7 Hamilton, *Painting and Sculpture in Europe*, 239.

8 On the Dadaists, see Dachy, *The Dada Movement.*

9 Eram, *The Autobiographical Pact*, 20.

10 Hamilton, *Painting and Sculpture in Europe*, 255.

of artists, including Joan Miró (1893–1983) and Salvador Dalí (1904–1989) in Spain, moved to Paris where, under Breton, they were organized in 1924 into surrealism. Their first exhibition was in 1925 in Paris with paintings from Picasso to Dalí.

In Paris, Miró's melding of abstract expressionism and surrealism influenced Dalí. By the late 1920s, Miró was calling for "assassination of painting," to break with the conventional and corrupt painting world, which Miró thought only served the wealthy.[11]

Miró and Dalí were different people. Dalí was immodest, ambitious, and clever at attracting attention through odd behaviour and appearance, and grand statements. As Dalí said, the only difference between him and the mad man is that he (Dalí) is not mad.[12] Miró was modest, intense, and a more gifted artist than Dalí. His paintings lacked ego and contained light, humour, elements of childishness, and spirituality.[13] Miró refused to belong to any artistic camp, like the surrealists. Breton is often quoted as saying that Miró, who had a "turbulent" entrance into surrealism in Paris, was "the most Surrealist of us all." Yet few commentators go on to note that in the same set of comments, Breton, in his typical egotistical manner, criticizes Miró essentially for not being a faithful foot soldier for his surrealism movement.[14]

Meanwhile, Breton and Dalí would clash, over politics and self-promotion.[15] In 1940, Breton gave Dalí a nickname, "Avida Dollars" (eager for dollars), an anagram of his name. Dalí, in bravado style,

11 On the "assassination," see Penrose, *Miró*, chapter 3.

12 Dalí loved to play the mad artist, with a long, waxed moustache and bulging eyes. He loved to tweak the noses of media interviewers and make outlandish statements. He captured public attention in a new age of mass media.

13 A review of a retrospective on Miró at New York City's Museum of Modern Art called his work "modernism for all" and "fun." In his resistance to pompousness, Miró was really anti-modern. See Peter Schjeldahl, "Modernism for All," *The New Yorker*, 11 March 2019, 70–2. A more recent exhibit, *Miró in Majorca: A Free Spirit*, at the Museum of Fine Arts in Quebec City in the summer of 2019, focused on Miró's incredibly productive period late in life. He used his abstract expressionism to convey an intense spirituality.

14 Breton, *Surrealism and Painting*, 36.

15 Breton disliked Dalí's self-promotion, fame, and lack of political commitment to communism, including his apparent sympathies with fascist leaders. Breton tried to kick Dalí out of his group. By 1940, Dalí had left surrealism, moving to the USA for almost a decade.

embraced “Avida Dollars” as a talisman. He said the term “rendered the rain of dollars fluid, sweet, and monotonous.”[16]

Surrealism’s history is populated with disagreements, duelling manifestos, and the clash of artistic egos. The painters argued over who were the true surrealists and their political commitments. Perhaps, they were too cocksure about their capacity to change culture. Yet they *did* have impact. They were despised by fascists and members of the Soviet Communist Party because the surrealists challenged authoritarian logic. Many surrealists paid for their political resistance.

“The Reign of Logic”

Breton and Dalí said they rejected reality and rationality. What did that mean?

They did not reject reality and rationality *tout court.* They rejected dominant views of reality and rationality which supported the status quo.

What views were those? As discussed earlier, the surrealists ran against the prevailing wind of positivism and utilitarianism. Both ideas were part of the rise of industrial rationality in France. Value was quantifiable. If not, it was a mirage.

For the surrealists, both the means and ends of current social thinking needed to be challenged, including the policies of government, academia, and the arts. In particular, the surrealists complained that techno-rationality did not assess the *ends* at which this thinking aimed. An art of the unconscious was welcomed because it ran counter to this technological, mechanical, materialistic culture. Techno-rationality, social Darwinian capitalism, and the safe, practical utilitarian values of the bourgeoisie blocked new thinking. They supported conservative forces, such as the military and the elites. The battle over ideas and values was ideological.

In 1924, Breton, chief theorist of surrealism, attacked rationalistic culture in his first of two manifestos on surrealism. He complained that the French (and other) people were “still living under the reign of logic but the logical processes of our time apply only to the solution of problems of secondary interest.” A fashionable absolute rationalism only allows people to consider “facts narrowly relevant to our experience.”

16 Dalí, *Diary of a Genius*, 67.

Yet, there is hope. Sigmund Freud had made a timely intervention. Freud brought back into the spotlight the role of the unconscious. To take the unconscious seriously is to question conventional views of rationality and morality that had put French culture in a cage. Surrealism designates a "pure mode of expression" issuing from the depths of humans, untainted by rational repression. For Breton, the "imagination is on the verge of recovering its rights." Alongside the liberation of the imagination, surrealism stressed desire, unshaped and unbounded by the conscious mind. Desire was the "authentic voice of the inner self," a path to self-discovery.[17]

In his manifesto, Breton wrote of the importance of the dream. "I believe in the future resolution of these two states, dream and reality, which are seemingly so contradictory, into a kind of absolute reality, a surreality, if one may so speak." Breton sounds much like the French poet Nicolas Rimbaud (1854–1891), viewing himself as a seer into a more intense reality.[18]

At the end of the manifesto, Breton provides two definitions of surrealism. The first definition defines it by stressing spontaneous thought: "Pure psychic automatism … to express … the real functioning of thought. Dictation of thought in the absence of all control exercised by reason, outside of all aesthetic and moral preoccupation." This method of writing directly from one's unconscious feelings has been called automatism.[19] The second definition stressed the superiority of irrational capacities: "Surrealism is based on the belief in the superior reality of certain forms of previously neglected associations, in the omnipotence of dream, in the disinterested play of thought." This was not far from Schoenberg's irrational inspiration.

17 Mundy, *Surrealism: Desire Unbound*, 7.

18 Robb, *Rimbaud*, 79–80. Rimbaud's *A Season in Hell* of 1873 influenced surrealists.

19 Automatism had a wide influence, including among a group of French Canadian painters in the 1940s, of which Jean-Paul Riopelle was a leading figure.

Dalí and the Ordinary World

I try to create fantastic things, magical things, things like in a dream. The world needs more phantasy. Our civilization is too mechanical. We can make the fantastic real, and then it is more real than that which actually exists.

Salvador Dalí[20]

Prior to Paris, in 1925, Dalí read Freud's *The Interpretation of Dreams* while attending art school. He described the book as "one of the capital discoveries of my life." As a Parisian surrealist, from 1929 to 1939, Dalí astounded the art world with irrational subject matter.

How did Dalí's paintings challenge what we think is real or rational?

One way was to paint irrational spaces. He painted the enigmatic within the familiar. He confounds interior and exterior settings or creates an improbable sense of scale and space. He paints humans on a beach, yet the arrangement of the figures is impossible, according to common sense. Dalí also disrupts the viewer's expectations. He invites us to look inside objects or into a hole, to be surprised at what we see, e.g., maggots or a severed woman's breast. Sexual images, like a nude young man, are injected into works on religious themes. In the early 1930s, Dalí developed a method which he called his "paranoiac-critical method" of interpretation. The artist invokes a paranoid state in the viewer by producing strange or disturbing images. The viewer feels she is being manipulated. In time, the viewer becomes aware of their participation in the viewing, their role in interpreting objects. As Aguer explains, "Subjectivity becomes the primary aspect of the artwork."[21]

In the 1940s, Dalí discovered how to paint optical illusions. For example, how to make a painting display two images. The title of his portrait, "Gala Contemplating the Mediterranean Sea which at Twenty Metres Becomes the Portrait of Abraham Lincoln," explains it all. Up close, the viewer sees Dalí's wife, Gala; from further away, it is the face of Lincoln. He also created "polymorphic" objects with many incongruent parts. For example, *The Great Masturbator* displays a big yellow head with fleshy cheeks and a large nose pressed against the ground. The face has

20 Quoted in the *Richmond Times-Dispatch* newspaper, Richmond, Virginia, 24 November 1940.

21 Aguer, *Dalí's World*, 3.

no mouth, and is replaced by some sort of grasshopper or other insect whose stomach is decomposing and contains ants, while a woman smells a man's genitals. All of this is *one* object. Or is it? For Dalí, magic is the power of the painter to "materialize the imagination in reality." He wrote, "Our super-mechanized age underestimates the attributes of the *irrational imagination*, which is still the basis of all discoveries."[22]

Through these techniques, Dalí challenged our perception of ordinary objects. Most of us assume that seeing is unproblematic, giving us objects whose properties are stable and obvious. Dalí undermines that confidence. He overwhelms the rational, categorizing, mind with multiple interpretations until it is delirious, creating a crisis around our understanding of the object. Outside surrealism, Picasso, as cubist, reorganized the object into non-conventional shapes that bore little resemblance to the ordinary object of perception. Through art, Dalí, Picasso, and others put perception and reality on trial.

Cubists, Dadaists, and surrealists had an intense preoccupation with objects. There was Duchamp's "ready-made" objects of art, such as a toilet urinal. Surreal objects arose through experiments in creating images, such as Max Ernst's "frottage" or Óscar Domínguez's "decalcomania." These techniques involved rubbing pencil or chalk on paper over a textured surface and interpreting the phantom image visible on the paper. In 1925, Breton, in his "Introduction to the Little Reality There Is," proposed creating objects that one comes across only in dreams. Breton, unlike Dalí, would become increasingly obsessed with strange objects and experiences. He was fascinated by dark irrationalism: he sought inspiration in the occult and Haitian voodooism. In his book *Nadja*, Breton, obsessed with a young woman, wanders the side streets of Paris looking for strange never-before-seen objects, "an encounter with the 'Marvelous.'"[23] Dalí wrote a surreal history of the object as surrealists were mounting the 1936 Surrealist Exhibition of the Objects in Paris. The exhibition displayed natural objects, found objects, mathematical objects, wild objects, and finally surrealist objects.

It has been said that surrealist theory "sought to re-enchant the universe."[24] If the object in all its strangeness is seen, we might see our

22 Cited in Aguer, *Dalí's World*, 3. Italics mine.

23 Jeanne S.M. Willette, *Art History Unstuffed*, https://arthistoryunstuffed.com/the-surrealist-object.

24 Ibid.

world anew and not reduce it to science or ordinary observations. Dalí, Breton, and the surrealists sought to revolutionize how we look at the world. Their motifs remain today, implicit in the work of artists such as Francis Bacon and the writing of magic realists.

SECTION 3: LOGICAL CONSTRUCTION OF THE WORLD

The ultimate goal of all visual artistic activity is construction! Architects, painters and sculptors must learn again to know and understand the multifaceted form of building.

Walter Gropius, Bauhaus founder[25]

While irrationalism constructed an aesthetic of the unconscious, rationalism was not in decline. We have seen that conservatives embraced industrial rationality to re-create order in society. But this was not the only rationalism on offer. To the contrary, a philosophical conception of rationalism was arising in architecture, design, and philosophy.

In Italy, for example, rationalist architecture emerged with a preference for geometric forms and ideal proportions. The architects abandoned the ornamental Art Nouveau style. Science was the basis of architecture. The spirit of Vitruvius was alive.[26] In Germany, the Bauhaus style of design, from furniture to buildings, was rational, functional, and then international. In Vienna, logical positivists wanted philosophy to become scientific. It would become one of the most powerful movements in modern philosophy.

Positivism of Pure Fact

The fact, as the basis for knowledge, was invented by experimental science in the seventeenth century. Francis Bacon was the champion of this new science. He explained the methods which would discover new facts. Scientists were not passive observers. They were active investigators, using experiments and measurements to force nature to give up

25 From the manifesto of the Bauhaus in its founding year of 1919. Also cited in Dutching, *Kandinsky*, 63.

26 See Kostof, *A History of Architecture.*

her secrets. Such knowledge would give men power over nature. This notion of science carried forward into the eighteenth century.

In the nineteenth century, this scientific stress on facts was given a name: positivism. Positivists sought positive knowledge. As noted earlier, its principal exponents in the first half of the 1800s were John Stuart Mill (1806–1873) in England and Auguste Comte (1798–1857) in France.[27] Mill defined positivism as such: "We have no knowledge of anything but phenomena, and our knowledge of phenomena is relative, not absolute. We know not the essence, nor the real mode of production, of any fact, but only its relations to other facts in the way of succession or of similitude."[28] Comte stressed verification of statements by fact. No fact, no intelligible sense. "All good intellects have repeated, since Bacon's time, that there can be no real knowledge but that which is based on observed facts."[29] For Comte, science was the culmination of the march of human thought from theology to metaphysics to positivist science.[30]

Positivism did more than admire the discovery of new facts. It denied there was any other type of knowledge about the world. Positivists took to heart Kant's dictum, in the previous century, that science (and the mind) knows *only* the sensible appearances of objects and regularities among the appearances. The mind cannot penetrate to the hidden essences of things, a reality behind what we observe. Fourier's mathematical laws of the diffusion of heat, for example, formulated regularities among phenomena without assumptions about the nature of heat. Ernst Mach in *The Analysis of Sensations* expressed his phenomenalism: "The world consists only of our sensations ... In which case we have knowledge *only* of sensations."[31] The table, the tree, and so forth, are "my sensations" and are constructed into beliefs about objects.

Consider what positivism excludes from the sphere of knowledge. It excludes theology, faith, metaphysics, what art or music teach us, ecstatic insights, what is known through emotions and feelings, occult beliefs, mysticism, and deliverances of the unconscious. It is a severe

27 The term "positivism" first appeared in 1831 in a document by the French Saint-Simon.

28 Mill, *Auguste Comte and Positivism*, 6.

29 Comte, *The Positive Philosophy*, 27.

30 Ibid., 25–30.

31 Mach, *The Analysis of Sensations*, 12.

rationalism, with a negative attitude toward irrational capacities. A belief is admitted through the gates of science *only* if it can be proved by fact and logic. Even if the psychological origin of an idea is a striking dream or an overwhelming mystical feeling, it cannot be regarded as knowledge, or as part of science, until it has been tested by positive methods.

Why this stringent empiricism? A major motivation was to distinguish true science from occult beliefs and philosophical speculations. The advance of science in academia and in society depended on being able to say how science was different (and better) than other disciplines.

In the second half of the nineteenth century, scientific positivism became even more strident. Efforts were made to reduce or eliminate the human influence in inquiry, almost entirely. The goal was the objectivity of *pure* fact, cleansed of all ideology, interpretation, and perspective. Hard nuggets of fact – these hard bits of reality – could not be rationally doubted and hence could adjudicate between scientific hypotheses. There was, in many scientific quarters, an almost religious veneration for the fact. "Sit down before a fact as a little child," wrote Thomas Huxley. "Be prepared to give up every pre-conceived notion, follow humbly wherever and to whatever abyss nature leads, or you shall learn nothing."[32]

Scientists gave birth to three types of pure objectivity: mechanical, aperspectival, and numerical.[33] Mechanical objectivity was objectivity achieved through machines. We discussed machine rationality earlier as part of social philosophies. Machine rationality also became part of science. Scientists were attracted to machines because they believed that machines recorded facts automatically, uncontaminated by interpretation. Among the instruments used were the camera obscura, lithographs, photoengraving, photographs, and X-rays. Scientists employed machines to create images of the body, biological and botanical species, and eventually elementary particles, stars, and embryos. Charles Babbage praised machinery because it avoided "the inattention, the idleness, or the dishonesty of human agents."[34]

A perspectival objectivity meant the transcendence of partial viewpoints, not the mechanical copying of facts but the reduction of distortion caused by local perspective. The scientist needed to "escape

32 Cited in Stephens, *A History of News*, 221.

33 For details, see Ward, *Objectively Engaged Journalism*, chapters 3 and 4.

34 Daston and Galison, "The Image of Objectivity," 81–127.

from perspective" to apprehend nature as it really is.[35] One way to do so was through peer review by scientific societies and journals. Science's internationalization encouraged the search for objective standards and terminology.

Finally, objectivity in the 1800s became defined by numbers. Numbers were favoured because they are abstract, impersonal entities, governed by formal rules of calculation that hold for all rational beings. This "trust in numbers"[36] was applied not just to mathematics and the natural sciences but to the nineteenth-century analysis of social patterns and problems.

The Birth of Logical Positivism

A philosophy is never a house; it is a construction site.

Georges Bataille[37]

Positivism gave birth to a scientific philosophy called logical positivism.[38] The aim was a systematic justification for objective, empirical science.

About 1928, a group gathered around Moritz Schlick at the University of Vienna, an Austrian scientist with a PhD in theoretical optics. Their meetings would form the Vienna Circle, the incubator of logical positivism.[39] Its 1929 manifesto was largely written by Rudolph Carnap (1891–1970) and influenced by Wittgenstein, Bertrand Russell, Gottlob Frege, and Mach.[40]

35 Daston, "Objectivity and the Escape from Perspective," 597–618.

36 For the rise of probability theory and statistics, see Porter, *The Rise of Statistical Thinking* and *Trust in Numbers*. See also Stigler, *The History of Statistics*, and Hacking, *The Taming of Chance*.

37 Cited in Noys, *Georges Bataille*, 59.

38 The term "logical positivism" came mainly from an article of the same name published by Albert E. Blumberg and Herbert Feigl in *The Journal of Philosophy* in 1931. Logical positivist Moritz Schlick called it "consistent empiricism," while fellow positivist Rudolph Carnap preferred "logical empiricism." It was also called neo-positivism.

39 For a laudatory yet still useful history, see Viktor Kraft, *The Vienna Circle*. Some of the members were Carnap, Friedrich Waismann, Feigl, Otto Neurath, and Kurt Gödel. It worked with the Society of Empirical Philosophy at Berlin led by Hans Reichenbach. Its main publication was the journal *Erkenntnis* (1930) which was renamed *The Journal of Unified Science* (1939–40), edited by Reichenbach and Carnap.

40 Mach's influence was so great that the first name for the group was Verein Ernst Mach.

The name of the group explained its mission: Positivists would use the new and rigorous techniques of logic, linguistic analysis, and mathematics to show how empirical knowledge is derived from perceptual experience.[41] Russell was responsible for much of the enthusiasm about philosophical analysis. In the early 1900s, he and Alfred North Whitehead published *Principia Mathematica*, which constructed mathematical notions from logical notions.[42]

Many of the logical positivists were scientists and mathematicians who knew little about the history of philosophy and were devoutly anti-metaphysical. For them, to be non-scientific was the intellectual equivalent of original sin. For about thirty years (1930–60) the movement virtually defined analytical philosophy. A journal was started; international conferences on the unity of science were held. The movement spread from Austria and Germany to England, Scandinavia, and the United States. The movement dissipated before the Second World War as its leading figures died, took up positions at other universities, or decamped to England and the United States to escape Nazi suspicions of the movement.

Logical positivism caught the spirit of its times. In the 1920s, both the political left and right in Austria and Germany were calling for a radical reconstruction of society after a disastrous world war. Among artistic liberals, there was an increase in experimentation. There was a decline in expressionism and a turning toward what was called New Objectivity in art and architecture.[43] Devotees sought to give Germany a modern face. In architecture, designers used glass surfaces and geometric composition. They preferred buildings that were practical, not weighed down by ornamentation or a complicated style. Romanticism was dead. Functionalism was rising. Architect Ludwig Mies van der Rohe,

41 These ground-breaking works on logic and mathematics were not available to the positivists of the early nineteenth century. For a summary of the emergence of mathematical formalism and formal logic, see Putnam, "Peirce the Logician." For the logical positivist's view of the role of logic in philosophy, see Schlick, "The Turning Point in Philosophy."

42 *Principia Mathematica* was published in three volumes in 1910, 1912, and 1913. It was based on logicism, the view that mathematics is reducible to logic.

43 New Objectivity art arose during the 1920s and included such artists as Max Beckmann and Otto Dix.

stimulated by America, designed skyscrapers with modern features.[44] The Dessau Bauhaus building was an example of New Objectivity.

For positivists, a modern society would be built on uncompromising new modes of thought that were practical, scientific, and technological. Carnap issued a call for "clarity, for a science that is free from metaphysics," for an attitude that "will win the future."[45]

Logical positivism was *not* a cautious extension of empiricism. Logical positivists wanted strong and strict distinctions between verifiable and non-verifiable, empirical and non-empirical, meaningful and meaningless. To make these distinctions, they employed unbridgeable dualisms. Picking up on Comte's stress on factual verification, they issued their famous theory of cognitive meaning: all meaningful statements about the world must be verifiable by direct experience, or they are literally meaningless. This dualism, in one swoop, cast all of metaphysics and most of traditional philosophy, including ethics, into the category of the meaningless. The logical positivists intensified Hume's distinction between "is" and "ought." Ethical statements about what ought to be were said to be emotive value judgments. The judgments cannot be verified by fact since they are a subjective expression of emotion. Logical positivists also presumed that it was possible to identify pure facts in experience. Facts were sense data, or facts were perceptions of external objects, prior to interpretation and theory.

Logical positivism could be belligerent.[46] In its early phase, logical positivists issued strongly worded *dicta* which attracted support from those who sought rigour in philosophy. But its intolerance for forms of thinking outside of natural science and logic made enemies in the humanities, social sciences, arts, traditional philosophy, and religious studies. Carnap, in *The Unity of Science,* portrayed many philosophical topics as "pseudo-problems." A.J. Ayer's overconfident *Language, Truth and Logic* in 1936, a popular work of philosophy, led the positivist's war on metaphysics. In the book, Ayer claims to have "explained the nature of truth." Within a few pages, he dismisses all of ethics as subjective emotion. Ayer later admitted that his arguments could have been

44 Pevsner, *An Outline of European Architecture,* 404–35.

45 Carnap, *The Logical Structure of the World and Pseudo-problems in Philosophy,* xviii.

46 Kraft countered the charge of belligerence by saying that the most controversial theses were not the views of all Circle members but the views of a subset of radical members such as Neurath. Kraft, *The Vienna Circle,* xx.

more persuasive if not presented in "so harsh a form" and that the questions with which *Language, Truth and Logic* dealt are not as simple as he once thought.[47]

Scientific philosophy did not *do* science. Science was empirical and synthetic. It said something about the world. Philosophy, like logic or mathematics, was analytical, the analysis of concepts and language.[48] Therefore, scientific philosophy was a logic of science, revealing the unity of science in a set of shared concepts and methods.[49] It analyzed scientific concepts, leaving empirical statements about the world to science. Moreover, philosophy employed its analytical powers to construct the world, i.e., to show how the mind moves from direct experience to scientific theory. In his early major work *The Logical Structure of the World*, in 1928, Carnap said the aim was a "rational reconstruction of the concepts of all fields of knowledge on the basis of concepts that refer to the immediately given."[50]

Logical Positivism and the Bauhaus

On 15 October 1929, Carnap arrived at the Bauhaus art school in Dessau, southwest of Berlin, to deliver a lecture.[51] A student of Frege, Carnap was by then a well-known leader of the logical positivists. His *The Logical Structure of the World* had become the bible of the new anti-metaphysical philosophy. He would lecture in a new and stunning building designed by Bauhaus founder Walter Gropius, a "citadel of high modernism."[52] The Bauhaus, founded in 1919, had moved to Dessau from Berlin as the school struggled with the Weimar government.

47 Ayer, *Language, Truth and Logic*, 5.

48 The philosophical distinction between the analytic (meaning of concepts) and the synthetic (statements about the world) was another distinction that the logical positivists turned into a dualism. Taking a page from Wittgenstein, statements about concepts were tautologies, i.e., true independently of experience. They did not say anything about the world. They simply explicated the meaning of terms. In contrast, synthetic statements described the world.

49 Carnap, *The Unity of Science*, 24–7.

50 Carnap, *The Logical Structure of the World*, preface to the second edition, vi–vii.

51 The German term Bauhaus literally means "building house." It was understood as meaning a "school of building."

52 Galison, "Aufbau/Bauhaus," 710.

Carnap would address the famed art school and faculty which would continue to teach until the Nazis closed the school in 1932. The Nazis accused the school of being too Jewish or oriental in spirit, a "germ-cell for Bolshevik subversion" and a designer of decadent modern architecture, among other things. The school was indeed known for its modernism. Many of its designs used simple, geometrical forms that avoided ornamentation. The school sought to bridge the divide between the teaching of fine art in the academies and the teaching of engineers and designers in more pragmatic institutions.

The belief that technological innovation and science could revive society was part of German intellectual life after the First World War. Gropius, as early as 1923, began speaking about a modern architecture that would produce a "complete spiritual revolution in the individuals" and a "new style of life." Architecture was not the continuance of a tradition but a product of industry and scientific specialists such as economists and statisticians. These ideas irritated the political right whose aim was to revive the traditional *volk* form of life prior to modernity, with large dollops of nationalism and racism.

Carnap's lecture was called "Science and Life." Carnap told his audience that he worked on the ideas of science and they worked on the visible forms of society. Yet the two enterprises are "only different sides of a single life."[53] Why did Carnap think that these Bauhaus intellectuals shared a "single life" with the logical positivists?

It was because the groups shared two things.

First, the members of both the Dessau Bauhaus and logical positivism sought to develop a modernism that emphasized what Galison calls "transparent construction," a building up from simple elements to all higher forms. The manner of construction itself would "guarantee the exclusion of the decorative, mystical, or metaphysical."[54] Although logical positivists differed on politics, they shared a deep interest in architectural notions. As a result, the logical positivists were the most frequent visitors to the Bauhaus, outside of visitors from art and architecture.

Second, the two movements faced the same enemies: the religious right, nationalists, volk theorists, and the Nazis. These conservative forces threatened a rationalistic, modernistic response to Germany's

53 Ibid.

54 Ibid.

problems. By stressing clear construction, whether of ideas or materials, the Bauhaus and the logical positivists had a political motivation. They hoped their approach would block the use of nationalist or historical ideas in philosophy and art. The logical positivist would build knowledge from reliable, simple observation reports to produce an anti-philosophy philosophy; the Bauhaus would combine primitive colour relations and basic geometrical forms to create an anti-aesthetic aesthetic around function. References to history, tradition, or the volk were avoided. During the 1920s and 1930s, the relationship between logical positivism and the Bauhaus was real and substantive.[55] In 1929, logical positivist Herbert Feigl, an official Vienna Circle visitor to the Bauhaus, praised the school's "new scientific world conception."[56]

Looking back, the Vienna Circle's manifesto was not a dry treatise. It was robustly political. It declared that the Circle seeks to make contact with the "living movements of the present" which are "well disposed toward the scientific world conception and turn away from metaphysics and theology." Its quarrel with traditional philosophy is due to "fierce social and economic struggles" between people of two opposite sides. One side holds fast to traditional social forms and outdated metaphysics, while the other side "faces modern times" and takes its stand upon empirical science. The traditionalists are the extreme irrationalists, the volkists, and fascists who threaten reason. Carnap and fellow positivists were trying to bring forward a modern form of life. While the surrealists would fight tradition with fantastic paintings and the unconscious, the logical positivists would use science. We now see an additional reason for the belligerence of logical positivists: the need to combat political enemies.

Such was the philosophical clash of ideas. However, it would be misleading to think that both sides lined up in a clear-cut war of ideas, with the logical positivists and the Bauhaus faculty playing, without exception, the role of admirable, freedom fighters. Below the philosophical level, there was the level of politics where imperfect individuals were caught in difficult, and sometimes compromising, situations.

55 The relationship did not end with Nazi Germany. When the Bauhaus reconvened as the New Bauhaus in Chicago, after fleeing the Nazis, the New Bauhaus acknowledged logical positivism as part of its design program. Galison, "Aufbau/Bauhaus," 711.

56 Galison, "Aufbau/Bauhaus," 716–17.

The closing of the Bauhaus did not happen overnight. As noted, the school had long been a source of controversy among conservatives. Conservatives disliked its designs, rejected a merger of fine arts and craftsmanship, complained about the Bauhaus's large number of international teachers, and opposed its attempt to design "minimal" but functional housing for the lower classes. Claims by Gropius, Paul Klee, and others that the Bauhaus was apolitical cut no ice with critics for whom the school was clearly left wing. Gropius stuck tenaciously to this apolitical claim even when safe in America, where he declined to take part in exhibitions that called attention to what was happening in Nazi Germany.

Scholar Peter Hahn argues that this caution was not entirely due to efforts to protect friends in Germany but because Gropius and other Bauhaus émigrés saw themselves as international exponents of modernism who could (and did) obtain prestigious positions in America. They were not desperate immigrants or political activists.[57]

Moreover, to survive after the school's closing, many Bauhaus staff took on less-prestigious design positions with the Nazi government. Kandinsky, like a number of students, thought the Bauhaus could be kept open through appeasement of Nazi authorities. For example, some students were willing to declare an oath of loyalty to their new political masters. Kandinsky wrote painter Willi Baumeister on 3 April 1933 proposing that modernist artists join the Campaign for German Culture led by the notorious Nazi ideologue Alfred Rosenberg. He also told Bauhaus student Werner Drewes that perhaps the German government would adopt the openness of Italian fascism to modern art, where "the new architecture and the new art (futurism) are recognized as Fascist art."[58] He would soon learn that this was a delusion. In 1937, the Nazis showed his work at their famous exhibition on "Degenerate Art" and fifty-seven of his paintings in German museums were confiscated. Like Kandinsky, Gropius hoped that the new Nazi state might follow the example of the Italian fascists in art. Gropius even contributed to the design of a Nazi racist exhibition in 1934 called "The 'German Volk.'" Bauhaus modernism could be combined with "Nazi-tainted subject matter."[59]

57 Hahn, "Bauhaus Exile," 221.

58 Hahn, *Bauhaus Berlin*, 126, 129–30.

59 Ibid., 217.

Yet, despite these complicating factors, the Bauhaus leaders and the logical positivists were, in general, philosophical opponents of the volk-supported Nazi regime. When the Nazis gained power over the Berlin region in the elections of May 1932, the writing was on the wall. The Nazis closed the school in September 1932 and cut off all government funding. The school attempted to carry on as a privately funded institution in Berlin but a police raid in April 1933 ended the Bauhaus in Germany, although it would revive in Chicago after the war.

By the mid to late 1930s, both the logical positivists and the Bauhaus faculty could see a Nazi apocalypse coming. Neurath, one of the founders of logical positivism, wrote to Carnap: "And behind it all stands Hitler ... Here comes God and Religion to the front and ancestral truths and the German *volk*, and what you need to do to stab a Jewish socialist with a knife between the ribs ... Oh Carnap! Oh World!"[60] The positivists and the modernists were on the run. Both in the Bauhaus and among the logical positivists, professors were resigning, fleeing, appeasing, or about to be arrested. In 1936, Schlick was murdered at his university by a deranged student.[61] Carnap, a socialist and a pacifist, emigrated to the United States in 1935, where he was a professor at the University of Chicago and eventually at UCLA in 1954. He refused a job offer from the University of California because, unlike Schoenberg, he would not sign the oath of allegiance.

The death of logical positivism as a philosophy was a fact by the early 1960s. Its main tenets were in dispute, members disagreed among themselves, and the dream of conceptually constructing the world from immediate experience seemed increasingly impossible as science became more theoretical and distant from direct human perception. In the philosophy of knowledge, logical positivism was replaced by relativism, constructionism, and historicism.[62]

60 Galison, "Aufbau/Bauhaus," 742.

61 Friedman, *Reconsidering Logical Positivism*, xii.

62 For an account of these new epistemologies, see my *Objectively Engaged Journalism*, chapters 3 and 4.

PART TWO

Irrational Publics

6

Apocalypse Soon

When bonfires glowed throughout the land every day to the glory of God and, in resplendent autos-da-fe, burned the wicked heretics

Fyodor Dostoevsky[1]

OVER THE PAST FOUR CHAPTERS I have looked at how cultures, and groups within those, swing back and forth between rationalism and irrationalism, like a pendulum.

In the next four chapters I pay attention to extreme irrationalism in two of three senses defined in chapter 1: irrationality as *against* reason and irrationality as bordering on the neurotic and psychotic, a losing touch with reality. I examine irrationality at the extreme end of the pendulum. I provide examples of extreme irrationality in religious groups, political movements, cults, and communes. The examples range from medieval Europe to contemporary America.

In this chapter, I discuss examples of two kinds: the apocalyptic irrationality that drove the crusades against the Muslims in the Holy Land and influences far-right groups today, and the heretical irrationalism that led to inquisitions against fellow Christians and alleged witches.

SECTION 1: APOCALYPTIC IRRATIONALITY

Apocalyptic publics share an ancient belief that the world will end soon in a cataclysmic event. Humans (or a sub-group of humans) will enjoy or suffer through, respectively, a paradise, i.e., a utopia, or a terrible world, i.e., a dystopia.

1 Fyodor Dostoevsky, "The Grand Inquisitor," *The Brothers Karamazov.*

The term "utopia" literally translates as "no place." Some utopian accounts are meant to entertain. Others are deadly serious, warning about cultural decline. Utopias may be written to moralize on some principle, e.g., to promote a society of shared property, to criticize the status quo, or to help citizens imagine another way to live. Utopias can incite reform on earth.[2]

Utopias are placed in the past, the present, or the future. Western literature is populated with paradises lost, such as the Bible's Garden of Eden, as well as paradise regained, as with Christ's Second Coming. The first literary reference to a golden age in the past is in Hesiod's poem *Works and Days* from the eighth century BC.

Some utopias are situated on the margins of the known world, such as Lilliput in *Gulliver's Travels*.[3] Some place the utopia in the sky. In *The Birds*, first performed in 414 BC, the Greek dramatist Aristophanes called his utopia "cloud cuckoo land." Two middle-aged men, disillusioned with life in Athens, persuade the birds to create a great city in the sky. Utopian writings stretch from Plato's myth of the island of Atlantis which sunk into the Atlantic Ocean to Francis Bacon's *New Atlantis* where scientists govern society. There is Thomas More's *Utopia* of 1516, which gave the genre its name.[4] In 1602, Italian philosopher Tommaso Campanella published *The City of the Sun* – a theocratic monarchy where all children, women, and goods were held in common. Other future writings purport to be scientific, predicting how human history will develop, whether the end state is a Marxist classless society or a totalitarian Third Reich. Some dystopias, as in Orwell's *1984*, depict an authoritarian society.

Visions of utopia have led to some of the worst forms of group intolerance. All depends on *what* the ideal is, *how* the ideal is fostered in human minds, and under *which* social conditions. Isaiah Berlin wrote that the twentieth century was shaped mainly by two factors: the development of the natural sciences (and technology) and "great ideological

2 For the types of utopias, especially in Greece, see Lauriola, "The Greeks and the Utopia."

3 In his 1726 novel, Swift locates Lilliput and Blefuscu, two fictional islands, in the South Indian Ocean.

4 In British and American literature alone, more than 3,000 specimens of utopian writing have been identified since 1516. See the introduction to More, *Utopia*, xx.

storms." The storms of extreme nationalism, communism, and fascism were storms created by utopian ideals. The ideals were propagated by leaders who became "prophets with armies at their backs."[5]

Yearning for the Millennium

Apocalyptic thinking is a form of utopian thinking that has had a long, harmful, and sometimes bizarre influence on Western society. It has been used to demonize Jews, Muslims, Freemasons, and institutions such as the United Nations. At its worst, apocalyptic thinking wanders far from its Biblical roots to induce a paranoid view of reality embraced by far-right militias, cult suicides, and lone gun terrorists.[6]

To base one's religious view on an apocalypse is sometimes viewed as an archaic way of thinking embraced by only a small number of religious eccentrics. Not so. Apocalyptic thinking is almost mainstream in many countries today. Its memes bound across social media.

Apocalyptic thinking takes on at least two forms: (1) apocalyptic millennialism based on ancient religious prophecies, and (2) modern paranoid fears of a new world order.

Apocalyptic millennialism is the ancient belief, in the Judaeo-Christian tradition, that Christ will return to earth at a time of apocalypse to establish a millennium of peace (1,000 years) before the end of time, when God judges all souls.[7] In the Bible, Mathew portrays the teaching of John the Baptist as a warning to "Repent for the kingdom of heaven is at hand."[8] Jesus engages in apocalyptic teachings, stating that certain things must come to pass before "the end."[9] Christians have tried to identify the date when the world will end. In England, the Fifth

5 Berlin, "The Pursuit of the Ideal," 1.

6 For the history of apocalyptic thinking in detail, see Cohen, *Cosmos, Chaos and the World to Come: The Ancient Roots of Apocalyptic Faith*, and Hall, *Apocalypse: From Antiquity to the Empire of Modernity*.

7 Two interpretations of the millennium existed in the Middle Ages. The millennium has not yet begun or, as Augustine said in *The City of God*, the millennium is already underway. It started with Christ's reincarnation. *City of God*, book XX, chapter 9, 907–14.

8 Matthew 3:1–2 in *The New Oxford Annotated Bible*.

9 Matthew 24:3–8 in *The New Oxford Annotated Bible*. See also Allison, *Jesus of Nazareth: Millenarian Prophet*.

Monarchy Men, a religious sect in the middle of the seventeenth century, predicted Christ's Second Coming in the year 1666. Isaac Newton proposed the year 2060. Many Mormons and Jehovah Witnesses believe we live in the "last days."

We have limited knowledge of the extent to which apocalyptic millennialism occupied the Dark Ages. It appears that, in the year 1000, Christian philosophers debated exactly when Jesus was born and when the apocalypse might occur.[10] However, we do know that millennialism revived at the end of the eleventh century.

Apocalyptic Sources

Where did these teachings come from? From religious prophesies only some of which are accepted by Catholic and Protestant churches into their canon of approved Biblical texts.

Judaism and Christianity have always had an eschatology, i.e., some conception of the last days of the world. The Judeo-Christian sources include the book of Revelation and the Old Testament's prophetic books, such as the book of Daniel.[11] The book of Revelation, written about 96 AD, describes an apocalypse where the Antichrist is defeated and Christ establishes a new Eden. Christ and the martyred saints, "souls who had been beheaded by the testimony to Jesus,"[12] would reign on earth for a thousand years before a general resurrection of the dead. Early Christians interpreted saints liberally to refer to themselves – the faithful.

Early Jewish and Christian sects regarded the millennium as (a) collective: enjoyed by the faithful as a whole; (b) terrestrial: realized on earth; (c) imminent: will come soon and suddenly; (d) total: will transform life on earth – it will be the perfection of life, not its mere improvement – and (e) miraculous: accomplished with help from supernatural agencies.[13]

10 See Palmer, "The Apocalypse in the Early Middle Ages."

11 Especially one particular section of the book of Revelation, 20:4–6, in *The New Oxford Annotated Bible.*

12 Revelation 20:4.

13 See Cohen, *The Pursuit of the Millennium,* 15.

Seeing themselves as the chosen people, it was natural for the Jews to respond to oppression with millennial prophecies of their triumph over enemies and endless prosperity under Yahweh, as a new Eden is created. The apocalyptic writings were directed particularly at the lower strata of Jewish society, to shore up their support. In chapter 7 of the book of Daniel, we read one of the earliest apocalyptic visions, from the second century BC. Palestine had passed into the control of the Syro-Greek dynasty of the Seleucids, which banned Jewish religious practices. In the dream of the book of Daniel, composed at the height of a Jewish Maccabean Revolt (167–160 BC), Daniel is said to dream of four beasts arising from the sea which symbolize four successive world powers. The fourth beast, with its ten horns, symbolizes the Greek kingdom, which will destroy the earth. The rule of the beast is ended by God who, in white clothes and with pure white hair, arrives on a fiery throne. God establishes a Jewish kingdom that rules over the whole world.

Christians began composing and collecting millennial prophecies in the first century AD, at the same time that many of them were joining sects outside the mainstream of the church. For example, an ascetic movement called Montanism, begun in 156 AD, spread across Asia Minor and into Africa, Rome, and Gaul. Its leader Montanus, experiencing ecstatic visions, proclaimed he was the Spirit of Truth which according to the Fourth Gospel would unveil the things to come. He summoned all Christians to Phrygia (in modern Turkey) to await the Second Coming of Christ. The non-appearance of the millennium did not crush the movement. Rather, leaders warned that it would come later, unexpectedly. Meanwhile, a series of important Christian writers advanced the millennium view, such as Irenaeus, Bishop of Lyons. Tertullian, a Christian apologist in Carthage, joined the Montanist movement. He wrote of a great portent: In Judea, people had seen a walled city in the sky every morning for forty days – a sign that the New Jerusalem was about to descend.

The central theme of these apocalyptic prophesies, Jewish or Christian, is that the world is a terrible place. The world is corrupted by tyrants and empires that are evil and demonic. The suffering will increase until the saints of God rise up and overthrow the tyrants.

As the church became an institution of the Roman Empire and the Second Coming did not occur, leaders from Origen to Augustine (and after Augustine) sought to separate church doctrine from the extreme views of many millennium sects. Augustine campaigned for inclusion of the book of Revelation in the Catholic canon, mainly on the belief that it was written by the Apostle John. Yet he also interpreted such texts as allegorical or symbolic, not the literal truth. Paradise was in heaven or in one's soul. Paradise was most closely approximated on earth by the church. Moreover, Christ came to make peace, not to act as a millennial warrior. Humans would receive their reward in the City of God, in the sky. These efforts failed to root out millennial ideas from popular religion.

The millennium may sound like a hopeful idea. Who would not want a paradise on earth? But the idea has a dark interpretation that preachers used to create militant, intolerant sects. The millennium was, and is, not just a religious phantasy. In its more militant forms, it was, and is, a *political* idea, a vision of God helping an oppressed group to overcome and then dominate their enemy. It is God-assisted revenge. The militant view of the millennium was not a hope for *all* mankind. It was a paradise intended only (or mainly) for one group, the faithful of God in the Judeo-Christian tradition, first the oppressed Jews and then the suffering early Christians. As paradise was being created, the faithful, as agents of a warrior Christ, would put many of the unfaithful to the sword. This was a strong political message at a time of profound persecution of religious groups and nations by tyrants and empires.

The unfaithful, however defined, were not secondary players in this cosmic drama. Frequently, they were interpreted as obstacles to the realization of the millennium. The faithful could assure their place in paradise and hasten the millennium by removing these obstacles, i.e., by taking action that apparently pleased God, such as suppressing Jews and Muslims. Millenarianism was an early form of the enemy stance, to be discussed later. It was a tribalism based on religious grounds.

Many of the Biblical millennium narratives are fantastical utopian writing using powerful, surreal images – of dark creatures emerging from the depths of the sea, of the Antichrist as a flying dragon, of the Four Horsemen of the Apocalypse, of a warrior God coming to restore justice, riding on clouds or a fiery chariot. Despite the hallucinogenic, ecstatic quality of much of the writing, the faithful considered them to be descriptions of reality. They were prophecies of things surely to come.

Crusade Mania: Populism

On 27 November 1095, Pope Urban II called for a crusade to the Holy Land to protect the Byzantine Empire from the advancing (Muslim) Turks.[14] His appeal was received warmly. People at his sermon in France volunteered on the spot, crying "God Wills It."[15] Urban II set 15 August 1096 as the date of departure by a coalition of Western European armies. He did not expect the enthusiastic response from ordinary people in England, France, and Germany. Before the First Crusade army could leave, a mob of paupers and peasants, badly armed and untrained, left for the Holy Land. It was called the People's Crusade. Excited that the crusade would bring on the millennium, the group slaughtered Jews and Muslims as they moved toward the Holy Land.

The People's Crusade was a reflection of serious religious dissent starting at the end of the eleventh century, due to deteriorating conditions for the European lower classes. Medieval Christian sects formulated what Norman Cohen calls a "revolutionary millenarianism" – a movement of mainly unrooted poor that would challenge traditional church and secular power and see Jews and other groups as scapegoats. Led by self-appointed holy men, sects looked eagerly toward the millennium, to rescue them from a harsh world. The Crusades provided a release for this pent-up populist enthusiasm.

This acute millennialism, catching fire among ordinary people, paupers, and even children, would cause pogroms during the crusades. At times, even the pope and military leaders could not restrain the desire of mobs to set out for Jerusalem, thirsty for salvation and captivated by dreams of the millennium and a New Jerusalem. Cohen summarizes the role of this millennialism during the early crusades: "So it came about that multitudes of people acted out with fierce energy a shared phantasy which, though delusional, yet brought them intense emotional relief that they could live only through it, and were perfectly willing to kill or to die for it."[16]

14 There were eight major crusades between 1096 and 1291. The attempt to recover the Holy Land ended in failure in 1291 with the fall of Acre, the last of four crusader states.

15 Historians continue to debate the pope's motives, including the possibility that he was trying to reunite Christianity under his leadership.

16 Cohen, *The Pursuit of the Millennium*, 88.

The First Holocaust

The People's Crusade was organized by Peter the Hermit of France and Count Emicho of Flonheim, Germany, among others. Peter the Hermit claimed to have a letter from heaven instructing him to crusade. He recruited widely from England, France, Flanders, and Lorraine.[17] He preached a "messianism of the poor" galvanized by an expectation of mass ascension into heaven at Jerusalem.[18] Miracles were said to occur as Peter the Hermit preached.[19] Leading the first of five sections of the People's Crusade, Peter the Hermit started with 40,000 men and women from Cologne in April 1096. He arrived at Constantinople by end of July. The crusade ended in October 1096 when the mob was slaughtered by Turkish troops in Anatolia.

When the People's Crusade approached the Rhineland, in the summer of 1096, a genocidal hysteria took over, resulting in the Rhineland massacres, which some historians call the first holocaust.[20] Crusaders destroyed many of the Jewish communities along the Rhine. Thousands of Jews were massacred, driven to suicide, or forced to convert to Christianity. In Worms, 800 were murdered. In Mainz, 1,100 more were killed. More Jews were slaughtered in Trier, Metz, and Cologne.[21] Jew hatred was so extreme that mobs invaded bishops' castles and palaces where Jews were hiding. Anyone preaching mercy for Jews was considered to have succumbed to Jewish bribery.

The barbarity went beyond the People's Crusade. When the First Crusade, composed not of paupers but of military crusaders, captured Jerusalem in July 1099, they massacred the Muslim and Jewish populations. Crusaders, "sobbing for excess of joy," with their hands still bloody from the massacre, gave thanks to God and then prayed in the Church of the Holy Sepulchre.[22]

17 Runciman, *A History of the Crusades*, 121–33.

18 Slack, *Historical Dictionary of the Crusades*, 228–30.

19 Asbridge, *The First Crusade*, 78–82.

20 Riley-Smith, *The First Crusade and the Idea of Crusading*, 50.

21 Estimates of the number of Jewish men, women, and children murdered or driven to suicide vary, ranging from 2,000 to 12,000. See Mentgen, "Crusades," 151–3.

22 Keen, *The Penguin History of Medieval Europe*, 119.

The intensity of popular support for crusades is shown by the so-called Children's Crusade of 1212. Scholars disagree on facts about the crusade, such as whether adults were part of the movement. Several myths and stories appear to have melded into one account. Traditional accounts tell of a young boy who begins to preach in France or Germany, claiming he was visited by Jesus. Jesus instructs the boy to lead a peaceful crusade of children to convert Muslims to Christianity. Arriving at the Mediterranean Sea, the group expects the waters to part, miraculously, so they can walk to Jerusalem. When the sea fails to part, merchants offer to transport them in boats. Instead, they take children to ports where they are sold into slavery, or the children are killed in shipwrecks. Modern accounts identify two movements of people of all ages in Germany and France. Each group – a group of 7,000 and another of 30,000 – was led by a shepherd boy. Neither group reached the Holy Land. One group reached Italy.[23]

Millennium Enemy Stance

What triggered the genocide of the People's Crusade?

One trigger was the insecure and frustrated position of the lower classes of medieval society as the twelfth century arrived. For decades, Western European poor had endured famine, drought, invading hordes, and the plague. Moreover, feudalism was weakened by increasing urbanization, population, and industrialization. While feudalism did not make peasants wealthy or independent, it did provide a familiar set of roles that reduced anxieties and gave life some order. The changes not only weakened this social structure but created a vast number of uprooted and unemployed journeymen, vagabonds, paupers, and peasants without land. To many of these people, the church, powerful and rich, was an object of suspicion. Moreover, medieval society was never without messianic preachers and wandering prophets typically consisting of lower clergy, petty nobles, monks who had left the monastery, and others. Some would claim to be the equal of the original Apostles and even Christ. People with deep anxieties were susceptible to these preachers

23 On the crusade, see Dickson, *The Children's Crusade*, and Russell, "Children's Crusade."

who used the millennium to explain the people's plight, blame others, and promise a wondrous future. Adding to the tension was the medieval penchant to see devils, spirits, witches, and other threats in nature at every turn.

The image of the enemy among participants of the People's Crusade, and other crusades, was the "peculiarly intense and unremitting hatred which in Christendom had been directed against Jewry above all other 'outgroups'" for centuries. Although the crusades were mounted, officially, against Muslim countries, the enthusiasm was easily canalized against the "wholly fantastic image of the Jew" which gripped the imagination of disorientated masses.[24] Crusade antisemitism was expressed by Godfrey of Bouillon, a Frankish knight and one of the leaders of the First Crusade. Godfrey said he avenged "the blood of the crucified one by shedding Jewish blood … completely eradicating any trace of those bearing the name Jew."[25]

Today, millennialism is reinvented and revised. For example, there has been a revival of rapture theology in North American evangelicalism. In this view, the Second Coming of Jesus will take place in two stages:[26] The first will be a secret rapture – a carrying away of all faithful Christians and the resurrected dead – to heaven. This begins a seven-year period of tribulation, during which the Antichrist will appear. The second phase occurs at the end of tribulation when Jesus will return to Earth in triumph and glory.

Millennialism is psychologically potent for at least two reasons. One, it provides an answer to the yearnings and anxieties of ordinary people. It feeds hope for revenge, stimulated by striking images. These images are easily manipulated by self-proclaimed prophets, since one can read into the narratives almost anything that one wishes to believe. Two, millennialism is potent because its narratives *are* irrational – they describe scenes that go far beyond ordinary reason and experience. These fabulous tales dispense with the need to consult science, factual evidence, or other religious texts. Believers are free to embrace the idea of an apocalyptic millennium in their imaginations. They can be reality averse.

24 Cohen, *The Pursuit of the Millennium*, 77.
25 See Geary, *Readings in Medieval History*.
26 See Johnson, *The Rapture*.

SECTION 2: HERETICAL IRRATIONALITY

Not all irrational intolerance in religion can be blamed on the notions of apocalypse and millennium. In Western Europe, from the late Middle Ages to the counter-Reformation, the church, in league with military and political leaders, committed large-scale acts of irrational intolerance aimed at nonconforming religious groups. Their actions, at times, amounted to genocide. In today's terms, many of the leaders, including popes and nobles, were guilty of crimes against humanity.

The medieval heretic was seen as a mortal threat to the one, true church; a corrupter of the faith; creator of schism in one Christian Europe under pope and emperor. The heretic was dangerous. Inhuman. Often a Jew. Probably a witch. Without doubt, an agent of Satan. Usually, the heretic was defined by religion as holding unorthodox beliefs. But the cause of enmity was not just religious or theological. There were secular causes. Persecuting heretics was about gaining their land, looting their properties, rising up the ranks of persecuting institutions, and protecting the power of kings and popes. The irrational enmity lit bonfires of human sacrifice across Western Europe.

A corrupt medieval church, rather than heal itself, conveniently projected its problems on others, on individuals branded as evil and heretical. In reality, the church was corrupted internally by its clergy. The church was captive to the same worldly urges that had caused Augustine, as an individual, to feed his "carnal habit." In the end, Christian leaders betrayed Christ's message of peace. They apparently saw no contradiction in exterminating entire groups of people in the name of a gentle Christ, celebrating the roasting of human skin at the stake while thousands watched the inhuman acts in city squares. These were not simply acts of faith (autos-da-fe), as the burnings at the stake were called. They were public displays of power, obscene acts of shared cruelty. They were part of a sweeping effort to create an inqui sitional theocracy to reinforce Rome. The object was to maintain control by using police state methods that strike fear into the nonconforming and induce paranoia among of the faithful.[27]

27 On the origin of Europe as a persecuting society and for the idea that the real causes for the persecution were secular, not theological, see Moore's *The War on Heresy* and *The Formation of a Persecuting Society*.

Development of Persecution

Heresy, in a religious sense, is a set of beliefs at variance with central beliefs of a dominant religion which defines what is orthodox.[28] In the sixth century AD, the Justinian Code, part of Roman law, defined the heretic as "everyone who is not devoted to the Catholic Church and to our Orthodox holy Faith."

Prior to the fourth century AD, the Romans persecuted Christians in waves between the Great Fire of Rome in 64 AD, which Nero blamed on the Christians, and Constantine's legalization of Christianity in the Edict of Milan of 313 AD. The converted Constantine would then be confronted by the problem of nonconforming Christian sects. The problem was so intense that he called the first ecumenical council to deal with the Arian heresy – the view that Christ was not an equal member of the trinity. He then enforced Catholic orthodoxy.

The Roman persecution of Christians was grounded in Christianity's monotheism. Christianity was incompatible with the Roman Empire's state religion, which was a form of syncretism, a mixing of many beliefs and gods. Rome did not require devotion to one god, but it did demand that a citizen's first loyalty was to the state. The state religion required, minimally, attendance at festivals of the state religion. But devotion to other gods was something Christians could not do. Also, Christians were open to members of any social class, which did not fit the social caste system of the Roman Empire. As well, Christian converts appeared to renounce their family and country.[29] Since Christians were forced at times to meet in secret, rumors abounded. Talk of Christians eating "the body and blood" of Christ and calling each other "brother" and "sister" suggested that Christians committed wicked crimes such as cannibalism and incest.[30] Pagans saw Christians as disloyal and a threat to state unity. Historian Edward Gibbon wrote, "By embracing the faith of the Gospel … they dissolved the sacred ties of custom and education, violated the religious institutions of their country."[31]

28 Heresy comes from the Greek word for "choice" or "thing chosen." In Christian, Muslim, and Jewish traditions the penalty for heresy has ranged from excommunication to death.

29 See Casson, *Everyday Life in Ancient Rome*, especially chapter 7, "Christ or Caesar."

30 See Fox, *Pagans and Christians*.

31 Gibbon, *The History of the Decline and Fall of the Roman Empire*, 309.

The pagan population worried that bad things would happen if the pagan gods were not properly worshiped. Tertullian complained that the Roman public thought the Christians were to blame for all disasters and would cry out, "Away with the Christians to the lions!"[32] Not all Christians ran from Roman persecution. The earliest Christian martyrs won fame, prompting other Christians to imitation, sometimes demanding governors to execute them. Church officials had to draw a distinction between solicited and forced martyrdom.[33]

When the church became the official religion of the empire in 380 AD, by the Edict of Thessalonica, the church could use state power to combat heresy. The church would change from being the persecuted to being the one who persecutes. It accused heretics of charges similar to the ones that Roman emperors once hurled at early Christians: charges of disloyalty and of being a threat to unity, only now it was the unity of the church that was paramount.

The Christianization of Europe in the early part of the Middle Ages occurred without intense, massive persecutions but it was hardly without clashes and battles. Christian kings such as Charlemagne in France and Olaf I of Norway acted violently toward pagans. Jews and Muslims were harshly persecuted and expelled from regions. The church mounted the Northern Crusades, campaigns from the thirteenth to fifteenth century by Teutonic Knights to covert the pagans in the Baltic Region. Their invasions encountered tough pagan resistance.

The persecution of Christian heretics by Christians resumed in the eleventh century. The level of religious dissent worried the Vatican. New sects were popping up in France, northern Italy, and elsewhere. Persecution began as early as 1022, when fourteen people were burned for heresy in Orleans, France.

Rationalizing Persecution

A medieval system for persecuting heretics needed a legal and philosophical basis. It was provided by Roman tradition, Christian theology, and features of medieval society.

32 Ehrman, *A Brief Introduction to the New Testament*, 36.
33 Bowersock, *Martyrdom and Rome*, 4.

Roman law prohibited non-religious forms of "heresy," such as arson, incest, sorcery, treason, and desertion from the army. For such crimes, the standard legal penalty was death by burning. This law was simply extended to Christians for religious crimes. With the Middle Ages, the revival of Roman law in twelfth-century Western Europe prompted leaders to pass laws legalizing the burning of heretics, e.g., in Lombardi and Sicily, and then across the Holy Roman Empire.

Creating a framework for religious persecution was made possible by the medieval blurring of church and state. Kings could claim to persecute with God's approval since they ruled by divine right, and the pope claimed he was God's representative on earth. In England, Henry VIII proclaimed himself to be both head of state and head of the Church of England. Many principalities were led by bishops or princes close to the church. The pope regularly called on monarchs to organize a holy war against a sect. The church had its own ecclesiastical courts that would hold inquisitions and then hand heretics over to the state for execution.

Apart from law, Christian theologians such as Augustine and Aquinas provided arguments for persecution which would be used by Catholics and then Protestants as the Reformation took fire. Augustine's original position was against persecution and in favour of rational argument to persuade heretics to see the truth. But, worn down by his clashes with nonconforming sects, Augustine advocated fines, imprisonment, banishment, and "moderate" floggings. He opposed the death penalty. In *City of God*, Augustine blames the devil for creating heretics. He writes indignantly about officials who "obstinately refuse" to correct the "pestilent and deadly dogmas" of heretics as if such people can be "retained indiscriminately in the City of God without reproof." Nonetheless, he says, these engagements with the enemies of the faith strengthen Catholicism.[34] Augustine's view that persecution was valid, and the only question was its severity, was accepted for over a millennium in Western Christianity.[35]

In 1270, when Aquinas composed his *Summa Theologica*, he went beyond Augustine and supported putting heretics to death. Aquinas portrays the heretic not as someone who has made a mistake but a

34 Augustine, *City of God*, book XVIII, chapter 51, 833.
35 Coffee, *Persecution and Toleration in Protestant England*, 22–3.

person who willfully, spitefully, refuses to admit the truth. Hence, the person is wicked and a corrupter of the faith.

It is worth quoting a passage at length:

> Wherefore if forgers of money and other evil-doers are forthwith condemned to death by the secular authority, much more reason is there for heretics, as soon as they are convicted of heresy, to be not only excommunicated but even put to death. On the part of the Church, however, there is mercy which looks to the conversion of the wanderer, wherefore she condemns not at once, but "after the first and second admonition," as the Apostle directs: after that, if he is yet stubborn, the Church no longer hoping for his conversion, looks to the salvation of others, by excommunicating him and separating him from the Church, and furthermore delivers him to the secular tribunal to be exterminated thereby from the world by death.[36]

These pre-Reformation arguments presume that there is only one true interpretation of the Bible, determined by the church. Since there is nothing more important than salvation, the heretic is a devil, a threat that should be eliminated. This is the view of society as an authoritarian theocracy. We are a long way from a tolerant society and individual rights of conscience.

Regrettably, the identification of heretics would often be mistaken, the means of elimination hideous, and the charge of heresy relative to country or religion. When the Protestant English burnt Joan of Arc at the stake for heresy, the French Catholic Inquisition declared her a martyr.

SECTION 3: HOLY FRATRICIDE

The Cathars

The church's irrational intolerance is disturbingly evident in its genocide of the Cathars, after a relentless twenty-year crusade, followed by eighty-eight years of inquisition.

36 Aquinas, *Summa Theological*, part II (2nd part), question 11, article 3.

The Cathars were an ascetic Christian sect that thrived in southern France and northern Italy between the twelfth and fourteenth centuries. Already in the eleventh century, Catharism had appeared in the Languedoc region of France. They were called Cathari, meaning those who are perfected or purified. They were also called Albigensians, after the city Albi in southern France where the movement took root.[37] They considered the church the embodiment of evil and sought a simple form of Christian devotion and lifestyle. They were Christian in being devoted to Jesus. But their religious ideas were often closer to other traditions, such as Persian Manicheism, Buddhism, and Gnosticism, the theology of an older Christian sect.

The Cathars should not be romanticized as perfect Christians. No doubt some members were less than perfect. Today, many of us would find some of their beliefs unpalatable. Nonetheless there were "among history's most poignant victims."[38]

In doctrine and practice, they were, for the church, heretical on many points. Like Manicheists, they were dualists: they separated the world into a spiritual realm that was light and good and a material world that was dark and evil. They believed in not one but two gods. There was a good god – the god of the New Testament – who created the spiritual world and a bad god – the god of the Old Testament – identified with Satan, creator of the material world. Humans were angels whose spirits had been trapped in the material world. Like Buddhists, they believed in reincarnation. Humans would endure the cycle of reincarnation until they achieve salvation through direct knowledge of the divine. Like the Gnostics, they held that a special knowledge of God – not the church, not the pope, not faith – would save people.

No priesthood was required. [39]

There were other heretical points of tension: The Cathars rejected the sacraments of the church and replaced them with a sacrament of their own, a ritual called the consolation whereby the person is "perfected" by being immersed in the spirit of God. The ritual served as baptism and then as last rites. The Cathars were devoted

37 It is debatable whether they referred to themselves as Cathars. In Cathar texts, the terms "Good Men," "Good Women," and "Good Christians" are used.

38 Baigent and Leigh, *The Inquisition*, 4.

39 Lambert, *The Cathars*, 21.

to Christ but not to the rest of the trinity, and they denied the incarnation of Christ.[40]

Although the church denounced the doctrines of the Cathars, its militant approach to the peaceful sect was prompted by the practical success of Cathar itinerant preachers, walking the countryside on foot, in gathering converts to their faith. Among the converts were nobles willing to defend them. By the early thirteenth century, it appeared that Catharism would replace Catholicism in southern France.

If the Cathars were popular, the church had only itself to blame. The general population saw the Cathars as honest, gentle, and virtuous, closer to the lifestyle of Christ and early Christians than the ubiquitous clerics of the institutionalized church. Cathar preachers did not bully or extort. They did not traffic in guilt or terrorize through threats of damnation; they demanded no bribes or fees. The church, on the other hand, was unquestionably corrupt. In 1219, Pope Honorius III described his priests as "worse than beasts wallowing in their dung."[41] In southern France there were churches where no mass had been said for thirty years. Priests carried out commercial transactions or maintained large estates. The Archbishop of Narbonne never actually visited the city or his diocese. Parish priests were badly educated. Senior members of the clergy took mistresses, travelled in opulent coaches, had large retinues, and lived like nobility.

"The Stick Will Prevail"

In the early twelfth century, a Spanish cleric called Dominic attempted to "fight zeal with zeal." He created a network of itinerant friars, the Dominicans, who, like the Cathar preachers, wandered the roads looking for converts. They were well-schooled in rhetoric and theology. Shortly after the start of a French crusade against the Cathars, Dominic gave a speech at Prouille, France, where the first Dominican monastery was established. He noted how his attempt to sing "words of sweetness" to the Cathars and the people of southern France had no effect. Hence, "where blessing is to no avail, the stick will prevail." Leaders and armies will gather against the people and cause "many people to die by the

40 See Peters, "The Cathars."

41 Lea, *A History of the Inquisition in the Middle Ages*, vol. I, 53.

sword, will ruin your towers, overthrow and destroy your walls and reduce you to servitude."[42] Dominic would be part of the coming "stick." He would travel with crusading armies and support the burning of heretics. He had blood on his hands.

Dominic's speech was a sign that the church was turning to organized violence after its peaceful attempts at reconverting the Cathars failed, and the efforts of successive popes to prompt local clergy and authorities to take stronger action fell on deaf ears. When Pope Innocent III (1160–1216) took up the papacy in 1198, he was determined to deal with the Cathars once and for all. The Dominicans would be the order to which he would turn.

Innocent III became pope at the height of the papacy's power. Innocent III was one of the most powerful men in Europe, and he would create new crusades. He had a dark Augustinian view of the misery of sinful humanity. As a cardinal, he wrote *On the Misery of the Human Condition*,[43] which listed dozens of kinds of wicked people, including heretics. He wrote that one can barely find a person who "does not return to his own vomit and rot in his own dung." Man is "born to punishment" and he becomes "fuel for the eternal fires, food for worms, a mass of rottenness." One must ask to what extent this view of human life affected Innocent's decision to launch genocide without an apparent twinge of conscience. Was it because a Cathar was just another depraved and disobedient wretch deserving punishment?

The trigger for a sacred war occurred in 1208. Innocent's papal legate Pierre de Castelnau was murdered while returning to Rome after excommunicating Count Raymond VI of Toulouse, who, in the legate's view, was too lenient with the Cathars. Pope Innocent III declared Pierre de Castelnau a martyr. He wrote the king of France, Philip II (or Philip Augustus), demanding a crusade to eliminate the Cathars. As reward, participants would get the same spiritual rewards as crusaders to the Holy Land, such as remission of sins, but more: they could keep confiscated land, no longer pay interest on debts, and if they committed any crimes, they would come under the protection of the papacy. The pope was offering "an implicit license to loot, pillage, plunder and

42 Cited in Baigent and Leigh, *The Inquisition*, 17. Also, Le Roy Ladurie, *Montaillou*, 78.

43 Innocent III, *On the Misery of the Human Condition.*

expropriate property."[44] Philip II declined to mount a crusade, but he allowed some of his blood-thirsty nobles to travel south. Thus began the Albigensian Crusade which repressed Catharism, killing thousands of men, women, and children.

In late June of 1209, an army of about 20,000 northern nobles, knights, soldiers, and adventurers had gathered on the Rhone. The crusade's spiritual leader was papal legate Arnauld Amaury, the abbot of Citeaux, a true religious fanatic with a love of murdering heretics. A French baron, Simon de Montfort, emerged as the military commander, a man of unstinting religious orthodoxy, having already fought in the Fourth Crusade (1202–04). He became feared for his ruthlessness.[45] For instance, in 1210 he burned 120 Cathars in the village of Minerve, who refused to recant. Prior to the sack of the village of Lastours, he brought prisoners from the nearby village of Bram and had their eyes gouged out and their ears, noses, and lips cut off. One prisoner, left with one eye, led the crusaders and the mutilated citizens into Lastours as a warning to the villagers.

Such was the leadership of this sadistic, marauding gang of murderers, bent on land, titles, and plunder. Their irrationality was on display on 22 July 1209, when they sacked the Cathar friendly city of Beziers, the first major military action of the Albigensian Crusade. When asked how the soldiers should distinguish between the Cathars and devout Catholics, Armaud is reported to have replied, "Kill them all. God will recognize his own."[46]

The Bishop of Beziers Renaud de Montpeyroux tried to avert bloodshed and negotiate with the army. He came back to Beziers with the message that the city would be spared if it handed over its heretics. The option was rejected. In the subsequent massacre, men, women and children perished. The doors of the church of St Mary Magdalene were broken down and the occupants slaughtered. In other parts of the city, thousands more were mutilated and killed. People taken as prisoners were blinded, dragged behind horses, and used for target practice.[47] Arnaud's written report to the pope was triumphant, gleeful.

44 Baigent and Leigh, *The Inquisition*, 11.

45 He was Lord of Montfort-l'Amaury in France and the fifth Earl of Leicester in England.

46 Moore, *Pope Innocent III*, 180.

47 Johnson, *A History of Christianity*, 252.

"Our men spared no one, irrespective of rank, sex or age, and put to the sword almost 20,000 people. After this great slaughter the whole city was despoiled and burnt, as divine vengeance miraculously raged against it."[48]

The massacre terrified the whole of southern France but the crusaders wanted extermination and plunder. So, the crusade carried on. On 15 August 1209, Carcassonne surrendered. Throughout the south, alleged heretics were burned, and anyone who opposed the burnings was hanged. Cathars, with support from some nobles, fought back and the control of towns changed hands. Simon de Montfort was killed in 1218 during the nine-month siege of Toulouse. The war continued. The crusade officially ended with the Treaty of Paris in 1229. The king of France took control over large tracts of land in southern France. Yet additional Cathar revolts erupted. On 16 March 1244, Montsegut, the most important remaining Cathar stronghold, fell and more than 200 Cathars were immolated on a pyre at the foot of the mountain on which the castle stood.[49] The last Cathar fortress, Queribus, fell in 1255. By that time, many heretics had fled to Catalonia and Lombardy.

Yet the Cathars remained active in the region, often melding into the general population. The church, not satisfied with military repression, organized an inquisition in 1233 to hunt down the remaining Cathars. Cathars who refused to recant were hanged or burnt at the stake. By the fourteenth century, pursued by an inquisition and abandoned by local nobles, the Cathar movement was exhausted. After 1330, the records of the Inquisition contain very few proceedings against Cathars. The last known Cathar leader in the Languedoc region, Guillaume Belibaste, was executed in the autumn of 1321. In 2016, the Roman Catholic Church formally apologized for the repression of the Cathars.

Raphael Lemkin, who in the twentieth century coined the word "genocide," referred to the Albigensian Crusade as "one of the most conclusive cases of genocide in religious history."[50] Mark Gregory Pegg said, "The Albigensian Crusade ushered genocide into the West by

48 Jacoby, *Bloodlust*, 29f. Also see Sibly and Sibly, *The Chronicle of William of Puylaurens*, 128.

49 Baigent and Leigh, *The Inquisition*, 13.

50 Lemkin, *Lemkin on Genocide*, 71.

linking divine salvation to mass murder, by making slaughter as loving an act as His sacrifice on the cross."[51] Strayer argued that the Albigensian Crusade increased the power of the French monarchy and made the papacy more dependent on it. This would lead to the Avignon Papacy.[52]

The madness of the heresy persecution of Christians spread across Europe for centuries, adopted by Catholics and then Protestants, by kings and queens. Why mad? Consider the favourite method for, as Aquinas termed it, "eliminating" a heretic from this world: death by burning. It could be burning at the stake, where you prayed to die by carbon monoxide before the flames reached you or you begged the public executioner to strangle you before he lit the fire. The executioner might also pour molten liquid down your mouth or ears, place you in boiling water, or put you inside a metal container that was then roasted on a fire.

Theocratic Tyranny

Across the twelfth century, heretical sects in Europe continued to emerge. The church was ready for serious inquisition beyond southern France. Inquisition would become a centralized and formalized church activity.[53]

In the beginning, "inquisition" referred to any legal investigation under Roman law, using a prosecutorial model whereby a judge or bishop conducts the inquiry.[54] Prior to the twelfth century, the church

51 Pegg, *A Most Holy War*, 195. Robert E. Lerner, in a review, argues that Pegg's classification of the Albigensian Crusade as a genocide is incorrect because it "was proclaimed against unbelievers … not against a 'genus' or people." The Cathars, however, were both unbelievers and a people. Lerner, "A Most Holy War."

52 Strayer, *The Albigensian Crusades*, 174. During the Avignon Papacy, from 1309 to 1376, seven successive popes resided in Avignon, rather than in Rome. Avignon was then a part of the Holy Roman Empire. The popes were under the influence of the French Crown.

53 The legal basis for the Inquisition was provided in Innocent III's papal bull of 1252 which authorized torture and under what conditions it should be used. By 1256, inquisitors were given absolution if they were overzealous in their use of the instruments of torture.

54 I use "Inquisition" to refer to the entire effort by the church in different countries. For specific inquisitions in countries, I use the lower-case, such as the "Spanish inquisition."

had long dealt with investigations into heresies. But inquisitions were ad hoc, locally directed (and therefore variable in process), and aimed at individuals or small sects. Torture was not used and execution was rare. Things changed dramatically in 1229 when Pope Gregory IX established the Inquisition of the Roman Catholic Church, based in Rome. In 1233, his papal bull gave the Dominicans the task of hunting down heresy. The first papal inquisition started in Toulouse in 1234. The pope established these papal inquisitions due to the failure of more informal and local methods of dealing with the Cathars, Waldensians, and other sects.[55]

Pope Gregory IX could not have imagined what he had started. The Inquisition would last eight centuries (up to the mid-nineteenth century in Italy) directed by about eighty popes. Its tyranny would spread around the world. It continues to live on in Rome as the "Congregation for the Doctrine of the Faith," which oversees the spread of Catholic doctrine.

The Inquisition would become the machinery for mass extermination. In the name of combatting heresy, thousands upon thousands of people would be killed, mangled, hanged, burned at the stake, tortured, bankrupted and socially ostracized, or sentenced to so-called lenient penalties. The bodies of deceased heretics would be exhumed and burnt. Languishing for years in prison on mere suspicion or dubious charges, accused by unknown informants, many alleged heretics would go mad, commit suicide, or die from abuse. The church banned book after book and often burned them. Painters created images that showed the Holy Ghost lighting the fires that burned the books. The prosecutors of the Inquisition were too often sadistic and corrupt inquisitors too little constrained by law. They oversaw a reign of terror and the construction of a theocratic police state within countries, turning

55 Scholars divide the Inquisition into the (a) medieval inquisition and (b) later inquisitions from the fifteenth century onward. The medieval inquisition dealt with isolated sects. The later inquisitions were reactions to the Reformation and the Catholic Counter-Reformation. The medieval inquisitions are also divided in two: episcopal inquisitions by bishops at a local level (1184–1230s) and the papal inquisitions under Pope Gregory IX's direction in the 1230s. The Spanish inquisition began in 1478, the Portugal inquisition in 1536, and an inquisition in Italy began in 1542. The Spanish inquisition was different in being run by the Spanish Crown. Sub-inquisitions were set up in European colonies such as Mexico and Goa in India.

neighbour against neighbour. In time, there would be inquisitions in almost every Europe country except England and Castile.[56]

Under Pope Gregory IX, the Inquisition became a permanent structure within the government of the church. It was centralized under the pope. The Dominicans, fanatical in zeal and totalitarian in spirit, ran the inquisitions, travelling to countries to act as inquisitors supported by local officials. They would be joined by the Franciscan Order. After 1200, a grand inquisitor – a Dominican or Franciscan friar who taught theology or law in a university – led each inquisition. The Dominicans and Franciscans turned out to be ruthless, often pathological, in their desire to kill for Christ. In 1234, the Dominicans of Toulouse planned a celebratory mass for their canonized founder, who died in 1221. Before the meal, while the clergy were washing, word came of a woman nearby dying of fever. She had received the consolation of the Cathars. Abandoning meal preparations, the Dominicans, along with the Bishop of Toulouse, rushed to the woman's house and burst into her room. After a conversation with the woman, the bishop declared her a heretic and demanded that she recant. She would not. "Forthwith … the vicar had her carried on the bed in which she lay to the count's meadow and burned at once."[57]

By 1235, public hostility to the Dominicans in Toulouse was so intense that a council expelled them from the city. The pope demanded their return. When they returned, in a vengeful spirit, they started an orgy of violence. The bodies of deceased people thought to be heretics were exhumed and cast out of their cemeteries, in front of the populace. As they dragged the stinking bodies through town, they cried out, "Who behaves thus shall perish thus." Then they burned the bodies "to the honour of God and the Blessed Virgin, His mother and the Blessed Dominic … (who) most happily brought about this work of the Lord."[58] The pagan ritual of human sacrifice was re-purposed as a joyous act of Christian piety.

56 Inquisitions were not successfully established in these countries because they had their own, non-Roman legal structure which did not allow torture.

57 Wakefield, *Heresy, Crusade and Inquisition in Southern France 1100–1250*, 216.

58 Ibid., 224.

The Inquisitor Cometh

Imagine how a grand inquisitor did his work. He descended like a deity onto a town, university, or abbot, often without warning. He entered the city gates in a solemn procession with secretaries, advisers, assistants, and armed escort. He would call people to a public place and preach a sermon on his mission. Then, as if it was a kind gesture, the inquisitor asked individuals to step forward to denounce themselves as heretics. Suspected heretics were given a "time of grace," usually fifteen to thirty days, to denounce themselves. If they did, they usually were accepted back into church with a penance to do. But they also had to furnish details on all known heretics.

The chance to denounce oneself was supposed to lead to lenient penalties. What was considered lenient? One penalty required the person to appear naked at Sunday masses and to be whipped by the priest before the congregation. Also, on the first Sunday of every month, he would be obliged to go to all the houses where he had met with other heretics and there be whipped again. More whippings were applied on religious feast days. These ordeals could last for the rest of his life until the inquisitor, who long ago had departed, remembered him and released him from his sentence.

Another penance deemed lenient was to go on a long pilgrimage or to spend between two and eight years fighting in a crusade. Also, a confessor might have to wear for the rest of their life a large saffron cross sewn into the breast and back of all garments, thereby exposing him or her to further ridicule. Another penalty was a fine, which could find its way into the pocket of the grand inquisitor. If an alleged heretic died before completing his penance, this was taken as a sign that God did not approve of the man's approach to his penance. His body was exhumed and burned. People accused of heresy had their property immediately confiscated. While in prison, the accused had to sell what he owned to pay for his stay in prison.

Upon arriving, the grand inquisitor set up headquarters and started hearing accusations and denunciations. It was a good opportunity for people to settle scores through false accusations. The inquisitor encouraged wives to denounce their husbands, children to denounce parents. If people named someone as a heretic, the accused would never know their names. An immense database was established on people, including previous criminal offences, and filed for future reference.

A suspected heretic could be confronted with a small crime he had committed thirty years before. As the authors of a book on the Inquisition stated, "Here was a blueprint for the kind of procedures whereby the modern state monitors its citizens."[59]

The opportunity for corruption by grand inquisitors was clear. In the province of Venice, the Franciscans became so corrupt enriching themselves with the property of alleged heretics that the pope stopped their activities in 1302. For inquisitors, forcing false confessions was better than admitting a person had been erroneously arrested. In Castile during the 1480s, up to 1,500 victims are said to have been burned at the stake as a result of false testimony. Keeping people in prison for long periods of time, without visitor's rights, often chained to a wall, was one way to get the required voluntary confession. What were some of the means of torture? There was water torture (forcing water down a person's throat). There was the rack, where chords wrapped around the prisoner's body (legs, arms, chest) could be tightened progressively to cause increasing pain. There was also the pulley. The victim's wrists were tied behind his back. The man was hung by his wrists, with weights on his feet. He would be raised slowly to maximize pain, and then dropped several feet abruptly, dislocating limbs. Ultimately, torture included anything that the sick imaginations of inquisitors could dream up. Inquisitors worked around a papal rule that a person be tortured only once by calling the end of a session a suspension of the session, allowing the inquisitor to renew the same session later.

The Inquisition's use of fear and revenge induced mass hysteria. The public was kept in a state of panic and dread, and everyone became a possible accuser or spy. In this climate, people were more easily manipulated and controlled. Not infrequently, whole sections of a community would confess en masse, full of paranoia and falling under the Inquisition's total control. In Toledo, in 1486, 2,400 people stepped forward en masse to denounce themselves. The Inquisition derived its energy from the "very populace it persecuted. Its power stemmed from a blatant exploitation of the weakest and most venal aspects of human nature."[60]

59 Baigent and Leigh, *The Inquisition*, 33.
60 Ibid., 69.

To ensure the maximum number of spectators, executions were performed on public holidays. Non-attendance made you a suspect. When the burning was over, there followed the "revolting process requisite to utterly destroy the half-burned body – separating it into pieces, breaking up the bones and throwing the fragments and viscera on a fresh fire of logs."[61] One reason for the extra effort was to ensure that no relic of the heretic was left behind. What was the aim of this staged drama? The 1578 edition of the *Directorium Inquisitorum*, an inquisitorial manual, stated that "punishment does not take place primarily and per se for the correction and good of the person punished, but for the public good in order that others may become terrified and weaned away from the evils they would commit."[62]

Women and Witches

When the Inquisition started to run out of heresies to prosecute, the inquisitors turned their attention to witches, stirring up public panic especially in difficult times such as during the plague or a devastating war. Scapegoats were found. Who was a more vulnerable target than a woman accused of being a witch?

The very idea of a church witch hunt was irrational. For centuries, the church had made belief in the reality of witchcraft a heresy. Then, a papal bull in 1484 recognized it as a reality. Suddenly, it became a matter of heresy if one did *not* believe in witchcraft. Once again, a conspiracy theory was invoked to produce the scapegoat. Magicians and female witches were the enemy, causing almost every sort of evil in the world, in a demonic pact with Satan.

Equally crazy – and I use the term literally – was the main instructional manual that inquisitors used to conduct witch hunts. It was a misogynist, obscene, and paranoid book called *Malleus Maleficarum* (*Hammer of Witches*).[63] Now the standard medieval text on witchcraft, it was written in 1486 by two Dominican academics and inquisitors, Heinrich Kramer, who once bragged he had condemned 200 female witches, and Jacob Sprenger, otherwise known for making popular the reciting of the rosary. The title of the book has a dubious history. There was an ancient

61 Lea, *A History of the Inquisition in the Middle Ages*, 552.
62 *Directorium Inquisitorum*, edition of 1578, book 3, 137, column 1.
63 I use the translation by Christopher MacKay, *The Hammer of Witches*.

book, the *Hammer of Heretics*, on how orthodox Christians smashed heretics of Christian doctrine. In 1420, inquisitor John of Frankfurt published *Hammer of the Jews*. *Malleus Maleficarum* was written to counter witchcraft sceptics. It would smash the conspiracy of female sorcerers threatening Christendom which is part of Satan's final assault on God during the "end times."[64] So popular was the book that thirty-four years after it was published, it had gone through thirteen editions.

Mackay's translation of the book has become standard. He provides a calm, scholarly introduction to the book, reviewing issues of authorship, the historical context, the influence of Satanism and apocalyptic thinking, and other issues. This helpful introduction cannot hide the fact that this book is a catalogue of violent, pathological fantasy without control. The authors engross themselves in descriptions of diabolic copulation, of intercourse with incubi, of sexual activities attributed to demonic forces. The book made official the mad myth of witches having magical powers enabling them to kill a man with their evil eye, to create hailstorms that ruin crops, cause lightening to strike people, and to cause impotence in men. Witches, who could fly through the air, liked to kill, boil ,and eat children. They even collected men's sexual organs.[65] The authors dilate on how witches sacrifice children.[66]

Here is where the scapegoat comes in. The book states that the devil cannot act alone but needs a human helper. Who were the helpers? Women. The authors were clearly terrified of women. They describe women as inherently weak, quick to falter in faith, and liars by nature. A woman is beautiful to view, but she is "contaminating" to the touch and "deadly to keep." All witchcraft comes from "carnal lust" which in women is "insatiable."

The Inquisition, whether dealing with heretics or witches, excelled in public propaganda. It used rhetoric to hide the true nature of some questionable practices. For example, inquisitors invented strange justifications for burning people at the stake, until it seemed like an act of kindness. Burning and torture was a swift route to salvation; when people are in agony from the flames, they will finally repent and then

64 MacKay, *Hammer of Witches*, 7.

65 For examples of such passages, see the book's part II, which describes the practices of sorcery.

66 MacKay, *Hammer of Witches*, 372–3.

be saved, reaching heaven. Wonderful. On this view, the inquisitor should be thanked. This is a terrible fake rationality.

Another inquisitional manual, from 1561, stipulated that torture be applied in accord with "the conscience and will of the appointed judges, following law, reason, and good conscience. Inquisitors should take great care that the sentence of torture is justified and follows precedent."[67] The brutal fact is that, in many cases, there was no rule of law and even less a concern for fundamental justice. To talk of reason in such circumstances is a mockery.

The Spanish inquisition was adept at using propaganda to stir up public outrage against Jews and Muslims. So much so that some of their antisemitic techniques were adopted by the Nazi minister of propaganda, Joseph Goebbels. For example, there is the infamous case of the Holy Child of La Guardia. On 14 November 1491, five Jews and six conversos (Jews who had converted to Christianity) were burned at the stake in Ávila, convicted of desecrating the host. They allegedly crucified a child and ripped out its heart. The purpose of their ritual was to neutralize the power of the Inquisition and send all Christians "raving mad to their deaths."[68] The Spanish inquisition published this trumped-up case in every city of Castile and Aragon, whipping up antisemitism to a peak of fury and fear. Three months later, in 1492, a royal edict ordered all Jews to convert or to leave Spain.

Unreasonable fears of heretics and witches spread across populations, "the psychological equivalent of the plague."[69] A few statistics indicate the extent of the carnage against heretics and witches. About 7,000 heretics were burned at the stake by the Inquisition as a whole.[70] In England, Henry VII executed many Catholics, including sixty heretics by burning. The Catholic queen, "Bloody" Mary I, burned at the stake 290 people between 1555 and 1558. Today, there are estimates that as many as 50,000 people were executed for witchcraft in Europe in this era.[71] The list of notables burned at the stake includes Jan Hus (1415), Joan of Arc (1431), John Frith (1533), William Tyndale (1536),

67 Karmen, *The Spanish Inquisition*, 188.

68 Baigent and Leigh, *The Inquisition*, 79.

69 Ibid., 119.

70 Caroll, *Constantine's Sword*, 357.

71 The peak period for European witch hunts was the century 1550–1650. The hunts ended in the first half of the eighteenth century.

Michael Servetus (1553), Giordano Bruno (1600), and Urbain Grandier (1634). The Anglican martyrs John Rogers, Hugh Latimer, and Nicholas Ridley were burned at the stake in 1555. Thomas Cranmer followed the next year.

The last execution of the Inquisition was in Valencia, Spain, in 1826. This was execution, by garroting, of a school teacher and former soldier Cayetano Ripoll, forty-eight, after being imprisoned for two years, for allegedly teaching Deism in his school.[72] Clergymen of the Spanish inquisition demanded Ripoll be burned at the stake for his religious offenses. However, the civil authority chose to hang him. Church authorities, upset that Ripoll had not been burned at the stake, placed his body into a barrel, painted flames on the barrel and burned the barrel, throwing the ashes into a river.[73]

If this not be madness, what is?

The Legacy: War and Demonic Rationality

After the burnings of heretics and witches, the Inquisition would evolve. The Reformation would take the internal Christian conflict to a new and higher level. When Martin Luther wrote his Ninety-Five Theses in 1517, Catholicism reacted the same way as it had to the heresies of the Middle Ages. The pope decreed in 1520 that Martin Luther was a heretic and excommunicated him. But things were different. The Reformation represented a massive revolt against the church that had political backing, especially in Germany. For the church, burning a few Christian heretics would not solve *this* problem. When it became clear that the Reformation could not be repressed by inquisition and excommunication, the fight became a battle between nations through wars of religion containing many massacres. One need only recall that the Thirty Year's War (1618–48), a ruinous war that involved many European nations, resulted in eight million fatalities from war, famine, plague, and out-of-control mercenary armies. It stands as one of the most destructive conflicts in history. In the previous century, the wars of religion in France killed three million people.

72 Law, *Humanism*, 23. Deists believe a supreme being created the world, but the creator does not intervene in the world.

73 See Schaff, *History of the Christian Church*, 552.

Meanwhile, massacres in the name of religion were common. The St Bartholomew's Day Massacre in Paris in 1572 prompted five days of killing, during which Catholics massacred Calvinist men, women, and children and looted their houses. Then it spread to other communities. About 2,000 Huguenots were killed in Paris and perhaps as many as 10,000 killed in all. King Charles IX announced that he had ordered the massacre to prevent a Calvinist coup. He proclaimed a day of jubilee to celebrate the killings.

The Reformation and its aftermath changed the target of heresy persecution. From the seventeenth century onward, the church came to define heresy in terms of intellectual activity. Earlier, faith was set against the irrational as demonic: that which was out of control, orgiastic, and frenzied. What lacked order. Witchcraft was feared because it was irrational and hard to control. With the Renaissance, Reformation, and then the Enlightenment, the demonic for the church was independent thinking by Renaissance sceptics such as Michel de Montague, Cartesian rationalists, and Enlightenment *philosophes* who used learning to question the church.

CONCLUSION: DOSTOEVSKY'S GRAND INQUISITOR

In chapter 2, I briefly mentioned Plato's authoritarian political philosophy in his final days. His view was not far from the attitude of the grand inquisitor in Fyodor Dostoevsky's parable, "The Grand Inquisitor." The same attitude existed among apocalyptic religious groups, among the persecutors of heretics, and in the theories of Joseph de Maistre.

To see the parallel, recall that Dostoevsky paints a portrait of the grand inquisitor of Seville, who arrests and interrogates Christ when he suddenly reappears on earth. His portrait is probably based on Tomas de Torquemada, the symbol of the Spanish inquisition at its most terrifying. Appointed in 1482, Torquemada would, until his death in 1498, have a power that almost equalled that of King Ferdinand and Queen Isabella. To impress, he travelled with fifty mounted guards and 250 armed men.

Dostoevsky uses the parable to dig deep into the philosophical issues surrounding a theocratic state staffed by grand inquisitors. Dostoevsky rightly makes the main theme our conflicting views about human nature. The grand inquisitor argues, to a silent Christ, that the latter's spiritual teachings demand too much of people. Christ teaches that people must seek to rise above their material desires and act according to a free conscience, making judgments on good and evil. People do not want this freedom and prefer to hand it off to authoritarian leaders.

The grand inquisitor says humans *enjoy* a life of obedience.

Given this conservative view of human nature, the actions of persecutors are not irrational or arbitrary. They are required. Dostoevsky's grand inquisitor requires us to come to terms with our view of human nature. For, if the grand inquisitor is right, then liberals, freedom-lovers, democrats, and many others need to change their philosophies.

7

Fascist Mind

Life unworthy of life.

Nazi slogan

Socialism is not Arcadian and peaceful. We do not believe in the sacredness of human life.

Benito Mussolini[1]

IN THE EARLY TWENTIETH CENTURY, fascism arose frightful and almost unsuspected, like a biblical monster from the depths of the sea.

New leaders and parties on both the left and right, with Benito Mussolini in Italy, Adolf Hitler in Germany, and Stalin in Russia, mobilized mass movements in the deepening chaos after the First World War. In Spain and Portugal, old-time dictatorship returned with Francisco Franco and Antonio de Oliveira Salazar. The term authoritarianism did not seem adequate to capture the new far-right. New terms were invented. They were called fascists and totalitarians.

It is wise not to get entangled in the academic quarrels over the definition of fascism, totalitarianism, and authoritarianism. We should not expect a crisp definition of political terms that garners full consensus. The political world is too complex and messy to reduce to water-proof categories. What we can do is identify features shared by clear examples.

In this chapter, I describe the fascist mind and provide examples such as the German *volk* ideologists of the nineteenth century and the genocidal Nazi doctors of the Second World War.

1 Ludwig, *Talks with Mussolini*, 151.

SECTION 1: RECOGNIZING THE FASCIST MIND

Fascio: Solidarity and Militancy

The term "fascism" is of Italian origin.[2] It refers to the authority and unity of the state or a militant group. It stems from *fascio*, literally a bundle. The word refers back to the Latin *fasces*, an axe encased in a bundle of rods carried before magistrates in Roman public processions to signify the unity and power of the state. Italian revolutionaries used *fascio* in the late 1800s to refer to the solidarity of militants. Peasants who rebelled against their landlords in Sicily in 1893–94 called themselves the *Fasci Siciliani.* The term was appropriated first by the left and then by the right. If mention of the left seems odd, remember that both Mussolini and Hitler used the left-wing term *socialism.* The first form of fascism was a trade union movement called syndicalism, with support from left-wing fascist intellectuals.[3] Towards the end of the First World War, left-wing nationalists, joined by Mussolini, worked to bring Italy into the war on the side of the Allies. They called themselves the Fascist Revolutionary League for Intervention Action. As the war ended, Mussolini used the term *fascism* to describe the mood of a small group of nationalist soldiers and pro-war syndicalists that saw Mussolini as their leader.[4]

With Mussolini, fascism moved to the right.

Fascism has an official birth date. It was born in Milan on Sunday, 23 March 1919 when war veterans, syndicalists, futurists,[5] and others gathered in a room overlooking the Piazza San Sepolcro to "declare

2 On the history of the term, see Gleason, *Totalitarianism*, 14–16.

3 Syndicalism was a radical part of the labour movement in Europe, most active in the early twentieth century. Syndicalists envisioned a post-capitalist state run by syndicates or trade unions of common people. See Gregor, *Phoenix: Fascism in Our Time*, 191.

4 Mussolini began as a member of the revolutionary wing of the Italian Socialist Party. In 1912, he was made editor of the party's newspaper, *Avanti.* Mussolini was thrown out of the party in 1914 by its pacifist wing for his continuing advocacy that Italy should enter the war.

5 Futurism, as mentioned earlier, advocated modernism, action, and political violence as necessary, while denouncing liberalism and parliamentary politics. See Hewitt, *Fascist Modernism*, 153.

war on socialism … because it has opposed nationalism." Mussolini called the movement Fasci di Combattimento or "fraternities of combat."[6] Some thirteen years later, Mussolini, now dictator, co-authored an essay, "The Doctrine of Fascism," with Giovanni Gentile, philosopher of fascism. It was published in the *Italian Encyclopedia* in 1932. In this entry, Mussolini writes that "this is the century of authority, a century tending to the Right, a Fascist century. If the 19th century was the century of the individual (liberalism implies individualism) we are free to believe that this is the 'collective' century, and therefore the century of the State."[7]

At about the same time, anti-fascist Italian journalist and liberal politician Giovanni Amendola (1882–1926) introduced the term *totalitario,* which became "totalitarianism" in English, in a 1923 article for his *El Mondo* newspaper. The term was used negatively, to complain that Italian fascists, like Mussolini, wanted something new: a state that wields total political power. Amendola died from an attack by bat-wielding fascist thugs while at an Italian spa in Montecatini. In contrast, Gentile approved of the term *totalitario* which he used to refer to the new fascist state and meant the "total representation of the nation and total guidance of national goals."[8] Mussolini, who also liked the term, said totalitarianism makes everything political: "Everything within the state, nothing outside the state, nothing against the state."[9]

Fascism is a kind of totalitarianism, and totalitarianism is a kind of authoritarianism, the oldest and broadest of right-wing political concepts. An authoritarian state is a state in which a single entity, e.g., an individual dictator, junta, or oligarchy of elites, monopolize political power. Historically, these authoritarian regimes have not tried to change the world radically, often seeing themselves as a defender of tradition or the status quo. Authoritarian leaders typically do not feel it necessary to become populist and excite the masses. The authoritarian state is concerned with holding power within a small group and as long as that

6 Paxton, *The Anatomy of Fascism,* 5.

7 Mussolini, *The Doctrine of Fascism,* 3.

8 Payne, *Fascism: Comparison and Definition,* 73.

9 Conquest, *The Great Terror: A Reassessment,* 249.

power is not threatened, the state may give society a degree of liberty.[10] For example, Francisco Franco, dictator of Spain from 1939 to 1975, is sometimes inaccurately considered a fascist. To be sure, he was ruthless. Franco secured power by killing 200,000 people between 1939 and 1945. Franco did make the fascist Falange the only party. But by the mid-1940s, Franco's Spain was more traditional and Catholic than fascist. Franco secured social control through the authority of the church, big landowners, and the army. In Portugal, dictator António de Oliveira Salazar ruled from 1932 to 1968. He directed an authoritarian government, the Estado Novo. He preferred a quiet, obedient public and a limited state. In 1934, he repressed a fascist movement, National Syndicalism, because he considered fascism a "cult of force" exalting the superiority of the state in social life.

In the twentieth century, totalitarian leaders led authoritarian states. They were *not* satisfied with political control of society. Totalitarian leaders wanted total control over most aspects of life: political, economic, educational, artistic, and religious. They wanted control over mass communications. The state is supreme. It prohibits other parties, restricts individual criticism and opposition to the state, and tends to rub out the distinction between public and private life. It recognizes no limits to its authority, and it uses terror, mass condemnation, and secret police to maintain order. Hitler and Mussolini on the right and Stalin and other Communist dictators on the left in the Soviet Union led totalitarian states.

We arrive at fascism, as a far-right, totalitarian ultra-nationalism. Fascism wants to be an extreme populism that galvanizes the masses to create a new and superior nation. Fascism is distinct in its totalizing, emotional irrationalism, its capacity to use myths, hatred, and propaganda to resurrect a nation.

Fascism as a political movement will always be associated with Benito Mussolini and Adolf Hitler. However, the mindset which motivates fascists was not created in the twentieth century. Fascist minds contain ideas and attitudes that rumble back through the corridors of history. The prosecuting Dominican friars in medieval times had a fascist, religious mindset.

10 Cinpoes, *Nationalism and Identity in Romania*, 70.

Five Properties of the Fascist Mind

The fascist mind has five main properties.[11]

The Mirage of the Great Nation: Fascism yearns to be part of a transcendent political mission, to create a great nation. It is an intense devotion to one's nation. Achieving national greatness overrides other goals and justifies almost any means. Fascism is fanatical.

Redemption from the Present: Fascism turns frustration with modernity into hatred, aggression, and revenge against the enemies of the pure volk and other scapegoats. The message of fascists to the German nation was you are a superior race. You have been great. You are not great now because of evil, impure, and conspiring others. *But you will be great, again.* Join us.

Fascist political redemption resembles religious redemption by the millennium. The yearning for a Christian millennium is replaced by a yearning for a thousand-year Reich. The devotion of the faithful to the church and the pope is replaced by a devotion to nation and führer.

Absolute Duty to Supreme Authority: The fascist mind wants, and needs, obedience and absolute duty. Complete loyalty to nation defines the true fascist patriot. The nation must be led by a militaristic, authoritarian government and a supreme leader. Collectivism rules, not individualism. The individual's petty desires and liberties weaken the nation. The lives of citizens acquire meaning through devotion to a fascist state. Obedience, sameness, and intolerance trumps criticism, plurality, and tolerance. To achieve great ends, leaders may go outside the restraints of law and ethics. Following the gentle virtues of Christ's Sermon on the Mount is replaced by following the hard, warrior philosophy of a great leader.

Extreme, Mass Populism: The fascist mind revels in populist adoration of the great, romantic leader. Rallies, rituals, and images excite the masses. Fascists go outside the law and democratic processes to seek "the acclamation of the street." Fascism learned how to channel the passions of people so they gave up on free institutions for "national unity, purity, and force."[12]

11 For a definition of fascism, see Paxton, *The Anatomy of Fascism*, 218.

12 Paxton, *The Anatomy of Fascism*, 216.

Passion over Reason, Action over Thought, Will over Restraint, Aesthetics over Ethics: What is real is the triumph of the will and action. There is beauty in the will and in violence when deployed to hasten the birth of the great society. Fascism is an anti-intellectual, romantic, dark irrationalism.

SECTION 2: VOLK IRRATIONALISM

At least a century of cultural and political developments prepared Germany and other countries for the fascists. In Germany and Austria, a reactionary conservatism that rejected modernity would become an antisemitic fascism.

The Volk

In Germany, the road to power for Hitler and National Socialism was prepared by the volk movement in the nineteenth century. Cultural despair stimulated the creation of a volkish philosophy that permeated German education and institutions. In the hands of Hitler, this cultural movement became a base of support. Volk irrationalism became fascist irrationalism.

It is difficult to capture the spiritual aura around the term "volk" in nineteenth-century Germany or to convey how it gave Germans a stabilizing sense of identity in a rapidly changing Europe. The term "Reich" had a similar aura. The volk were not just citizens who happen to live in a state, i.e., a populace. There were indigenous Germans who shared a culture rooted in the land. Volk philosophy relied on the myth that there was a homogeneous, pure Germanic race going back to a golden age in medieval times. Volk members claimed to be the true Germans.

Rootedness was stressed by the first philosopher of the volk, Herder.[13] Contrary to Herder's intention, a lack of roots in a particular landscape would be used to deny volk status to Jews, the Roma, and other minorities who did not reside in one place. Another criterion was the vexed concept of blood lines. There was no precise test for race or blood lines. There was no scientific test for being a member of the volk. But that did not matter. People *wanted* to believe in a pure volk. In practice,

13 Herder, however, was not a proto-Nazi. He was a pluralist who recognized the volk of many nations. He opposed German nationalism's "savage spirit of conquest." Herder, *Letters for the Advancement of Humanity*, 377.

people used parochial and subjective criteria. Members of the volk were assumed to be white and Christian. They had a German last name and German parentage. They shared such superficial features as blond hair and high cheekbones.

Volk philosophers claimed that the volk were a race of people who had a special, spiritual relationship with their land and with nature. Like the romantics in art, Germans turned inward and developed the myth of the deep and superior German soul. As we will see, German thinkers like Paul de Lagarde and Julius Langbehn claimed that members of the volk could connect with mystical, cosmic energies. Nature was pantheistic, something alive, a source of creativity for true Germans.

Volk mysticism satisfied a deep German desire for transcendence. Germans wanted to be part of something great. They wanted to be part of something spiritual, something greater than practical government, economic reform, democratic debate, and adaptation to the modern world. Materialism, liberalism, or progress were not enough. Such concerns lacked the vaunted spirituality of the German soul. What would suffice? A cultural revolution led by a revitalized volk, taking the nation in the opposite direction of liberalism and modernity. We know where this revolution led, tragically. But, in the middle 1800s, promoting the volk appeared to be an unobjectionable desire to preserve German culture against modernity.

The volk movement, which evolved in stages across the 1800s, consisted of an unlikely collection of individuals and groups. Among the shapers of the ideology were frustrated academics, social misfits, philosophers who embraced irrationalism, theorists of culture and race, and people who claimed to intuit the spiritual essence of the volk. Some groups delved into the occult and practised nature mysticism, sun worship, and theosophy. Some called for a Germanic religion. German utopians created back to the land communities.

Writers, like Berthold Auerbach (1812–1882) and Dietrich Echart (1868–1923) – the later becoming Hitler's crazed mentor – wrote popular novels and plays that idealized the German peasant close to nature, in the tradition of Rousseau and Tolstoy.[14] Other adherents looked to Richard Wagner's music to speak for the greatness of the

14 In 1912, Echart adapted, with popular success, Ibsen's Norwegian tale of peasant Peer Gynt. Gynt was now portrayed as an honest German peasant struggling for salvation.

volk. Importantly, educators created a youth movement that carried the volk ideas forward.

Toward the end of the 1800s, Aryan theories of race, using anthropology and phrenology, became popular and were deemed scientific. One could determine the inner quality of a race's (or a person's) character from their external features and appearance. Not surprisingly, writers claimed that the Aryan race was the most beautiful and pure, and there should be no mixing of races. The Jew, the lowest and ugliest race, threatened the purity of the German people.

By the time of National Socialism, the idea of a superior, German volk, exclusive of Jews and wealthy capitalists (and liberals), was accepted across the nation, ready to be exploited by Adolf Hitler.

German Anti-Modernity

The German turn towards conservativism was not limited to volk philosophers or organizations. It was a society-wide discontent with modernity and Germany's place in it.

Modernity was particularly troublesome for Germans who saw their country as a fragmented, second-rate European power which, in their view, was not corrected by the Treaties of Paris in 1814–15 or the leadership of Bismarck. After the First World War, the imposition of the Treaty of Versailles, the weakness of the Weimar Republic, and the economic crisis would rub more salt on the pride of Germans.

Philosophically, the stormiest critique of modernity and its decadence had come from Nietzsche. German conservatives began to read his works in the early 1900s. Nietzsche was not a proto-Nazi. Nietzsche would not have supported a nostalgic view of the German past or an imaginary perfect volk. He would have scoffed at the idea that the Nazis were supermen. But he was a resource for Nazi ideology. His works, sometimes written with passion rather than scholarly qualification, were easily re-formulated as Nazi dogma. His ideas of beyond good and evil, of a will to power, and of a superman were wide open for fascist exploitation. His philosophizing "with a hammer"[15] became Nazi philosophizing with a racist hammer.

15 The title of one of his last books is *Twilight of the Idols, Or How to Philosophize with a Hammer.*

The revolt against modernity attracted a following in Germany because there was a good deal of truth to the criticism. Life *had* become materialistic and impersonal. Modern mass societies and their huge, industrializing cities, *were* soulless. Just look at all the strangers and unrooted workers streaming into the enlarging German cities. Did they not dilute the unity and character of the nation's people?

The opposition of German conservatives to modernity is captured in their antipathy to cities like Berlin. In the early 1900s, Berlin was the stereotype of a city spoiled by modernity, the first city that never slept, a city without shame. Thousands of male and female prostitutes worked the dozens of cabarets, casinos, and dance halls which swayed with the new jazz. Visitors could choose from a smorgasbord of sexual perversions. An extreme decadence seemed to take hold of the city, in the despair that followed the loss of the war. Even the bourgeoisie, former symbols of moral rectitude and social order, joined in the "social abandon."[16] If neither liberalism nor the war would cure problems, then why not drown oneself in a libertine's life of excess pleasure. One night in 1928, Joseph Goebbels walked around the cabaret district and returned home to write, "This is not the true Berlin … the other Berlin is lurking, ready to pounce."[17]

Where could Germans turn to reverse the decline? When the present threatens and the future cannot be faced, one looks backward. Nostalgia takes over. As Germany was becoming a modern military and economic force, Paul de Lagarde and others were nostalgic about an old Germany of hamlets close to the spirits of nature. Stern comments, "Few societies in the modern world were so remote from reality as the Germans in the years of the empire."[18] The cultural despair rose to such heights that, as mentioned, the start of the First World War was for many a great relief from insufferable modern life.

Fascism captured the growing power of volkish philosophy and its hatred of modernity. By 1933, many Germans were ready to hand the struggling German government to a strong man. Even the German philosopher Martin Heidegger would join the Nazi party and, as chancellor of the University of Frieberg, implement the Nazi program for

16 Weir, *Decadence*, 94.
17 Ross, *The Rest Is Noise*, 197–8.
18 Stern, *The Politics of Cultural Despair*, xxvii.

universities.[19] In recent years, evidence that Heidegger's Nazism was extreme and was not separate from his philosophy has surfaced due to the publication of his letter and diaries, such as the *Black Notebooks* in 2014.[20] Generations had come to believe that implementation of volk ideals was the *only* solution to Germany's problems.[21] Citizens became so wedded to an ideology that "they lost sight of civilized law and civilized attitudes toward their fellow men."[22]

Philosopher Eugen Diederichs called volk conservativism a "new romanticism."[23] Volkism was attractive because it was *not* logical. People were ready for passion and action, spurred on by resentment and prejudice. Will and violence defined the soul of mankind.

Bring in the irrational.

The Conservative Radicals

The swing to the right was apparent in many artists and composers of the new music, discussed in chapter 4. Authoritarian sentiments went beyond Arnold Schoenberg. Frustration at the impotency of democracy fed the delusion that complex problems could be solved by a great political leader or führer. As Ross writes, "As in prior periods of cultural and social upheaval, revolutionary gestures betray a reactionary mind-set."[24]

The German musical avant-garde at the turn of the twentieth century were individuals that can be called conservative radicals. They claimed their compositions were works of genius, at odds with accepted norms. Yet they were drawn towards conservative and authoritarian views of politics and society.

For some time before Schoenberg, the marriage of German music and arch-conservative politics had been consummated by Richard

19 Heidegger joined the Nazi Party on 1 May 1933, ten days after being elected rector of the University of Freiburg. In April 1934, he resigned the rectorship and stopped taking part in Nazi Party meetings. He remained a member of the party until the end of the Second World War.

20 On the notebooks and Heidegger's extreme Nazism, see Wolin, *Heidegger in Ruins.*

21 Mosse, *The Crisis of German Ideology*, 202–3.

22 Ibid., 8–9.

23 Cited in ibid., 52.

24 Ross, *The Rest Is Noise*, 42.

Wagner. Wagner's antisemitism was well-known. His *Judaism in Music* was an antisemitic tome that made it difficult for Jewish composers like Mahler and a young Schoenberg to be accepted.[25] Wagner's music inspired the German volk and the dreams of far-right fanatics.

As noted in chapter 4, the writings and personal correspondence of leading composers display a strong misogyny[26] and traditional social biases.[27] Antisemitism was generally accepted and always close to the surface. Fear of the developing modern face of women is evident in the musical portrayals of women in Wagner, Straus, Schoenberg, and Puccini – from the dangerous Salome to the incestuous Electra. In the 1930s, many leading Western artists, like many leading industrialists and politicians, were attracted to the strength of the emerging fascist leaders, Mussolini and Hitler, although a number of them would live to regret such political blindness. Stravinsky, Eliot, Pound, Toscanini, Schoenberg, Kandinsky, and others were attracted to aesthetic fascism, the *idea* of a system that would preserve musical (and other) traditions.

Stravinsky grumbled in 1933 that his work was being ignored in the new Germany despite his strong "negative attitude toward Communism and Judaism."[28] Stravinsky hated the Bolsheviks for robbing him of his Russian land. In 1930, at a public event in Italy attended by Mussolini, Stravinsky proclaimed to the world that no one "venerates" Mussolini more than he and "he is the one man who counts nowadays in the whole world." He renders homage to the Duce and calls him "the savior of Italy and – let us hope – of Europe."[29] Stravinsky deeply feared

25 On Wagner's antisemitism, see Katz, *The Darker Side of Genius: Richard Wagner's Anti-Semitism.*

26 Misogyny was part of the culture. For example, Freud's analysis of the "hysteria" of Dora (Ida Bauer) is a classic work of psychoanalysis. Freud is shockingly insensitive to the plight of a young women who, by the age of thirteen, becomes the sexual target of several men, aided by her father. Freud thinks Dora is hysterical, suffering from a woman's incapacity to find pleasure in sexual feelings. Dora is the one with the problem, not the men. Freud, *Dora*, 21–2.

27 Conservatism among creative people in the twentieth century was not new. Dalí was a strong believer in the irrational and a radical critic of art, yet he was far from radical in his politics or religion. As his life went on, he gravitated towards his childhood Catholicism and looked favourably upon the Spanish dictator Francisco Franco.

28 Heyworth, *Otto Klemperer*, 13.

29 Cited in Taruskin, "The Dark Side of Modern Music," 32.

social disorder caused by mass revolutionaries and a levelling of society by the masses. How could high culture survive in an "age of rampant proletariats"?[30] By the middle of the 1920s, Stravinsky was declaring himself to be an anti-modernist where modernism was equated in politics with the Bolsheviks and in music with both romanticism and Schoenberg's atonal works. He allowed his spokesman to describe him in print as "the dictator of the reaction against the anarchy into which modernism has degenerated."[31] He was the Mussolini of music.

For his part, Toscanini was lauded for stepping down as head of the Bayreuth Festival in protest against the Nazis. But he was no democrat. He was an aristocratic musical dictator who bullied orchestras into fascist-like obedience – a style the fascists liked. He charged extravagant fees. As a result, the musicians in his orchestras took a pay cut. Puccini called him "the God."

Kandinsky, despite his trumpeting of abstractionism and art as transcendence of the material world, was attracted to fascism in the real world of politics. Kandinsky in Paris supported a Paris lecture in 1935 by futurist Filippo Tommaso Marinetti. Artists scorned Kandinsky for supporting the fascist Marinetti. But Kandinsky celebrated futurism's "abstracting modernism." He found "Italian Fascism not incompatible with modern art and modernism."[32] He supported Italian fascism *after* he had moved to France in 1933, now that the Bauhaus was closed – by fascists.

One of the strangest manifestations of authoritarianism was the case of Heinrich Schenker (1868–1935), the Austrian music theorist who, despite being a Jew, avidly supported Hitler and his brownshirts. He died in 1935 before the Holocaust began. Nonetheless, in a letter to a pupil in May 1933, he proclaims the "historical achievement" of Hitler in eliminating Marxism. He hoped that, some day, there would be a musical version of Hitler. Musical "brownshirts" would "exterminate the musical Marxists" because "art and the masses have never belonged together."[33]

30 Taruskin, "The Dark Side of Modern Music," 32.
31 Lourié, *Sergei Kousevitzky and His Epoch*, 196.
32 Buenger and Holz, "Antifascism or Autonomous Art?," 70.
33 Taruskin, "The Dark Side of Modern Music," 34.

Meanwhile, in New York, Dalí was criticized as a reactionary – a surprising term for someone thought to be radical. In 1941, Nicolas Calas[34] accused Dalí of apostasy since he no longer believed in basic surrealistic principles, and he had rediscovered Spain, Catholicism, and neoclassicism.[35] Progressive artist Walter Quirt, Breton, and others called him a fascist. They disliked Dalí's ghostly painting, *The Enigma of Hitler*. Dalí didn't help matters when he "confessed" that "Hitler turned me on in the highest."[36] There was also Dalí's declaration of allegiance to Franco's Spain. Breton took steps to throw him out of his group of surrealist artists as Dalí decamped to America. What was one of Dalí's responses to critics? He took a page out of Schoenberg's political handbook. Dalí claimed he was apolitical. "I was definitely not a historic man. On the contrary I felt myself essentially a-historic and a-political."[37]

Unfortunately, this love of authoritarianism, mixed with prejudice, arrogance, and aristocratic values, would cause allegedly great men to be attracted to terrible, stupid ideas. Take the case of Otto Weininger, a Jew who converted to Christianity and whose ideas would be used by Nazis against the Jews. In 1903, he shot himself in the house where Beethoven died. He revered the composer. This theatrical death prompted other suicides, as had the suicide of Goethe's (fictional) young Werther a century before. The suicide made Weininger's unfinished doctoral thesis, called *Sex and Character*, a bestseller. The main argument was that Europe suffered from degeneration because of the sexuality of women. Jewishness and homosexuality were signs of a feminized, weak society. Only a masculine genius could redeem the world. Wagner, the book claimed, was "the greatest man since Christ."

According to Weininger, the human personality has masculine and feminine aspects. Masculinity is active, productive, conscious, moral, and logical, while femininity is passive, unproductive, unconscious, amoral, and alogical. Female life centres around the sexual function, whether the woman is a prostitute or a mother. The duty of the male,

34 Nicolas Calas was the pseudonym of Nikos Kalamaris, a Greek American poet and art critic and Trotskyite.

35 Calas, "Anti-Surrealist Dali," 3. See also chapter 6.

36 Dalí, *The Unspeakable Confessions of Salvador Dalí*. Calling them confessions is questionable. Dalí said outrageous things to attract press coverage. It is difficult to know when he was being sincere or not.

37 Dalí, *The Secret Life of Salvador Dalí*, 357.

or the masculine aspect, is to become a genius. To do so, one must abandon sexuality for the abstract love of the absolute, or God, which men find within themselves. This incoherent book was read and taken seriously by the likes of Ludwig Wittgenstein and James Joyce, along with Schoenberg and his pupils.

Weininger's ideas figured into Wittgenstein's life. Wittgenstein sought the status of genius. He wanted to be perfect and to produce great works. This was one reason why he left Cambridge University and went into exile in Norway, so he could focus on his thoughts. Wittgenstein also was neurotic in sexual matters. He struggled to express sexual desire to another person.[38] For Wittgenstein and Weininger, there is primarily the duty to self. This is romanticism gone dangerously selfish, a narcissism easily twisted into a "pure" Aryan ideology, the Nordic superman. What lies behind the duty to self is the erotic absolute – the attraction of giving one's entire life over to one, absolute ideal.

As Hitler came to power not all Jewish artists were upset or fearful – not yet. Some were impressed by Hitler's willingness to change the stagnant Weimar republic. Some cheered Hitler's war victories. Some Jewish composers sought to appease the Nazis and soon faced the terrible choice between saving one's principles and saving lives.

For instance, when Hitler came to power in 1933 Richard Strauss (1864–1949) was a world-renowned composer. He said, "Thank God. Finally, a Reich Chancellor who is interested in art." He accepted a Nazi appointment as head of the Reich Music Chamber and principal conductor of the Bayreuth Festival, well-known for its antisemitic history. At Bayreuth, Strauss replaced Toscanini.

Ross bitingly says that Strauss, born a Catholic, became a model Jewified German, "a prize exhibit of Nazi culture" who attended Nazi functions. Strauss wrote a letter to Hitler calling him "the great designer of German existence."[39] His defenders note that Strauss hoped to be apolitical, and to resist the worst Nazi effects on German music. At first, he thought he could be apolitical, creating music under any government. More pragmatically, he could promote copyright protections for composers and ignore bans on the works of Debussy, Mahler, Mendelssohn, and others. More urgently, Strauss wanted to use his influence to save

38 Monk, *Ludwig Wittgenstein: The Duty of Genius*, 90.

39 Ross, *The Rest Is Noise*, 334, 338.

Jewish relatives from the concentration camps. Strauss claimed, as Schoenberg would, that his art was not affected by politics. He justified his official position as an effort to "prevent great disasters."

His apolitical stance soon became untenable. In 1935, Strauss wanted a Jewish librettist, Stefan Zweig, for his opera *Die schweigsame Frau* (The silent woman). In June of that year, Zweig wrote Strauss that he had to withdraw from the project because of Strauss's affiliation with the Nazis, in particular his position as the head of the Reich Music Chamber. Strauss wrote to Zweig complaining of the "Jewish obstinacy" which caused Zweig to feel solidarity with the Jews of Germany. The Gestapo intercepted the letter. Strauss had to resign from his post. Ross calls Strauss's downfall "a supremely painful case of aestheticism confronted with reality."[40]

Strauss's influence was enough to save his immediate family, including his daughter-in-law, but not dozens of his relatives. To his credit, he refused to sign documents kicking Jews out of the Reich Music Chamber. Yet he did sign a denunciation of Thomas Mann. In 1936, he wrote and conducted the "Olympic Hymn" at the opening of the Olympics in Berlin before Adolf Hitler. Ultimately, Strauss had to grovel before Nazi ministers. Strauss privately dismissed Goebbels as a "pipsqueak."[41] However, in 1933 he dedicated an orchestral song, "Das Bächlein" (The little brook), to Goebbels, in order to gain his cooperation in extending German music copyright laws from thirty years to fifty years.[42] In 1941, he was heard to disparage the operettas of Franz Lehar, composer of *The Merry Widow.* Hitler loved his music. Goebbels called Strauss to a humiliating meeting before other composers: "Lehar has the masses, you do not," screamed Goebbels.[43]

Meanwhile, as Schoenberg was adjusting to American life in the mid-1930s, two of Schoenberg's best students, Alban Berg and Anton von Webern, were adjusting to Nazism. Berg was not sympathetic to Hitler's program, but he played up his Aryan origins to the Reich Music Chamber.

Webern's image in the years after the Second World War was positive – a transcendent music that had survived depravity. Yet, by the late

40 Ross, "As If Music Could Do No Harm."
41 Reuth, *Goebbels,* 402.
42 Kennedy, *Richard Straus,* 281–2.
43 Ross, *The Rest Is Noise,* 357.

1970s there was growing evidence that he had supported the Nazis. His Nazi sympathies were known much earlier to German composer Karl Hartmann, who for a while studied privately under Webern. In 1942, he cut short his studies with Webern because the latter kept talking about politics, saying that "any kind of authority should be respected" and that citizens should recognize the authority of their state "at any price."[44] Webern's letters show him reading Hitler's *Mein Kampf* with great excitement and praising Germany's war effort. Webern welcomed the Nazis into Vienna. He greeted the Nazi invasion of Denmark and Norway with orgasmic writing: "This is Germany today! But the *National Socialist,* to be sure. Not just any one! ... Yes, *a new state it is ... It is something new! Created by a unique man!!! ... Each day becomes more exciting!*"[45] His tragic disillusionment would come later.

SECTION 3: THREE HORSEMEN OF THE GERMAN APOCALYPSE

The Germany that we love and that we yearn to see has never existed and perhaps never will exist.

Paul de Lagarde[46]

The ideology of the volk movement was largely the work of three German intellectuals in the nineteenth century. Ideology in this period always ran a fever, comprised of forceful ideas intended to attract acolytes. The writings of these three men contained diatribes, hatreds, mystical feelings, personal yearnings, dehumanizing depictions of groups, and dogmatic appeal to special intuitions – an authoritarian form of scholarship. Their writings show what happens when an ideology worships at the altar of nationalism, glorifies the will, and ignores reality to revel in the irrational. One gets demonic ideology. One gets millions of dead on the ground.

These three writers were most active from the middle of the nineteenth century to the threshold of German fascism in the 1920s. They were, chronologically, Paul de Lagarde (1827–1891), a biblical scholar who created a mystical philosophy of volkism, spread antisemitism,

44 Moldenhauer and Moldenhauer, *Anton von Webern,* 540–1.

45 Ibid., 527.

46 Cited in Stern, *The Politics of Cultural Despair,* 27.

embraced pan-Germanism, and sought a German religion; Julius Langbehn (1851–1907), an art historian, failed academic, and psychopath who explicitly embraced irrationalism and raged against the modern age; and Moeller van den Bruck (1876–1925), esthete and historian. His book, *The Third Reich*, gave the Nazi party its messianic goal.[47]

The members of this unholy trinity were cultural malcontents. All three were isolated individuals, blaming their troubles not on themselves but on the world, and paranoid of conspiracies. All three made a virtue of their failures, playing the role of the alienated intellectual misunderstood by lesser minds. All three men despised modernity, liberalism, and democracy, the bourgeoisie, communism, and the proletariat. Their proposed reforms tended to be abstract, meager, and far from reality. They sought refuge in an imaginary idea of Germany. All were fascist minds before fascism became a political party in Germany.

Whatever their weaknesses, these men were skilled at capturing the hearts of an ailing nation. They used passionate language to express the frustrations of the time. Late in life, Lagarde received plaudits as the father of volk philosophy. The German leaders who would come later thought they were acting according to Lagarde's principles. After the First World War, agricultural settlements were founded to maintain Lagarde's idea of a Germanic volk. During the Second World War, an anthology of his work was distributed to soldiers. Later, Langbehn's book *Rembrandt as Educator* was wildly popular, read by millions in the early 1900s. Bruck, because of *The Third Reich*, was hailed as the prophet of Germany's messianic mission.

I call these writers the three horsemen of the German apocalypse because they were the sign of an impending catastrophe. They exchanged political reason for messianic, political fantasy; they exchanged traditional Christianity for political religion. In the end, this ideology led Germany over a cliff and into the abyss. By the end of the Second World War, Germany was shattered and divided by foreign powers. The yearning for a new unity would end in the tragic burdening of the nation, for eternity, with the guilt of the Holocaust.

The formulation of volk ideology by these writers consisted of three leaps. (1) A psychological leap: constructing a political ideology based

47 In these portraits, I have benefitted from reading George Mosse's *The Crisis of German Ideology* and Fritz Stern's *The Politics of Cultural Despair.*

on personal intuition and resentment; (2) a metaphysical leap: constructing a racist utopia from mystical metaphysics of the volk; and (3) a political leap: constructing a political morality of hardness to pursue the Nazi utopia.

Fritz Stern, a leading authority on these writers, has said the trinity used cultural despair to create a politics of organized hatreds. The fatal moment came when they leaped from "despair to utopia across all existing reality ... [which] gave their thought its fantastic quality."[48] Not satisfied to join the critics of modernity, they become prophets of German messianism. Their ideas, often a cover for frustration and mental illness, infiltrated the political environment of fin-de-siècle Germany.

Psychological Leap: From Personal Isolation to Volk Religion

Lagarde's life began badly in Berlin.[49] He was born in 1827 into an old Saxon family. Only twelve days later, his mother, eighteen years of age, died. The family had lost a daughter the year before. His philologist father, Wilhelm Botticher, went into a deep grief. For the rest of his life, he was a cheerless, Jew-hating Christian who despised his son, blaming him for his wife's death. Two maternal great-aunts brought up the young man. The break between father and son never healed. When called to his father's deathbed, Lagarde was troubled that he could not manufacture the least feeling of grief. Lagarde would write that his childhood was "immeasurably sad" and "far from people," driving him to live in a world of books and dreams.[50] Nevertheless, Lagarde would be influenced by his father's thought and antisemitism, while acquiring his temperament of being both irascible and sentimental.

As a student in the 1840s, Lagarde was deeply religious, although he rejected traditional Christianity. Politically, he initially supported the Prussian conservativism of king, aristocracy, and military. He rejected the liberal revolution in 1848. He would eventually break from this tepid conservatism and become a more radical conservative, an outsider belonging to no political camp. At the universities of Berlin and then Halle, he enjoyed reading the romantics and set a career path that

48 Stern, *The Politics of Cultural Despair*, xi.

49 He was born Paul Anton Botticher. In 1853, he adopted the name of his great-aunt, Ernestine de Lagarde.

50 Stern, *The Politics of Cultural Despair*, 5.

would make him a biblical scholar and orientalist of some renown. Yet the struggles of his country imprinted on his mind a terrible pessimism about Germany's future.

His isolation from and dissatisfaction with almost everything around him grew. He became bitter. For years, universities declined to give him a permanent position forcing him to teach in a gymnasium, a post he felt was below his talents. He blamed a conspiracy of professors against him. At other times, he explained it as the inability of lesser minds to appreciate his ideas. In truth, he was projecting his own tendency toward combativeness, intrigue, and calumny. He was difficult to work with, arrogant, and a number of his publications were not top-notch. He would brook no disagreement and raged against negative reviews of his work. His scholarly methods did not fit – and he made no effort to make them fit – the scientific and rational ethos of his colleagues. He dismissed the writings of colleagues as discourses on minor topics. He dismissed their rational, theological debates. He made broad assertions such as the Jews have no soul and the Persians have the greatest soul. When colleagues asked for evidence for such prejudice, Lagarde replied he knew this by intuitively grasping general truths amid detail. He had, as Stern said, "soaring pretensions, fragmentary performance."[51]

Ironically, this isolated arch-conservative, divisive in his personal life, would become a voice for unity among the German volk. The future of the nation depended not on economic development or on a Marxist classless society. It depended, he thought, on a revival of idealism – of the capacity of the people to revitalize the volk, the authentic Germans. German unity would be based on common spiritual values. What Germany needed was increased inwardness, a spiritual revolution, a new Germanic religion.

The new religion would emphasize the pre-modern values of old Germany, of a medieval-style life of closeness to nature, of personal relations with others, of tradition and rootedness, of community and collectivity. Lagarde took up the myth of the Germany peasant seeking salvation. These ideas were set against the values of liberalism, individuality, and materialism. Lagarde projected on to a fantastical, ideal volk the fellowship and affection he gravely desired but could not express to friends and colleagues. He projected all positive values on to a perfect

51 Ibid., 25.

volk world. To the task of revitalizing the volk, Lagarde would dedicate himself with the fervour of a Protestant reformer. After 1871, the year of German unification as an empire, Lagarde would publish some fifty writings warning that Germany was never so divided and calling for a volk revolution.

The younger Langbehn would eventually join Lagarde in preaching the primacy of the volk. But his writings were more volatile and his mind more unstable. In 1851 he was born in a Schleswig town, then in Danish control, and now part of northern Germany. His father was a philologist who taught at the local gymnasium. Shortly after his birth, Danish officials fired his father because of his German patriotism. From then on his family struggled with poverty, settling in nearby Kiel. Langbehn did not suffer the harmful family isolation that marked Lagarde's youth, but they shared mental traits. Both were disenchanted with the status quo and uneasily followed conventions. Both were combative, and both had grandiose views of themselves. However, unlike Lagarde, Langbehn would develop severe mental problems – narcissism, paranoia, and psychopathy.

As a student at the University of Munich, Langbehn was bored with chemistry and the sciences but fascinated by the talk of artists. It led to a doctorate in art history. But his entire, and intermittent, life as a student was tumultuous and strained the patience of academic advisers. His Munich dissertation advisor, the archeologist Heinrich Brunn, saw Langbehn's intellectual strengths but also started to speak of his "megalomania."[52] Brunn sought to obtain academic grants for Langbehn but the latter would alienate funders with his arrogance. Langbehn chafed at the thought of being chained to an academic position and formulated great, unrealistic plans for future work. When Brunn suggested a more practical plan, Langbehn erupted in anger.

By 1880, Langbehn had to find employment, but, disdaining work, he resolved not to work at all. Instead, he proposed that his friends and colleagues, seeing his greatness, would provide him with money to live. Meanwhile, he would "construct the future."[53] He would undertake a reform of German culture and a rebirth of the German people. Such ambitions clashed with the reality of his life. Now living alone, without

52 Ibid., 101.
53 Ibid., 103.

recognition, he was a failed academic. Langbehn developed a narcissistic obsession with the self. He would sit for hours before his portrait, caressing it.[54] He was paranoid. He feared that, unless he prepared his own special diet, his enemies would poison him. He went to extremes in everything. He shocked friends by calling for a reintroduction of slavery and a subjugation of lower races. Like Lagarde, he inwardly craved friends and affection but he rebuffed them. He was a dictator to his friends. Friends either agreed with him completely or they were jettisoned. His disciple, Benedict Momme Nissen, who lived with him, wrote that "when he commanded, I had to obey."[55] His personal need for dictatorial powers led him to favour a dictatorial leader, a messiah for the nation. At times, he imagined himself as this messiah. His sanity was questioned by friends.

Yet despite these mental issues, he completed his book. Published in 1890, *Rembrandt as Educator*[56] was another attack on civilization and reason. But its wild style made it popular. The book was a "rhapsody of the irrational," written in a Nietzschean ecstasy.[57] It was a tirade against intellectualism and science and in praise of the volk and artistic sensibility and the lost German virtues of childlike simplicity and subjectivity. Rembrandt, celebrated as a German, was to be the model German individual. Art was the highest good and the true source of knowledge and virtue.

Langbehn's psychopathic mind is evident during a bizarre attempt in the winter of 1889–1900 to take over the care of Nietzsche at an asylum in Jena.[58] He implored Nietzsche's mother to leave her son in his care. Frau Nietzsche welcomed him warmly at first and authorized his visits to the asylum. For two weeks, he talked with Nietzsche every day. Then he started to poison Frau Nietzche's mind against the attending physicians. He insisted on having exclusive care of Nietzsche and Nietzche's mother would have to sign an oath to never communicate with her son except by his permission. This was beyond the pale. She rejected his demands. Langbehn left Jena shortly thereafter when

54 Ibid., 104.

55 Mosse, *The Crisis of German Ideology*, 45.

56 The book was styled after Nietzsche's "Schopenhauer as Educator," which is part of Nietzsche's *Untimely Meditations.*

57 Stern, *The Politics of Cultural Despair*, xii.

58 Ibid., 107–8.

Nietzsche, being lectured by Langbehn, flew into a rage and stormed out of his room. When Langbehn's art-based utopia did not appear, he joined a Catholic order. The former radical spent his remaining years in the traditional arms of the church.

The Metaphysical Leap: From Life Force to Racism

The theory of German unification developed by Lagarde and Langbehn was unlike previous romantic musings about the volk. It was not poetry about a past era. It was a hard-edged political view based on metaphysics. It referred to transcendent entities and unseen forces known through mystical insights.[59]

As seen, positivists rejected unverifiable metaphysics. However, the three horsemen would have no truck with positivism. They constructed a mystical, non-rational philosophy. It was a metaphysics that Kant had shown, a century before, was beyond the limits of reason.[60]

Why is the metaphysics of these volk ideologists important? Because the metaphysical ideas were used in three important ways. One, the metaphysical ideas, such as the capacity to commune with cosmic energies, explained why the volk were special among the races. The Nazi view of a supreme volk was not far away. Second, metaphysical distinctions between soul and body and spirit and matter would be used to denigrate other non-volkish groups. The Jews and others were said to lack soul or connection to the spiritual world. Third, these distinctions would support an irrational epistemology. Ecstasy, visions, insights, and religious emotion were the methods of volk knowing.

LIFE FORCE

Primary among these metaphysical concepts was the notion of a life force that runs through nature, which science cannot know or measure. Langbehn thought individuals could participate in a pulsating, energetic life-force, the source of creativity, by participating in the life of the volk. As he stated, "With a dose of mysticism one can gild the life of a nation."[61]

59 I have no objection to mysticism as heightened awareness in contemplation, in listening to music, or in other experiences. My concern arises when such experiences enter the political arena. The horsemen crudely employed mysticism to support a racist philosophy.

60 See Kant, *The Critique of Pure Reason.*

61 Mosse, *The Crisis of German Ideology*, 41.

Langbehn tied his ideas closely to theosophy, founded by Helena Blavatsky and Henry Olcott in 1875. Theosophy believes that knowledge of God can be achieved through spiritual ecstasy, direct intuition, or special individual relations. The extrasensory world is the true world. Langbehn, like many others at this time, was fascinated with Emanuel Swedenborg, an eighteenth-century Swedish engineer turned mystic. Swedenborg, who claimed to commune with dead people, thought that God, the world, and humans were one – they were spiritual phenomena.

RACISM

Lagarde and Langbehn regarded the volk as an exclusive race, the true Germans.

Racism and nationalism were present in Lagarde's definition of Germany: "Germany is the totality of all German-feeling, German-thinking, German-willing Germans. In this sense, every one of us is a traitor if he does not consider himself personally accountable in every moment of his life for the existence, fortune and future of the fatherland, and each is a hero and liberator if he does."[62] Who were the people preventing the volk from reviving? The Jews.

> One would have to have a heart of steel to not feel sympathy for the poor Germans and, by the same token, to not hate the Jews, to not hate and despise those who – out of humanity! – advocate for the Jews or are too cowardly to crush these vermin. Trichinella and bacilli would not be negotiated with, trichinella and bacilli would also not be tortured, they would be destroyed as quickly and as thoroughly as possible.[63]

Langbehn agreed. Nature and race were identical. Volkish virtues were gifts from nature and transmitted through blood inheritance. Jews were polluting the purity of volk blood. They had been estranged from the vital flow of life spirits and their souls had petrified. Since they lacked a soul and could not re-establish contact with the life force, Jews could not retain virtues like honesty and loyalty. Jews were "pest and cholera" and "arch-fiends."[64] Jews had to be exterminated.

62 Lagarde, *German Writings*, 101.

63 Ibid., 53.

64 Mosse, *The Crisis of German Ideology*, 44.

The difficulty of objecting to this line of thinking is that it is metaphysical and driven to promote the volk. Rational argument and facts are of no avail against these rhapsodies of the irrational. Truth was whatever advanced the volk. "I have no use for abstract truth," said Lagarde. "I want to liberate my people."[65]

Volk metaphysics adopted the romantic view of humans as creatures of will. Lagarde says, "The core of man is not his reason, but his will … For like everything that is good, knowledge only enters through the will, whose wings are sensibility and imagination, and whose driving force is love."[66] Love would be the weakest force in the years to come. As National Socialism developed, the "will" became an "all-encompassing metaphysical principle."[67] A religion of the will is evident at the huge Nuremberg rally in 1934 whose theme "The Triumph of the Will" became the title of Leni Riefenstahl's infamous film.

Yet, as with the earlier romanticism, German irrationalism left unanswered the great questions: A will to do what? Freedom for what?

Leaping into the Abyss: From Total War to Apocalypse

If the volk revolution occurred, what would society look like?

In formulating practical aims, the three horsemen revealed the reality averse, irrational, dream-like nature of their thinking about concrete reality. All ignored detailed, serious, analysis of economic, technological, and other factors that were defining their age. They *did* want a fierce strong leader, such as a monarch or führer, to compel unity and achieve Germany's destiny to be the greatest nation in the world. Lagarde thought society should be organized into medieval estates, with the working classes transformed into artisans. "Oh, what a delightful time the Middle Ages were, when everything was learned under the guidance of masters," wrote a nostalgic and deluded Lagarde.[68] Medieval Germany was delightful. The belief that modern industrial Germany could retreat back to medieval feudalism was, literally, insane.

Langbehn's scheme was no better. He thought Germany should abandon industrialization and urbanization for an agrarian society ruled

65 Ibid., 13.
66 Ibid., 37.
67 Stern, *Hitler: The Führer and the People*, 70.
68 Mosse, *The Crisis of German Ideology*, 35.

by a monarch. There would be no bourgeoisie, no proletariat, and no landed nobility. But he had few concrete notions of how this would come about. What about equality among citizens? "Equality is death," replied Langbehn.[69] What if certain groups or the state disagreed with this totalizing plan? If necessary, the state, or any group, could be crushed like an eggshell if it opposed the volk's national destiny.

Bruck and the Third Way

By the early 1900s, Moeller van den Bruck's scheme for Germany surpassed those of Lagarde and Langbehn. He came of age in the 1890s as Langbehn's book emerged. He too longed for a new German faith. During the Weimar Republic, writers and politicians sought a third way as an alternative to capitalism and Marxism. Bruck would provide a third way using the emotional, spiritual term "the Reich."

Bruck was born in Solingen, central Saxony. His paternal grandfather was a landed gentleman, his uncles were Prussian army officers, his father an architect in the civil service.

When young, he was expelled from his gymnasium, a major disappointment to his family who wanted him to follow in one of the family's professions – army or ministry. They repudiated him. At the University of Leipzig, he was bored by lectures, even lectures by the great psychologist Wundt, preferring to read Nietzsche. At the end of his under-whelming academic studies, he left Germany to escape military service. He spent twenty years wandering, writing, thinking about Germany and interacting with intellectuals and artists in places like Paris. In the French capital he was repelled by scepticism and came under the influence of exiled poet, apocalyptic prophet, and mystic Dmitry Merezhkobsky. The Russian poet, a leader of the symbolist movement, spoke of the need for a spiritual revolution, an idea that would resonate with Bruck. Merezhkobsky asserted that one should reject "the rational in favour of the intuitive" and exploit the "spirituality of a symbol." Thought, as spoken and rational, lies. In poetry unspoken things affect us through the beauty of symbols.

The modest fortune that Bruck inherited, plus money from freelance writing, allowed him to avoid steady employment. It allowed him to be

69 Ibid., 51.

an outsider, thinking of himself as Nietzsche's prophet of the superman, Zarathustra. He began to write on culture and history, seeking, like Lagarde and Langbehn, to capture the spirit of his age. Like Langbehn, he believed the zeitgeist reveals itself through great artists. As the First World War began, he was working on *The Prussian Style*. Published in 1916, it embraced nationalism. The essence of Prussia was "the will to the state."

A Plea for Revolution

In *The Third Reich* of 1923, Bruck caught the spirit of the times. He considered calling the book *The Third Way* or *The Third Point of View* but then recalled a German myth about Reichs. The three Reichs were: the Holy Roman Empire, the German Empire, which ended in 1918, and a future and permanent Third Reich.

At the beginning of *The Third Reich*, Bruck called for a true, German revolution. Not the German revolution of 1918 that ushered in the Weimar Republic. But a spiritual revolution, a new empire. It made him the darling of the conservatives and emerging fascists. Bruck states that "instead of government by party we offer the ideal of the Third Empire … the dawn of a German Age in which the German People would for the first time fulfill their destiny on earth."[70] Germans needed to be fired by an ideal from their past which pointed towards future greatness.

The book was a call, at times a desperate plea, to political action. The idea of a third empire is "misty, indeterminate, charged with emotion," he wrote. It will remain a dream unless Germans translate it into "concrete reality." The French may have had their liberal revolution, but now the Germans must have their first political revolution of the spirit.[71] Germany, Bruck thought, must find a way between the extremes of communism and American capitalism. Destroy the political parties and democracy. Depoliticize the proletariat by somehow persuading them to return to the values of the volk. Reject science, materialism, and modernity.

With Bruck, German thought turns from sentimentality to aggression. Nothing must stand in the way of the Third Reich.

70 Bruck, *The Third Reich*, 13.
71 Ibid., 17.

The book is also an indictment of many presumed enemies, now familiar to the reader: liberals, Jews, "intellectual blockheads" who believe in peace and the League of Nations, freemasons who assert a "bogus rationalism."[72] Liberalism was a fraud that the foes of Germany had conspired to introduce into the German body politic. He repeated the myth that these intellectuals and liberals were to blame for Germany's defeat in the First World War. Consequently, he writes, "a suspicion broods over the country that the nation suffered betrayal."[73]

The ending of the book resorts to grandiose bombast. In a "sinking world" the German "seeks his salvation." Bruck wants to preserve "imperishable" Prussian values. He construes fighting for a German Reich as fighting for the "cause of Europe" since Germany is the centre of Europe – an assertion at which many French and other Europeans would look askance. The revolution is for "the Germany of All Time, the Germany of a two-thousand-year past, the Germany of an eternal present which dwells in the spirit."[74]

Bruck would not live to see the success of *The Third Reich.* He despaired at its mediocre initial reception. The book did not catch fire until it was reissued in 1930. Meanwhile, the times were dark. The Nazis received almost two million votes in the election of May 1924; in December, they attracted less than a million votes. In 1925, he died by suicide.

Bruck's political and cultural writings are, perhaps, the best of the three horsemen. *The Third Reich* is the completion of his cultural criticism over decades. Despite their obnoxious doctrines and strident language, Bruck's writings at least attempt to argue rationally, not wildly like Langbehn. His writings are more informed by reality and the state of Europe than the writings of Lagarde.

Warrior Morality

For Bruck, as well as for Lagarde, men – not women – reached the highest peak of life when they acted as warriors. Bruck's view of mankind combined a simplistic model of Nietzsche's superman with social Darwinism. Fighting alone makes a man. Society changes but human nature, with its fierce instincts, is unchangeable. Bruck wrote, "Fighting

72 Ibid., 25, 84.
73 Ibid., 77.
74 Ibid., 264.

is magnificent ... Battle gives us ... our greatest kings and best heroes ... Eternal peace would be insupportable – it would be boredom, a yawning that would give us merely the philistine."[75]

Since suffering was necessary for creativity, then prosperity and the slackness of modernity was a disaster for culture. The struggle of war had the same positive, reviving effects on people as spiritual self-conquest. The liberal view of happiness, if achieved, would cause humans to "cease being fighters."[76] Grounding *The Third Reich* was Bruck's pessimistic view of human nature: a creature that is violent and needs discipline. He believed in the inequality of men, their inherent limitations, and their irrationality.

The Horsemen's Legacy

The three horsemen show how psychology, philosophy, and politics can contribute to war and horror. They show how views of art and history can produce new political philosophy with concrete impact on society. A psychology of personal isolation and frustration encouraged the idea of a pure volk and then a racist metaphysical ideology. The ideology, once it entered the political domain, prompted a religious-like pursuit of a German utopia. Pent-up psychological pressures found a release through political visions. These visions were as far from reality as the thinkers were from the economic and other realities of their turbulent times. Bred on fantasy, irrational prejudice, and fierce tribalism, the Germans leapt into the abyss.

The horsemen were learned and intellectual but they failed as rigorous thinkers. Due to upbringing, social context, and inherited traits, they lacked the discipline and temperament to master the objective methods of knowledge. They were unable to transcend their subjectivity and their prejudices. Not for a moment could these geniuses question their self-serving presumption that Germans had the deepest of souls, while the rest of the Western world were superficial materialists; not for a moment could they do without their presumption that Germans were a superior race. Not for a moment could they consider that there might be no such thing as a pure volk. They were self-absorbed, often

75 Stern, *The Politics of Cultural Despair*, 189.
76 Ibid., 195.

self-pitying, figures unable to live without mystical assurances and nonexistent spirits. They had a shameful disregard for facts, common knowledge, scientific method, and the strengths of other races and cultures. Their power was derived from the power of their passions, not their arguments.

They could think only in narrow ideological ways, using biased, simplistic characterizations of liberalism, democracy, and the Enlightenment. Ethically speaking, despite their solemn religiosity, they were incapable of caring about the equality or justice of others. Right came from the needs of the volk or the barrel of a German gun. Justice was only a concern when they perceived a need for retributive justice for the volk against trumped-up scapegoats, like the Jews. They did not have the honesty to recognize that the troubles with their nation were not the result of conspiracies but largely the result of their nation's own inadequacies and of global conditions beyond direct control. Rather than adjust Germany to modern realities, they retreated into a fantasy world.

It will remain one of the great tragedies and mysteries of modern times that such flawed men, with such putrid ideas, could attract the support of a great nation like Germany. They were anti-intellectual intellectuals – the most offensive kind – whose failures teach us the danger of the tyranny of unreasonable passion supported by fake rationality.

SECTION 4: THE KILLING PROFESSION

This world is not this world.

Auschwitz survivor

The Nazi Doctors

We dive deeper into the fascist mind by examining groups that participated in Nazi genocide.

One group were the Nazi doctors who sterilized and killed millions of people.[77] At Auschwitz alone, doctors murdered about one million people. Moreover, dentists and doctors who arrived at Auschwitz and other extermination camps as inmates were ordered to help the Nazi

77 In this section, I benefited from Lifton's *The Nazi Doctors*. See also Spitz, *Doctors from Hell*; Schmidt, *Karl Brandt: The Nazi Doctor*; and Mitscherlich and Mielke, *Doctors of Infamy*.

doctors. It is not my intention to recount the disturbing events called the Holocaust[78] nor redescribe the doctors' disturbing procedures. Rather, I ask how did the Nazi doctors, members of a well-educated profession who had taken the Hippocratic Oath, become leaders in genocide?

When the Nazis took power, they ended the careers of 7,000 Jewish doctors in Germany. By 1942 more than 38,000 German doctors, half the total number of doctors, had joined the Nazi party. The Holocaust could not have happened without them. Killing and experimentation became medical procedures performed by licensed doctors. At trials of doctors, after the war, the argument was made that there was no international law to differentiate between legal and illegal human experimentation. This led to the Nuremberg Code on human experimentation of 1947. After the war the German Medical Association, to its shame, blamed Nazi atrocities on a small group of 350 doctors. Some doctors changed their name to avoid responsibility. A minority of doctors were criminally charged. The most infamous of all, Josef Mengele, escaped. He would spend the rest of his life in South America.

The Nazi killing of Jews, the Roma, homosexuals, mentally ill patients, and many others required more than the acquiescence of educated, professional classes. It required the *active* participation of physicians, psychiatrists, dentists, engineers, lawyers, transportation officials, hospital staff, and the civil service.

The doctor killings increased in intensity and scope over several steps. It started with the forced sterilization of people who had diseases or disabilities. One of the first laws of the new Nazi government, enacted in July 1933, was called the *Prevention of Offspring with Hereditary Diseases.* It required the sterilization of the mentally handicapped, the mentally ill, repeat criminal offenders, physically disabled, people with epilepsy and Huntington's chorea, and so on.[79] Hitler wrote, "The *volk*ish state must see to it that only the healthy beget children … Here the state must act as the guardian of a millennial future … It must declare as unfit for propagation all who are in any way visibly sick."[80]

Next came the killing of "impaired" children in hospitals and the killing of "impaired" adults, mostly collected from mental hospitals.

78 For a history of the Holocaust, see Hilberg, *The Destruction of the European Jews.*

79 Taulbee, *War Crimes and Trials*, 60.

80 Cited in *Lifton, The Nazis Doctors*, 22.

The murders occurred in centres equipped with carbon monoxide gas. This program was extended in the same centres to "impaired" inmates of concentration and extermination camps. Then commenced the mass killings, mostly of Jews, in the extermination camps. By 1941, senior Nazi officials began issuing stronger and stronger directives to not only kill Jews but to kill *all* Jews.

To understand the active participation of doctors, consider what the physicians did at Auschwitz. Although doctors presided over the murder of one million victims, the thousands of official Auschwitz documents fail to use the word "kill" or "killing." Instead the term "euthanasia" was commonly used – incorrectly – to cover over the harsh reality.

Doctors selected who would live or die as people arrived at the camp or later in the camps. They supervised the killing in the gas chambers and decided when the victims were dead. They sent to the gas chambers terminally ill people and people with contagious diseases. They directed or carried out the direct killing of debilitated people on the medical blocks through phenol injections into the bloodstream or into the heart. They signed death certificates falsely stating that the victim had died from a disease or physical problem. Doctors, such as Mengele, undertook research and medical experimentation on camp inmates without permission and often without the patient's knowledge.

Doctors consulted regularly on how to keep the selections running smoothly and how many people to keep alive to fulfil the slave labour requirements of the I.G. Farben operations at Auschwitz. They planned the burning of corpses so as not to strain the camp's crematorium. In making the selections, they literally had god-like power over life and death. This omnipotence appealed to sadists like Mengele who would walk the selection ramp with a riding crop in hand, shouting "left" or "right" – to the gas chambers or not. When he separated families and members of the families wept and begged for mercy he would brutally beat the pleaders.

What was new about such medicalized killings was not the unethical behaviour of doctors. Throughout history, doctors have been part of state sponsored killings and the mistreatment of people. Soviet Union psychologists claimed that political dissenters were insane and forced them into mental hospitals. CIA-employed psychologists conducted drug and other experiments on unsuspecting patients. Nor was sterilization, eugenics, and the idea of separating "unfit" individuals from the population a new idea. For example, by 1920, twenty-five states in the United States had laws for compulsory sterilization of the criminally insane and other people regarded as genetically inferior. Leading German physician advocates of "racial hygiene," such as Fritz Lenz, would complain that their country lagged behind American systems of sterilization.

What was new was the scope and systematic nature of the killings, amounting to genocide, and involving many levels of society. For perhaps the first time, doctors had a central role in the planning, staging, and execution of a genocidal project based on a (false) biomedical model of racial hygiene. For doctors to willingly, and often enthusiastically, join the killing teams meant their fascist minds were irrational. But how did this come about, psychologically?

Biocracy

> The Führer holds ... the duty of the physician is or should be one of racial leadership.
>
> Martin Bormann, Hitler's personal secretary[81]

The goal of National Socialism under Hitler was biocracy.[82] A biocracy is a secular, biological version of theocracy. A theocracy is rule by priests who claim an absolute divine right to power. A biocracy is rule by a (presumed) biologically superior race of men, especially their rulers. Nazi biology contained the idea of purity of blood, and the idea of eliminating inferior human types. The biological language of contamination, disease, and degeneration is extended to politics and the health of the nation. This promiscuity of ideas supported Nazi genocide rhetoric.

None of this Nazi racial biology had scientific validity. But in an era of eugenics, social Darwinism, cultural discontent, and nationalism the ideas attracted many people already predisposed to dislike Jews, Roma, Blacks, and other minorities. Nazi racial theory contained three concepts that spoke to a frustrated German populace. (1.) The idea of a national *cure*: Aryan Germans are a master race but, presently, they are an organism that is ill, or diseased, and a cure must be found. The cure is a purification and revitalization of the Aryan race. The nation is so ill that

81 Lifton, *The Nazi Doctors*, 22.

82 Ibid., 17.

the cure must be total, all or nothing. (2) The idea of a *great aim*: The cure is a means to something transcendent – a strengthening of a master race whose great nation dominates the world, creating a new human. Biocracy was a means to a "mission of the German people on earth."[83] (3) The idea of *killing as therapeutic*: Killing "inferior" humans is a means to the renewed organic health of the German nation.

Medical imagery was used repeatedly in Nazi speeches and volkish propaganda. A Nazi poster showed Hitler in a white doctor's coat, a stethoscope in his pocket, with a legend describing him as physician to a diseased nation.[84] In *Mein Kampf*, Hitler states, "Anyone who wants to cure this era, which is inwardly sick and rotten, must first of all summon up the courage to make clear the causes of this disease."[85] Jews were agents of "racial pollution" and "racial tuberculosis" and parasites causing sickness, degeneration, and death in the host countries. They were the "eternal bloodsucker," "vampire," "germ carrier," "people's parasite," and the "maggot in a rotting corpse."[86] The cure, then, must be radical.

Some people think of Nazi ideology as a form of social Darwinism. But the Nazis rejected much of Darwin's theories and went further than the social Darwinians. The Nazi regime disliked the Darwinian idea that all humans – white, Black, Christian, or Jew – evolved from a common ancestry, as that theory threatened the idea of a unique, master race. Also, Darwin's ideas do not entail that a superior species, however defined, will survive in the future. Often what species survives under natural selection is due to chance mutation and fortuitous adaptation, not a matter of racial superiority or manly strength. Moreover, what the Nazis wanted was control over human evolution itself. They wanted to replace God or nature as the entity that selects and shapes the future of the human race. The Nazis wanted control over life and death, over the evolutionary process itself, over the biological human future.[87]

From the beginning, the crude Nazi biology of breeding implied the elimination of certain polluting species. Heinrich Himmler compared the task of Nazi leadership to the task of the "the plant-breeding

83 Hitler, *Mein Kampf*, 397–8.
84 Robins and Post, *Political Paranoia*, 276.
85 Hitler, *Mein Kampf*, 435.
86 Ibid., 150, 300–8, 312–13.
87 Lifton, *The Nazi Doctors*, 17.

specialist who, when he wants to breed a pure new strain from a well-tried species that has been exhausted by too much cross-breeding, first goes over the field to cull the unwanted plants."[88]

We can explain Auschwitz in many ways. We can focus on the sadism of the camp leaders and guards, and we can look at the bureaucratic methods of killing which helped to depersonalize the murdering.[89] But these causes are insufficient to explain the doctors' conduct or psychological adaptation to the camps. Lifton's interviews with Nazi doctors reveal that they saw themselves as part of the healing practice of medicine. They were killing to preserve life. As one doctor stated, "Out of respect for human life, I would remove a gangrenous appendix from a diseased body. The Jew is the gangrenous appendix in the body of mankind."[90]

Doubling Up: "A Fidelity to Evil"

Lifton provides a piece to the psychological puzzle of how the doctors coped. He directs our attention to a basic human capacity when faced with difficult moral decisions. It is called "doubling." Doubling, he says, facilitated genocide.[91]

Doubling, for Lifton, is the human capacity to divide the self into two functioning wholes so that a part-self can act as the entire self, even as the part-self "disavows" the other. Doubling indicates that a person is under serious psychological stress and moral discord caused by immersion in an extreme environment where they must make a decision to do evil or not. Divided within themself, the person faces a mental and moral meltdown. So, the person separates the warring elements within their psyche. The result is two selves. One self is the ordinary, decent self who is a parent, a professional, a community supporter. This self follows accepted moral principles. The other, second, self is forged in

88 Cited in Krausnick, *Anatomy of the SS State*, 14.

89 Killing by gas chamber is, relatively speaking, more impersonal than soldiers killing Jews face-to-face. Nazi doctors had noted that soldiers on the eastern front who directly killed Jews became mentally ill. This was one argument for gas chambers.

90 Cited in Lifton, *The Nazi Doctors*, 16. Also see Lingens-Reiner, *Prisoners of Fear*, 1–2.

91 Lifton takes his idea of doubling and the human desire for immortality from psychologist Otto Rank. See Rank, *Beyond Psychology*, and Lifton, *The Nazis Doctors*, 418, 466.

the heat of an extreme situation. It is a self that is willing to act unethically. It is our dark side, ready for "fidelity to evil."[92] This self makes a Faustian bargain. It agrees to do things that the prior, decent self would repudiate. In return, the person survives (and perhaps prospers in) the extreme environment. The second self takes control and rationalizes its evil ways.

Doubling is a universal human capacity. William James, in his *The Varieties of Religious Experience,* discussed the phenomenon of the "divided self" – people who have "an incompletely unified moral and intellectual constitution." He quotes from French novelist Alphonse Daudet's *Notes sur la Vie*:

> "Homo duplex, homo duplex!" writes Alphonse Daudet. "The first time that I perceived that I was two was at the death of my brother Henri, when my father cried out so dramatically, 'He is dead, he is dead!' While my first self wept, my second self thought, 'How truly given was that cry, how fine it would be at the theatre.' I was then fourteen years old."[93]

The duality of the human mind is part of German philosophical and literary traditions.[94] Goethe, in *Faust,* writes, "Two souls, alas, reside within my breast. And each withdraws from and repels its brother."[95] There is Robert Louis Stevenson's *The Strange Case of Dr. Jekyll and Mr. Hyde* and Dostoevsky's novella *The Double.* Today, with more than a century of psychoanalysis behind us, it is common for psychologists to talk of troubled individuals as divided.[96]

Doubling can be adaptive and important, such as when a combat soldier needs to arouse his most fierce instincts to kill others. But it can also become unrestrained evil, overtaking the decent, prior self from within until it speaks for the whole person. It can also link up with narcissism and other abnormal tendencies.

92 Lifton, *The Nazi Doctors,* 428.

93 James, *The Varieties of Religious Experience,* 173.

94 Lifton, *The Nazi Doctors,* 428.

95 Goethe, *Faust,* part 1, 40.

96 See, for example, Ronald D. Lang's account of schizophrenia as the outcome of a divided self. It is the tension between two personas within us: our authentic, private identity and the false sane self that we present to the world. Interestingly, Lang thinks that, in many cases, it is our modern world that is irrational, not individuals. See Lang, *The Divided Self.*

How does doubling apply to the Nazi doctors? The doctors were immersed in the extreme, death-haunted, environment of the extermination camp. Even if they were Nazi supporters, they could not, psychologically, avoid the impact of life-and-death decisions that they had to make every day nor eliminate the experience of direct killings of disabled people and children. They had the constant reminder of the gas chambers and the smoke (and smell) from the crematorium. Supporting such evil conduct was a visionary Nazi ideology, collectively affirmed and associated with calls for utmost loyalty to the volk. It was supported by the collegiality of the doctors after the day's killings were over, as they shared their loyalty over heavy drinking. Their drinking numbed the feelings but did not entirely eliminate the images of the day's work. The fact that doctors could play God – or they could be God acting like a doctor – was satisfying to subconscious power-seeking impulses, and it stimulated narcissistic doctors such as Mengele. For others, it must have been an incredible feat of psychological self-delusion to avoid the reality of their actions. Upon going home after the war, when their prior self would re-emerge, the psychic dissonance must have been, perhaps late at night, unbearable.

What changed in doubling was not the reality of the camp but the meaning of that reality. Selections were interpreted as a necessary healing of the nation. Killing was therapeutic and life-giving, and murder was not murder, it was euthanasia. In a strange dialectic, doctors probably kept both selves in operation. A doctor needed his Auschwitz self to function in the camp, and he needed his ordinary self to maintain his image of himself as physician, husband, and a decent person. This schizoid dialectic took a mental toll on the person but, in an extermination camp, some doubling – some "dissolving of psychic glue"[97] – was required to avoid a complete mental meltdown.

It has been said that Nazi individuals skillfully avoided guilt and conscience. Perhaps it is better to say that conscience was transferred to the rationalizations of the Auschwitz self. The Auschwitz self did the dirty work and provided the requisite rationalizations. Conscience was given new priorities: absolute patriotism to Germany, duty to ideology, and professional cooperation with other doctors in one's camp.

97 Lifton, *The Nazi Doctors*, 422.

The Erotic Absolute

How to explain the monstrous strength of the people's allegiance to Nazi ideology?

One key factor was the erotic absolute: humans channel their energies towards one, absolute ideal. The herd mentality of authoritarianism is caused by a masochistic excitement generated when people prostrate themselves, submissively, to an absolute power – a God, a führer, a guru, a dictator, a utopian goal.

The attraction to one ideal contains a powerful impulse to obey or to require obedience. There is a felt eroticism in the act of submission. This submission, as the grand inquisitor noted, allows individuals to escape from their freedom – and such people enjoy the submission. German totalitarianism excited this attraction to the erotic absolute: the submission to an apocalyptic, religious-like, goal – the German master race. This is erotic political absolutism.

Erotic absolutism occurs in many places.

Stanley Kubrick's 1971 dystopian crime film *A Clockwork Orange* is set in a future England.[98] Alex and his Droogs spend their nights getting high at the Korova Milkbar. Then they set out to do "a little of the old ultraviolence," while warbling "Singin' in the Rain," forever changing people's mental image of that happy song. Jailed for bludgeoning to death the wealthy Cat Lady with a phallic sculpture, Alex agrees to behaviour modification techniques so as to be set free. He is conditioned to abhor violence. He returns to a violent, sadistic world defenceless, and attempts to commit suicide by jumping out of a window. He awakes in a hospital to find himself no longer averse to violence and sex. Alex thinks about violent acts and imagines himself having sex with a woman in front of an approving crowd. He says to himself, "I was cured, all right!"

In Orwell's *1984*, O'Brien, a member of the Inner Party, spies on and arrests Winston Smith for thoughts of rebellion against Big Brother. During Smith's interrogation, an attempt to make Smith love Big Brother, O'Brien explains that the basis of Big Brother's authoritarian system is sadism – enjoying the process of making other people suffer and submit. "The intoxication of power," says O'Brien, "the thrill of

98 The film is based on a novel with the same title by Anthony Burgess, published in 1962.

victory, the sensation of trampling on the enemy who is helpless. If you want a picture of the future, imagine a boot stamping on the human face – forever."[99]

In 1940, Arthur Koestler's novel *Darkness at Noon*[100] appeared after Stalin's Great Purge of 1936–38 and the Moscow Trials. At the trials, revolutionary communist heroes and party supporters were accused of participating in a conspiracy against Stalin and the Soviet Union. During the purge, millions died or were sent to the Gulag.[101]

Koestler, a former journalist and communist, cannot help but ask what was the attraction of communism? In my terms, a good part of it was the erotic absolute where three powerful urges came together: a complete theory of meaning for life in difficult times, a high moral aim – justice for much-abused working people – and a sadistic–masochistic bowing down to sadistic leaders and following the party without question. These three things, so vital to human psychology – meaning, justice, and order – lifted a moral burden off individuals. They no longer had to make individual judgments or question orders. Adopting Sartre's "bad faith,"[102] they justified what they did by appealing to something external, such as the unstoppable march of history described by their totalizing ideology.

Ideologically, Communist theorists used an extreme rationality (or rationalization) to justify any means that helped to realize a communist society. It was a moral gamble: One bets that, in the future, a great classless society will look back and absolve the immoral actions that made it possible.[103] It did not turn out that way. All bets were lost. Sadism, power-seeking, paranoia, and other all-too-human factors perverted the implementation of the pure ideology. Communist Marxists, those great critics of capitalist ideology, turned out to be among the world's greatest abusers of ideology. As the main character in Koestler's

99 Orwell, *1984*, 350.

100 Koestler, *Darkness at Noon.*

101 The Moscow trials were a series of three Stalin-ordered show trials between 1936 and 1938 against Trotskyists and members of Right Opposition of the Communist Party of the Soviet Union. Dozens were tried, many of them executed. Many were former Bolshevik party leaders and top officials of the Soviet secret police. Most defendants were charged with conspiring with Western powers to assassinate Stalin and other Soviet leaders, break up the Soviet Union, and restore capitalism.

102 Sartre, *Essays in Existentialism*, 148.

103 On *Darkness at Noon* and this moral gamble, see Kirsch's "Assassin's Creed."

novel, Nikolai Salmanovich Rubashov, says, "Our principles were all correct, but our results were wrong. This is a diseased century."[104]

In the Moscow trials, innocent defendants admitted that they were guilty as charged. They deserved punishment for betraying the party. Why confess? Why accept the judgment of a corrupt and murderous party? They knew they would be executed, so could fear have been a motive? Did they finally succumb to endless interrogations? Were they protecting others? Perhaps they remembered their guilt in committing other atrocities, prior to and not associated with their formal charge. I conjecture that, in at least some cases, the erotic absolute was again doing its eerie, covert, psychological work. At least some of the accused were still controlled by a deep, subconscious need to belong to something great – something absolute – and to follow orders. Moreover, to oppose the party, at this point, would have made everything they did and lived for a mirage. Better, it seems, to continue to follow the myth of the great party. Significantly, Rubashov, in his final statement to the trial judge, after admitting to his charges, asks what he is dying for. "Absolute nothingness" confronts him. "There is nothing for which one could die, if one died without having repented and unreconciled with the Party and the Movement. Therefore, on the threshold of my last hour, I bend my knees to the country, to the masses and to the whole people."[105]

Whatever the reason, the moral is beware of complete theories of life, absolutely proclaimed. Beware of "ends justifies the means" reasoning. Beware of ideologies that ask you to eliminate your personal conscience and hand over your judgment to the whims of a powerful leader and his party. Beware of your vulnerability to ideas that give you some meaning in life. Beware of feelings of guilt and the lurking attraction of the erotic absolute.

Now, let us return to Hitler's Nazism. Here the psychological attractiveness was due to the convergence of three psychological tendencies: (1) *power*: a desire in humans to assert their life power; (2) *erotic arousal*: the arousal (often unconscious) of the willingness to obey absolute leaders and ideas or to be an absolute leader; (3) *seeking utopia*: the ancient millennial promise of an apocalyptic project of world

104 Koestler, *Darkness at Noon*, 52.
105 Ibid., 199.

significance.[106] The yearning for the erotic political absolute is part of the Nazi state of mind. As Rosenberg said about Nazi Germany, people were ready to march in a column to anywhere, as commanded.[107] If the people were ready to march like automatons, the Nazi party had lots of help, such as Nazi sympathizer and propagandist film maker Leni Riefenstahl. She produced the infamous *Triumph of the Will* on the 1934 Nuremburg rally. People like Riefenstahl made fascism fascinating and erotic in its absoluteness.[108]

I believe many Nazi doctors succumbed to the lure of the Nazi erotic absolute. Being a Nazi was both masochistic and sadistic. Sadistically, Nazi officers and doctors enjoyed the assertion of their power over life and death, combined with the erotic-tinged, masochistic obeying of Hitler, a father figure. Such enjoyment was triggered by specific causes that we have discussed above, such as frustration with German culture. The erotic absolute made Nazism attractive to educated Germans, even if they disliked the Nazi thugs and were sceptical about Nazi's "scientific" racism.

The erotic absolute, in many cases, speaks to the desire for immortality. Many people seek immortality by having children who will live on after them, by creating lasting social reforms or new institutions, by creating works of art, by writing philosophy books, and so on. Some seek it in being part of a grand political movement. Recall that O'Brien in *1984* declares the eternal hatred embodied in the party outlives the mere individual. "The Party is immortal." Similarly, the Third Reich gave frustrated Germans a chance to participate in a great historical movement. Nazism promised revolutionary immortality in the millennialism of the Third Reich. The Nazi yearning for the erotic absolute merged with apocalyptic millennialism, to the point of psychosis.

106 Psychoanalysts like William Reich attributed fascism to sexual repression. But fascism cannot be explained by sexual repression alone. See Reich, *The Mass Psychology of Fascism*, especially chapters 1 and 2.

107 Rosenberg said that the new German style "is the style of a marching column, no matter where, or to what end, this marching column may be directed." Cecil, *The Myth of the Master Race*, 147.

108 American writer Susan Sontag rips apart the tissue of lies and excuses that Riefenstahl made about her role in popularizing Nazism – her lame half-truths, which she recycled up to her death in 2003. She even claimed that *The Triumph* was apolitical – purely an artist's attempt to create works of art. A debasing of the slogan "Art for art's sake." See Sontag, "Fascinating Fascism."

Hitler's own apocalyptic psychosis was so deep that we can ask whether, in his final days, Hitler sought a *Gotterdammerung* that would destroy his own country. From his bunker, Hitler began ordering the demolition of all industrial, transportation, communications, and supply facilities. Thousands would have been killed if his orders had been obeyed. It would have been a totalizing fire to dramatically mark his death and the end of his hopes for the German people.

His yearning for apocalypse – an insane bonfire for his vanity – failed only because Albert Speer and others intervened.[109]

109 See Speer, *Inside the Third Reich*, 444–60.

8

Paranoid Tribes

Paranoia strikes deep
Into your life it will creep
It starts when you're always afraid
Step out of line, the men come and take you away

"For What It's Worth," Buffalo Springfield[1]

PARANOIA IS AN UNDERRATED CAUSE of social conflict and irrationality even though it has contributed to almost every murderous leader and every murderous mass movement of the twentieth century. A substantial percentage of the public regard paranoia as a strange mental illness of individuals in mental institutions and hospitals. What is not appreciated is how many paranoid people – we can call them functioning paranoids – walk the streets of our cities, work next to us in offices, direct institutions, and lead governments.

Paranoia, at varying levels of intensity, affects political and military leaders, foreign policy decisions, and religious gurus. Social paranoia, the paranoia that infects groups, is a constant danger for democracies and the global community. Leaders use conspiracy theories to induce paranoia among groups and promote violence.

Paranoia as a factor in irrationality has been lurking in the text of previous chapters. In this chapter I draw it out from the shadows. I shine a light on paranoia-in-society.

1 "For What It's Worth," a protest song by the rock band Buffalo Springfield, 1966.

SECTION 1: PARANOIA'S KEY ELEMENTS

Definition

Paranoia is typically classified as a form of narcissism. It is a mental disorder characterized by (1) persistent delusions of persecution or grandeur; (2) the projection of intense and upsetting feelings on to others; and (3) a grave, reality-averse suspicion of others, especially strangers, who become the paranoid person's persecutors or enemies. These strangers are constantly plotting against him. They do not realize his greatness. This makes vigilance, the discerning of conspiracies, and hostility a necessity. The paranoid lives in a world of suspicion, enemies, and constant danger. He is the central character in a dark drama.

The paranoid's suspicion of others causes hyper-alertness to the environment. Robbins and Post describe the paranoid: "Like a submarine on patrol in hostile waters, its periscope constantly scanning the horizon for the enemy, the paranoid searches constantly for subtle clues of danger."[2] The paranoid sees the other as not just a rival or competitor but an enemy that deserves to be opposed aggressively. The paranoid operates with a distorted image of the other, constructing a "pseudo-community" of enemies.[3] Why is paranoia associated with narcissism? Because the paranoid has a dominant, ego-centric view of life. Everything has meaning only in reference to the paranoid and their ego. The paranoid rejects evidence that he is *not* the object of conspiracy because of his narcissism. It is better to be the centre of a conspiracy than to be ignored, to be unimportant, to be a nobody.

How does the paranoid construct an enemy? I will have a theory on this matter in upcoming chapters. For now, we can focus on the mechanism of projection. Humans frequently project onto others the negative feelings they have about themselves, such as their faults, their conflicting emotions, their shameful sexual feelings, and weaknesses. These feelings can be caused or enhanced by bad parenting, disappointments in life, and rejection by friends and colleagues. The paranoid personality begins in individuals with deep psychological conflict, a conflict so strong it must seek relief. Relief is accomplished by externalizing these

2 Robins and Post, *Political Paranoia*, 7.

3 Cameron, "The Paranoid Pseudo-Community."

traits. It is not me but the other person who is weak or aggressive; it is not me but other people who have aberrant sexual desires. Projection, then, is a way to deal with psychological dissonance. Our intolerance and hate towards ourselves becomes an intolerance and hate towards others. If suspicion is the hallmark of paranoia, projection is one of its main mechanisms.

Projecting negative feelings onto specific groups is another way to externalize conflict. A group, rather than an individual, is the object of my projection. Consider the conflicted individual who is psychologically overwhelmed by conflict. Life lacks a meaning, and his insignificance is offensive to his narcissistic element. Such a person is emotionally desperate for some answer or explanation of his plight. At this point, ideologies, conspiracies, and paranoid depictions of strangers enter the psychological drama. Such a person is vulnerable to manipulation. He is told by leaders, demagogues, and ideologues that his troubles – in fact the trouble with his whole society – are due to the malevolent influence of other groups, like Jews, communists, homosexuals, Blacks, immigrants, or elites. Not only do these messages provide an external explanation for one's troubles, they suggest a solution: kill, attack, harm, repress, discriminate against, or otherwise deal with these enemy groups. Meanwhile, individuals get caught up in groups that share these beliefs and feelings. The emotional contagion of the group validates the person's projections. In the long run, group paranoia can lead to extreme tribalism.

Social paranoia becomes political paranoia when this mindset treats political rivals as conspirators and enemies. Leaders use paranoid messages to spark a crusade against dangerous or unpatriotic groups.

In the seventeenth century Blaise Pascal, that sharp observer of mankind, recognized the reality of projection and the anger it produces.

> Man would fain be great and sees that he is little … would fain be perfect and sees that he is full of imperfections … The embarrassment … produces … the most unjust and criminal passions imaginable, for he conceives a mortal hatred against that truth which blames him and convinces him of his faults.[4]

4 Pascal, *Pensées*, 67.

One does not have to be insane to be paranoid. Mental disorders come in degrees of intensity and debilitation. In 1912, English psychiatrist Bernard Hart published what would become a popular textbook on the psychology of the insane. Interestingly, he argued that the irrationality of the normal citizen and the insane is a difference in degree.[5] The insane person's irrationality is just more obviously in conflict with reality than the irrationality of ordinary people. Both entertain weird beliefs. Yes, the insane are more resistant to counterfacts, but, Hart adds, the supposed sane sectarian in political life is also resistant to counterargument.[6]

Phantom Terrors

Paranoia and fear have a long history. As noted earlier, citizens of the Roman Empire suspected the early Christians of constantly conspiring against the state. The Inquisition would stir up group paranoia against Jews and heretics. Tudor England (1485–1603) was a period wracked by political paranoia. It had a mania for conspiracy theories. Leaders were constantly on guard against real or perceived traitors. Smith's *Treason in Tudor England: Politics and Paranoia* shows how paranoia seeped into all layers of society; fathers advised their sons, "Love no man: trust no man." Georges Lefebvre's *The Great Fear of 1789* deals with the paranoia, panic, and social chaos in rural France caused by the revolution and by exaggerated fears that the aristocracy would return to power. Adam Zamoyski in *Phantom Terror* describes how, after Napoleon was defeated, the leaders of European states kept people in line by evoking the fear that the terrors of the French Revolution would return.[7] Paranoia was rampant in Stalin's Russia and in the enemy-is-near mentality of US president Richard Nixon.

Conspiracy!

Conspiracy theories sustain paranoia. They are called theories because of their speculative nature. Often, they amount to no more than an exaggerated fear.

5 Hart, *The Psychology of Insanity.*

6 Ibid., 98.

7 Zamoyski, *Phantom Terror,* xiii.

A conspiracy theory is an explanation that posits an unusual or unlikely cause of an event without strong evidence. There exists, for instance, some sinister conspiracy against the people, who are unaware of such machinations. Maybe communists are poisoning the water supply. Maybe the United Nations is a front for globalists that want a repressive, world government. Maybe a mass shooting at an American school is fake news from a liberal media that wants to remove the citizen's right to bear arms.

Conspiracy allegations gain traction from the fact that conspiracies *do* exist in the world. Tutor monarchs were not wrong to believe there were traitors in their midst. Nations *do* conspire against each other. During the Second World War, the allies conspired to assassinate Hitler. Moreover, most conspiracy theories contain some truth or plausibility. It *is* possible that Kennedy was assassinated by a secret cabal. In the fall of 2018, the Metropolitan Museum of Art (Breuer) in New York City mounted an exhibition called *Everything Is Connected: Art and Conspiracy*. It documented extensive efforts by Americans and artists to reveal government conspiracies against groups and individuals. Many of the conspiracies did exist. Others did not.

Consider Senator Joseph McCarthy speaking in 1951 on the communist conspiracy that was allegedly undermining the United States:[8] "How can we account for our present situation unless we believe that men high in the government are concerting to deliver us to disaster? They [mistaken acts and decisions] cannot be attributed to incompetence."[9]

The defining characteristic of conspiracy theories is *not* that there is no basis for a specific fear or concern. McCarthy's communist "witch hunt" was driven by paranoia *because* there were real dangers to democracy during the Cold War. It was probably true that there were communists in the United States working against the government. The problem was how McCarthy opportunistically took advantage of the tensions of the Cold War to induce paranoia in Americans and to accuse innocent people, far beyond the facts available.

8 On McCarthy, see Wicker, *Shooting Star*.

9 Hofstadter, "The Paranoid Style in American Politics," 23.

In paranoia, the danger is exaggerated, out of proportion to reality. And alternate explanations are dismissed too quickly. Conspiracy theories thrive where there is an absence of facts making it impossible to conclusively prove a hypothesis. This allows alternate explanations to circulate. Most importantly, they thrive where the conspiracy theories support our deep prejudices. The mind is closed, not open, to a full and rigorous review of the facts.[10]

Therefore, a test of a conspiracy theory is whether theory holders allow their hypothesis to come under open, full, and robust evaluation by existing knowledge and by people outside their circle. You know you are dealing with a dubious conspiracy theory when people dismiss inconvenient facts and continue to believe it *against* strong counterevidence.

Another test is whether the theory's investigation amounts to a fixed conclusion in search of evidence rather than a hypothesis open to the test of fact. As Karl Popper stressed, an important feature of objective thinking is seeking to falsify one's hypotheses.[11] The rational person adjusts beliefs to facts; the paranoid, irrational person adjusts facts to fit their beliefs.

There is a troubling and deceptive insincerity among many holders of conspiracy theories when they talk about their love of evidence, as if they were sincerely committed to norms of rational inquiry. Many are not so committed. They are dogmatists for a cause and willing to use shabby methods. They think that simply adding together a convenient fact from here and there amounts to scientific method. There is no need for rigour. One preaches to like-minded people and gets a free pass on tough questions.

In politics, conspiracy theories are popular because they work. A good number of people will believe a falsehood that plays to their biases if it is dramatically presented and repeated over social media. If people intensely dislike Barack Obama, for racial or political reasons, no amount of evidence will persuade them that he is not a Muslim or that he was born in the United States.

Conspiracy theories are irrefutable to those who cling to them. There is little difference in mindset between the medieval person who reads

10 See Rokeach, *The Open and Closed Mind.*

11 Popper, *The Logic of Science*, chapter 4.

portents of a coming apocalypse into unusual natural events and the paranoid person today who reads portents of a coming new world order into statements by leaders. Conspiracy theorizing seems irrepressible, no matter how much we come to know the world, scientifically.

Aristotle's Conspiracy?

One of the strangest conspiracy theories in American history was constructed by political activist, perennial presidential candidate, and fraudster Lyndon LaRouche (1922–2019).

How to sum up this apocalyptic demagogue? One gets dizzy trying to follow his ideological swerves from far left to far right, his career changes, his numerous publications, his organizations, his political initiatives, his harassment of critics, and his crazed conspiracy accusations.

As a young man he started as a Marxist and then became a revolutionary socialist, a Trotskyite, and a labour organizer. Then he became a management consultant and successful businessman.[12] In the 1970s, he started his main far-left group, the National Caucus of Labor Committees (NCLC). The ultimate political aim was to get support from labour unions and overthrow the government. He and his staff also developed an extensive network of international contacts and provided intelligence to governments. He founded the US Labor Party. By the 1980s, he was leading fascistic, antisemitic groups. He ended in prison for fraud. Amid this activity, he ran for president eight times, once from prison. He died at ninety-six.

LaRouche's 1988 biography was entitled *The Power to Reason.* It was a paranoid mind's search for greatness based on a pretense of superior intellect, plus the use of intimidation and unreason. Nonetheless, thousands of Americans joined his movement. Thousands of people voted for him. In his lifetime, he was called a racist, fascist, and cult leader. One of his biographers, Dennis King, said he was a danger to democratic institutions.[13] He is a case study in political paranoia, a nexus of paranoia, narcissism, and megalomania familiar to psychiatry.

12 On how he came to read philosophy, why he became a Marxist, and his work as a management consultant, see his *The Power of Reason.*

13 See King, *Lyndon LaRouche and the New American Fascism.*

Here is a summary of LaRouche's main conspiracy theory.[14] It begins in a most unlikely place – a dispute between two ancient philosophers, Plato and Aristotle, on the nature of truth. According to LaRouche, Plato and his followers believe in absolute or pure truth, which amounts to a belief in certainty and firm standards in the world. Aristotle and his followers believe that truth is uncertain and relative, and therefore they are the opponents of standards. Everything in the world hangs on this conflict. If people do not believe in certainty and pure truth – defined as LaRouche's truth and LaRouche's standards – there can be no progress. Humanity will slip into a self-destructive hedonism.

Where does the conspiracy enter? It begins with the conspiracy of dastardly Aristotelians who, yesterday and today, fool the people with false beliefs. Elite Aristotelians distract people from the truth in order to retain their power and wealth. They promote false doctrines such as moral relativism and psychotherapy. They promote drugs and degraded entertainment such as pornography, jazz, and acid rock. The British musical invasion led by the Beatles was an Aristotelian conspiracy.

For LaRouche, Platonists are men of reason and technology, and they support man's conquest of nature; Aristotelians are men who prevent the advance of reason, technology, and the control of nature. LaRouche dumps every major thinker, economist, philosopher, writer, composer, and statesmen into one of two categories – an advocate of Platonism or Aristotelianism. Among the Platonists are Jesus, Bach, Shakespeare, Leibniz, Franklin D. Roosevelt. Benjamin Franklin, Alexander Hamilton, Abraham Lincoln, and Ronald Reagan. Aristotelians are Hitler, Adam Smith (who apparently encouraged capitalism to spread hedonism), Jeremy Bentham (founder of "hedonistic utilitarianism"), and the entire British empirical tradition from Hobbes to Hume. Aristotelians today include the American Civil Liberties Union, the right-wing John Birch Society, the FBI and the CIA, and, the "master" of the FBI and CIA, the British Intelligence services. Part of the conspiracy is physicist Werner Heisenberg whose uncertainty principle holds that the movement of small units of matter cannot be predicted.

But there is hope: If humans defeat the Aristotelians, they will become perfect and enjoy a reason-based millennium.[15]

14 See Johnson, *Architects of Fear*. Also, see Robins and Post, *Political Paranoia*, 196.
15 Robins and Post, *Political Paranoia*, 198.

Paranoid Megalomania

What is interesting is not whether this theory is true. Any sane person should walk away from this ridiculous theory, its crude analysis of Plato and Aristotle, and its implausible attempt to wedge all thinkers and public figures into two categories. What is interesting is how LaRouche exhibits, in his conduct, the features of a paranoid and narcissistic leader.

To begin with, he conjured up "assassins" from all over the world devoted to killing him. He hired body guards. When people criticized him, his narcissism kicked in, prompting million-dollar libel suits against mainstream media. He instructed his followers to harass critics and write scathing attacks in his publications, such as *New Solidarity*.

In 1983, he moved from New York to a large estate near Leesburg, in Loudoun County, Virginia, where he was protected by guards carrying semi-automatic weapons. Roads were blocked by concrete barriers. Local people who complained about his militia and their weapons were accused of being communists, homosexuals, drug pushers, and terrorists. Incredibly, he accused the Leesburg Garden Club of being a nest of communist sympathizers. Asked why he needed the guns, he replied that without the guns "assassination teams of professional mercenaries now being trained in Canada and along the Mexico border may be expected to start arriving on the streets of Leesburg … If they come, there will be many people dead or mutilated within as short an interval as 60 seconds of fire."[16] Who was trying to kill him? The queen of Great Britain, for one. Also, Zionist mobsters, the Mossad, the US Council of Foreign Relations, the Rockefellers, Colonel Gadhafi, Henry Kissinger, Soviet Union leader Yuri Andropov, and Ayatollah Khomeini of Iran. He was, indeed, a central character in a dark drama.

Perhaps the paranoia and narcissism originated in youth. Born to Quaker parents in Rochester, New Hampshire, his Quaker oath to never fight made him a target of bullies at school, resulting in him spending time alone reading philosophy. Whatever the reason, the narcissism made him insufferably (and, at times, stupidly) arrogant. He said that, when studying at Northeastern University in Boston in the 1940s, his teachers "lacked the competence to teach me on conditions I was

16 Quoted in Matthew Wald, "Man Who Calls Queen a Pusher Worries Town," *Montreal Gazette*, 14 April 1986.

willing to tolerate."[17] He backed Ronald Reagan's Strategic Defence Initiative (SDI) and tried to persuade Soviet Union officials to join the project. When the Soviet Union collapsed, he said it was because the Soviet Union ignored *his* advice on SDI.

His narcissism required grandiose, delusional beliefs about himself. For example, he claimed he was the greatest economist and forecaster ever. He demanded that his followers devote themselves to his movement, shape their marriages according to his wishes, and place their possessions and bank accounts at his disposal. In the 1970s and 1980s, he created an international intelligence-gathering network, and the information was sent to government officials, among others. His political movements, such as the NCLC and then the US Labor Party, could be violent, attacking both right-wing groups and rival left-wing groups. Members took training in self-defence and the use of weapons. Some members underwent brainwashing and "ego-stripping" so they could be shaped into socialist acolytes. By 1977, he moved the US Labor Party from the left to the right. The party, with 1,000 members in fifty offices in the United States, became fascistic – an extreme-right, anti-semitic party.[18] Meanwhile, he made contacts with the Ku Klux Klan, the Nation of Islam, and the far right Liberty Lobby.

What about reason? What ideas issued from his great Platonic mind? A hodgepodge of irrational and socially harmful ideas, pronounced with great certainty and mixed with conspiracy innuendo. In 1976, when Legionnaires' disease broke out in the United States, he said it was a continuation of the swine flu outbreak and senators who opposed vaccination were suppressing the link to the swine flu as part of a "genocidal policy." His presidential platform in the same year predicted financial disaster by the 1980s, accompanied by famine and the virtual extinction of the human race within fifteen years. At a political meeting in 1979, this man of "reason" promised to transform the world through high technology. "We are going to have Manhattan projects and NASA Projects and every dirigiste, Federally-directed, scientific crazed program we deem necessary."[19] He claimed that Ronald Reagan's campaign

17 LaRouche, *The Power of Reason*, 33.

18 On the fascist strain in LaRouche's views, see King, *Lyndon LaRouche and the New American Fascism.*

19 At the opening of the National Democratic Policy Committee, 1979. The political action committee was the agency through which LaRouche campaigned in US elections.

staff in October 1980 conspired with the Iranian government during the Iran hostage crisis to delay the release of the fifty-two American hostages held in Iran, so as to help Reagan beat Jimmy Carter in the presidential election.

In the mid-1980s, he made AIDS a central policy. He treated AIDS like a disease that is easily communicated by casual contact or through insects. This suggested that HIV-positive people were extremely dangerous. He advocated a wide testing of school and health workers and the quarantine of HIV-positive people. His advocacy group PANIC (Prevent AIDS Now Initiative Committee) sought to have AIDS entered on the list of California's communicable diseases. The proposal was put on state election ballots in 1986 and 1988. It failed both times but the proposition received a high of 2 million votes in 1986. He called on government to make him director of an AIDS emergency response unit that would be funded with millions of taxpayers' dollars.

Meanwhile, this man of reason opposed environmentalism. Climate change was a scientific fraud. He opposed the impeachment of President Bill Clinton as a plot by the British Intelligence to destabilize the US government. He argued that the 11 September 2001 terrorist attacks were an "inside job" and an "attempted coup d'etat." Elements within the US sought to start a war against Islam.

Then the roof fell in. After raids on his offices in Virginia and Massachusetts, he was convicted of fraud and tax evasion, and, in 1989, he began serving a long prison sentence. He was released on parole in 1994. Of course, he treated the convictions as a conspiracy against him. For a time, he shared a prison cell with TV evangelist Jim Bakker. Bakker said LaRouche believed the cell was bugged. Bakker said, "To say LaRouche was a little bit paranoid would be like saying that the Titanic had a little leak."[20]

Surveying his controversial public career, we can see how it lines up with our characterization of social paranoia. LaRouche, like many paranoid leaders, begins with a youthful trauma that prompts him to stand apart from everyday social life and friendship, retreating into a world of thinking and growing resentment. At the same time, narcissism, probably a latent trait, develops as a response to the hostile world, ending in delusional and grandiose beliefs about one's greatness. This paranoia–narcissism complex exhibits additional psychological traits

20 Quoted in April Witt, "No Joke," *Washington Post*, 24 October 2004, W12.

which we see in LaRouche: arrogance, difficulty in working with teachers and superiors, fierce rejection of criticism, rejection of conventions as below oneself, and then the development of conspiracy theories to explain a world set against oneself. Finally, this complex finds expression and relief in political action and leadership where it wreaks havoc. He works on people's sense that their world is collapsing and extreme measures by a strong leader are necessary. As is typical, there is no shortage of "facts" and arguments and theory. What is missing is an impartial rationality guided by rigorous method, not philosophical intuitions and abstraction. He demands absolute fidelity of members of the movement. His success was due in part to sadist-masochist traits in society and the attraction of troubled individuals to a leader's certain and emotional explanations, which activates prejudices.

What is different in LaRouche's case is his stress on Platonic reason and his use of philosophical ideas to define a conspiracy. He had the capacity to place events within an abstract, philosophical explanation that attracted people looking for meaning, not critical debate. Yet, this appeal to reason is all smoke and mirrors, created by a troubled mind. In truth, his actions, beliefs, and paranoid mindset show that irrational forces – such as a desire for control and worship by followers – were the actual driving forces in his life and political work.

SECTION 2: GOD'S PARANOID TRIBES

Paranoid irrationality is well known to occur in extreme groups, dominated by leaders demanding complete obedience from members. From outside the group, one struggles to see why people find the leader's charismatic powers and his teachings so persuasive as to completely alter one's life and negate one's freedom. From the inside, the leader is perceived as a holy or inspired person who has special insights into reality and where the world is going. His paranoid and megalomaniacal pronouncements are seen as great truths. Typically, the group is seeking an apocalypse, as a threatening world closes in on them. The group bears the marks of a cult, an insidious form of group irrationality.

On 18 November 1978, hundreds of Americans – men, women and children, members of the Peoples Temple cult in Jonestown, Guyana, on the northeastern coast of South America – died after drinking a cyanide-laced soft drink on the order of their leader, Jim Jones. Jones and his wife also died. About eighty members survived either as defectors or as loyal members at the cult's headquarters in Georgetown, capital of Guyana. Survivors returned to America to an oppressive media blitz and derision from fellow citizens.[21]

Drinking the Kool-Aid: Jonestown

The Peoples Temple saga begins with the charismatic preacher Jim Jones. He was born in 1931 in Crete, Indiana, to a passive father, James, injured by mustard gas in the First World War, and a strong mother, Lynetta Putnam, who ominously said she married to give birth to a "savior."[22]

Jones struggled with a lonely childhood in Depression-stressed Indiana and developed an intense interest in religion, which created a difficulty in making friends.[23] Childhood acquaintances remembered him as a "really weird kid" who was obsessed with religion and death. He was also a voracious reader who studied Stalin, Marx, Mao, Gandhi, and Hitler.[24] Later, in one of his lectures to followers, Jones described his youthful loneliness and anger – a message that connected with his largely poor and neglected followers. "I was ready to kill by the end of the third grade … I was so fucking aggressive and hostile … Nobody gave me any love, any understanding." He complained that his parents never went with him to school events. "Alone, I was always alone."[25]

Although he had a fundamentalist upbringing, Jones moved away from religion as a young person until 1952 when, newly married, he was attracted to the Methodists because of their support for "racial groups." Within months he was a student pastor at a Methodist church in Indianapolis. In the 1950s, Jones, a young Indianapolis minister, preached an unusual blend of the gospel and Marxism. He became known to liberals as an effective Christian activist. He rose up the ranks of society. In 1960, he began his public career as head of the Indianapolis Human Rights Commission. In 1965, Jones moved his church, the Peoples Temple, to northern California, where he was involved in politics

21 For the full story of the Jonestown cult, see Reiterman and Jacobs, *Raven: The Untold Story of the Reverend Jim Jones*, and Guinn, *The Road to Jonestown*.

22 Zee, "The Guyana Incident," 347.

23 Kilduff and Javers, *The Suicide Cult*, 10.

24 Reiterman and Jacobs, *Raven: The Untold Story of the Reverend Jim Jones*, 24.

25 Ibid., 17.

and became a prominent Bay Area leader. He would become the chair of the San Francisco Housing Authority. The *Los Angeles Times* named him Humanitarian of the Year.[26]

But the darkness in his mind had not disappeared.

From the beginning, Jones sought out the vulnerable, the disadvantaged, the confused, and the rejected. Many of his followers were poor, had few personal ties, and had suffered from racial discrimination. They found in Jones "a promise of strength and redemption" while Jones benefited from their attention. He made the transition from a loner to the leader of a group of adoring followers.[27] But by the 1960s, Jones started to struggle with mental problems. He was obsessed with fears and fantasies, extremely suspicious of co-workers, and detected anger and betrayal around every corner. He hired bodyguards. He became riveted on the issue of nuclear war. About 1961, he experienced a horrifying vision of a nuclear explosion and read an article on safest places to be in case of nuclear war.[28] Sometimes, he would cry if he heard an airplane. He tentatively moved to Brazil. The problems were exasperated by his increasing addiction to drugs.

This convergence of factors – private neurosis, a receptive audience of distressed people, and his need to find a safe home – led him to a fateful decision: he announced he would form a therapeutic community in a place far from the threat of nuclear war. It would be a "socialist paradise" and a "sanctuary" from the media scrutiny in San Francisco. The Peoples Temple would "replace corrupt, racist, oppressive societies that were doomed to destroy themselves."[29] There was a promise of faith-healing and a future millennium. However, there is also evidence he left the United States to escape an in-depth investigation into criminal activities by his ministry.[30] Despite allegations linked to the investigation, Jones left California as a figure respected for setting up a racially mixed church that helped the disadvantaged. About 68 per cent of Jonestown's residents were Black. Jones also started to propagate his belief in what

26 See Klineman, Butler, and Conn, *The Cult That Died.*

27 Robins and Post, *Paranoid Politics*, 117.

28 Wright, "Orphans of Jonestown," *New Yorker*, 70.

29 Ibid.

30 It appears that David Conn, an ordinary citizen in California, had obtained information about criminal activities by Jones and had passed the data on to government and four reporters.

he termed "Translation" once they were in Jonestown. He and his followers would die together and move to another planet to live blissfully. To gain such advantages, however, members must turn their property and income over to Jones.

When the government of Guyana allowed his group to settle in an isolated area of the country, Jones and about 1,000 followers created a community in the jungle.

A Totalitarian Town

From the beginning, Jonestown was not going to be just another religious community. It was to be a highly ordered cult. Marital and family bonds were discouraged, and sexual promiscuity was encouraged. Jones humiliated male followers by making love to their wives in front of them. He required women to make themselves sexually available to him. Everyone called him "Dad" and he was to be their primary love object. This was an erotic totalitarian society. Jones maintained control by having spies keep detailed information on members. While members were at services, Jones's loyalists would break into their houses, read their mail, go through their garbage, and examine medical cabinets.[31] Individuals reported dissenters to Jones. Communication with the outside world was forbidden or controlled, with Jones warning about the danger of attacks by outside mercenaries or CIA "fascists." Leaving Jonestown was not allowed and was deemed treasonous.

Gradually, Jonestown began to spiral downward, becoming a fearful environment where Jones grew ever more psychotic. His services were incoherent emotional tirades which exalted his greatness and humiliated his followers:

> You are stupid piss-ants and reptiles, who are lower than the primates … you make your whoopee, while I do something much more significant, because I know exactly what's going to take place. I have made big plans, honey … You fuckers … you don't know how clever I am. I made plans for your treason long ago, because I knew I couldn't trust nothing, only Communism, and the principle that is in me – that's me.[32]

31 Wright, "Orphans of Jonestown," 71.

32 Reston, *Our Father Who Art in Hell: The Life and Death of Jim Jones*, 244.

These offensive services, however, may have brought some members closer together, as they caught the contagion of Jones's "paranoid siege mentality."[33]

Nevertheless, there were serious problems. Internally, Jones faced diminishing conversions, resentment for his dictatorial style, and worries about his increasingly psychotic behaviour and drug use, which included barbiturates and amphetamines.[34] Externally, the outside world was starting to intervene. A few members escaped and raised an alarm. Families of Jonestown members feared for their safety. Congressman Leo Ryan of San Francisco flew to Guyana and toured Jonestown where he met with a number of disaffected members. When they tried to leave, Jones's armed guards, called the "Red Brigade," shot and killed Ryan, three journalists who had accompanied him from the US, and one Temple defector at the airport.[35] *Now,* all of America was paying attention and a full-scale investigation would be launched.

Before Ryan's visit, Jones had staged several fake "loyalty tests" in which members, including children, were gathered and told they were under attack and were to commit suicide by drinking a poisoned soft drink. After Ryan's assassination, almost all of the community including Jones assembled and drank the poisoned drink, freely or through coercion. It was no fake test. Some 909 inhabitants of Jonestown, 304 of them children, died of cyanide-laced, grape-flavoured Flavor Aid, in and around the settlement's main pavilion.

On a taped recording of the suicide, recovered by the FBI, Jones tells members that armed "intelligence" men would "parachute in here on us," "shoot some of our innocent babies," and "they'll torture our children, they'll torture some of our people here, they'll torture our seniors." According to escaped Temple members, children were given the drink first by their own parents; families were told to lie down together. When some members cried, Jones said, "Stop these hysterics. This is not the way for people who are socialists or communists to die. No way for us to die. We must die with some dignity." Jones can be heard saying death is "just stepping over into another plane," and "a friend."

33 Robins and Post, *Paranoid Politics,* 118.

34 Wright, "Orphans of Jonestown," 75.

35 For the story of one survivor of the attack, see Speier, *Undaunted.*

At the end of the tape, Jones concludes, "We didn't commit suicide; we committed an act of revolutionary suicide protesting the conditions of an inhumane world."

Apocalyptic Terrorism: Aum Shinrikyo

On 20 March 1995, seventeen years after the Jonestown cult debacle Aum Shinrikyo, a Japanese apocalyptic cult, shocked the world by releasing deadly sarin gas on five Tokyo subway trains during the morning rush hour.[36] People choked, convulsed, and thirteen died.[37] About fifty-four were seriously injured and perhaps as many as 6,000 were less seriously injured.[38]

It was not the group's first gas attack and not its first act of violence. Since at least the mid-1980s, this fanatical "new religion," led by the charismatic but deranged Shoko Asahara, had been involved in a campaign of escalating violence in Japan, from threating, harassing and kidnapping, to druggings, murders, and now mass murder.[39]

What made the attack especially frightening was that the cult was acting on behalf of their guru and his "vast plan for salvation."[40] Their ultimate aim was to bring the world to an end by prompting an apocalyptic final battle of good and evil, which would leave the guru and a

36 The cult's name means, roughly, "Aum Supreme Truth" or "Aum Teaching of Truth." Aum derives from a Sanskrit syllable. In Buddhism, aum refers to primal forces in the cosmos. It is often used as part of a mantra. In 2000, the organization changed its name to Aleph, a reference to the first letter of the Phoenician, Hebrew, and Arabic alphabets.

37 For a detailed account of the cult, see Kaplan and Marshall, *The Cult at the End of the World: The Terrifying Story of the Aum Doomsday Cult, from the Subways of Tokyo to the Nuclear Arsenals of Russia.*

38 Precise estimates are not available because many victims were reluctant to come forward.

39 There is debate over whether or when to use the negative-sounding term "cult" and replace it with "new religion." In Japan, "new religion" applies to religions established since the late 1800s. They begin with the vision of an ordinary person who borrows ideas from many religions. A cult is not just a new religion. As Lifton states, Aum Shinrikyo is a cult because it exhibited three features: (1) totalistic or thought-reform practices; (2) a shift from worship of spiritual principles to a person – a guru; (3) and the combination of a spiritual quest from below and exploitation (sexual and economic) from above.

40 Lifton, *Destroying the World*, 3.

small band of loyalists standing. The world was so evil that God would help the cult – the pure ones – wipe out almost everyone on the planet. They would re-start civilization and create a utopian society. To this end, the cult had been stockpiling weapons, seeking to purchase a nuclear bomb, and learning to manufacture chemical and biological weapons of mass destruction. The spectre of global apocalyptic terrorism emerged on the world's stage.

Medieval apocalyptic crusaders could only wait for the millennium. This relatively small crusading cult[41] could *actually* force Armageddon to occur.

In July 2018, after two decades in prison and having exhausted all appeals, Asahara and twelve followers were executed by Japan as punishment for the 1995 attack and other crimes. But the volatile mix of paranoid, fanatically religious, and world-hating followers remains a threat.

Seeking the Erotic Absolute

At the centre of this irrational cult was Asahara, yet another charismatic leader who was paranoid, violent, and megalomaniac. Yet another man frustrated in early life, now lusting for power and greatness and perhaps immortality; yet another man able to disguise his power-seeking beneath holy visions that attracted confused disciples ready to prostrate themselves before the erotic absolute.

Like Jones, Asahara was charismatic and paranoid. He "saw dark conspiracies everywhere promulgated by Jews, Freemasons, the Dutch, the British royal family, and rival Japanese religions."[42] Despite paranoia, Asahara, like Jones, was able to work at a high intellectual level. Like Jones, he was a skilled con man, adapt at lying, fraud, and deception, taking a sadistic pleasure in controlling others. Like Jones, Asahara would retreat into psychosis when the environment threatened. But, unlike Jones, Asahara struck back at the world.

41 In the mid-1990s, Aum Shinrikyo claimed 10,000 members in Japan, 1,400 in Russia, and a handful in West Germany, Sri Lanka, and the United States. Between 1990 and 1995, it staged at least fourteen chemical and biological attacks of varying size and impact. Current estimates of the size of its successor, Aleph, range between 1,000 and 1,600 members, mainly in Japan.

42 Goldwag, *Cults, Conspiracies, and Secret Societies*, 15.

In 1955, Asahara was born Chizuo Matsumoto, the sixth of seven children, to an impoverished family in Yatsushiro, Kumamoto, one of Japan's southmost main islands. Afflicted with congenital glaucoma, he had no sight in one eye and impaired vision in the other. His parents sent him to a school for the blind until he was twenty. In a school for the totally blind, he used his partial vision as an advantage, to become a dominant and violent student, resentful of failure. By then he already with a few followers. He said he wanted to be the prime minister of Japan.

After school, Asahara worked as an acupuncturist and masseur in Tokyo while immersing himself in the revolutionary writings of Mao Zedong. He started a lucrative Chinese pharmacy. He would marry and have twelve children.

How did Asahara find religion? In his writings, he says that one day he came psychologically to a turning point, asking what living was for: "Is there anything absolute, does true happiness really exist in the world? … [M]y soul was looking for enlightenment." He "awoke … the desire to seek after the ultimate, the unchanging." Then, Asahara gives this poignant tale a megalomaniac's twist: He characterizes his spiritual journey as the overcoming of many obstacles, "discarding everything." And, he adds, this required "great courage."[43] He says he spent eight years on the road to enlightenment – a tale that no doubt resonated with new acolytes who themselves were searching for the ultimate. Any ultimate.

In 1981, at twenty-six, he joined Agonshu, one of Japan's most successful new religions. He became fascinated with Nostradamus, a sixteenth-century astrologist and physician who predicted that the world would end in 2000. Asahara was an emerging guru. But in 1982, two years before he founded his own religious order, Asahara was arrested for selling fake medicine. He served a brief jail sentence and went into bankruptcy, which caused humiliation and resentment. He kept reading Mao and Nostradamus and studied fortune telling, Taoist medicine, and mysticism.

In 1984, Asahara began a new religious order, Aum Shinsen no Kai, in his one-bedroom apartment in Tokyo, offering yoga and meditation classes. It would grow into a monkish order. He changed his name from

43 Cited in Lifton, *Destroying the World*, 18.

Chizuo Matsumoto to Shoko Asahara and renamed his group Aum Shinrikyo in 1987. Many lay followers joined. Asahara began to promote himself, appearing on TV and on magazine covers and by visiting famous spiritual leaders such as the Dalai Lama. The yoga practitioner and teacher became a charismatic guru with long flowing hair and beard. He wrote books, such as *Beyond Life and Death* and *Supreme Initiation.* He was invited to lecture at universities. The cult attracted a substantial number of graduates from Japan's elite universities and was called a "religion for the elite."[44] Asahara combined New Age ideas such as empowerment with ancient Hindu and Buddhist mysticism, Nostradamus, and the book of Revelation, which was attractive to young people.

In 1985, at thirty, he had a life-changing vision while walking along the ocean: A deity appeared and ordained him as "the god of light who leads the armies of the gods" in an ultimate war to destroy darkness and bring about a utopian kingdom of spiritually realized people.[45] This excited his latent megalomania. In 1992, he declared himself to be Christ,[46] Japan's only fully enlightened master, and the Lamb of God.[47] His growing belief that his cult must bring on the apocalypse touched on the hope, fear, and paranoia of his followers, while never letting them grow idle. He explained disasters, such as the Kobe earthquake in January 1995 and the decline of the Japanese economy, as signs of bad karma and the coming end of the world.

The Total Cult

As in Jones's group, new disciples of Aum Shinrikyo had to make themselves completely dependent – psychologically and physically – on guru Asahara. They lived ascetic lives, adopting celibacy (despite the guru's non-celibate life). They had to hand over property and income to the guru, separate themselves completely from family, leave their jobs, and live in the cult's facilities. Individuals replaced their name with a Sanskrit name. They renounced the world for a small, closed society.[48] In the

44 Lewis and Petersen, *Controversial New Religions,* 16.
45 Lifton, *Destroying the World,* 20.
46 Snow, *Deadly Cults,* 17.
47 Partridge, *The Re-Enchantment of the West,* 300.
48 Lifton, *Destroying the World,* 24.

facilities, life was spartan: long meditation and breathing exercises, prostration to emphasize one's unworthiness, demanding work, two small meals a day, and irregular sleep. There were violent practices such as immersion in very hot or cold water, hanging by one's feet for hours, and solitary confinement in a small, hot cell with no bathroom. Members endured many types of initiations including drinking (often unknowingly) LSD to induce visions. Members would confess to the cult that they had failed to understand the full meaning of their guru. They would try harder. Leaving the group was difficult and dangerous.

Asahara's megalomania knew no bounds, and it was enhanced by adoring followers. He presented himself as the world's greatest spiritual leader, a combination of Shiva, Buddha, and Christ, and he was, apparently, a genius in almost every field of endeavour. Members even made claims that he had a unique DNA, and his blood had special properties that could be transmitted to disciples who drank it.[49] This megalomania led him to weapons of mass destruction.

Lifton believes the power of the Aum Shinrikyo environment was due to "ideological totalism"[50] where everything is controlled on an all-or-nothing basis. This environment had the following features:

1 *Milieu control*: All information and communication are controlled, so reality is defined by the group.
2 *Mystical manipulation*: The guru, through close associates, uses drugs and other means to induce mystical experiences.
3 *A demand for purity*: In the world and in persons there is absolute division between pure and impure, the good and the bad. Only the guru was pure. The rest of the cult tried perpetually to improve their purity.
4 *An ethos of confession*: Members were continually confessing before others their shame and guilt in not being pure.
5 *Sacred science*: The guru insisted that his ultimate spiritual truths could be proved by science, and such truths formed the ultimate science of human behaviour.
6 *A loading of the language*: The guru and cult twisted words such as "truth" and "defilement" to give them their own cultish meanings.

49 Ibid., 27.
50 Ibid., 25–6.

7 *Doctrine over the person*: All individual beliefs were subordinate to the cult's ideological claims. To doubt the guru was due to the disciple's remaining "defilement."
8 *The dispensing of existence*: The guru and his doctrine determine who has the right to live and those who do not and therefore may be murdered. Like the Nazi doctors, the cult killed to heal, i.e., killing was an altruistic act. In killing, the cult gave the victim a better chance for a higher level of existence upon rebirth. The cult came to believe that no one outside the cult had a right to exist because they were not related to the guru and therefore remained hopelessly defiled.[51]

Within this totalism, disciples found meaning. It could be psychologically exciting to devote oneself to the cult's extreme asceticism, a discipline that gave meaning to unhappy lives.

The Guru and Me

The cult was based on the psychology of guruism – on the totalitarian relationship between a supreme spiritual leader and his disciples. To understand guruism, or secular versions such as the cult of the führer, one begins by embracing a paradox: the guru is both "everything" and "nothing" in this relationship. Everything because it is the guru's charisma, authority, and ideas that control the cult. No guru, no cult. Nothing because the guru is nothing without disciples. The guru is created by the "hunger of his disciples."[52] When some of Asahara's closest associates turned on him as police closed in on the cult, the guru became psychotic because he could not withstand the loss of his source of identity and power: his believers. The guru figure, from Jones to Asahara, needs disciples to hold himself together psychologically. The extreme guru lives on the edge of personal fragmentation, paranoia, and mental meltdown. His fantasy world is both fragile and incredibly resistant. The guru and his believers deeply need each other. Thus, lies the secret to their bond.

The other psychological secret to the cult is their freedom to be radical and unrestrained. For whatever reasons, both the guru and his

51 See Asahara, *Supreme Initiation: An Empirical Spiritual Science for the Supreme Truth*.
52 Lifton, *Destroying the World*, 11.

disciples are unmoored in modernity, adrift from traditional institutions and practices. While this may be stressful, it can also introduce an intoxicating whiff of freedom, a freedom to pursue power, purposes, or resentments long frustrated by society. The guru is free to create whatever theology he wants, without careful scholarship, institutional correction, or external standards. Asahara could warp ancient texts, such as the book of Revelation, to his visions and desires, just as the crusading, non-mainstream preachers did in the West centuries ago. Also, the guru can give his uprooted disciples, cut off from society, any direction he chooses. He becomes a free "floating guru."[53]

British psychoanalyst Anthony Storr describes the guru type as a spiritual teacher who works from personal revelation, perhaps a vision provided by a deity. The revelation, which has transformed the guru's life, usually comes after a period of distress or illness in his thirties and forties. There is suddenly a sense of certainty, of having found the truth. He emits an aura of one who knows. The guru now promises new ways of self-development, new paths to salvation, always based on his own experience.[54]

Asahara was a Japanese phenomenon,[55] but he also used the human universal psychological repertoire of feelings, desires, and motivations plus the long-standing attraction of humans to apocalyptic visions. The fantasy of collective apocalypse is always a temptation for disturbed minds that despise the world so much they feel compelled to destroy it. In destroying it, they express a "desperate quest for immortality."[56] Moreover, as Ian Reader has argued, the Aum phenomenon also draws on the violence inherent in strong religious views – a violence ready to break through. Reader notes how after the Tokyo subway attack almost every critic of Japanese society blamed the attack on his favourite beef with the country – some blamed the education system, the Japanese media, the commercialism of mainstream culture, and so forth. Yet they ignored a more universal feature: a religion that separates itself from the world and treats it as an enemy; a religion that divides the world dualistically into good or bad, contaminated or pure. Such a religion – which we have seen elsewhere in this book – will almost certainly lead

53 Ibid., 12.
54 Ibid., 13.
55 See Reader, *Religious Violence in Contemporary Japan: The Case of Aum Shinrikyo.*
56 Lifton, *Destroying the World*, 9–10.

to, and even encourage, a conflict with the world. Groups like Aum, given their religious beliefs, come into friction with the world and that friction develops into violence.[57] The violent capacities of extreme religion are the same as the violent capacities of extreme politics, and this extremism is defined by an absolute ideology.[58] At the bottom of everything is psychological absolutism: the psychological attraction to absolute forms of religion and thought to resolve deep inner conflicts and uncertainties.

SECTION 3: TOTAL PARANOID SOCIETY

Collective Purification

Irrationality and social paranoia exist outside of cults. The twentieth century gave us the terrible spectacle of entire societies going paranoid and virtually mad. Inhumane but cunning leaders induced paranoia and hatred across entire populations and then sent them on a campaign of merciless, bloody social purification against innumerable "class enemies." Atrocity after atrocity would be justified by a crude consequentialist reasoning that anything was justified if it was a means to the ultimate end – an illusionary, glimmering vision of socialist utopia. The goal was a total remaking of humanity and society through mental and moral slavery to a collectivist, fascistic ideology. And, if ideology was not sufficient for control, there was always terror and torture.

In Germany, Hitler created a Nazi version of collective purification. Socialist leaders after Hitler would attempt similar grandiose social engineering. Their vision was, of course, different: a classless society of equals where everyone's needs were met. But the methods and reasoning were similar. First, there was Stalin's paranoid Soviet Union, and then Mao Zedong's revolutionary China, followed by Pol Pot's Cambodian holocaust, modelled on Maoism. Mao and Pot were the true heirs of Stalinist thinking, not the leaders of the Soviet Union after Stalin died. These three experiments in remaking society not only failed in the long run but killed more than sixty million people. Add Hitler's ten million murders and we are in excess of seventy million people.

57 Reader, *Religious Violence in Contemporary Japan*, 224–49.

58 On the violence embedded in religion, see Rapoport, "Some General Observations on Religion and Violence."

Killing, unfortunately, was not the whole story. In China and Cambodia, Mao and Pol Pot oversaw the repression of minorities, torturous prisons, famine, forced collectivization, cruel public humiliations, the clearing of cities, the robbery (or destruction) of people's property and personal possessions, book burnings, the destruction of churches and temples, the searing pain of families divided, and out-of-control young guards of the state beating up elderly people.

Leaders and their goon squads, trained in cruelty, would turn entire countries into moral wastelands, where mercy, sympathy, and dignity were rejected as weakness or liberalism. Freedom of thought, moral values, and truthfulness were the discredited ideas of the bourgeoisie. Leaders learned to rule by fostering hate among people, by using people's weaknesses. Mao and Pot did not have to organize intelligence units like the KGB. The people *themselves* collectively monitored dissent and attacked the enemies in their mist. All in the name of purifying their culture of foreign or "rotten" influences. The more that soldiers, officials, and the zealous public exercised the forces of dark irrationality within them, they more they grew to like it.

Mao's Not-So-Great Leap

The inhumanity and irrationality of Mao Zedong's utopian project is evident in his catastrophic economic policy the "Great Leap Forward" and then his fascistic cultural project, the Cultural Revolution – both within the first twenty years of his rule.

The Great Leap Forward, between 1958 and 1962, aimed to rapidly increase China's grain production and transform China into an industrial power. The plan was initiated nine years after Mao had stood on the Gate of Heavenly Peace in Beijing and proclaimed the People's Republic of China. There was hope that, after civil war since the 1930s, China would be united and peaceful. Also, many thought a planned socialist economy might eliminate poverty and improve conditions for citizens. Such optimism was quickly squashed. The Great Leap Forward led to the deadliest famine in history and the deaths of between twenty and forty-five million people.

In 1957, Mao predicted that China would surpass Britain in steel production and its grain production would increase dramatically. To double China's steel production in one year, the government encouraged every family to set up a backyard steel furnace to double China's steel production in one year. Families put steel house implements – knives, pots – into the furnaces. It was a farce. Much of the melted-down steel was unusable, and the agricultural harvest suffered from a lack of workers who had been diverted into steel production.

The attempted grain revolution fared no better. By 1958, peasant farmers had formed cooperatives which were integrated into huge communes of 50,000 people. Private ownership of land was abolished. The huge harvests never came, for numerous reasons including Mao's mistaken and unshakable belief that grain seeds should be planted close together. Mao doggedly refused to believe that the program was in trouble. He staged events for cameras that appeared to show strong grain growth.[59] Propaganda that China had surpassed American grain production meant that grain exports were doubled. By 1960, peasants, even in villages close to Beijing, were starving and many were too weak to work in the fields, although state granaries had enough grain to feed everyone. Many committed suicide out of despair. The official line that the harvest was abundant kept the granaries shut to ordinary people. The 1959 harvest was at least 30 million tons less than the previous year's harvest. When told of the loses and the suicides, he remarked, "People who try to commit suicide – don't attempt to save them! ... China is such a populous nation. It is not as if we cannot do without a few people."[60]

In response to the Great Leap fiasco and its political fallout, Mao would launch the Cultural Revolution in 1966. The Leap's failure damaged Mao's reputation. Senior party officials, such as State Chairman Liu Shaoqi and General Secretary Deng Xiaoping, sought to marginalize Mao, making him a symbolic figure or revolutionary theorist. Mao is said to have worried that this new ruling class was distant from the people – a remarkable claim given his uncaring response to the famine. Mao disliked Shaoqi's relaxation of collectivization and liberal measures such as allowing greater freedom of thought. In the end, it seems to have been an old-fashioned battle for power, with Mao seeking revenge on his critics. Mao began the Cultural Revolution, ostensibly, to remove counterrevolutionary elements in Chinese society. He would purge the leadership and the party and destroy their supporters. Lasting ten years,

59 See Becker, *Hungry Ghosts: China's Secret Famine*, 144–5.
60 MacFarquhar and Schoenhals, *Mao's Last Revolution*, 110.

it was a brutal class struggle that killed millions and began Mao's cult of personality.

The idea was to mobilize the young to become a sword of vengeance against landlords, teachers, and established officials – anyone who was of the wrong social class, i.e., not a peasant or proletariat. The youthful Red Guards would lead the charge. In colleges and schools, Maoist student Red Guards were encouraged to denounce their teachers and party officials. Mao began wearing their uniform as he presided over huge rallies in Tiananmen Square. Mao encouraged the young to take apart society and start again.

The tyranny of the arrogant, ideologically blind Red Guards has been documented and recounted.[61] Traditional Chinese culture was attacked, especially the influence of Confucius. The Red Guards destroyed most of the temples in China. Almost all schools and universities were destroyed and young intellectuals living in cities were sent to the countryside to be "re-educated" by the peasants, where they performed manual labour. In people's residences, books and works of art were destroyed. Libraries were ransacked and books burned. The Red Guards felt free to attack anyone – old women, young girls, former teachers. Many of the attacked had to publicly admit (falsely) to being a spy, while enduring cruel and humiliating abuse. Like all totalitarian regimes, the Maoist regime sought to weaken family ties and bonds among friends and colleagues. It encouraged friends to report friends and children to report on their parents. This was the socialist version of the medieval Inquisition. Intellectuals had to publicly apologize for teaching false Western ideas. Hundreds of thousands of people, perhaps millions, perished in the violence of the Cultural Revolution. In August and September 1966, 1,772 people were murdered by the Red Guards in Beijing alone.[62]

When Mao called for a "bombarding of the (government) headquarters," a terrifying incident unfolded. Liu Shaoqi was dragged from his house and his wife was forced to dress up, grotesquely, as a capitalist. His shirt torn open, the head of state was pulled around by his hair, his head brought near to the ground. He was slapped in the face and kicked. Shaoqi was then forced to criticize himself before 10,000 students in

61 See Wen, *The Red Mirror* and Chang, *Wild Swans.*

62 MacFarquhar and Schoenhals, *Mao's Last Revolution,* 124.

the Great Hall of the People while Mao listened, like Stalin would do, behind a curtain. When Mao emerged on stage to thunderous applause, he refused to even look at Shaoqi. The head of state, who had diabetes, developed pneumonia and was initially refused medicine. But Mao's wife insisted he be kept alive for the Ninth Party Congress in 1969, where he was denounced as a traitor. Then he was allowed to die in agony.[63]

The attacks involved unprecedented mass participation, such as jeering at "enemies of the people" at sport arenas. The fierce psychology of the irrational crowd, excited by revolutionary ideology, was one cause, as was the sadistic love of domination and the pleasure of seeing people humiliated.

Throughout this irrational anarchy of dark forces from hell, Mao stood behind the Red Guards' expression of "their indignation" at the exploitation of workers by class enemies such as landlords, capitalists, and their lackeys. He wrote that the exploitation "fully justifies any rebellion against the reactionaries. I am firmly behind you."[64]

Mental Slavery

The Maoist revolution required that people abandon their freedom to think, doubt, and debate. They must abandon rational practices, such as changing a belief when facts showed otherwise. They were required to become rigidly reality averse: to accept reality *as* defined by an absolute ideology protected jealously – because power was at stake – by tyrannical forces of the state. If, under Mao, many Chinese citizens lived like intimidated citizen-slaves in their own country, now they were asked to accept mental slavery. The state social engineers were not satisfied with external conformity to society; they wanted to socially engineer the very thoughts and inward nature of humans through propaganda, terror, torture, and the threat of re-education.

The mental slavery began at the top in Mao's imperial court where few dared to disagree with the socialist leader who lived like an emperor, with his swimming pool and specially made bed and a ready supply of books, especially about Chinese emperors. He was supplied with a steady

63 Zhisui, *The Private Life of Chairman Mao,* 489–90.

64 Letter to the Red Guards, 1 August 1966. In Ch'en, *Mao Papers,* 115.

parade of young women to satisfy his sex drive. He demanded, and received, flattery as a great philosopher and poet, as well as a great leader. Staff had to tell him about each other and repeat their conversations to each other. While lonely and wanting conversation, he also was too paranoid to be close to other leaders or to have friends. His food was tested for poison.

What happened to anyone who tried to question Mao's bulletproof Marxist view of reality is clear from the case of Peng Dhuai, minister of defence. By 1959, Peng was speaking out against Mao's denials of famine. Peng had a heated meeting with Mao where he said Mao was like Stalin, sacrificing people to impossible production targets. Mao then attacked him as an "anti-party element." Peng had to write a self-criticism. He was placed under house arrest. During the Cultural Revolution, he was tortured and killed.[65]

It may be thought that complying with official dogma was simple: verbally and publicly repeat the official doctrines but hold a different set of beliefs inside one's mind. Yet the indoctrination was so constant and invasive that people began to doubt themselves. People started to fear stepping out of line even in their own personal thoughts, banishing questions from their mind.[66] In 1951, China began an effort at "thought reform" directed at Chinese intellectuals and universities. It put psychological and physical pressure on people to change their views. Intellectuals were forced to stand in handcuffs and chains for days, without sleep. Psychological techniques included humiliation, e.g., having to eat with your mouth from a dog's bowl. They were forced to denounce their former ideas. Gradually, exhausted individuals began to accept – if not fully believe – the official ideas, if only to avoid trouble.[67]

One of the most excruciating self-criticisms was that of Professor Chin Yueh-lin, educated at Harvard University and a teacher of formal logic in China. His written confession in 1952 admits to following the decadent philosophy of the bourgeoisie and its "game of concepts." He apologizes for being concerned with the validity of arguments.

65 Glover, *Humanity*, 287.
66 Chang, *Wild Swans*, 359.
67 Lifton, *Thought Reform*, 36–45.

In short, he apologized for being rational and objective. He was a "criminal for having sinned against the people." The mission of a philosophy department, he said, was to train propaganda personnel to disseminate Marxism.[68]

The Maoist approach to the mind is the old doctrine of the blank slate that we discussed earlier. Ironically, while Western intellectuals insisted that the blank slate metaphor best protected our image of humans as free and autonomous, Mao saw the metaphor as indicating that the human mind, or the Chinese people, was ready to be shaped by ideology: "A blank sheet of paper has no blotches, and so the newest and most beautiful words can be written on it, the newest and most beautiful pictures can be painted on it."[69]

Part of the slavery was the destruction of a person's previous moral identity, which stood in the way of full acceptance of propaganda and state actions. The goal was to develop revolutionary citizens who were willing to abandon their former human decency and attachment to truthfulness, mercy, kindness, sympathy, autonomy, and respect for human dignity. Under Mao and the Cultural Revolution, the state set out systematically to discredit such values by saying they originated in liberalism and bourgeoisie society. They were the dreaded values of Communist China's class enemies.

What values should replace sympathy and universal human dignity? The revolutionary values of hardness, the warrior ethic. Also, an unwavering capacity to be cruel, including an emotional detachment from the harm one causes to others, even if they are one's former teachers or neighbours. One's private life and personal feelings – not just one's personal beliefs – were to be changed and controlled creating an amoral citizen. Mao promoted this hardness. He warned followers of the danger of being nice to a "beautiful snake"; he told the Red Guards to "be violent." His slogan was "Mercy to the enemy is cruelty to the people" – a twisting of the meaning of words that we saw in the rationalizations of the Nazi doctors. It has been said that Mao loved continual upheaval by the people because of his "voluntarianism" – his belief that great masses of people could effect great change. But that is not quite the

68 Yueh-li, "Criticizing My Idealistic Bourgeois Pedagogical Ideology." Cited in Glover, *Humanity*, 293–4.

69 Mao Zedong, *Sixty Points on Working Methods*, Internal Party Document, circulated in Beijing, 1958. Cited in Spence, *The Search for Modern China*, 577–8.

whole story. Psychologically, Mao was a paranoid sadist who loved domination and continual destruction. He is probably the best political example of Freud's death instinct, an instinct for destruction. Mao himself lacked the capacity for human feeling and warmth. This incapacity was rationalized as a hardness *only* against the enemy. "We don't object to humanitarianism in its entirety," Mao once told his doctor. "We are simply opposed to practicing humanitarianism on the enemy."[70]

The fanaticism that drove Maoism has been described by Lifton as a desire for "revolutionary immortality."[71] In this view, there is a universal human desire for meaning, vitality, and life, which struggles against death or inner deadness. Individuals desire their life to not only go well on a daily basis but to have some ultimate meaning or purpose. This desire is satisfied by a sense of immortality, by feeling connected to what has come before me and what will come after me. This sense of immortality may be felt by having children or participating in a great social undertaking, such as a revolution. Social revolutions can give members an exhilarating feeling of vitality, power, and meaning. This explains the intensity of the revolution and the willingness to create a cult of the leader. To maintain this vitality and sense of immortality, the revolution must never end but must be perpetual. To keep the revolutionary zeal alive, enemies must be perpetually found and opposed to so as to maintain energy.

These extraordinary psychological factors help to explain the acute amoralism of Mao and his followers and their inhumane calculations of how many might have to die for their cause. Mao, for example, thought that there were about 30 million enemies of the people in China, among a population of 600 million. Mao applied this reasoning, worryingly, to the atomic bomb. In a speech, he said he was willing to lose 300 million Chinese people in an atomic war. Although this was half the population, the country would produce more people.[72] This was the attitude of "dispensing" with human existence seen in the Nazis and the Aum Shinrikyo. To do so, one must be, as Nietzsche prescribed, "hard" and willing to be "birds of prey."

70 Zhisui, *The Private Life of Chairman Mao*, 140.
71 Lifton, *Revolutionary Immortality*.
72 Glover, *Humanity*, 297.

SECTION 4: THE CAMBODIAN HOLOCAUST

The Faceless Leadership

When Pol Pot's Khmer Rouge revolutionaries defeated government troops and entered Phnom Penh in April of 1975, two weeks before the fall of Saigon, one of the world's most secretive, paranoid regimes would take power in the heart of Southeast Asia. While Mao and his Communist officials were brutal and totalitarian, Pol Pot's communists would come to be seen as deranged, dark, and bizarre and, if possible, even more brutal and blood thirsty.

But there was another striking difference: Pol Pot and the Khmer Rouge leadership were not well known to outsiders and they appeared to like it that way. Few pictures of or interviews with Pot existed; he was secretive and avoided the spotlight. There was no cult of the leader, as with Mao during the Cultural Revolution. There were no staged public appearances of a god-like leader acknowledging his adoring followers. There was no little book of Pol Pot sayings. Moreover, it appeared that the Khmer Rouge were led by a group of people in which Pol Pot had an important role but lacked tyrannical rule over senior officials. Khmer Rouge leadership has been called the "cult of nonpersonality" and "collective paranoid leadership."[73]

Pol Pot was born Saloth Sar in 1928 in the northern province of Kompong Thom, a strong Khmer region that was moderate in politics yet opposed to foreign influences.[74] He adopted the nondescript, common name Pol Pot (similar to John Smith) as he became leader of Cambodia. His father would be considered, by Cambodian standards, a rich farmer since he had a reasonable amount of land to farm. Unlike other leaders studied so far, he had, by all accounts, a relatively happy youth. No deep trauma. Rather than work the fields, he was sent to a monastery and then a Catholic school where he was a poor student. At twenty-one, in 1949, he enrolled in a Paris school, then joined the French Communist Party. He formed the Cambodia Communist Party in 1960. From 1967 to his victory in 1975, he fought the French and the pro-American Cambodian governments. In 1969, the Khmer Rouge

73 Robins and Post, *Paranoid Politics*, 253.

74 See Chandler, *Brother Number One.*

numbered only 4,000 but by 1975 there were enough members to defeat government forces. Their victory was helped by the American bombing of the country as an extension of the Vietnam War. The bombings led peasants to support the Khmer Rouge.

Many of the Khmer Rouge soldiers were young, uneducated peasants with a resentment for anything Western or upper class – anything beyond their own narrow experience. As in China, sympathy and humanity was driven out of their character by a "training in cruelty," which included playing cruel games. Many of the soldiers apparently loved to torture cats and small animals. Gradually, soldiers became "addicted to torture."[75]

Some of Pol Pot's colleagues portrayed him as a plodder – self-effacing, hard-working, efficient, but otherwise unremarkable. They underestimated him, and maybe that is what he wanted. Pol Pot had a thirst for power. He was introspective and highly reclusive. He "delighted in appearing to be what he was not – a nameless face in the crowd."[76] He was obviously a skilled organizer off and on the field of battle. He had to be a tough infighter to maintain power within the Khmer Rouge. Like the other leaders we have seen, he was paranoid, haunted by fear of assassination, and had a great fear of being poisoned. This quiet man, we must not forget, was responsible for the holocaust to come, including the murder and torture of at least 12,000 people at Tuol Sleng prison.

He constructed a fascist state with a racist, nationalist, socialist ideology. Khmer Rouge Cambodia showed that a colourless leadership could be as dangerous as a nation led by a strutting führer.

The Madness of Purity

Before Pot's regime ended about two million Cambodians – a quarter of the population – would be killed or would die as a result of Khmer Rouge policies. On a per capita basis, Hitler and Mao do not come close to Pol Pot as a mass murderer. In the past, there had been plenty of foreign and non-Khmer dominance of Cambodia. This helps to explain why the Khmer Rouge attracted members and why the Khmer Rouge were full of hatred. Nor was suspicion (or even a degree of paranoia)

75 See Sihanouk, *War and Hope: The Case for Cambodia.*

76 Short, *Pol Pot: The History of a Nightmare*, 6.

unreasonable if we review the history and politics of Cambodia and surrounding countries. There was plenty of justified suspicion among the leaders of Cambodia, Vietnam, and China. However, under the Khmer Rouge the level of murderous pogroms and the searing hatred exhibited in the killing went beyond all human bounds.

What drove the Khmer Rouge was an unquenchable thirst to purify their country of all non-Khmer influences of any kind. Once in power, the aim of purification would govern all actions. In April 1975, the new government, triumphant, blamed Cambodia's problems on foreign enemies, where "foreign" was interpreted liberally as "non-Khmer." Once again, millennial thinking played a role. The government contended that once contaminating, foreign elements of society – Chinese, Vietnamese, Thai, Western – were eliminated, a perfect society would emerge. It would be a pure Cambodia called Kampuchea (land of the Khmer). Two forces were dominate: a hatred of *everything* non-Khmer (or non-ethnic Cambodian) and an idealization of Khmer culture. Pol Pot declared that Cambodia would isolate itself from the world and its population would become, for the most part, peasants. What was rural was good; what was urban was foreign, Western, and contaminating. This was a call to go back to the land with a vengeance. It was as unrealistic as Paul de Lagarde's belief that modern Germany should once again become a medieval-like land of peasants and artisans.

From the start, it should have been clear to anyone familiar with the complex history of Cambodia, alternating between self-rule and foreign occupation, that this pursuit of a purified Cambodia was impossible. The Khmer had retained their ethnic distinctiveness, but they had integrated many non-Khmer and external influences from the West, from Vietnam, and so on. It was not possible to untangle these influences and isolate a racially pure culture.

The policy of purity soon led to irrational and destructive actions. The decision to make Cambodia a totally agrarian country led to the forced, chaotic evacuation of cities, sending the unprepared population into the countryside to form collectivized farms. In Phnom Penh alone, nearly two million people were evacuated. At the French hospital of Calmette in Phnom Penh, patients were forced to leave the centre and join the crazed exodus.[77] They walked into the countryside with their

77 See Ponchaud, *Cambodia, Year Zero*, 22.

bandages, or they were pushed on beds with their drips still attached. Nearly 10,000 died during the evacuation of Phnom Penh.

Within two months, the population of many towns and cities had been moved, until about 95 per cent of the population were on collective farms. Families were separated, and people were sent into unpopulated areas known for malaria. City folks, without any aptitude for working the land, were asked to be productive peasant farmers. In the forced march into the countryside, many people died or became violently ill due to near-starvation or diseased through lack of sanitation or filtered water.

Like Mao, the Khmer Rouge wanted to totally recreate Cambodia. Khmer Rouge documents often talked about Mao's Great Leap Forward. Pot visited Maoist China in the early years of the Cultural Revolution and was impressed.[78] Like Mao, Pot agreed that the people needed to be re-educated, the family should be undermined through communal living, and citizens had a duty to spy on each other.

So, 1975 was Year Zero, a year to begin the dismantling of foreign influence. Money and private property were banned (as Western and corrupting). The government provided no compensation for the property they took over or for the work that citizens did. It closed schools, monasteries, and churches. Travel, reading, writing, and public entertainment were restricted and even international telephone, telegram, and cable links were cut. International mail was neither sent nor received. Regular airline service ended. The borders were closed and mined. Medicines and pesticides were no longer imported, causing a malaria epidemic. Foreigners found in the country were killed. The killing included not only long-standing enemies such as the Vietnamese but also Indian and Pakistani students and merchants, and American, Australian, British, and New Zealand sailors ashore.

Enmity towards *anything* that seemed to go beyond the rural identity of the Khmer reached absurd heights. Anything that suggested the person was from the upper classes, could lead to death, prison, or discrimination. A person was thought to be non-Khmer if they wore glasses, jewelry, or a watch, if they used a ballpoint pen or had soft hands. Women with long hair were suspected as non-Khmer. The expression of emotions was discouraged and romance had to be approved by

78 See Quinn, "Explaining the Terror."

the authorities. As usual, language was twisted. When people were taken to a place to be executed, officials used euphemisms such as asking them to "help us collect fruit" or "to come with us for further study."

Many Cambodians were not fooled. The phrase "Angka (the Khmer Rouge) kills but never explains" became popular.[79]

Rotten and Dirty

This xenophobic regime used the promiscuous language of cleanliness and rottenness to explain irrational policies. Money, eyeglasses, and telephones were dirty and to be eliminated. A Khmer Rouge radio broadcast summarized Cambodian history as such: "For thousands of years the colonialists, imperialists, and reactionary feudalists have dragged us through the mud. Now with victory … we will smell good again."[80] Enemies were "rotten fruit" that spoiled the entire basket of fruit. One report, probably by Pol Pot, said there was a "sickness inside the Party." Enemies were "microbes" that the party would locate and eradicate.[81] A popular slogan on radio shows and at Khmer Rouge meetings was, "What is rotten must be removed," eerily echoing the Nazi use of organic and biological metaphors.

Like Mao's means–ends reasoning, Khmer Rouge slogans implied that it is better to kill an innocent person than risk allowing an enemy to live. Shoot first; (perhaps) ask questions later. Another slogan stated, "One or two million young people are enough to make a new Kampuchea."[82] Human existence was, once again, dispensable, a matter of calculation.

The Khmer Rouge ideology explicitly linked Khmer Rouge blood with hatred and the killing of enemies. A few lines from their anthem, surely one of the most disgusting and irrational of all anthems, indicates the theme: "Bright red Blood which covers town and plains … Sublime Blood of revolutionary men and women fighters! The Blood changing into unrelenting hated."[83]

79 Chandler, *The Tragedy of Cambodian History*, 259.
80 Burgler, *The Eyes of the Pineapple*, 58.
81 Glover, *Humanity*, 306.
82 Ponchaud, *Cambodia, Year Zero*, 86, 92.
83 Cited in Becker, *When the War was Over*, 219.

One might predict that when a paranoid regime with a grand vision fails to achieve its projections, it would double down on its alleged enemies and foreign conspirators.

This is what happened as the Maoist-inspired Four-Year Plan, developed in 1976, failed quickly and miserably. The Khmer Rouge became obsessed with conspiracy as the explanation. The crop harvest in the country's best area of farmland, the Battambang area, was supposed to double. Why? Because ideology said it would. The ethnically pure workers, inspired by the Communist government, would supposedly double their effort. However, they would be deprived of "Western" fertilizers and insecticides. Moreover, the workers were brutalized, ill-fed, and without farming experience. But the government blamed capitalist habits and traitors.

Meanwhile, political officials and soldiers grew ever more sadistic and deranged by revolutionary passions. It meant even worse treatment of prisoner-workers and more casual executions. As failures mounted, the government broadcast more triumphant speeches while blaming spies for any problems. Then the paranoia turned inward. Pol Pot's forces started to accuse members of the army and the party of conspiracy. Purges and fighting erupted. Cambodia was starting to implode. By 1978, Cambodia was a teeming state of paranoia. The Khmer Rouge leaders "believed the enemy was everywhere."[84] The Khmer Rouge government made detecting and eliminating enemies their one obsession, abandoning talk of building a new Cambodia. The holocaust continued until, in January 1979, Vietnamese forces rolled into Phnom Penh. The carnage was ended. But Pol Pot and his Khmer Rouge would carry on. They retreated to a jungle base near the Thai border but would never threaten government again. Pot died under house arrest in 1998.

84 Becker, *When the War was Over*, 221–2.

9

American Helter-Skelter

THE POLITICAL MYTH OF THE UNITED STATES is that its War of Independence created a completely different kind of country, compared with the monarch-ruled countries of Europe – the Old World. Its Enlightenment Constitution, supported by a Bill of Rights, would ensure a country of fair dealing, in which every citizen was free and equal under God; a country in which citizens would be prepared to pursue not only their own happiness but the greater, common good. *E pluribus unum*: Out of many, one.

The new America would leave behind the hierarchies, aristocracies, and Old World hatreds. America was to be exceptional. It was historically important proof that the birth of democracy did not have to end in a bloodbath like that of the French Revolution. It was, as religiously inclined people would say, a gleaming city on the hill, a New Jerusalem, where anyone, if they worked hard, could be president. Liberty and opportunity for all.

It would be a millennium on earth.

As with all ideal myths, reality never lives up to it. From America's beginning, Old World prejudice and tribalism would travel to the new land. The Puritans sought religious freedom *for themselves*, not all.[1] They wanted to form *their own* Bible-based society. Puritan hegemony in the Massachusetts Bay Colony lasted for at least a century. They were

1 See Bremer, *Puritanism*. In December 1620, Pilgrims from Britain created Plymouth Colony, south of Massachusetts Bay. The main era of settlement was between 1630 and 1641, when about 21,000 additional Puritans arrived, while others settled in Virginia and the Caribbean. Eventually, the New England immigrants organized the Massachusetts Bay Colony.

as suspicious and intolerant of other religions or groups, such as the aboriginal population or French Catholics, as their former persecutors in the Old World were of them.

Old World hatreds infected the politics of the pre-independence founding states. By the eighteenth century, conspiracy theories against Catholics, Catholic monarchs, Jews, Freemasons, and then Blacks tainted public discourse, undermining high-minded talk of a new world for all. In 1787, when the founding fathers gathered in Philadelphia, their Constitution was not, as myth would have it, the result of noble and tolerant sentiments around the table. It was a tough political compromise in the face of a nation falling apart due to parochialism and self-interest.[2] The Constitution expressed the founders' fears of ordinary people, prompting the inclusion of elite measures, such as an electoral college. Class, racial, and political bias shaped this populist document.

Then, in the nineteenth century, slavery, supported by violent hate groups such as the Ku Klux Klan, put the lie to claims that America would be the home of a new and great social experiment, a refuge for the persecuted and huddled masses. After a brutal civil war, the issue of Black rights was shelved to allow partisan politics to go on. But racism would never let the country rest.

These early irrationalities would carry on into the twentieth century in many violent and strange forms. Right-wing religions turned Christianity from a religion of brotherly love to a religion of hatred of non-white minorities. Racist groups arose on all sides – from the white Christian Identity movement to the Black Nation of Islam. During the Cold War, groups like the John Birch Society would advocate a narrow anti-Communist patriotism, while supporting Senator McCarthy. That American society had a dark side was shown by the shocking actions of paranoid cults. They committed mass suicide or killed innocent people in a defiant helter-skelter rejection of the world. Fantasies replaced reality. Religions promised that UFOs would someday transport the select to heaven. Meanwhile, in the countryside, paramilitaries armed themselves for Armageddon and, in their paranoia, feared a conspiracy to create a world government.

2 See Klarman, *The Framer's Coup: The Making of the United States Constitution*, especially chapter 1.

By the late 1990s, in mass media, every sort of demagogue, self-proclaimed prophet, and philosophy to save alienated moderns was put forward, producing best-selling self-help books. The idea of informed citizens carefully reflecting on the direction of their country was replaced by masses of people following the latest trends – no matter how ridiculous – through the new media of television, the internet, and then social media. Rational, informed, and patient politics was found to have a feature repellant to an age of immediate gratification and public image: It is, well, boring. Not the latest thing. Not easily summarized in a slogan. It requires hard thought and perhaps a change in one's biases. Modern prophets and extremists were, and are, the equivalent of yesterday's snake-oil salesman, but they are more damaging and dangerous.

The nation, or a good part of it, was, and is, losing touch with reality.

Extreme groups not only violate the lofty language of the Constitution, they also damage the country's capacity to respond to serious issues. In the 1960s, the right wing portrayed the Vietnam War as a war to stop communism. It was a war that every patriot must support, even as the madness of that blood bath seemed to carry on without end, and the nation tore itself apart. War opponents were traitors. Then after the country's defeat in the war, many people turned their backs on returning veterans. Meanwhile, in many cities, the reasonable demands of Blacks in the civil rights movement – demands guaranteed by the Constitution – met fierce opposition. It revealed the extent of hard-core racism in American society.

By the turn of the twenty-first century, extreme politics – where your political opponent is an enemy of the state – became mainstream, supported by media who either shared the ideology or used conflict to attract audiences. The country became politically polarized, and the new social media helped extreme groups dominate daily discussion. Many of the contemporary groups were motivated by the same Old World fears and tribalism that reached the shores of America in the seventeenth and eighteenth centuries.

The shift to polarized and extreme messaging began to eat away at a prior understanding of why there should be self-imposed limits to political strategies and partisanship. Leaders like Donald Trump began to ignore basic rights and the rule of law to play to their intolerant political base. The country's large economy and military might maintained America as a world power but the nation's egalitarian democratic culture began to erode. America no longer has moral credibility globally on many issues ranging from immigration to human rights.

We have yet to see where this new irrationalism will take the country. But we do know that, within America, there were and are dark prejudicial strains in its body politic, which continue to disrupt and threaten its democracy. It should not be underestimated. In this chapter, I select some examples of this embedded irrationality. We have already seen examples: McCarthy's purge of Communists, Jonestown, and the LaRouche movement.

SECTION 1: EARLY HELTER-SKELTER

Mass Panic in Salem

Social irrationality was at work early in the history of America, in the Salem witch trials – a mass hysteria that overtook the Puritan area of Salem in colonial Massachusetts, in 1692. More than two hundred people – all Puritans – were accused of witchcraft and of those more than fifty confessed. Some nineteen people were executed (fourteen women and five men). At least five people died in jail. The trials were not the first. Some twelve women had been executed in Massachusetts and Connecticut previously during the seventeenth century.

The Salem executions occurred at a time when people were inclined to see devils and evil powers behind worrisome events. As noted in chapter 3, European witch hunting peaked in the mid-1600s. Belief in devils, witches, magic, and sorcery was common. The Puritan religion stressed the reality of supernatural forces and human vulnerability to evil spirits. Equally important was that the Salem accusations seemed to reveal a devil-directed plot against citizens. Magic, white or black, had long been part of Western society, but the real fear was a certain type of black magic: people make a pact with the devil, who then seeks to undermine Christian society and bring on the apocalypse.[3]

Fears of devil-inspired sorcery began in Salem Village in January 1692 when a group of young girls, some as young as eleven, fell strangely ill. They were unable to speak and see and fell into convulsive fits involving

3 For attitudes towards magic in this era, see Thomas, *Religion and the Decline of Magic*.

grotesque distortions of the necks, arms, and back along with choking, temporary amnesia, and loss of hearing and touch. An enslaved West Indian woman, Tituba, was asked to treat two of the girls. She did, by having them serve a "witch cake" made with the girls' urine to a family dog. The convulsions ceased. Ministers in the village were not at all pleased at the cure. They were alarmed that an enslaved person was using magic at the request of a church member. Then more girls came forward claiming they were influenced by witches.

Many of the accused, including Tituba, confessed to witchcraft and implicated others. Panic took root. George Burroughs, a former Salem Village minister, was accused of having presided at witches' Sabbaths. He was brought back from Maine in May 1692, tried, and hanged.[4] A new governor, Sir William Phips, fearing a conspiracy of the devil, appointed a court to hear the cases. The court met on 2 June 1692, to hear the case of Bridget Bishop. She was convicted and hanged on 10 June. Another eighteen people were hanged by 22 September 1692. Although the cases were contested, the judges believed the village was under satanic attack. Detailed confessions of devil meetings and other dark events only served to intensify the panic.

Many puritans interpreted the confessions as a sign that the devil was provoking an apocalypse. Recent events reinforced this belief. Were not the pagan Indians in revolt? Were not French Catholics and Quakers coming into God's Massachusetts colony? Perhaps the British Crown, ever the persecutor of Puritans, would take a large share of their growing prosperity through taxes and other means. In general, it was a time when many feared a loss of autonomy through repression or invasion. Richard Godbeer wrote that the "predisposition … to locate evil outside the self" was the key to understanding the events in Salem.[5] We know this predisposition as the paranoid predisposition, aided by projection.

What ended the circle of accusation and trial? One factor was the growing number of accusations. It was hard to believe that *so* many people in a small community could be witches. Second, the accusations began to name elite members of society – including Governor Phips's

4 Hansen, *Witchcraft at Salem*, 119.
5 Godbeer, *The Devil's Dominion*, 203.

wife. Phips suspended the trials on 22 September 1692. He dismissed the court and began to release prisoners on bail. In May 1693, the governor issued a general pardon to the surviving accused.

The Salem trials show that paranoia is not purely a matter of belief. It expresses current social hierarchies and prejudices. One can see such factors at work by asking, who was likely to be accused of being a Salem witch? The answer, generally, is the most vulnerable, the most easily victimized people who were outsiders or different in some way. Some of the victims seemed to fit the features of feared groups, e.g., Tituba practised magic by reading fortunes; others had curious lifestyles. Also, victims were arrested because the accusers would benefit from their demise. Accusation was a way of settling a score, as we saw with the Inquisition. In the end, even well-respected citizens were accused and harmed. When the contagion of paranoia seeps into daily life, almost no one is safe.

The Salem panic was an eruption of social paranoia which normally lies beneath ordinary life in villages and towns. It was (1) a conspiratorial delusion (caused by the devil and his agents); (2) a great hostility (against presumed witches); (3) prompted by millennial thinking – the devil had chosen Salem to begin his pre-millennial attacks; (4) grandiose: Salem would defeat the devil and save Christianity.

The Paranoid Style

Historian Richard Hofstadter was one of the first historians to apply psychiatric terms, like paranoia, to American history. He said the political rhetoric of early American groups employed a "paranoid style" that combined "heated exaggeration, suspiciousness, and conspiratorial fantasy."[6] This style is not limited to right-wing groups. The term applies not only to leaders with disturbed minds but also includes the use of "paranoid modes of expression by more or less normal people." Hence, the term "paranoid," usually limited to clinical evaluation in hospitals, can be recognized as a significant phenomenon in public life.[7]

6 Hofstadter, *The Paranoid Style in American Politics and Other Essays*, 3–40.

7 Ibid., 4.

Hofstadter begins by recalling McCarthy's accusations. Then Hofstadter asks us to consider examples of this style from the nineteenth century. He cites a Texas newspaper article of 1855 which warns of a massive Roman Catholic conspiracy against the US government:

> It is a notorious fact that the Monarchs of Europe and the Pope of Rome are at this very moment plotting our destruction ... and that our Executive head is tainted with the infectious venom of Catholicism ... These minions of the Pope are boldly insulting our Senators ... propagating the adulterous union of Church and State ... spewing out the bitterest execrations on all Protestantism. The Catholics in the United States receive from abroad more than $200,000 annually for the propagations.[8]

One of Hofstadter's early examples was the alleged conspiracy of the illuminists and Freemasons to eliminate established religion and overturn existing governments.[9] As mentioned earlier, illuminism was a pro-Enlightenment movement started in 1776 by Adam Weishaupt, a law professor in the University of Ingolstadt in Bavaria. Perhaps naively, it sought to bring human affairs under Enlightenment rationalism, mixed with an anti-clerical stance. Its humanitarianism was influential in Masonic lodges. In Europe, anti-Enlightenment conservative movements, characterized illuminism and Masonry as subversive and devilish. Unfortunately, this exaggerated response took root in New England among clerics and others. They sought to raise an alarm about the same alleged devilry in Jeffersonian (Enlightenment-based) democracy.

Americans first learned about illuminism in 1797 from a book published in Edinburgh and then New York by Scottish scientist John Robison. Its title was *Proofs of a Conspiracy Against All Religions and Governments of Europe, Carried On in the Secret Meetings of Free Masons, Illuminati, and Reading Societies.* Robison proclaimed a "great and wicked project fermenting and working all over Europe." Illuminism was committed to the corruption of women, free sexual activity, and the violation of property rights. It had concocted a tea that had a secret substance that "blinds or kills when spurted in the face." They made a stench bomb for filling a bedroom with "pestilential vapors."

8 Ibid., 8.
9 Ibid., 10–11.

These claims were false. But paranoid prejudice does not need truth. The American illuminism panic of the 1790s had begun. Preachers and conservative leaders in the USA began to spread the conspiracy theory. Preachers in pulpits in dozens of towns and cities denounced the illuminists as the Anti-Christ, as if the members of this peaceful, Europe-based group were everywhere across the land.

Hofstadter also points to anti-Masonic movements in the USA during the 1820s and 1830s. These extended the country's obsession with conspiracy. The extension, however, changed the nature of the panic. The idea of a Mason conspiracy had influence beyond New England. The conspiracy was a folksy movement that played well in rural America. It decried the Masons as a traitorous secret society, a conspiracy against republican government. As Catholics were said to be loyal to the pope, Masons were said to be loyal to their cause. Masons constituted a separate government within existing federal and provincial governments. Officials and sheriffs who were Masons would not charge Mason criminals. Somehow, the press was so muzzled by the Masons that news of their treachery was not published. People ignored the fact that the Masons were not alone, as a civic society, in having their own structure and practices. So did innumerable Protestant and Catholic groups.

Further, it was not enough for people to critique Masonry or ask about its practices. Not at all. The early paranoid style prompted people to go much further and say Masonry was an apocalyptic movement that was helping the arrival of the Anti-Christ. No sooner had the Mason hysteria calmed down when another plot against American values was discovered among Catholic Jesuits.[10] The same creation of an enemy, the same paranoid exaggeration, and the same intense hatred, re-emerges. These anti-Catholic feelings were strengthened by a growing nativism among "Yankee Americans" to maintain an ethnically and religiously homogeneous society that was Protestant and committed to individualism.

Two books published in 1835 described the new danger. One was *Foreign Conspiracies Against the Liberties of the United States* by Samuel Morse, the inventor of the telegraph, and the other was the *Plea for the West* by Lyman Beecher, father of Harriet Beecher Stowe, abolitionist

10 Ibid., 79–81.

and author of *Uncle Tom's Cabin.* Morse said Austria (or the Catholic Hapsburg Empire) was sending Jesuit missionaries to the United States to undermine support for republican government. This would pave the way for a member of the House of Hapsburg to be emperor of the United States. "Austria is now acting in this country," Morse warned. "A conspiracy exists" that cannot be easily defeated by guns or forts.

Beecher thought that the Christian millennium could occur in the United States, depending on how things developed in the western portion of the country. The plea was for the country to make this Western region Protestant not Catholic. Protestantism was in a life-or-death struggle with Catholicism. This meant a quick response to stop a great tide of Catholic immigrants, hostile to free institutions, from swamping the country. They were sent by the Catholic "potentates of Europe" creating violence, filling jails, crowding poorhouses, and quadrupling taxes. These Catholics would soon be able to vote, in the thousands.

This anti-Catholicism was made more graphic by what Hofstadter called the "pornography of the Puritan" – erotic tales of Catholic sexual impropriety and libertine lifestyles.[11] Eroticism enhanced the hatred. No doubt, there was some truth to claims of improper Catholic sexuality behind closed doors. The same could be said of Protestant clergy. But, for the anti-Catholics, there was, apparently, no end to the perversity of libertine priests. Strange things happened inside confessional boxes. One could only imagine what nuns got up to in those licentious convents. One of the most popular books of the era was by Maria Monk, entitled *Awful Disclosures*, published in 1836. Monk wrote that she escaped from the Hotel Dieu nunnery in Montreal after witnessing terrible things, such as the murder of infants born to priests and nuns. The book was attacked and defended. It continued to be read and believed even after her mother testified that Maria was "addled" since she was a young girl, due to a self-inflicted head injury. Maria died in prison in 1849 after being arrested in a brothel as a pickpocket.[12]

Anti-Catholicism was also strong in the 1890s. The American Protective Association blamed the 1893 depression on Catholics who allegedly made a run on the banks. It issued a bogus encyclical attributed to Pope

11 Ibid., 21.
12 Ibid., 22.

Leo XIII instructing American Catholics on a certain date in 1893 to exterminate all heretics – a myth that persisted into the twentieth century. Anti-Catholicism would remain an enduring strain, re-emerging in the 1960s with fears that John Kennedy, if elected president, would march to the tune of the pope.

SECTION 2: ORIGINS OF THE RACIST RIGHT

"The Mud People"

A second wave of Old World religious hatred crossed the Atlantic to America in the second half of the eighteenth century. It was racist, paranoid, and irrational. From its ideas there grew, in twentieth-century America, bigoted and belligerent religious sects and racist groups.

The movement began as "Anglo Israelism" in Great Britain in the late nineteenth century. Its influence in Britain peaked in the 1920s, when it was popular among the British establishment. Today it is reduced in size and influence, with a modest headquarters in Putney, South London.

An early influence were the ideas of English writer John Wilson (1799–1870). The Anglo-Israel Association was founded in Wilson's home in London in 1874. In his *Lectures on Our Israelite Origin* of 1840, Wilson argued that the lost tribes of Israel migrated to Northern Europe and eventually to the British Isles. They gave rise to the Israelite race of Northern Europeans. They were superior to the Jews of the southern kingdom of Judah. Of all the races that make up the Northern Europeans, the most important are those in the British Isles. They are the chosen people, who followed God's will in creating a worldwide British empire for him.[13]

We should also note the influence of two writers in the mid-1900s, although they were not members of the Anglo-Israelism movement. They created concepts and language around which antisemitism in the USA would build its message. In 1864, Irish lawyer Dominick McCausland (1806–1873) published *Adam and the Adamites*. He called the descendants of Adam "the Adamic race" – white, gentile Europeans. This is a phrase still used in extreme American religions. As well, Alexander

13 Robins and Post, *Paranoid Politics*, 183.

Winchell (1824–1891), a Methodist minister and geologist, published *Adamites and Preadamites, Or, A Popular Discussion* in 1878. He divided humanity into the inferior Black race who preceded Adam, the "pre-Adamites," and the "noble and superior" white race that came after Adam. Extreme religious views, such as Christian Identity, use his conceptualization to call Black people the "mud-people."[14]

These views were attractive to teachers and evangelical ministers in the 1890s.[15]

Onward Unchristian Soldiers

By the early 1900s, groups from the Ku Klux Klan (KKK) to Christian Identity combined religion and racism.[16] Their members were mainly white, with a background in fundamental Christianity.

The persistence of dark irrationality in America is evidenced by the fact that the KKK has existed as three klans since its founding in Pulaski, Tennessee, in 1865.[17] The white supremacist hate group reached a peak in 1925 when it is estimated that there were between three million and six million members. Today, the KKK's religion is essentially the Christian Identity theology. It advocates for white nationalism, Nordicism, anti-immigration, and anti-Catholicism.[18] The allies of the KKK include such dark-sounding groups as White League, European Kindred, Aryan Brotherhood, Knights of the White Camelia, Red Shirts, and the Nazi Lowriders.

The success of the KKK in the 1920s was due, in part, to Reuben Sawyer (1866–1962), an American clergyman and a leader of the Ku Klux Klan in Oregon. He was an important advocate of Anglo-Israelism. He lectured widely to promote the Ku Klux Klan. He defended the ideas of the "Second Klan" which reviled "foreign influences" and advocated for a "cleansed and purified Americanism."[19] Who were the

14 See Langer, "The American Neo-Nazis Movement Today."

15 For example, in 1890 Charles Totten, a teacher of military science at Yale University, founded a periodical called *Our Race: Its Origin and Destiny*, which repeated the view that the British were descendants of the lost tribes.

16 See Barkun, *Religion and the Racist Right.*

17 The dates for the three clans are 1866–71, 1915–44, and 1946–present.

18 See Guterl, *The Color of Race in America, 1900–1940.*

19 Barkun, *Religion and the Racist Right*, 23.

dangerous foreign influences? The Jews. According to Sawyer, the Jews were plotting the end of Christianity. They were Bolshevists forming a "government within a government." Or, they were Shylocks using finance to gain control of Christians. Therefore, he concluded, the Ku Klux Klan should destroy them.

Christian Identity is a common theology for many white racist churches, a doctrine that combines fundamental Protestantism and paranoid, racist ideas. Christian Identity churches hold that the Bible teaches the superiority of Aryans.[20] Jews and Blacks are at the same spiritual level as animals. Aryans are God's chosen people and Jesus was not a Jew. Jews are, according to Jarah Crawford, a proponent of the Christian Identity bible, a "race-mixed, polluted people not of God," and they are "the children of Satan, the serpent seed line."[21]

Like its predecessor Anglo-Israelism, Christian Identity believes that Aryans are decedents of the lost tribes of Israel and are on earth to do God's work, a special calling. The apocalypse is approaching and it will be a battle between Aryans and Jews, the forces of good and evil, respectively. Ayrans have been directed by God to warn people of the dangers of Jews and Blacks, and to destroy them.[22]

In the 1930s and 1940s, the Christian identity movement was on the rise. In the 1960s, the theory of the satanic origin of the Jew was fully developed. The ideology used the pre-Adam and post-Adam distinction. The serpent in the Garden of Eden was the devil, and original sin was Eve's sexual relationship with the serpent. This has led to two "seedlines": the noble and good (and gentile white) descendants of Adam and the Black or Jewish descendants of the serpent. Cain was born out of the Eve–serpent relationship. He was the first Jew and passed on his penchant for evil to all of his descendants. Christian Identity, therefore, is a delusional belief in a worldwide Jewish conspiracy supported by the devil. Hence, in this view, there must be a final battle to destroy the seed of the devil. In the meantime, Christian Identity's political agenda includes replacing human law with Biblical law.

20 "Aryans" are defined as people having a Nordic or Alpine racial background, especially residents of the Scandinavian and Germanic countries, plus the British Isles. However, in practice, any gentile white person would be accepted.

21 Cited in Barkun, *Religion and the Racist Right*, 131.

22 Barkun, *Religion and the Racist Right*, ix.

SECTION 3: FEARING DYSTOPIA

From Russia, Without Love

Seeking a utopian millennium has spurred groups to kill presumed enemies. In the second half of the twentieth century, the fear of the opposite – an approaching dystopia – became a powerful political force on both the left and right. On the left, George Orwell, fearful of the rise of totalitarianism, would write his dystopia novels – *Animal Farm* and *1984* – which warn that modern trends could lead to a fascist state where individuality was crushed.

Orwell's novels, however, were not irrational. They were clear-eyed writings about where political trends might lead humanity. There was no racism, no paranoia, no unbridled hatred of Jews, Blacks, or other minorities. No calls for holocaust. But on the right, especially in America, fear of dystopia *did* spark irrational ideologies and movements.

Among the early right-wing dystopia movements were the American anti-communist groups. A leader in this area was the John Birch Society, especially at the height of the Cold War in the 1950s and into the 1960s. The John Birch Society has been called a "soft paranoid" movement[23] because they do not attack people or set off explosives but provide an ideological home for like-minded people. But don't let the term "soft" fool you. These homes for ideologues have impact on society.

The John Birch Society was founded in 1958 in the middle of the Cold War by Robert Welch, a retired candy magnate, who was consumed by fear of a communist conspiracy.[24] Welch's fear of communism went back to 1938 when he read a journalist's memoirs about the repressive Stalin government – Eugene Lyon's *Assignment in Utopia*. By the early 1950s, Welch was demonizing Soviet leaders as "predatory beasts." He became a supporter of Joseph McCarthy.[25] In 1958, Welch met with eleven friends. The transcripts of the meeting were published in 1961 as *The Blue Book of the John Birch Society*. It became the society's bible. Welch and friends became the founders of the society. They called their group after Captain John Birch, an army intelligence officer killed by

23 Robins and Post, *Paranoid Politics*, 190.

24 On Welch and the Birch Society, see Broyles, *The John Birch Society: Anatomy of a Protest*.

25 Welch, *May God Forgive Us*, 61.

Chinese Communists just before the end of the Second World War. They remembered him as the first casualty of the Cold War. Welch told the founding meeting the group had only a few more years before the communists took over America, and the society was to elect a new leader if he was killed by communists.[26]

Welch's society, at the height of its popularity, produced a newsletter for 67,000 subscribers. He stepped down in 1983 and was followed by other leaders. In 1991, despite the demise of the Soviet Union, the society's newsletter still had 21,000 subscribers. The enemies of the society were supporters of the civil rights movement, the United Nations, and the sponsors of Earth Day. In September 1991, the society warned of a planned "complete socialist takeover of the greater Los Angeles area."[27]

Militias and Armageddon

By the 1970s, a more extreme response to dystopia arose in America. People formed paramilitaries against the federal government, which they believed was in league with a world-wide conspiracy to eliminate their liberties. The ideas behind the militias went back to Anglo-Israelism, to Christian Identity theology, to the Ku Klux Klan, and other groups. The predominant concern of the militias was the federal government, while antisemitism and racism adopted a lower profile. Yet these themes could never be separated. For instance, militias were suspicious of central government because they accepted the myth that it was run by Jews.

A forerunner of the militias was the now defunct Posse Comitatus, an anti-government movement that recognized no public official above the level of sheriff. It began in 1969 in Portland, Oregon as the Citizen's Law-Enforcement Committee to protest taxes and challenge the authority of the federal government over local government. They offered legal assistance in tax evasion. The movement evolved into the national Posse Comitatus which was organized in Michigan in 1972. Over the next decade, chapters were formed in almost every state. Members believed that the county was the proper seat of government (hence "Posse

26 Welch, *The Blue Book of the John Birch Society*, 181.

27 Rose, "Will Communists Take Over in 2002? Ask a John Bircher," *Wall Street Journal*, 2 October 1991, A1.

Comitatus" or "power of the county"). The Posse opposed state and federal laws and considered the IRA and income tax "Communist and unconstitutional." Posse doctrine advocated firearms and survival training in preparation for Armageddon, an approaching nuclear holocaust which is the goal of the "Communist-Jew run government."[28]

Posse had no central leader or governance system. It was a loosely affiliated web of chapters, often known by other names. The average Posse member was religious, a tax protestor, a loner, and self-employed. Most hated Blacks and Jews. Members had to be white, Christian, and required to state they were patriotic and interested in law and order, as defined by Posse. The group justified the killing of federal officials as a "defence of freedom" which is "not murder anymore than a soldier killing in war."[29]

The development of militia mentality can be observed in a wide range of groups such as Aryan Nations, Christian Patriots, The Order, and the National Vanguard, a West Virginia neo-Nazi group. Aryan Nations is an antisemitic, white supremacist terrorist organization that was originally based in Hayden, Idaho. Richard Girnt Butler founded the group in the 1970s, as an arm of the Christian Identity organization, Church of Jesus Christ–Christian. This church was opposed to what it called the Church of Jesus Christ–Jew. Each July, members receive indoctrination in Christian Identity ideas. Its magazine, *Calling Our Nation,* has accused Jews of committing human sacrifice and recycles the satanic Jewish conspiracy principles.

In 1983, a neo-Nazi terrorist, Robert Mathews, split from Aryan Nations to form his own group, "The Order," a violent, tax-protesting, neo-pagan cult that also called itself the Brotherhood of Silence. Their principal concern was the danger of the "genocide of the white race" at the hands of the Jews, "the devil's children." The Jews were controlling the USA through their domination of banks and media. Members of the Order took an "oath of violence" to achieve Aryan victory over the Jews, claiming "no fear of death, no fear of foe." They were in a "state of war" and united by a "blood covenant." To finance a guerrilla campaign, the Order started robbing banks and making counterfeit

28 Yeager, "Armageddon Tomorrow: The Posse Comitatus Prepares for the Future," 17.

29 Lake, "An Exegesis of the Radical Right," 98.

money. In 1984, they robbed a Brinks armoured car and then murdered Alan Berg, a Jew and a radio talk show host in Denver.[30]

The FBI caught up with Mathews at his home on Whidbey Island in Puget Sound, north of Seattle, Oregon. He refused to surrender to law-enforcement officials. A helicopter dropped an explosive onto the house and Mathews died in the fire. Liberty Net, a neo-Nazi online network, made Mathews a hero. It carried his last message: "By the time that my son had arrived [was born] I realized that white America … was headed for oblivion unless white men rose up and turned the tide."[31]

The books and mail-order catalogues of the racist right indicate the irrational, overheated emotions that drive these organizations. A popular book, yesterday and today, is the putrid *The Turner Diaries*. It was written by William Pierce under the pseudonym of Andrew McDonald. Pierce was chief of the American Nazi Party in the 1960s and mentor to Robert Mathews. He was a physicist who left academia to campaign against Blacks and Jews. Since it was published in 1978 white supremacists frequently quote the book. It has inspired numerous hate crimes and acts of terrorism. It is the bible of white supremacists.

The novel starts with a foreword set in 2099, a century after a global race war. The book quotes from a recently discovered diary of Earl Turner, the novel's protagonist, a member of the white revolutionary movement that caused these events. The story relates how Turner and his militants brought about an apocalyptic overthrow of the US federal government (called "the System"), ignited a nuclear war, and engaged in a race war that took place first in North America, and then the rest of the world. The war leads to the extermination of non-whites.

The plot is an ugly triumphalist fantasy. In the final section of the book, millions of American Blacks, Jews, and Latinos are hanged on lampposts on the "Day of the Rope," and California is liberated by the explosion of a nuclear bomb. The novel also describes the hangings of thousands of white women who were partners of non-white males. Each woman wore a necklace with a placard that read, "I defiled my race." By 1996, the book had sold more than 200,000 copies. Timothy McVeigh, who bombed the federal building in Oklahoma City on 19 April 1995, killing 168 people, was influenced by the *Turner Diaries*.

30 Barkun, *Religion and the Racist Right*, 228.

31 Lake, "An Exegesis of the Radical Right," 102.

He used a fertilizer bomb that is similar to a bomb described in the *Diaries.* In the novel, the weapon is used to blow up an FBI building in Washington, DC.

The *Diaries* are a mad man's fantasy of gore and violence. The ideas encouraged helter-skelter, American style.

The New World Order

The paramilitaries and other racist-right groups hold in common at least three beliefs: the right to bear arms, suspicion of the federal government, and a coming dystopia. What distinguishes these far-right groups is *how* they hold such beliefs. These beliefs are held by many reasonable Americans. Many people believe the right to bear arms is a constitutional right. Suspicion of a central or federal government has always been a theme in American politics. We often have legitimate reason to be suspicious of what some federal institution may be doing.

But far-right groups take such beliefs to the extreme. They exaggerate. They turn legitimate worries into apocalyptic paranoias, such as a just-around-the-corner defeat of (white) civilization. So white people need to start arming and training themselves out on the frontier. The right to bear arms is extended to mean the right to stockpile weapons, to do military training, and to create survival compounds. The federal government is the source of all political evil and a danger to the country, and citizens can rightfully ignore the laws of the land to defend their liberties. The coming Armageddon is a vast conspiracy to create a new world order.

What is this new world order?

This is not Woodrow Wilson's or Winston Churchill's idea of a progressive new world order after a world war – a chance for Western civilization to start over again. It is not the idea that there should be international bodies such as the United Nations to prevent future world wars or to coordinate efforts by nations to address common problems. It is the idea of a grand conspiracy to create a totalitarian world government that will crush nations and crush individual freedoms.[32] In this view, secretive groups, leaders, powerful institutions, and elites – right

32 The idea of international agencies was never about crushing nations. See Mazower, *Governing the World.*

now – are laying the groundwork for world government. They work behind fronts and corporations that appear legitimate. The new world order will not be a Christian millennium or paradise. It will be the reverse. The Anti-Christ will win. Evil power will reign, and world armies, perhaps orchestrated by the United Nations, will march into nations.

World domination is the real, hidden aim.

Studies describe American far-right militia as having a "frontier state of mind" where people want to live in small communities apart from authorities. This frontier mentality believes government is a monolithic entity determined to destroy their lifestyle with taxes, gun control, and help to minorities. There is also a fear of being contaminated by people (and government) who do not share the militia's ideology, race, or values.[33]

Extreme groups oppose the new world order by circulating conspiracy theories that accuse a shifting menagerie of people and groups of being part of the world domination cabal: Jews (described as "international financiers"), global corporations, United Nations soldiers (who we call peacekeepers), Wall Street, the United States Federal Reserve and Foreign Relations Council, liberals, atheists, Muslims, progressives, communists, and cosmopolitans. The belief that the world will end becomes an ultra-conservative, political paranoia that finds its way into public thinking on almost anything from gun laws to abortion. Religion, politics, and prejudice come together in a perfect storm.[34]

As seen, in the eighteenth and nineteenth century, the American right accused Freemasons, Jews, and liberals of promoting an internationalist conspiracy. In the Cold War era, fears of a new world order sparked anti-communist hysteria and support for Senator Joseph McCarthy. The John Birch Society claimed that the governments of the United States and the Soviet Union were controlled by a cabal of global corporations and Jews. When the Soviet Union failed in the 1990s, these groups shifted their animosity to globalists of any kind. American televangelist Pat Robertson had a best-selling book in 1991, *The New World Order*, which warned that Wall Street, the Federal Reserve system, the Council on Foreign Relations, the Bilderberg Group of European and

33 See Stern, *A Force Upon the Plain.*

34 This is not to deny that some people liked the idea of a world government. Writer H.G. Wells advocated for a technocratic world state and a planned economy. But Wells was no secret and violent conspirator. He published his views.

North American leaders, and the Trilateral Commission, an international discussion group,[35] were working towards world government. These conspiracy theories supported and encouraged the rise of the militias and the "patriot movement."[36]

The beliefs of the extremists are strengthened by government–militia confrontations. By a crazy self-fulfilling logic, the groups set up camps and carry out actions that cause government to intervene; the groups refuse to cooperate or surrender to federal officials and violence occurs, not unexpectedly. Then the groups' leaders point to the use of force as evidence of a federal government seeking to destroy liberties and the sign of a coming final battle. The groups cite regularly such confrontations and immortalize the right-wing leaders, such as the 1992 Ruby Ridge confrontation where federal agents killed the wife and child of white supremacist Randy Weaver at Ruby Ridge, Idaho. They also love to cite the US government's clash with Branch Davidians in Texas in 1993, discussed below.

Paranoia is rampant among these groups. For some militants, the barcodes on federal highway signs are secret codes for the UN army when it moves in to take over the United States. Groups also worry about government surveillance by "black helicopters" and satellites. One conspiracy theory believes that the military embedded microchips in the buttocks of right-wing members during their military service. These chips now send signals to satellites on the location of these members and other information. Timothy McVeigh spoke in earnest about the biochip in his buttocks.[37] The "new world order" opponents spread their anti-government conspiracies at gun shows, at conferences, on AM radio shows, and on the internet.

35 The Bilderberg Meeting is an annual conference established in 1954 by Prince Bernhard of the Netherlands "to foster dialogue between Europe and North America." Participants are European and North American political leaders, experts from industry, finance, academia, and the media. The Trilateral Commission is a non-governmental, non-partisan discussion group founded by David Rockefeller in July 1973 to foster closer cooperation among Japan, Western Europe, and North America.

36 See Mason, *The New World Order: The American Patriot Movement, Globalization and Resistance.*

37 The conspiracy theorist Phillips O'Halloran has described in detail how the chips work. Cited in McHugh, "Conspiracy Theories Grow."

Finally, these movements are a response to the feminist movement and similar progressive causes which gathered strength in the second half of the twentieth century. These causes threaten the "Rambo" militia men[38] and their need for rigid social hierarchy where the man-of-the-family is an unquestioned tyrant. This fear of a changing world is one reason these groups hate the cities and modern life, with their social movements. As seen, liberal decadents and surrealists have also opposed modernity but for different reasons and through different methods.

Ideologically, this extremism is grounded in three connected myths: rural or Wild West romanticism, the ideal of rugged individualism, and America as historically special or exceptional.

The myth of the Wild West, the original frontier, has been exploited in countless novels and Hollywood movies. According to myth, this huge region was settled and run by rugged individuals, either as fiercely independent settlers or as armed gunslingers on horseback, quick on the draw. This myth borrowed from the afore-mentioned ideal of natural man promoted by Rousseau. No doubt the settlers were strong-minded people and had to be able to do things for themselves. But much of the settlement required that groups cooperate to erect towns in wild places or to circle the proverbial wagons to fend off attacks by Natives. Somehow, the movies never explained why the Natives are restless or angry, despite the fact that the settlers were, without notice or compensation, taking over land that had been home to Indigenous peoples for centuries. Natives were blood-thirsty barbarians who just happened to be in the area.

Also, myth ignores the fact that many of the settlements depended heavily on financial, food, security (the US cavalry), and transportation assistance (the coach and railway) not to mention the communication assistance of the post office and telegraph. Where did such support come from? From *non-frontier* cities and government officials back east. The romantic ideal of the West being won by dominating gunslingers or a US marshal who takes on a gang of thugs by himself was exaggerated. Whatever security could be mustered was often due to community participation. Thirty men with guns in a town will soon eliminate a rugged lone gunman.

38 In the 1980s and beyond, the movie series Rambo was the favourite of far-right groups. See Robins and Post, *Paranoid Politics*, 212.

Moreover, the romanticism misunderstood individualism as an extreme freedom to do whatever one wanted. And the notion of America as special ignored distinct and admirable features of other countries in the world, some as close as Canada to the north. Today, this American form of arrogance, an intentional ignorance of others, remains in the culture. Many Americans continue to accept without question the patriotic slogans that they are the freest people, and the greatest nation, in the world.

Conspiratorial ideas about a new world order continue to find their way into unexpected places, e.g., the explanation of John Kennedy's assassination. The result is a dangerous stew of half-baked ideas, uniformed interpretation, and paranoia.

SECTION 4: FROM CULTS TO MASS SHOOTERS

The emergence of irrational cults in America was clear in the Jonestown suicides. However, Jonestown was only one of a number of gruesome events due to cults.

Crazy Cults

Many people are familiar with the name of cult murderer Charles Manson. What some do not know is that Manson was not just crazy and the leader of a criminal gang. He became head of a counterculture, apocalyptic gang with a mission to kill people as part of destroying the "bourgeoisie world." Manson ranted, "One by one this fucked-up society is stripping my loves from me. I'll show them! They made animals of us – I'll unleash these animals – I'll give them so much fucking fear that people will be afraid to come out of their houses."[39]

In mid-1967, he formed what became known as the Manson Family, a quasi-commune based at first in a bus in California. Manson and his cult became famous when they killed nine people at four Los Angeles locations in July and August of 1969. In one incident, four members of the Manson Family invaded the home of actress Sharon Tate, married to director Roman Polanski. They murdered Tate, who was eight and

39 Ibid., 278.

a half months pregnant, along with four friends, including an eighteen-year-old, who were visiting at the time.

When he formed the Family, Manson was an unemployed ex-convict who had spent half of his life in prison. He was a minor songwriter in Los Angeles. The rock group the Beach Boys almost signed Manson to their record label. For a period of time in 1968, Manson and his family – in reality a bus of young men and women living a libertine lifestyle – got to know the Beach Boys through drummer Dennis Wilson, who was impressed with Manson's songs. A summer was spent partying and playing songs, but Manson's weird behaviour eventually frightened away band members.[40] When the Beatles released their *White Album* in 1968 Manson believed that thirteen of the songs were addressed to him personally. The drug-addled mind of Manson interpreted Paul McCartney's manic song "Helter Skelter," about getting high and coming down, as a warning about a pending apocalyptic race war in which white supremacy will finally triumph. When someone suggested that his commune should be filmed, Manson loved the idea but insisted that images of Hitler's Third Reich be inserted into the film.

Manson kept telling his followers that he would soon lead them to a great new world, but as time passed the followers grew impatient. So, Manson decided to do something drastic, quickly. He ordered the "Sharon Tate murders." He and his followers, who were mostly young women, believed the murders would help precipitate an apocalyptic war.

Unfortunately, Manson didn't just become notorious. He also became a symbol of insanity, violence, and the macabre in popular culture. The fascination that people have with dark irrationality was evident in the public's interest in Manson. After he was charged with the crimes, recordings of songs written and performed by Manson were released commercially. A number of musicians covered his songs, including the rock band Guns and Roses. He served out his life sentence in a California prison and died at eighty-three in 2017.

About twenty-five years after the Manson murders, David Koresh, leader of the Branch Davidian religious cult, died, along with seventy-nine others, on 19 April 1993. Their deaths occurred when an almost two-month-long siege by federal and Texas state officers, as well as the

40 See Hewitt, "The Beach Boys Nearly Sign Charles Manson to Their Label."

US military, came to a fiery end at the group's compound at the Mount Carmel Center outside Wacó, Texas.[41] The siege started when the US Bureau of Alcohol, Tobacco, and Firearms sought to serve arrest and search warrants for illegal possession of firearms and explosives.

Once again, we see psychological patterns perceptible in other cults previously described. Koresh was born Vernon Howell in Texas in 1959.[42] His childhood and youth seemed designed to undermine his self-worth and create a vengeful, paranoid leader, like Jim Jones. It was marked by rejection and lack of stability. As a youth, he was handed back and forth between his mother and grandmother, living in a number of places from Dallas to Houston. His stepfather was a macho ex-prisoner who beat him. Diagnosed with dyslexia, he struggled with school. He dreamt of being a rock star.[43] Then finding fundamentalist religion, he was entranced by the book of Revelation and the apocalypse. Eventually, he started to think of himself as a religious prophet. He became a congregational leader, but he annoyed some church goers with his dogmatic religious views. He proved to be a spellbinding preacher. After an internal power struggle, Koresh emerged as leader of the Branch Davidians in 1987 at the age of twenty-eight. He began to live with a harem of young girls, some as young as twelve. They believed he was Jesus Christ. The girls had a duty to allow him to plant his divine seed to fill the House of David. As in Jonestown, husbands were honoured to send him their wives and parents were honoured to send him their daughters. Allegations arose that Koresh was guilty of child abuse and statutory rape.

In the meantime, Koresh turned the church grounds into an armed compound and began training people for the apocalypse. He claimed that he was the seventh and final angel, destined to be the agent of God who brings about the end of the world. The triggering event would occur at his compound, during an attack by the US army. He urged followers to prepare for the final battle, which would a result in the world being consumed in fire and purified so that Christ could return. People who believed in Koresh would find paradise in the New Jerusalem.

41 Reavis, *The Ashes of Waco*, 13.

42 In 1990, Howell changed his name to David Koresh. Koresh is Hebrew for Cyrus, the Persian king who allowed the Jews to return to Palestine.

43 As a young person he got a band together. He once wrote a song called "Mad Man from Waco" in which he talks about a "Prince of Hell."

As the siege began, Koresh was paranoid, grandiose, and delusion, moving in and out of reality. The attention of the FBI and the media boosted his narcissism, and the guns and other weapons of the officers seemed to confirm his prophesy of a final battle. The self-fulfilling logic of apocalyptic thinking was about to run its terrible course.

Four years after the Waco siege, another irrational cult would make headlines for the dearth of its members. Only this time, the manner of their deaths would be eerily peaceful. In late March 1997, thirty-nine bodies were found at a mansion in Rancho Sante Fe, outside of San Diego. It was the largest mass suicide to occur in the United States. The dead were members of a group called Heaven's Gate.

How they died was striking. It was orderly, well-planned, and apparently without struggle. There was no mayhem and no resistance as in Jonestown. They drank a deadly potion and left this plane of existence. Members believed they would be picked up by a UFO and transported to the gates of Heaven.

With Heaven's Gate, we have another totalizing environment, and behind it all was an apocalyptic vision. The group's co-founders were Marshall Herff Applewhite and Bonnie Lu Nettles. Applewhite met Nettles in the early 1970s during a stay in a psychiatric institution.

Applewhite, like other cult leaders, was paranoid and a megalomaniac. Nettles was older, a nurse, and a born-again Baptist interested in the occult, astrology, and metaphysics. They renamed themselves Bo and Peep and took a six-month road trip across the United States.

In 1974, they assembled a wandering cult. For the next two decades, they lived in many places in Southern California. They used the new technology of the Internet to share their beliefs with a wider audience and also to make a living, designing websites. Although Nettles died in 1985, Applewhite kept the group together. By the 1990s, the group became reclusive and recruited followers online. Applewhite told followers that he was the second coming of Jesus Christ, that God was an alien, and that they were living at the end of the world.

Heaven's Gate members committed suicide over three days. Police found their bodies on 26 March 1997. Wearing black track suits and sneakers, they ate applesauce laced with barbiturates and washed it down with vodka. They then put bags over their heads and purple shrouds over their bodies and lay down to leave their bodies, or earthly vehicles, behind. They did not think they were killing themselves. They were transitioning to another level of existence. They were freeing their souls so they could ascend to a spacecraft, a UFO – a "cloud of light" – flying in the wake of the Hale-Bopp comet which was passing by Earth. The UFO would take them to a new home in space. Heaven, apparently, was a physical place that could be reached by a UFO.

Commentators noted how orderly, non-violent, or "gentle" the three-day process had been. Yet suicide is violent in its own way. It is self-destruction. Moreover, they had a violent attitude toward their bodies. Eight of the male members had themselves castrated before leaving for heaven. The Next Level was a place without gender. Probably, the members did not know that the castration idea originated in Applewhite's troubled sexual past. Applewhite was fired as a music professor in 1970 after university officials learned he had sex with a male student. He sought cures for his homosexual urges. The conflict between his homosexuality and his married life caused a mental breakdown. Now, he wanted to find a way to have a Platonic relationship with members. Castration would make that easier. The group, unaware of this background, saw castration as a religious ideal, and they instituted a strict "no sex, no human-level relationships" rule.

CONCLUSION: KILLING AMERICANS AT PRAYER

Today, cults, racist leaders, and militias continue to attest to the deep, abiding legacy of Hatred Americano. Only now, a different kind of irrational force has been added to the mix, and it is killing hundreds of people. No, not the foreign terrorist, but the domestic, irrational terrorist. It is the lone gunman who uses military guns and other weapons to carry out delusional apocalyptic goals, seething with hatred against innocent citizens – usually entire strangers. The paranoid loners are inspired by online websites about Hitler, terrorist groups, recycled conspiracy theories about Jews and Blacks, and other sordid material. They walk into a school, a workplace, or a church and open fire on unarmed and peaceful men, women, and children. Then, the mass shooters use social media to upload images of their actions, captured on a smart phone, to the internet. There, they claim to have avenged some terrible group or thwarted some terrible threat – all the while believing they have achieved heroic status and media immortality.

The psychological determinants for mass shooters are not new. Often, the shooters have apocalyptic visions, have turned their failures in life into racist hatred, and now have a world of global media – countless irrational hate sites – to feed (and confirm) their angst and paranoia. They may stumble on the *Turner Diaries* or some ancient and invalid tale of Jews killing Christian children. They fall back into a medieval form of irrationality. Beset by their mental discontent, they have neither the capacity nor the will to assess online material objectively. Nor do they want objectivity. They want someone to blame.

Equally depressing is that there appears to be no political pathway to respond to the mass shootings. Neither the racist right nor the Christian right will help America respond to these killings. The right to bear arms movement, fostered by rifle associations, right wing groups, and anti-government paranoia, make sure no legislation will be introduced to reduce the slaughter. Apparently, the right to bear arms trumps the right not to be shot when at prayer.

The fact that America cannot effectively respond to the crisis shows the extent to which America is not only polarized but tottering on the verge of public irrationality. Many birds are coming home to roost. If killing kids in schools does not prompt most citizens to revaluate laws and principles, you have a society that is reality averse *in extremis* and is paralyzed by an irrational mindset among many citizens.

PART THREE

Explaining Irrational Publics

10

Engines of Unreason

Everything is the way it is because it got that way.[1]

We are biological and our souls cannot fly free.

Edward O. Wilson[2]

I HAVE WRITTEN ON THE NATURE of rationality and irrationality, the tension of rationality and irrationality in culture, and examples of extreme irrationalism. It is time to develop a view of the causes of this pendulum and its most extreme manifestations.

My viewpoint is philosophical naturalism, defined in chapter 1. It fits well with the scientific naturalism that followed Darwin's momentous investigations into the evolution of species. The founding discipline of the sciences of the human is evolutionary biology under Darwin's idea of natural selection. In the mid-1900s, a genetic reformulation of Darwinism arose with the great synthesis of Darwin and Mendel. The gene became the mechanism for inherited characteristics pruned by natural selection.[3] This synthesis was secured intellectually by Theodosius Dobzhansky, Julian Huxley, Ernst Mayer, William Hamilton, and others.[4] Today, the theory of DNA-based reproduction and evolution shows its power from ecology and genetic engineering to the insights gained from the Human Genome Project.[5] Natural

1 A phrase credited to biologist D'arcy Thompson. Cited in Dennett, *Darwin's Dangerous Idea*, 220.

2 Wilson, *On Human Nature*, 1.

3 To get a sense of how gene-orientated is today's evolutionary biology, consult the research papers in the recent book by Arber, *Evolutionary Biology*.

4 On the place of evolutionary theory in biology, see Sober's *Philosophy of Biology*.

5 The Human Genome Project was a scientific project to determine the human genome, completed in 2003. One finding was there are about 22,300 protein-coding genes in humans.

selection "unifies all of biology and the history of the planet into a single grand story."[6]

In the second half of the twentieth century, new evolutionary sciences, from sociobiology to evolutionary psychology, narrowed the distance between biology and the social sciences (and the humanities). Controversy flared, especially where writers applied their ideas to human society, such as Edward O. Wilson's sociobiology – applying biological principles to social behaviour, from ants to humans.[7] Some of the claims of sociobiologists were overreaching and provocative, e.g., predicting the reduction of the social sciences to principles of biology. The bravado invited attack, including criticism from noted evolutionists such as Stephen Jay Gould.[8] Also, there were spurious attacks on Wilson's views as genetic determinism, fascist, and anti-female. In the 1980s, evolutionary psychology arose with less controversy, followed by new disciplines about the connections between mind, brain, and ethics: neuroethics, psychiatric neuroethics, neuroscience, moral cognition theory, and evolutionary psychopathy.

I introduce a philosophical theory, a general framework for making sense of irrationality and intolerance. It is a set of conjectures derived from these leading evolutionary theories. Philosophical frameworks bring together a plethora of specific findings so we can grasp where our knowledge of certain phenomena stands. Therefore, my framework is not a scientific hypothesis tested through prediction and precise methods. This hard work occurs in the sciences. My view draws out the implications of the human sciences. It is not science.

Over the next two chapters I provide two connected approaches.

First, in this chapter, I offer an evolutionary explanation of the origins of irrational intolerance. I trace irrational intolerance back to primordial mental adaptations that are universal to our species. Extreme psychological traits are understood as extreme motivational systems that developed because they were adaptive. In the next chapter, I offer a psychological explanation of how these adaptations express themselves in concrete situations. This requires looking at triggers and enabling conditions.

6 Dennett, *Darwin's Dangerous Idea*, 20.

7 See Wilson, *Sociobiology: The New Synthesis*.

8 Gould had praise for Wilson's *Sociobiology* and its explanation of altruism. But Gould was "very unhappy" with the last chapter on humans. Gould thought Wilson was suggesting a biological determinism, via genes. See Gould, *Ever Since Darwin*, 252.

SECTION 1: THE ADAPTIVE MIND

In every human mind, whatever the intellectual development, there remains an indeterminate background of primitive mentality.

Lucien Levy-Bruhl[9]

A Conjecture and Three Hypotheses

Why resort to evolution?

Because extreme irrationality is a capacity of human nature, and human nature is a product of evolution.

My naturalism holds that there must be an evolutionary story that explains the emergence of our species and our mind. This story explains mental traits that cause irrational intolerance such as extreme aggression, hostility, paranoia, and tribalism. Whether we can discover the complete details of that story cannot be known in advance. But, already, an outline of the story has been sketched by evolutionary psychologists and others.[10]

I advance a two-fold conjecture:

Primordial origins: The psychological dispositions of irrationality and irrational intolerance are so strong, so emotive, so raw, and all-but-universal in the species that their origin is to be found in early human history. They are primordial in origin and still part of our human nature. Thus, today, they can be activated by triggers in a person's personality and environment.[11]

Maladaptive traits: When activated in modern times, the traits that cause irrational intolerance are often maladaptive for individual, society, and species. Joyce in *The Evolution of Morality* captures my perspective: "Psychological mechanisms productive of adaptive behavior in a prehistoric past may, when operating in creatures no longer living in such an environment, result in different, surprising, and/or maladaptive

9 Lévy-Bruhl, *How Natives Think*, 28.

10 See Buss, *Evolutionary Psychology: The New Science of the Mind.*

11 Interestingly, urban people often discover their animality by accident, e.g., when a bear attacks us while we are walking in the forest. People who have had such experiences talk about how they felt deep animal-like impulses to survive, to fight or to flee. For an engaging discussion, see Maxim Loskutoff, "The Beast in Me," in the *New York Times*, 17 August 2018.

behavior."[12] Given that extreme intolerance is part of our inheritance as a species, it will not disappear soon.

These conjectures, if true, catch sight of a large irony. In a sophisticated world, we use media technology to activate our oldest and most primitive prejudices: our fear of the stranger and our tribalism toward groups of strangers.

I explore these conjectures with the help of three hypotheses:

THE ENGINES OF UNREASON HYPOTHESIS

I locate the source of irrational intolerance in the engines of unreason: the traits of (1) excessive aggression and (2) group contempt. These traits literally cause unreason or irrational conduct. The traits that are the engines of unreason are the hard side of humans, what we have called dark irrationalism. The traits belong to our "Darwinian self," in contrast to our softer, more sociable side which features empathy and altruism. The engines of unreason are psychological adaptations by our ancestors to the problems they encountered in their primordial environments. Given the right conditions today, these traits erupt into our social and personal lives causing havoc and harm. They are engines of unreason in a world that needs engines of reason.

THE ENEMY STANCE HYPOTHESIS

The engines of unreason, when activated, create a specific mindset in individuals and groups. I call it an enemy stance. Other people and other groups are regarded as enemies that must be overcome, resisted, or eliminated.

THE COMMUNICATION VIOLENCE HYPOTHESIS

The origins of intolerant public communication, which I call communication violence, are found among the engines of unreason. Early in human history, the use of hostile or manipulative symbols and language capacities was prompted by the need to arouse the enemies of unreason for self-defence or group defence.

12 Joyce, *The Evolution of Morality*, 5.

Human Nature as Basic Repertoire

My analysis stands or falls on the validity of two notions: human nature and psychological adaptations acquired through evolution.[13]

Perhaps no notion in biology and the social sciences has caused so much unproductive and fierce debate than the idea of human nature. So, before I present my theory, I need to explain how my approach avoids the typical objections to talk of human nature.

Accepted as a fundamental fact during the Enlightenment, the idea of human nature was attacked in the twentieth century as presuming a deterministic view of humans that denies individuality and the role of culture. Also, it was alleged that appeals to human nature support hierarchical or racist societies as natural. Historically, the latter charge is correct. But this does not rule out an alternate conception of human nature that is not associated with racism or the justification of the status quo.

It is hard to avoid making *some* informal assumptions about human nature in everyday life. We presume that people prefer, as a matter of human nature, pleasure over pain. They identify more closely with kin than strangers. They rise to anger if treated unfairly, are frustrated when they meet obstacles to goals, and are prone to rationalize their questionable actions. This is a folk psychology that presumes we have a common nature.

Human nature is also a concept of philosophy, theology, and other disciplines. The Western history of ideas is populated with theories of human nature, from Judeo-Christian notions of a God-made human nature to scientific notions of an evolution-made human nature. Political philosophies, such as liberalism and communism, make assumptions about human nature.

By human nature, I mean those innate capacities, proclivities, and evolutionary adaptations that are the common heritage of healthy infants born into our species. The development of these innate traits occurs as the individual grows and interacts with the world. I agree with Pinker's definition of human nature as a "complex system of cognitive and emotional faculties, implemented in the brain which owe their basic design to the processes of evolution."[14]

13 On human nature as "the central premise" of evolutionary psychology, see Barkow, Cosmides and Tooby, *The Adapted Mind*, 5.

14 Pinker, *The Better Angels of Our Nature*, xxiii.

Coming from the humanities I think of human nature as an inherited repertoire of abilities for performing the drama of life, i.e., for responding to a complex environment. How we use this repertoire varies from person to person, culture to culture.

What belongs to human nature? The traits can be placed in six categories:

(1) PHYSICAL HUMAN NATURE

Humans have similar bodies, from organs to muscular structure, and these parts have a distinctive organization into a complete organism. Humans share a genome. They also have common physical and material needs to survive.

(2) INSTINCTUAL AND DESIROUS HUMAN NATURE

Humans have a basic set of instincts and desires such as the instincts for food and sex. Even the smile appears to be a species-wide instinct, as do many phobias such as fear of snakes. We also have desires for warmth, security, activities that bring pleasure, the avoidance of pain, and social approval. The instincts and desires can be conscious or unconscious.

(3) COGNITIVE AND EMOTIVE HUMAN NATURE

Humans have cognitive capacities such as perception, conceptualization, memory, habit, reasoning, and decision-making. Humans share a core of emotions such as fear, anxiety, anger, aggression, empathy and sympathy, plus moods such as depression, boredom, or exhilaration. Humans have conative powers, such as the capacity to will that I do something.

(4) SYMBOLIC, RATIONAL HUMAN NATURE

Humans are innately conscious and capable of thinking symbolically and rationally. Humans represent things in linguistic terms and they use symbols to mathematically measure the world, to think logically from premise to conclusion, and to have forethought. They use symbols to express their image of themselves and the world, to produce art, ethics, and science. Humans have innate propensities to form habits, to develop a personality, and to prefer certain mindsets.

(5) REGULATIVE HUMAN NATURE

Humans are innately reflective and self-conscious. Consequently, humans have the capacity to evaluate their beliefs and actions. They regulate their behaviour.

(6) SOCIAL HUMAN NATURE

Humans have innate social traits. They appear to have a near universal desire to live in groups and to prefer their group over other groups. In many societies, they display empathy and sufficient willingness to cooperate to allow society to exist. They also live in social hierarchies where they worry about their status.

These components of human nature are designed – by nature – to express themselves differently in different contexts. They are capacities with potential. One and the same trait can be realized in many ways.[15] The capacity to love or to show anger is expressed differently from culture to culture.

My view of human nature is anti-dualistic. It refuses to see the explanation of the mind as a forced choice between nature or nurture. It refuses to think of the explanation of human conduct as a forced choice between attributing it mainly (or solely) to genes or mainly (or solely) to culture. Moreover, my view rejects the dualism that the human mind, upon birth, is either a blank slate or it is a mind crammed with innate ideas.[16] These sterile dualisms, and the quarrels they sparked, have taken up too much of our time.[17]

Fortunately, there is an alternate perspective which I call *interactionism.* This interactionism is becoming the approach of the best theorizing about humans today. It explains human traits through a nuanced interaction between human nature, experience, and the environment. Traits develop within the organism–ecology interface.

The idea of human conduct as fully formed by genetic inheritance cannot withstand serious scrutiny. This form of explanation does not even work where the role of genes is known to be large. For example, consider the genetic metabolic disorder phenylketonuria (PKU) which is caused by an enzyme deficiency and can result in severe mental retardation and seizures. It can be avoided by providing the infant with an appropriate diet.

On the other hand, the idea of the human, or the human mind, fully formed by culture and experience cannot withstand serious scrutiny. The infant arrives in the world with a large number of genetically

15 See Polger and Shapiro, *The Multiple Realization Book.*

16 For a rebuttal of blank slate theorists, see Pinker's *The Blank Slate.*

17 On the sterile nature of these dueling dualisms, see Dennett, *Freedom Evolves,* 157–8.

specified innate reflexes and tendencies, such as an instinct to seek warmth and food and a desire to attach to their mother.

If you still think human nature is a myth, consider this fact: every page of *Gray's Anatomy*, dealing with our physical structure, applies to every human on the planet.

The real issue is not whether nature or nurture is in complete control but to what extent biology and the environment influence humans in general and in specific cases. Furthermore, the great question today is not *if* there is a human nature but what we want it to be. As Habermas said, humans have, for the first time, the capacity to *change* their nature by altering, deleting, and splicing genes.[18] The question "Who are we as a species?" becomes "Who do we want to be?"

To understand human nature in this interactionist manner is the best antidote to the misuse of the idea of human nature.

Probable Universals

Given organism–environment interaction, what does innate mean?

It means innate is a probability concept. An innate trait is an endogenous trait which, under certain conditions, is likely or probable to appear. For example, it is highly probable that our innate capacity to learn language will develop in childhood at a standard rate as long as we are in a supportive environment where a specific language is used by parents and others.

By now, we are familiar with talk about how a feature like the colour of one's eyes or a physical disorder such as Down syndrome is inheritable (through genes) as a percentage, e.g., the colour of your eyes has a heritability of almost 100 per cent. Talk of percentages means that both internal and external factors are in play. A genetically determined trait is a trait that differs from other traits as a result of the presence of one or more distinctive genes. But to what extent is the trait gene determined? Moreover, how many types of causes – genetic, chemical, environmental, social – converge to produce the trait? One cannot *abstract* human nature from its concrete and complex anchor in the world.

Genes create *general* predispositions or susceptibilities to certain things, e.g., a susceptibility to cancer. The rest is filled in by experience

18 See Habermas, *The Future of Human Nature.*

and the environment. There is no gene that makes individuals prefer a Big Mac burger or prefer Times Roman font when typing an essay. I, like others of my species, have inherited a predisposition to fight if provoked, but I have no gene that says I must fight Tom, that bigmouth at my local pub.

The idea of genetic determinism is violated everyday by humans. We rebel against basic instructions from our genes and instincts. Humans commit suicide. They engage in altruistic conduct detrimental to their genetic fitness – a soldier jumps on a grenade to save his troupe. Even if genes are "selfish," as the evolutionary biologist Richard Hawkins famously wrote, this does not entail that humans are necessarily (and only) selfish.[19]

Does saying a psychological or social trait is innate entail that it is universal – that every person or society manifests the trait? No. Given the complexity of evolution and the probable nature of innate mechanisms, it is best to talk about traits that are generally true of the species or of human culture. I prefer the term "species-wide" rather than "universal" given the long and thorny debate about universals in the history of ideas.[20] Innate mechanisms tend to express themselves "absent any environmental variation to cause divergence."[21] But we should allow for exceptions, e.g., genetic defects rob an individual of a species-wide capacity. Some people incorrectly deny that aggression is innate (or has a significant genetic component) because it appears that a tiny minority of societies are pacific. But, innateness is a "measurable probability that a trait will develop in a specific set of environments" not the certainty it will develop in all environments.[22]

Nonetheless, universality, or near universality, may tell us something. It suggests that an innate mechanism is operating. The near universality of morality in societies and the early capacity of children for moral judgment does not *entail* that morality is innate, let alone that there is a gene for morality. But it suggests that the capacity to make moral judgments has an innate component. Anthropologist Donald Brown has found that cultures around the world share hundreds of traits, from

19 See Dawkins, *The Selfish Gene.*

20 See Armstrong, *A Theory of Universals.*

21 Wright, *The Moral Animal,* 137.

22 Wilson, *On Human Nature,* 100.

romantic love and food taboos to the mourning of the dead.[23] Not every cultural commonality reflects a corresponding innate mechanism. But the commonalities give us a reason to investigate the role of human nature and innate factors.

SECTION 2: ROOTS OF UNREASON

How do we use this naturalistic, interactionist framework to explain the engines of unreason?

First, we identify the main traits (or adaptations) to be explained. Second, we examine existing knowledge about psychological adaptations in ancestral ecologies, especially as it relates to these traits. Third, we provide a plausible evolutionary view of why these traits evolved to become part of human nature and why they may be maladaptive today.

Nine Key Traits

In previous chapters, I indicated here and there that a number of traits need explaining, such as reality averse beliefs and extreme emotions. Here is a full list of the traits that typically characterize irrationally intolerant people:

Disturbing sense of vulnerability: There is disturbing psychological vulnerability or uncertainty beyond the normal sense of vulnerability natural to the human organism. There is a severe lack of self-esteem, often caused by events in youth and early adult life.

Mounting inner conflict and external frustration: The uncertainty is increased as people struggle with conflicts between their inner desires and their ideal self-image, defined socially. This psychological condition is exacerbated by thwarted aims and social rejection. Alienation arises, and life may come to lack meaning. This discontent may prompt a retreat into isolation. The person may develop the loner syndrome where the person begins to fantasize about themselves as great but misunderstood. The frustration requires release.

Projection and suspicion: The level of psychological conflict is reduced through the projection of one's troubling traits and conflicts on to other individuals or groups. The person adopts a suspicious stance to society,

23 Brown, *Human Universals*.

alert to other groups as threatening. Narcissism and paranoia are often components of the mindset. They may grow in strength over time, at times becoming delusional and psychotic. The person also displays extreme emotions and inappropriate responses such as high levels of fear, irritability, impatience, anger, inflammatory language, and unwillingness to dialogue or compromise.

Discovery of a single, unquestionable meaning to life: The person becomes entranced by a utopian goal, a sense-making but simplistic ideology preached by a father-like leader. The goal, which can be millennial and apocalyptic, is often fantastical and reality-averse. Some individuals develop a delusional sense of being a divine prophet or a long-awaited great leader.

Creation of an enemy – the threat of decline and contamination: The suspicion and ideology lead to the identification of an enemy group that is said to threaten the individual and/or their group. A strong tribalism results, defining society in terms of we versus them. Scapegoats are found. The enemy group is blamed for a decline in, or contamination of, culture, which requires that the disease be eradicated. The promiscuity of ideas, defined in chapter 1, plays a harmful role here, allowing leaders to link groups of people with notions of contamination, disease, and what is unnatural. The dominant political view is that politics is a war of tribes, to be won at all costs. Politics is a sequence of zero-sum battles.

Symbiotic relation between guru and followers: The "all yet nothing" guru psychology (see chapter 7) creates acolytes for a guru or prophetic leader who is thought to have special traits and knowledge. The guru is all or everything for the group. Yet the leader is nothing without his followers and their ardent belief in his powers and vision. Absolute loyalty is required.

Twisted logic: Achieving the goal of one's ideology is all important. The end justifies almost any means. The ordinary meaning of language is corrupted to rationalize unethical actions, such as portraying the killing of innocent people as helping the victim.

Sanctioning of violence and discrimination: Achieving the end requires fierce aggression hatred, and a willingness to threaten and attack (verbally or physically) the targeted group or a willingness to support others who do so. In many cases, the perpetrators of violence come to be fascinated by dark and destructive impulses, and a sadism evolves. The great end justifies going outside the law and social morality.

Totalizing environment, authoritarianism, and the absolute. Irrational intolerance thrives in cults, militia, and other groups that come to exercise total control over members. They become reality averse *in extremis.* Giving others such control is more likely if the person has an authoritarian personality that values sameness and obedience. Attachment to the leader, or to the cause of the favoured group, is a form of erotic absolutism – the love of prostrating oneself before a presumed absolute leader and values.

Not all nine features are exhibited by every irrationally intolerant person or group. But a core of these features is displayed in most cases. The traits may become so extreme that the person is functioning under a mental disorder or pathology.

One way to look at the list of features is to divide them into three groups. (a) *Inner conflict*: a struggle that calls for a release of frustration through projection and the creation of an enemy to hate. (b) *Group identity*: the dynamics of joining a group, such as absorbing a tribal ideology, and playing a role in the totalizing guru–acolyte structure. And (c) *acting on one's ideology*: violence, discrimination, and absolute loyalty.

Another way to look at these traits is to see them as all exhibiting one property: extremism – extremes of fear and anger, extremes in conduct.

I begin my evolutionary approach to this nine-fold mindset by considering the group features of early humans.

Vulnerability and the Group

Early humans lived at an elemental level of life. Individuals needed traits that helped them survive as individuals. These are traits of individualism. They also needed traits that helped them be part of cohesive groups. These are traits of groupism. Both sets of traits co-existed, by necessity.

An important feature of humans is that they are born almost entirely helpless as infants. In primordial times, this required parents and the tribe to spend a lot of resources on rearing the infant and then the child. It still does. What the new human has going for it is a set of instincts, reflexes, and bodily structures that express the organism's innate desire to exist and to develop. From birth, humans are characterized by a tension between an instinct to develop, eat, and grow – to exist as an individual in its environment – and the individual's vulnerability to damaging events or deadly objects in the environment. This is a vulnerability of which the individual soon becomes aware. This tension is the crucible out of which human psychology develops, and it is a drama played out until death. Vulnerability puts its stamp on human society. Society supports the young individual while calling on the latter, when older and capable, to return the favour by supporting society and other individuals.

This individualism is sometimes called egoism. Spinoza recognized the centrality of organic individualism centuries ago when he wrote, "Everything, in so far as it is in itself, endeavors to persist in its own being."[24] Schopenhauer crisply defined egoism as "the urgent impulse to exist, and exist under the best circumstances."[25] In my view, individualism or egoism is a great, biologically based, impulse which becomes self-interest when we add rational thinking to the process. The individualism of the just-born human organism is not conscious or selfish. It is an organic, inchoate desire to sustain existence, which requires assistance from the environment. The development of individualism is the gradual turning of the organism outward to the world, a strong instinct to persist and to persist well as one becomes a full adult member of one's community. The necessary organic individualism of the infant becomes, in time, a conscious and understandable concern for one's person or ego. The individual learns, within a culture, how to compete with others for limited resources and social benefits. However, without an innate zeal for maintaining and maturing individuality from the beginning of life, our species would have perished long ago.

Evolution, however, did not leave us there, as individuals seeking to advance only ourselves. And it is a good thing that it did not. As Hobbes made clear, unrestrained individualism leads to a war of all against all. Schopenhauer thinks egoism is essentially selfish in the extreme.[26] Selfish egoism is the "gloomy side of human nature" – what I call the Darwinian side. People only care for their own pleasure, and they exhibit extreme traits, such as hatred, envy, malice, and cruelty toward others.

24 Spinoza, *Ethics*, part III, proposition VI, 136.

25 Schopenhauer, *The Basis of Morality*, part III, 75.

26 Schopenhauer says acts of egoism and acts of moral worth "absolutely exclude each other." My individualism takes a different view, arguing that individualism (or egoism) can express itself selfishly or not. Schopenhauer, *The Basis of Morality*, 83.

Schopenhauer notes that selfish egoism is so much the opposite of morality that society must use every available tool to restrain it, from the threat of police action to the wrath of a mythical god. The essence of ethics is to understand the psychology of humans, what causes them to act well or poorly, and how to support moral, non-egotistical, character. What matters is supporting a "morality of the heart."[27] Only then should one worry about detailed rules, codes of ethics, and theories of morality. As Schopenhauer states, "To preach morality is easy, to found difficult."[28]

Fortunately, a morality of the heart, e.g., as exhibited in compassion, evolved because evolution developed not only our egoistical impulses but also our cooperative, social side. This is groupism, the desire to belong to groups, and the development of traits that support group existence and development.[29] Groupism is responsible for developing empathy, sympathy, reciprocity, and loyalty to one's group. But to live in groups, individuals had to restrain their individualism, their unrestrained pursuit of goods that favour only themselves. How did this restraint come about?

Explaining the emergence of restrained individualism, cooperation, and eventually morality is a major pastime of ethicists and evolutionary theorists.[30] One answer is this: Prudentially, early humans gained a fitness advantage by cooperating, especially in a hostile ecology. Cooperating groups survived better than conflicted groups or lone individuals. Evolution selected for cooperating groups of individuals, making sure social traits would become species-wide adaptations. But the story cannot be that simple. One wonders how cooperation grew in the first place among individuals who made their survival and self-interest a paramount value. How did cooperation arise when defecting

27 However, with Schopenhauer there is an important limit placed on supporting moral character. In his view, character is "fixed and unchangeable" and hence people are, by nature, (1) virtuous or not, and therefore (2) virtue cannot be taught. I disagree with both of these propositions. Schopenhauer, *The Basis of Morality*, 80, 123.

28 Schopenhauer, *On the Will in Nature*, 128.

29 Haidt says humans are "groupish." They love to form all manner of groups, from teams to nations. Haidt, *The Righteous Mind*, 190.

30 See, for example, Joyce, *The Evolution of Morality*; Frans de Waal, *Primates and Philosophers*; Greene, *Moral Tribalism*; and Wright, *The Moral Animal*.

from cooperation could be, at least on some occasions, advantageous?[31] How did trust and reciprocity get a stable foothold in groups?

To address these questions, evolutionists have sought more complex accounts of human interaction. Robert Trivers, in his classic paper, "The Evolution of Reciprocal Altruism," explained reciprocal altruism as acting in a manner that temporarily reduces one's fitness while increasing another organism's fitness, with the expectation that the other organism will act in a similar manner later.[32] Other evolutionists talk about mutual benefit – where all actors benefit from cooperation, such as a group of people rowing a boat to shore. Altruism is where an actor incurs a cost to benefit another. Selfishness applies to an actor who benefits by inflicting a loss on a recipient. Actions are spiteful where an actor incurs a loss to inflict a cost on another.[33]

Reciprocity seems easy to explain. If you scratch my back, I'll scratch yours. The trouble is that reciprocal acts take place over time. That requires trust. Why should I trust you to scratch my back *after* I have scratched yours? Hobbes said men will only maintain reciprocal agreements if there is a ruler to punish defectors. Therefore, theorists have used game theory and computer-generated games of cooperation to show what cooperative strategies lead to stable forms of reciprocity.[34] One finding is that reciprocity may fail in one-time interactions. Strangers may defect after you do something nice for them. They may pick your pocket and disappear. But reciprocity is more likely to develop if we look at people who have interactions over time, such as people who work together or live in communities. Actors come to know each other, allowing a mutual confidence to grow and making defection costly. Determining the reliability of others to reciprocate may have been one of the first uses of gossip – to gather information on the

31 This is the well-known free rider problem of how society deals with individuals who benefit by not cooperating. They avoid paying their fair share of taxes or gain support from social programs to which they are not entitled.

32 Economists use "strong reciprocity" to refer a form of altruism where members of a group punish violators even though they gain no benefit (and may incur a cost) for their actions. They do it to support the group. See Bowles and Gintis, "The Evolution of Strong Reciprocity."

33 For further clarification of these terms, see West, Griffin, and Gardner, "Social Semantics."

34 Robert Axelrod's *The Evolution of Cooperation* popularized the application of computerized game theory to the problems of cooperation.

character of cooperators. Hobbes was not entirely wrong. Force and punishment have supported reciprocity throughout history. But it is applied not only by kings or coercive states. The social hierarchies of early human society used shunning, complaining, threatening, and punishing to restrain defectors. Eventually, with reciprocity in place, more robust forms of social relations appeared, such as primal forms of altruism and love. And then morality.

Is it likely that reciprocal stances would be favoured by natural selection among early humans? Yes. Consider how prehistoric humans as hunter-gathers fitted into their ecology.[35] They lived in small groups that consisted of several families of a few dozen people. Yet their home territory could be as large as 3,000 square kilometres – the range of a wolf pack, but a hundred times larger than the home range occupied by a troupe of vegetarian gorillas. Hence, reciprocating associations of humans increased their evolutionary fitness.

Yet the co-existence of soft and hard traits could never be taken for granted. Human association, from the beginning, was a fragile balance between cooperation and fighting.[36] Primordial humans and their groups were not always at each other's throats. There is evidence that they worked together to make better tools and they formed bands of one hundred or less to roam for food. Within groups, young males would have to restrain their sexuality and aggression and adopt more complex social skills. Over time, humans began interacting with social groups located far away. Some 130,000 years ago, there were groups who, although living 300 kilometres apart, exchanged goods and resources.[37] Also, early humans, male and female, were directly involved in families and in the extended care of infants. This helped to establish empathy as an emotional capability and eventually an adaptation. De Waal's work on the psychology of chimpanzees and other primates has found what appears to be early forms of the human emotions of sympathy, compassion, empathy, and care for distressed members of kin.[38] We can think of primordial prosocial (cooperative) and non-social

35 On the role of ecology, see Nettle, "Ecological Influences on Human Behavioral Diversity"; and Nettle, *Evolution and Genetics for Psychology*.

36 See Bourke, *Principles of Social Evolution*.

37 See Dunbar and Shultz, "Evolution in the Social Brain," and "Bondedness and Sociality."

38 De Waal, *Primates and Philosophers*.

(aggressive) behaviours as different strategies and adaptations that serve human survival, given the human niche in the ecology.[39]

Balancing the traits of individualism and groupism was a constant concern.

Within groups, violence erupted over mates and social standing. But often the impact of the fighting was moderated by ritualized fighting where a competitor lost a challenge but was not killed. Who or what maintained this balance? There was no police force, no written commandments, and no philosophies of cooperation. Rather, what was appropriate was a matter of evolved social behaviour. There were group norms and approved behaviours – an early, implicit, proto-morality – enforced by social hierarchies. Also, selective pressures would have developed social anxieties about conduct that harms the group or mating. If excluded from the group, individuals would have had less chance to mate and have progeny.[40] Group cooperation helped groups to be uncooperative toward other groups, deemed to be rivals or threats. A major function of group cooperation was to enable collective aggression against other groups, from small-scale fights and raids to all-out wars between enemy coalitions.[41]

The need to get this balance between individual and social traits right was a life or death affair. Aggressive traits were needed when danger arose, but those would be maladaptive if they caused excessive defections and group in-fighting.

Extremism: Individual and Tribal

So far, my tale of human developments ends on a somewhat positive note. Early humans developed individual and group traits and balanced them to survive and reproduce, despite an unforgiving environment. But if this *is* the story, what about fierce aggression, hatred, and the rest of the hard traits? Not enough has been said about them. The adaptations of individualism and groupism do not explain the origins of the

39 See Hawley, "Ontogeny and Social Dominance," and "The Duality of Human Nature."

40 See Baron and Richardson, *Human Aggression.*

41 See Bowles and Gintis, *A Cooperative Species.*

engines of unreason. It seems, as American humourist Ogden Nash once wrote, "You can't get there from here."[42]

Actually, you can get there from here. But you have to add to the mix an important feature of our ancestors: the capacity for extremism. Extremism in emotion, in thought, and in behaviour. It is *these* traits that create tribalism and intolerance. Why did they evolve? Why do humans have the capacity to become terribly angry or full of fury, willing to physically attack another person? Such responses evolved to serve an adaptive function. It was not enough for individuals to feed themselves and work in groups. The human ecology required that individuals and groups had the capacity to exhibit traits to an extreme degree. It was not enough for groups to promote cooperation. The milder traits were not sufficient to ensure human survival and the all-important replication of genes.

Groups needed their largest and strongest members, usually male, to engage rival groups or predatory animals, either to kill the latter for food or to not be eaten by them.[43] To do this, one must be fierce and aggressive. One must be capable of arousing oneself into extreme states of anger and hatred. These states increased fitness. The advantage of having extreme traits would cause them to proliferate in the species and become adaptations. They would become part of human nature.

The same case can be made for the origins of traits that define tribalism. Tribalism is an extreme loyalty to one's group and an extreme bias against other groups. Today, tribalism expresses itself as extreme nationalism and patriotism. The threat of rivals bonded groups into fighting units, ready to attack and gain the resources of the other tribe, or ready to defend their group's own resources and mates. Tribalism consisted in a deep suspicion of other groups, based on a need to clearly separate us from them.

Lorenz argued that, with the development of weapons during the Stone Age the capacity to successfully attack (or defend against) other human groups became the most important selective factor in human development. He notes that, across the Paleolithic and Stone Age eras,

42 Nash, *You Can't Get There From Here.*

43 There has been a debate in evolutionary theory as to whether primordial humans developed as "man the hunter" or "man the hunted." See Sussman and Hart, *Man the Hunted.* For my story, the debate doesn't matter. Both forms of behaviour required Darwinian traits.

almost every new tool, such as the capacity to control fire, was used as a weapon against others. This need for cohesive groups may have encouraged the development of in-group friendship and comradery, similar to the way that members of a military unit in dangerous territory develop strong bonds.[44] Threats encountered in the wild encouraged male-dominated social hierarchies with strong leaders. This is, I suggest, the origin of the human propensity toward authoritarian social structures and the authoritarian personality.

More recently, the search for ancient DNA has reinforced and brought back into focus how much of human evolution was due to violent mass migrations across Europe, North America, and elsewhere. The migrations were brutal events as the migraters replaced, by attacking and killing, resident populations.[45]

We sometimes wonder why people today have the capacity to harm others, to hate, to be out of control angry, to believe conspiracies about others, and to use weapons of war. From an evolutionary view, there is no mystery. Evolution developed us as suspicious, hyper-alert creatures who have a propensity to hate, to harm, and to be violent. Causing harm, originally, had adaptive advantage. To eliminate one's rival was a harsh but effective survival strategy. Recall Nietzsche's assertion that humans should be like "large birds of prey" who carry off a small lamb without twinges of conscience.[46] This bird of prey attitude is always possible for humans because it is part of human nature. As Trilling said, "Somewhere in the child, somewhere in the adult, there is a hard, irreducible, stubborn core of biological urgency, and biological necessity, and biological reason that culture cannot reach."[47]

Early in our history, extreme individualism and tribalism were pre-wired into our brains as adaptations. In modern times, Darwinian traits became difficult to control. Modern humans in Darwinian mode see *too many things* as a threat and regard too many situations as requiring an aggressive response. Darwinian mindsets prompt modern societies to support war, genocide, and paranoid leaders. Human history and morality are largely a record of how these moderate and immoderate traits have competed to influence human behaviour.

44 Lorenz, *On Aggression*, 209.
45 See Reich, *Who We Are and How We Got Here.*
46 Nietzsche, *On the Genealogy of Morals*, first essay, 29.
47 Trilling, "Freud: Within and Beyond Culture," 13.

SECTION 3: MIND DESIGN

I have used broad evolutionary ideas to conjecture how extreme traits originated in early humans. I now employ more specific concepts from the evolutionary theory of mind.

In the mid-1900s, discovery of the genetic basis of natural selection strengthened evolutionary biology's large-scale story about the evolution of life on earth. But evolutionists struggled to apply these highly general theories to small-scale phenomenon. There was plenty of evolutionary speculation about humans but not a lot of empirical data and research to back it up. However, by the time that the first edition of Buss's *Evolutionary Psychology* was published in 2008, research into how evolution shaped our minds was mounting.[48] I will use two concepts. First, the foundational concept of evolutionary psychology, psychological adaptation, and second, the concept of a motivational system.

Design for Fitness

The design of life on earth arose in a complicated, nonconscious way over billions of years. There were many failed experiments, evolutionary dead ends, bloody competition, and, luckily, a sufficient amount of success to lead to our species, after more than four billion years of life on earth. Your body – all thirty-seven trillion cells of you – is the result of many incremental biological adaptations that were not pre-designed. You, and the person next to you, are marvellous products of inadvertent design. Despite this randomized, non-conscious natural process, humans emerged as mind-endowed, rational, self-conscious creatures, the only species that has figured out its natural history. The implication for understanding the human mind is profound: If natural selection shaped our brains (and bodies), then natural selection also shaped our minds.

How to explain this design of mind? The paradigm I employ comes from evolutionary sciences such as evolutionary psychology, evolutionary anthropology, and evolutionary psychopathology.[49] Evolutionary

48 On how evolutionary psychology developed as we approached the twenty-first century, see Buss, *Evolutionary Psychology*, viii.

49 For the foundations of evolutionary psychology, see Barkow, Cosmides, and Tooby, *The Adapted Mind.* Evolutionary psychopathology explains mental disorders as due to neural and psychological mechanisms shaped by natural selection. See Del Giudice, *Evolutionary Psychopathology*.

psychology differs from sociobiology by focusing not on social behaviour but on psychological mechanisms that underlie the behaviour.[50] The premise is that the current design of our minds consists of psychological adaptations to primordial environments, under pressure from natural selection. The primal adaptations included anger, empathy, ritualized fighting, long-term care for children, and cooperation within and among groups.[51]

Psychological adaptations are analogous to physical adaptations in that they spread across the species because they improved an organism's lifetime reproductive fitness[52] or the total number of offspring that survive to maturity.[53] Traits that enhance fitness are adaptive. Traits that reduce fitness are maladaptive.[54] All traits have costs and benefits. The bowerbird builds an elaborate bower to attract a female. The pair have a "sexual moment" lasting a few seconds. They never meet again. To be adaptive, a trait can have costs, but it must provide a positive net

50 For examples of recent research, see Buss's *The Handbook of Evolutionary Psychology*.

51 This search for basic adaptations is the "adaptationist program." Gould attacked the program as presuming that natural selection produces the optimal design. See Gould and Lewontin, "The Spandrels of San Marco." Ernst Mayr replied that natural selection produces only "reasonably well adapted" traits. Mayr, "How to Carry out the Adaptationist Program," 324. Marcus said evolution selects the "fittest solution that was readily available." Marcus, "Survival of the Fittest?," 8.

52 Hamilton, "The Genetical Evolution of Social Behavior." Natural selection as individual reproduction is not a complete theory. There are traits such as reciprocity, self-sacrifice, and altruism that involve a loss of individual fitness. To address this paradox, evolutionists use Hamilton's notion of natural selection as promoting inclusive fitness or kin selection. This is the individual's contribution to its own fitness and its contribution to the reproductive fitness of kin.

53 Fitness calculation becomes complicated when you figure in population growth and fluctuations in the environment. See Hunt and Hodgson, "What Is Fitness and How Do We Measure It?"

54 Williams, *Adaptation and Natural Selection*. Adaptations can be structural, physiological, or mental-behavioural. Structural adaptations are changes to the structure of the organism, such as bipedalism in humans and the giraffe's long neck. Physiological adaptations include development of immunity to a poisonous plant or a digestive system that can process a wider selection of food. Behavioural traits include the singing of songbirds or their capacity to follow migration patterns, or the instinctive cry of the human infant.

contribution in terms of reproductive fitness.[55] Not *everything* is an evolutionary adaptation. Some traits are by-products of successful adaptations, like the sound of my heart beating. Gould called these by-products "spandrels."[56]

Psychological Adaptations

Psychological adaptations are a species of evolved psychological mechanisms (EPMs). An EPM is any psychological mechanism developed through evolutionary processes.[57] EPMs include spandrels and vestigial traits that no longer promote fitness.[58] Psychological adaptations, however, are information-processing and response-generating mechanisms that continue to enhance fitness. They serve the brain, the chief information-processing organ. Del Giudice describes the mind "as a network of evolved information-processing mechanisms whose function is to control and regulate behavior."[59] Information mechanisms take certain types of data as input and transform it into other kinds of data as output. For instance, human memory takes experiences (sense data) and stores them as retrievable memories (i.e., other forms of data).

We are all familiar with psychological mechanisms. Take denial, where a person refuses to believe their doctor when told they have a fatal disease. Take false humility to impress others and to conceal one's arrogance. These mechanisms are adaptations that are cognitive, behavioural, or social. Social adaptations include sexual strategies, such as "impress the female" dancing by male birds; subconscious responses,

55 Jabr, in "How Beauty Is Making Scientists Rethink Evolution," explores claims by some evolutionists that natural selection cannot explain the costly efforts that birds like the bowerbird and peacock make to look beautiful and attract mates. However, for an evolutionary account of beauty, see Prum, "Duck Sex and the Aesthetic Evolution."

56 A spandrel is a by-product of the evolution of some trait. It is not an adaptation; it has no evolutionary function. Gould and Lewontin, in "The Spandrels of San Marco and the Panglossian Paradigm," used "spandrel" to label such by-products. Originally, "spandrel" is an architectural term for a triangular space between the tops of two adjacent arches in a cathedral. Spandrels have no architectural function. They are by-products of construction.

57 See Barkow, Cosmides, and Tooby, *The Adapted Mind.*

58 In biology, "vestigial" means a part of an organism that no longer performs a function, such as the wings of kiwis.

59 Del Giudice, *Evolutionary Psychopathology*, 30.

such as repressed envy at another's success; conscious responses, like fear and empathy; and instincts that are highly innate, such as a phobia for snakes. Incest avoidance and physical aggression are evolved behavioural adaptations; sexual jealousy is an innate instinct, including the male disposition to guard its mate. Heuristic problem solving (thinking by using shortcuts, such as stereotypes) is a cognitive adaptation. Sometimes, psychological adaptations are a hybrid of cognition and learned behaviour. Noam Chomsky regards language as an innate psychological capacity stimulated by exposure to a particular language at birth.[60] Jean Piaget's theory of cognitive stages, from somatic behaviour to abstract thinking, explains how children acquire innate psychological adaptations *over time*. "Intelligence is adaptation," Piaget writes, calling the structures of intelligent development "functional invariants" that amount to a "particular instance of biological adaptation."[61]

The influence of an adaptation can be unconscious and emotive, not conscious and cognitive. For example, humans avoided incest long before science pointed out the heavy physiological penalty of inbreeding in terms of children diminished in body size, muscular coordination, and academic performance.[62] Natural selection favours outbreeding. Generations of humans have felt the taboo as an instinct based, unknowingly, on genes and natural selection.

What do adaptative explanations look like? Take, for an example, Aaron Sell's treatment of anger. Earlier, I asked the simple question, Why do we get angry? Sell argues that anger is a psychological mechanism that organisms employ to gain advantage when they come into conflict. Sell says anger is the "output of a cognitive mechanism designed by natural selection to negotiate conflicts of interest among organisms."[63] What is the problem that anger is supposed to address? Among humans, it is where a person unthinkingly or unjustly causes you to incur a cost or to lose a benefit. The person fails to take you and your interests (and feelings) into account. How can I get this person to give my interests more weight? One response is to display anger. Anger may prompt the person to recalibrate the weight they place on my interests.

60 See Lenneberg, Chomsky, and Marx, *Biological Foundations of Language*, vol. 68.

61 Piaget, *The Origins of Intelligence in Children*, 3–4.

62 Wilson, *On Human Nature*, 37.

63 Sell, "Applying Adaptationism to Human Anger," 53.

Sell hypothesizes that the anger response began with animals and early humans in primordial times. The scenario is this: Animals of the same species compete for the same finite resources in an environment – from food to mates. Where the organisms are not kin and reciprocity is not involved, natural selection designs organisms to be aggressive birds of prey, i.e., to gain resources without regard for the harm done to competitors. But before the animal acts, evolutionary theory holds that it typically considers how much they value the resource and the fighting ability of its competitor. For example, a sea lion will stop chasing a penguin in the water if the penguin eludes capture over an extended period of time. The exhausted sea lion will stop the pursuit, concluding that the bird is not worth the effort.

Something similar happens with anger. Displays of hostility indicate to the aggressor that he will incur a cost if he tries to grab a resource and run. Anger is a sign of willingness to resist and, if necessary, fight. This may prompt the aggressor to modify their actions. Hence, anger, where it works, is adaptive, increasing the fitness of the angered animal.

Sceptics of adaptive explanations worry that it is too easy to tell a story about how a trait became an adaptation. Gould complained that too many evolutionary accounts were like Rudyard Kipling's *Just So Stories* for children, e.g., how the camel got its hump. Scientific explanations should not be imaginative stories that lack verification.[64] This is a question about evidence. When can we be confident that an adaptation exists? Schmitt and Pilcher point to two methods: (1) Adaptations should exhibit "special design" – a design that effectively addresses a particular problem and increases fitness; and (2) the explanation is consistent with existing knowledge, especially evolutionary science.[65] "Just So" stories do not meet the requirements of (1) and (2). Also, an adaptation explanation is a "historical narrative" of the emergence of a feature. The events have occurred in the distant past and cannot be directly observed. So adaptationists use the common method in science of "inference to the best explanation."[66]

64 See Kipling, *Just So Stories*. Gould made the complaint in "Sociobiology: The Art of Storytelling."

65 Schmitt and Pilcher, "Evaluating Evidence of Psychological Adaptation."

66 Mayr, "How to Carry Out the Adaptationist Program," 325, 328.

The evolution of humans can be studied by describing how humans adapted to changing eras and ecologies. The sum total of adaptations in an era is called the "human adaptive complex."[67] What was the adaptive complex of primordial humans? The complex included (1) increasing capacity to exploit high-quality food sources, e.g., large game, through techniques based on learning and technology; (2) evolution of a large brain that allowed for learning and data storage; (3) a multigenerational system of knowledge transfer from grandparents to parents to children; (4) bi-parental investment in the care of children; (5) agreements among kin and unrelated individuals which permit food sharing and group coordination and reduce mortality.

My claim, then, is that we should regard the extreme traits, central to irrational intolerance and tribalism, as psychological adaptations and part of the human adaptive complex. The extreme capacities were successful in promoting the reproductive fitness of our species in a primordial ecology. If they had *not* been successful, they would not have become species-wide and would not be around today, a part of human nature. Hence, extreme anger and aggression, extreme tribalism, and our penchant to see strangers as potential enemies were adaptations important to human group survival in a hostile, primordial environment. It is the task of evolutionary psychologists and other scientists of the human to develop new research and revealing hypothesis about how these adaptations occurred. The conceptual framework is sound. Now we need to fill in the portrait with inventive, empirical study.

Motivational Systems

I call attention to one type of inventive thinking in evolutional psychology. It is research into motivational systems.

Motivational systems are patterns of organized behaviour across a species, from the beaver's production of a dam to human mating rituals. They are called motivational systems because the entire sequence of behaviour is under motivational control. They are aroused and maintained by certain motivations. Motivational systems are psychological adaptations of the human brain to problems posed regularly by

67 See Kaplan, Gurven, and Lancaster, "Brain Evolution and the Human Adaptive Complex"; and Lancaster and Kaplan, "The Endocrinology of the Human Adaptive Complex."

the environment. These psychological adaptations are embedded in human nature and are ready to emerge given the right conditions and triggers.

Some motivational systems are relatively simple. Human infants innately seek the goal of attachment, i.e., to maintain physical proximity to the parent. In some animals, this is called imprinting. Humans are motivated to seek things necessary for survival, such as food and security. We are motivated to fight when threatened and cornered. Where the systems are relatively complex the organism as a whole is involved. It seeks goals, tracks progress toward the goals, and learns how to respond to obstacles and opportunities.[68]

The concept of motivational systems prompts us to think holistically. Rather than think about *a* motive, for example pleasure, as an isolated feeling, the idea of motivational systems encourages us to think of motivation as referring to a coordinated response over time with feedback. It is an interconnected system of beliefs, instincts, emotions, and goals that adapts to external conditions.

Roughly, the causal path is this: An organism's motivational system is aroused by cognitions and desires within a situation. They suggest a motive or goal. For example, the organism desires to avoid a threat in its environment. Once aroused, the motivational system triggers additional cognitions and emotions. The organism coordinates a suite of mental and bodily sub-systems that result in behaviour. The study of motivational systems must address two basic questions: (1) *when will it become activated*, given internal and external cues, and (2) *how it will respond to ambient conditions*, i.e., how will it get around obstacles, or how intense will the response be? Each motivational system has its "rules of engagement" with the world.[69] Today, theorists talk of "triggers" or "enablers" of certain kinds of behaviour. But the trigger is only one stage in the process by which a motivational system directs the organism to a goal.

From this perspective, emotions are not inert, subjective feelings that are inside me, something I happen to have. They are dynamic, causal elements that help the brain coordinate responses. They perform

68 See Aunger and Curtis, "The Anatomy of Motivation."

69 Del Giudice, *Evolutionary Psychopathology*, 35.

functions for the motivational system.[70] One function is to present to the agent an evaluation of the goal, some positive or negative valence. Emotions suggest the object is something to be pursued or something to which we should be averse. Many of these valences harken back to past experience and primordial adaptations, such as the emotions of fear and disgust. Another function is to prompt other mechanisms. For example, fear activates, almost instantly, physiological changes in circulation, respiration, and digestion; it increases perceptual acuity and improves the detection of threats, while making salient the objects that fall under the categories of "dangerous" and "safe." A basement may suggest safety in a storm. Moreover, fear activates knowledge of the threat and memories of possible escape strategies; it may prompt actions (e.g., running for your life) accompanied by facial expressions that warn others of danger.

Extreme Motivational Systems

In *Evolutionary Psychopathology*, Del Giudice provides a table of motivational systems in humans.[71] All systems consist of innate adaptations. The table helps us understand how extremism can be a feature of our motivational systems.[72]

Each of Del Giudice's fourteen systems has a "proximate goal" and associated emotions and feelings. The systems range from the "aggression system" and "security system" to the "reciprocity" and "curiosity" systems.

In my view, the systems that could contribute to severe intolerance are (1) the aggression system, (2) the fear system, (3) the security system, (4) the disgust system, (5) the status system, (6) the mating system, (7) the affiliation system, and (8) the acquisition system. Systems that

70 On the functional role of emotions, see Tooby and Cosmides, "The Evolutionary Psychology of the Emotions and their Relationship to Internal Regulatory Variables."

71 Del Giudice, *Evolutionary Psychopathology*, table 21.1, 38–9.

72 The table builds upon pioneering work on the evolutionary theory of motives by Robert Aunger and Valerie Curtis. In their "The Anatomy of Motivation," they regard motives as psychological mechanisms to produce behaviour that solves "evolutionary important tasks in the human niche." By looking at human ecology, they identify eight human needs which lead to a list of fifteen motives.

could contribute to cooperative behaviour or groupism include (1) the caregiving system, (2) the pair bonding system (long-term sexual partners), and (3) the reciprocity system.

Here are a few examples from Del Giudice of how these systems could lead to extremism. The goal of the aggression system is to counter threats or gain resources by threatening or inflicting harm. It includes harming others as prey. Its associated emotions are anger, rage, and excitement. Success (reaching the goal) provides relief or satisfaction; its failure leads to frustration. The fear system exists to avoid immediate threats, while the security system restrains fear to allow for surveillance of the alleged threat. The security system of the mind seeks to detect and prevent potential threats, the way anti-ballistic systems seek to correctly appraise threats from foreign countries. The emotions of the security system are anxiety, wariness, and apprehension. Success means relief and safety; failure means fear and guilt. Meanwhile, the status system seeks to improve one's social status and the ability to display dominance, power, or prestige. It can activate the emotions of anxiety, ambition, envy, or embarrassment. Success entails pride and admiration; failure means shame or sadness.

These systems are the psychological basis for the development of extreme systems. Extreme motivational systems *exaggerate* pre-existing feelings, emotions, and responses developed by non-extreme motivational systems. Given the right triggers and conditions, aggression becomes fierceness. The emotions of being irritated or frustrated become rage and hatred. Fear becomes excessive and may become paranoia. Systems for security go into overdrive producing an extremely wary stance to the world.

The goal of the disgust system, for example, is to avoid contact with pathogens or toxins (pathogen disgust), to avoid undesirable sexual contacts (sexual disgust), and to condemn moral violations (moral disgust). The arousal of this system prompts emotions of disgust, repulsion, or nausea. Successful avoidance brings relief, while failure activates discomfort, shame, or guilt. Here we have, in psychological form, the system that is behind one of the major traits of irrational intolerance: fear of decline and contamination by the enemy group. It is also the evolutionary explanation of the promiscuity of ideas where people or things we do not like are associated with things we find disgusting. Systems meant to prevent disease or contamination by being careful with what one eats and how one lives become an extreme disgust at other people as *literally* toxic, unclean, and a severe security threat. A useful disgust mechanism becomes an extreme disgust that defines tribalism.

One evolutionary study has found that xenophobia could be due, in part, to disease aversion. Studies of xenophobic persons today were linked to chronic and contextually aroused feelings of vulnerability to disease, which motivated negative reactions to foreign peoples.[73]

All of these motivational systems can be taken to extreme lengths. In fact, one definition of mental pathology is the exaggerated development of ordinary mental traits until they amount to paranoia or psychosis. All humans have such extreme dispositions which can be aroused by the right type of triggers and external conditions, causing them to erupt in modern life.

Aggression as Primal Adaptation

Aggression is such a central part of extremism that theories of mind need to look at how and why it became adaptive. Aggression is a motivational system where individuals or groups act with the intent of physically or psychologically harming others. Violence is extreme aggression.

Aggression, anger, and other hostile attitudes originated in the need of primordial humans to confront, deter, and, as Sell says, negotiate conflicts. It also helped them to screw up the courage to defend against groups seeking access to their resources. Tooby and Cosmides argue that aggression provides animals with two classes of benefits: it eliminates or disables others who might reduce its fitness; and aggression can be used as bargaining power, e.g., threats may induce others to hand over resources. Two emotions are associated with these benefits: hate and anger. Hate is an emotion associated with impairing others, while anger is in the service of bargaining. There may also be a distinct motivation system called rage which prompts combat behaviour or motivates crimes of passion.[74]

Theories of aggression are of three kinds: instinctual, socio-cultural, and interactive.

73 Faulkner, Schaller, and Duncan, "Evolved Disease-Avoidance Mechanisms and Contemporary Xenophobic Attitudes."

74 Tooby and Cosmides, "Groups in Mind," 191–2.

At the turn of the twentieth century, instinct was established as a concept in psychology. British psychologist William McDougall, in his popular *An Introduction to Social Psychology* of 1908, made aggression an innate instinct, related to frustration. However, the most famous instinct theory would be written by Freud.[75] Freud started with the view of aggression as the result of frustration. But he eventually thought that aggression expressed a "death instinct"[76] to destroy or damage. The destructive instinct is either aggression against oneself (self-hate or masochism) or aggression against others.[77] Earlier, I used this conceptual scheme to explain, at least in part, the Nazi doctors and other extreme groups.

Freud, when commenting on the death instinct and civilization, would not shrink from drawing the obvious, but negative, conclusions from his ideas: "The bit of truth behind all this – one so eagerly denied – is that men are not gentle, friendly creatures wishing for love, who simply defend themselves when attacked, but that a powerful measure of desire for aggression has to be reckoned as part of their instinctual endowment." Just consider the atrocities of the Huns, the Mongols or the Christian crusaders, or ponder the First World War, says Freud. If you do, you will "have to bow your head humbly before the truth of this view of man." For Freud, there is no hope of eliminating men's aggressive instincts. Society can only try to divert them away from war. If you think Freud's view is too strong, read Barbara Ehrenreich's *Blood Rites* on the "passions of war." Humans are attracted to war as a feeling. It is the "ecstasy of war," an almost sacred test of loyalty and "blood sacrifice." Humans engage in "the sacralisation of war" or "war worship."[78]

In 1938, frustration theory would make a comeback. The new theory was published in *Frustration and Aggression* by John Dollard and a group of psychologists. The group called their theory the frustration–aggression hypothesis. Its basic postulate was "the assumption that *aggression is always a consequence of frustration.*"[79]

75 Psychoanalyst Alfred Adler theorized that sadomasochism consisted of an "aggressive drive" as well as a "striving for power" and a "striving for superiority." On the aggressive and non-aggressive traits of character, see Adler, *Understanding Human Nature.*

76 Freud, "Beyond the Pleasure Principle," 275.

77 On the two-instinct theory, see Freud's *Beyond the Pleasure Principle.*

78 Ehrenreich, *Blood Rites: Origin and History of the Passions of War.*

79 Dollard et al., *Frustration and Aggression*, 1. Italics in the original text.

After Freud, the idea of aggression as instinct was carried forward by ethologists such as Konrad Lorenz and by the anthropologist, playwright, and science writer Robert Ardrey.[80] Lorenz said aggression is so prevalent among animals and their weapons so diverse that aggression must have arisen "under the selection pressure of a species-preserving function." Aggression is one of the instincts, like hunger and sex, which preserves the species.[81] In modern life, the continued high level of aggression among humans at a time of atomic bombs means that aggression may switch from a species-enhancing trait to a species-ending trait. A few decades after Lorenz, Erich Fromm, in *The Anatomy of Human Destructiveness*, claimed that humans have a death instinct that leads to pathological forms of aggression beyond those encountered in animals.

This instinctual approach to aggression would be challenged in the second half of the twentieth century by social constructivists who objected to talk of human nature, for reasons noted above. Anthropologist Ashley Montagu asserted, inaccurately, that Lorenz and other evolutionists painted a portrait of humans as "Man the Killer" and humans "cannot be otherwise."[82] Meanwhile, Albert Bandura developed a social learning theory which claimed that aggression, as shown by his "Bobo doll" experiments in the early 1960s, was learned when children observe aggressive adults. [83]

Where do we stand today? The way forward is the aforementioned approach of interactionism which combines innate and social factors into a more complete theory. There is no denying the genetic–instinctual component. We have known for a long time that animals can be bred to be fiercely aggressive by breeding the most aggressive offspring with each other. We know that identical twins are more similar than fraternal twins in their aggressive tendencies and criminal records. We know that men are more disposed to aggression than women, in a manner than cannot be reduced to social learning. More recently, genetic (and other)

80 See Lorenz's *On Aggression* of 1963 and Ardrey's *The Territorial Imperative* of 1967.

81 Lorenz, *On Aggression*, 38.

82 Ashley-Montague, *The Nature of Human Aggression*, 3.

83 It was called the Bobo doll experiment because children watched an adult act aggressively (or not) towards a Bobo doll. The toy gets up by itself to a standing position after it has been knocked down. On social learning theory, see Bandura's *Social Learning Theory* and Social *Foundations of Thought and Action.*

studies show that genes, brain anatomy, hormones, and neurotransmitters are involved in anger and aggression. Yet, at the same time, we have plenty of studies showing that culture and society determine when and how aggression is expressed.

Today, leading research into aggression is, fortunately, interactive. For example, Anderson and Bushman proposed an integrated approach to studying aggression called the "general aggression model."[84] It shows how different aspects, psychological and social, can be linked conceptually. Current textbooks on aggression feature a rich mix of research on the genetic–environment nexus.[85]

Interestingly, Edward Wilson provides an example of interactive theorizing on aggression, despite the inaccurate image of his views as reducing all behaviour to innate biology. In his chapter on aggression in *On Human Nature,* Wilson argues that there is no unitary form of aggression but rather several kinds of aggression with different biological mechanisms.[86] Nonetheless, humans are innately predisposed to strong aggression, war, and violence. Humans have a "marked hereditary predisposition to aggressive behavior."[87] But then he adds the interactive thought: aggression is a "structured, predictable pattern of interaction between genes and environment."[88] Aggression in humans was like a "pre-existing mix of chemicals ready to be transformed by specific catalysts." Much of the most dangerous forms of aggression, e.g., in military or criminal assault, is learned behaviour. Yet this learning is prepared by our biological nature. For Wilson, the particular forms of violence are not inherited. What is inherited is "an innate predisposition to manufacture the cultural apparatus of aggression." Culture gives a particular form to aggression. Humans, Wilson states, "fabricate aggressive cultures."[89]

Wilson says that, to recognize the conditions that aroused primordial aggression are "largely obsolete" is not to banish these propensities. Humans must undertake a rare pathway in psychological development that leads to mastery over "the profound human tendency to learn violence."[90]

84 Anderson and Bushman, "Human Aggression."
85 See Shaver and Mikulincer, *Human Aggression.*
86 Wilson, *On Human Nature,* 103.
87 Ibid., 99–100.
88 Ibid., 105.
89 Ibid., 115.
90 Ibid., 119.

Tribalism

I cannot end this chapter without a few words on tribalism. Talk of tribalism as a form of group aggression is popular today in the media and in popular works of psychology.[91] The term "tribalism" suggests a form of behaviour with a long ancestry. However, the idea of tribalism in scientific psychology is not old. It was only at the turn of the twentieth century when psychologists began to theorize about the fact that people are prone to divide individuals into rival groups. In his best-known work *Folkways* in 1907 William Summer at Yale University, one of the first American sociologists, introduced the terms "we-group" and "others-group."

> Each group nourishes its own pride and vanity, boasts itself superior, exalts its own divinities, and looks with contempt on outsiders. Each group thinks its own folkways the only right ones, and if it observes that other groups have other folkways, these excite its scorn.[92]

Pragmatist William James said that, in many respects, man is the most ruthless and ferocious of beasts. "Two souls" are within his breast: one is sociability and helpfulness; the other is jealousy and antagonism. "Hence the gory cradle … in which our race was reared; hence the fickleness of human ties, the ease with which the foe of yesterday becomes the ally of today."[93] Later, in the 1940s, anthropologist Arthur Keith said humans were governed by a "dual code" – the parochial imperative to protect one's own people, and the duty to destroy one's enemies. Moral conscience is "the instrument of the group."[94]

Talk of dual codes evolved into the distinction of the in-group and the out-group made popular in the mid-1900s by social psychologists Henri Tajfel and John Turner. They found that people can create in-groups in a matter of minutes, even where the basis for solidarity are arbitrary or invented characteristics, such as preferring certain paintings.

91 For example, see Greene, *Moral Tribes: Emotion, Reason and the Gap between Us and Them.*

92 Sumner, *Folkways*, 13.

93 James, *The Principles of Psychology*, vol. 2, 409–10.

94 Cited in Ardrey, *The Territorial Imperative*, 287–8.

The social roots of aggression are in the conflict between in-groups and out-groups.[95]

Recent theorizing in evolutionary psychology explains tribalism through the lens of primordial group conflict. One theory is the male warrior hypothesis.[96] The theory holds that intergroup conflict gave men a chance to access the mates and territory of opponents, which increased status. Therefore, conflicts created selection pressures for psychological mechanisms in men to initiate intergroup aggression. Also, Tooby and Cosmides discuss ancient human coalitions to explain the roots of war and morality. They note that intergroup conflict among chimpanzees suggests that the ancestors of humans have been practising war for at least six million years. Natural selection, they claim, built the human "coalition psychology" – innate adaptations to regulate within-coalition cooperation and coalition conflict with other groups. This innate psychology expresses itself in war, politics, group psychology, and morality.[97]

95 See Tajfel and Turner, "An Integrative Theory of Intergroup Conflict."

96 McDonald, Navarrete, and Van Vugt, "Evolution and the Psychology of Intergroup Conflict: The Male Warrior Hypothesis."

97 Tooby and Cosmides, "Groups in Mind."

11

Constructing the Enemy

Mass movements can rise and spread without belief in a God, but never without belief in a devil.

Eric Hoffer[1]

IN THE PREVIOUS CHAPTER, I used my engines-of-unreason hypothesis to explain how extreme traits arose from adaptations in primordial ecologies. My explanations remained at a general level of thinking. Even if extremism expresses evolutionary adaptations, we still want to know, more specifically, why certain forms of extremism emerge in different forms in different situations. We also would like to know more about the extreme mindset. What is the role of personal experience, individual differences, triggers, and varying social ecologies?

I provide a psychological model that outlines the relationship among these psychological, social, and innate factors. I examine the mindset of the enemy stance or the construction of the other as enemy.

SECTION 1: CONSTRUCTING THE ENEMY STANCE

Mindsets and Stances

A mindset or stance – I use the terms interchangeably – is a psychological mechanism that helps individuals interpret and respond to the world or some part of it, such as politics. A mindset is a way of *apprehending* the world, a holistic result of experience, i.e., of thinking, emoting, and evaluating.

1 Hoffer, *The True Believer*, 91.

Almost every experience is holistic. Our experience is rarely one, isolated cognition or one, private emotion. Even a moment of abstract thought is tinged with some type of emotional quality, perhaps some sadness as a conclusion is drawn or some excitement at a new idea. Beliefs and attitudes mingle to create evaluative judgments about the objects of apprehension. We paint an evaluative gloss on all that we experience. Emotional colourings are baked into our judgments about things. Our natural experience of the world, prior to analysis, is rich and wide in texture. The positivists' factual description of experience as narrow fact may have its philosophical purposes, but we should not forget that it is an abstraction whose existence presumes a wider apprehension of the life-world around us.[2]

The connections among our psychological capacities are essential to everyday experience. Emotions and beliefs are connected by a two-way street. If I believe I am in danger, I feel anxious; if I dislike you, I believe negative statements about you.[3] Our beliefs and values are also holistic in structure. Beliefs and values form systems, like a web with nodes.

A mindset is, then, a holistic apprehension of my world. Given the mindset, I like or abjure certain things; I promote or avoid certain things. A mindset means I have a disposition to respond in generally predictable ways to people, problems, and situations. By noting someone's mindset, I am identifying a *pattern* in the person's evaluative apprehension of the world. For example, my mindset about organized religion may be described as sceptical. What does that mean? It means that I am disposed, whenever the topic arises, to make negative comments about organized religion and to be sceptical about its theological claims or values. This mindset affects my actions: I do not attend a church, and I do not financially support a particular religion. In having a mindset, I adopt a certain posture or stance towards the world.[4]

Mindsets are shaped by our society. Not all of this shaping is useful. For example, in teaching ethics at university, professors encounter

2 On wide experience and its implications for philosophy and ethics, see my *Objectively Engaged Journalism: An Ethic*, chapter 5.

3 Nussbaum defines emotions as "intelligent responses to the perception of value." Nussbaum, *Upheavals of Thought*, 1.

4 The popularity of "stance" is due to art. Painters and sculptors gave their portraits or sculptures of people a stance or attitude, from which we might infer their personality. Stance is defined in dictionaries as a person's posture, especially when deliberately adopted.

students with a negative mindset regarding the topic, a mindset derived from their culture. They believe that morality is not an area for objective, rational reflection. Much of teaching, then, is the fostering of new and better mindsets.

Groups also exhibit mindsets. In a community that has suffered from a mass shooting, many citizens adopt a common mindset. They grieve together and adopt common ways of expressing their shock and support. A lynching mob also has a common mindset. So does a cult. During war, entire nations may take a hostile stance toward the enemy, a mindset that demands unquestioning patriotism from all citizens. Moral mindsets stretch across centuries, such as groups that endorse Christian ethics.

Three Terms

The construction of the other as enemy is the adoption of a stance towards certain groups, especially where social and political issues are in question.

Each of the terms – construction, other, and enemy – needs a preliminary exposition.

CONSTRUCTION

The stance is a psychological construction. It develops in peoples' minds. It consists in extremely negative apprehensions of others in the social environment. Intense feelings devolve into stereotyping, scapegoating, and maybe paranoia. The mindset, once adopted, is resistant to change. It impairs the objective functioning of one's mind.

Many beliefs do not cause violence. But beliefs about groups as threats do enable violence. A mob has high levels of emotion that spread like fire across a group. How do such emotions arise in the first place? One method is to draw a provocative image of the person to be lynched. For example, male racists who lynched enslaved Black people in nineteenth-century America spread the lie that the men were secretly fornicating with white men's wives or daughters. This belief raised anger in the mob, triggering pre-existing biases.

OTHER

The construction is social because it is a judgment about a group. The judged group is treated as an other. The other is not part of my favoured group – my race, my ethnicity, my religion, my nationality, my gender, my sexual orientation. The judging group adopts an intense attitude of suspicion towards the other, and this leads to intolerance. Even where someone ridicules the physical appearance of a targeted group, e.g., that the group belongs to a race with small brains, the motivation for such physical slurs is usually social – hatred of strangers, or tribalism.

ENEMY

The enemy stance treats the targeted group as more than an other.

It views the group as an enemy to other groups or the whole nation. The enemy is said to be (a) a physical or political threat; (b) an illegitimate obstacle to goals; (c) subversive of high values, or (d) a contaminant of the purity or greatness of one's society. Or, a combination of (a) to (d). The enemy stance is Darwinian hardness in modern society. The perception of someone as enemy is not a factual error that, when pointed out to people, will end the hostility. This mistakenly assumes that the people in question are holding this stance on a rational basis, i.e., based on facts and objective thinking.

The term "enemy" signals that a war-like mentality is being embraced to deal with matters of society and democracy. Society (and politics) is viewed, literally, as a war among groups. The war is verbal, ideological, economic, and at times physical. A warrior ethic prevails.

Among the strongest feelings in the enemy stance is the pleasure of hating. In 1831, English social commentator William Hazlitt gave a wonderfully frank acknowledgment of the reality of hating in his *The Pleasure of Hating*. Hazlitt provides example after example from ordinary life of how people *actually* love to scheme against others and criticize rivals behind their backs. Civilized humans, he says, may not be inclined to overtly kill others, as in primordial times, but they cannot give up the pleasure of hating and of hostility. Religion is turned into bigotry, patriotism is an excuse to carry "fire, pestilence, and famine into other lands." Without "something to hate, we would lose the very spring of thought and action."[5]

With the enemy stance, this pleasure in hating is directed at a specific group.

5 Hazlitt, *The Pleasure of Hating*, 108, 105.

Enemy Stance: System and Components

Figure 11.1 presents the model as a whole. The diagram is a conceptual map of the factors involved in a full explanation of irrational intolerance. It depicts the basic components of the enemy stance. It incorporates the nine key traits of irrational intolerance discussed in the previous chapter.

The components are grouped according to three levels of causal influence. Level 1 contains the conscious components of the mindset itself, from attitudes to triggers. This is the surface psychological level at which the stance operates among individuals. Level 2 consists of underlying psychological conditions of two kinds: personality and mental disorders. Level 3 is the deepest and oldest level. It consists of primordial traits embedded in human nature.

Level 1: The Mindset

Level 1 is the convergence of three general factors: (1) *psychological inputs,* i.e., the psychological history of a person or group and their extreme attitudes and traits; (2) the *mental and social ecology* which consists of the belief systems, ideologies, and value systems that surround the person or group, as well as triggers for extreme responses; and (3) *intolerant outputs* – extreme motivational systems and the actions they prompt.

The attitude is called the "ego war mode." Ego is used to note, as Beck has stressed, that many intolerant people are, despite their loyalty to a group, intensely concerned about themselves.[6] They are at the centre of a great drama. Reasoned queries about the person's stance, or disagreement with their beliefs, are taken as personal attacks and rarely forgotten.

The ego adopts a hyper-alert war mode as described above. It is wary of the social environment, especially of other groups. Fear of threats is a common trigger for the enemy stance, and it leads to inappropriate levels of aggression. In this wariness, one recognizes the primordial hyper-alertness of early humans to a dangerous environment.

6 On the relation of hate and the ego-centric bias, see Beck, *Prisoners of Hate,* chapter 2.

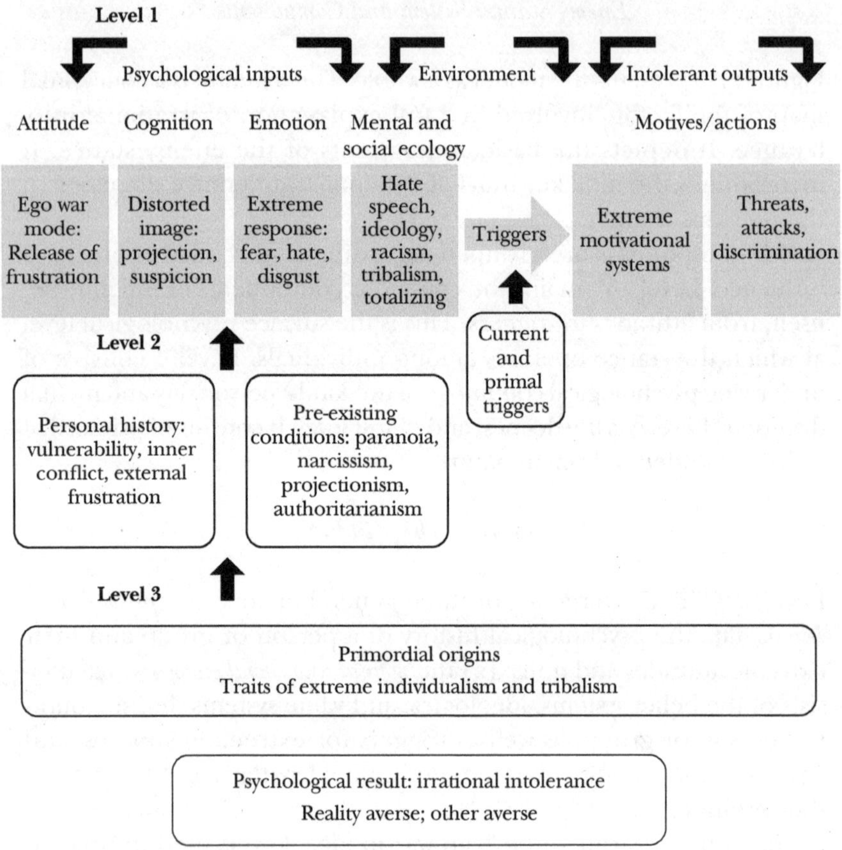

Figure 11.1 Enemy stance – the three levels.

Primordially, all stimuli had to be assessed quickly and dualistically as either friend or foe, threat or non-threat. One errs on the side of safety, even if it results in false alerts.

Today, this alertness continues to exist and can have valid application. A person rightfully senses danger in an alleyway; a woman suspects the taxi driver is a sexual predator. When a threat manifests itself, we can choose fight or flight.[7] As noted, if we decide to fight, we must mobilize

7 In 1963, Cannon, in *Wisdom of the Body*, explained aggression as an adaptive response to dangerous circumstances – the fight or flight reaction.

all of our resources. The combat soldier, like primordial warriors, must rouse himself to kill the enemy when face to face. Here Darwinian traits come rightfully to the fore. These are real enemies. The problem, however, is that the enemy stance is fuelled by an overheated surveillance system. The extremist sees too many things as a threat. The surveillance system is applied to others who are not threats but selected on racist or other grounds. The primordial alert system is today appropriate in only a small percentage of situations. We are no longer hunter-gatherers with spears.

The enemy mindset is shaped significantly by our ecology. The ecology is physical, ideational (or cognitive), and social. Individuals are more likely to express irrational intolerance if supported by their society. Individuals are more likely to endorse extremism if their mental ecology consists in extreme ideas regularly circulated by prominent leaders. Triggers arouse these tendencies. Leaders may use public media to prime a public to go to war by accusing the enemy of brutal acts against co-nationals. Other triggers are better called enablers. They include economic distress, social frustration, polarization in politics, social inequality, propaganda in the media system, and an authoritarian personality threatened by pluralism. Sometimes, we do not know the strength of a society's prejudice until a trigger brings it out into the open. Recall the hostility directed at Jackie Robinson by white Americans when he broke the Black barrier in professional baseball.

Finally, the mindset results in outputs. Extreme motivational systems of disgust and aggression, once aroused, call for action. Some bigoted people may remain relatively passive, joining intolerant groups online to share ideas, but they do not take action. Others may participate in intolerant acts or settle for supporting groups that do act intolerantly. In the diagram, action refers not only to bodily action or physical attacks but also to people joining extreme groups, voting for intolerant leaders, sharing online fake or prejudiced stories, and a willingness to accept (or support) undemocratic measures. The action could be the use of social media to intimidate people who question intolerant leaders.

Level 2: Underlying Psychological Conditions

The psychological profile that underlies the mindset and its outputs on Level 1 includes one's personal history and pre-existing conditions such as paranoia.

Personal history includes genetic predispositions, upbringing and education, and culture. Did personal experience make me suspicious of strangers or bitter towards other groups? As discussed in previous chapters, these are also psychological disorders associated with extremism and intolerance, such as a susceptibility to paranoia and narcissism. My claim is not that all people who adopt the enemy stance are psychotics. My claim is that pathological tendencies can lead people to adopt the enemy stance. Pathologies promote irrational, maladaptive, or reality averse thinking.

Level 3: Primordial Origins

At the base of the system is human nature, with its innate adaptations and extreme psychological traits identified in chapter 10. The primordial traits give individuals a propensity to adopt extremism. Not all people will express that propensity in action, and, in individuals, we can expect the propensity to have different strengths. The existence of a general propensity, even if innate, does not, by itself, explain why the propensity emerges in this person at this time in this location. To be that specific, the explanation needs to take into account factors on Level 1 and 2.

SECTION 2: THE PLEASURES OF SOCIAL ORDER

One trait that is of special importance to the enemy stance is the need for social order. In chapter 4, I noted an analogy between musical rationalism and political rationalism. A love of the Rameau system of musical tonality reveals an ideology that loves order and hierarchy. I said that this corresponds to a love of social order. What is not loved is disorder, anarchy, chaos, unruly masses of people, messiness, freedom, spontaneity, and breaking the rules.

The desire to find an order or ratio in one's world is not pathological. It is necessary for humans. But this desire can become so strong that it favours authoritarian government, social hierarchy, and absolute leadership. The medieval social hierarchy was supported by classes of people at the top of the hierarchy, to their own advantage. The fascist mind loves a total order in society under a total leader. The love of order can become a lifelong attraction to the erotic absolute.

Authoritarianism: The Values

A person's display of extreme traits and ideological conformity is often attributed to personality. It is argued that some personalities are susceptible to demagogic leaders and hate-based ideology. Personalities are defined by broad dispositions to act in certain ways, e.g., to be an introvert or extrovert. In chapter 4, I described Schoenberg's personality as that of an "authoritarian prophet."

Authoritarianism referred to a way of governing before it was used to denote a type of personality. Authoritarianism, as a political term, is not simply the belief that some people must have authority in society. Unless one is a radical anarchist, this strikes one as obviously true. In complex modern societies, some people and some institutions – law makers, police, the justice system, political leaders, educational institutions – must have authority for society to go well. These people have authority – either legitimately derived or gained through force – to perform actions on behalf of society and the state. Investing people with authority is necessary to avoid anarchy or arbitrary injustice in a populace of strangers with conflicting interests.

Authoritarianism is the belief that, in society, there should be a lot of authority around, such as strong laws and powerful law-enforcement officials. Their orders and laws should be applied in a top-down manner that requires obedience from citizens. Authoritarianism, like liberalism, is a philosophy of how society and its government should be structured – how people in charge should act and the extent of their powers. In an authoritarian state, government has the right, if it wishes, to monitor private lives, restrict individuals, and intervene in the economic, cultural, and political domains of society. Liberty – freedom to act in ways outside the coercive power of the state – should be restrained. When discussing authority in society, the debate is usually not about the philosophical definition of authority.[8] It is something more practical. The debate is over this: In this society, *who* should have authority, *how* should authority be exercised, and *what* are the limits on authority?

8 Arendt has noted that authority is hard to define because "authority has vanished from the modern world." We no longer can fall back on "authentic and indisputable experience common to all." Totalitarianism arose against the background of a general, dramatic "breakdown of all traditional authorities." See Arendt, "What Is Authority?"

Authoritarianism is one of the oldest and most prevalent ways of structuring human societies. By comparison, liberal ways of organizing society are recent experiments. As John Stuart Mill said, one can ask of any society to what extent are people's freedoms limited by coercive state authority.[9] The answer to that question determines to what extent your society is authoritarian or non-authoritarian.

Psychologically, authoritarianism defines a type of personality, a personality that literally loves or needs authoritarian structures at home, in the workplace, and in society.

Why does the authoritarian want so much authority to exist? The authoritarian person may say that it is necessary. They fear themselves and others when not policed. The hard side of human nature needs to be controlled. Another cause, perhaps not conscious, is that one's personality is inclined towards authoritarian structures. This inclination may be due to the factors discussed in this book: a disposition towards an enemy mindset, underlying psychological features that seek security, sadomasochistic impulses, and the operation of the enemies of unreason, which cause us to be overly aggressive and dominating.

What are the primary values of authoritarianism in the political sphere? They are obedience to authority; security; sameness in values, practice, and lifestyle; law and order; loyalty to nation (or group); and maintenance of the status quo. One set of values and laws should be enforced by strong and uncompromising leaders or militaries. Opposed to authoritarianism are the values of freedom, individuality and creativity, independence and autonomy, changing the status quo, pluralism in thought and value, and critique of authority.

Recently, the return of authoritarianism around the world has led to a renewed focus on fascism and its causes. For example, legal scholar Cass Sunstein edited a book called *Can It Happen Here?* Philosopher Jason Stanley published *How Fascism Works*. Former American secretary of state Madeleine Albright wrote *Fascism: A Warning*.

The Authoritarian Personality

Theories of authoritarian personality go back at least to herd psychology as developed by the French conservative and science popularizer Gustave Le Bon in the late 1800s. In his pioneering *The Crowd*, Le Bon

9 Mill, *On Liberty and The Subjection of Women*, 84.

argues that, in a crowd, the individual's autonomy and critical thinking powers are set aside for obedience to the group, which becomes an irrational mob.

For Freud, authoritarianism is obedience to a "primal horde" – an innate tendency of the human mind. Freud describes the instinct as such:

> The leader of the group is still the dreaded primal father; the group still wishes to be governed by unrestricted force; it has an extreme passion for authority; in Le Bon's phrase, it has a thirst for obedience. The primal father is the group ideal, which governs the ego in place of the ego ideal.[10]

About forty years after Freud wrote on the herd instinct, Eric Fromm defined the authoritarian attitude as the personality of someone who "affirms, seeks out and enjoys the subjugation of men under a higher, external power" whether this power is a state, a leader, natural law, the past, or god. Fromm viewed the authoritarian person as a sadomasochist who feels pleasure in submission to authority and in the subjection of underdogs. Fromm said individuals are seeking to "escape from freedom" which can be frightening and demanding. Modern life is isolating, and it lacks absolute certainties to assuage doubtful minds. "This isolation is unbearable," writes Fromm and encourages humans to "escape from the burden of his freedom into new dependencies and submission."[11] Similarly, psychoanalyst Rollo May thought modern man's "age of anxiety," which is an era of "hollow people" lonely and anxious, is caused by the deep changes and confusions caused by modern life.[12]

Arendt saw totalitarianism as an authoritarian assault on the individual conscience and sense of responsibility. The moral person – an individual capable of making choices on principle – is replaced by a follower of an authoritarian leader.[13]

Adorno and others, in *The Authoritarian Personality*, asked what made up a "fascistic individual" and what constitutes "anti-democratic thought." The detailed study surveyed American citizens, supplemented by in-depth interviews. The study found that the authoritarian personality

10 Freud, "Group Psychology and the Analysis of the Ego," 260.
11 Fromm, *Escape from Freedom*, viii.
12 May, *Man's Search for Himself*, 7.
13 Arendt, *The Origins of Totalitarianism*, 451.

is comprised of nine dimensions, including submission to authorities, belief in rigid categories and stereotypes, belief in the power and toughness of good leaders, and hostility in general toward humans and strangers.

Recently, Christian Fuchs, in *Digital Demagogues,* used the work of Fromm and Adorno, among others, to construct a model of right-wing authoritarianism. It has four dimensions. (1) *Authoritarianism in leadership*: belief in strong authorities and hierarchical leadership. (2) *Nationalism and ethno-centrism*: belief in the superiority of a particular community as a nation or ethnicity. (3) *The friend–enemy scheme*: The national community is defined in opposition to enemy out-groups. (4) *Conservative patriarchy*: a belief in conservative values, e.g., traditional gender roles, sexism, and patriotism.[14]

The "Authoritarian Dynamic"

A recent theory of authoritarianism sees the authoritarian personality as having a need for sameness. The authoritarian personality is the enemy of pluralism of almost any kind. Psychologists Karen Stenner and Jonathan Haidt, in putting this theory forward, argue that the rise of right-wing populism is not due to economic distress or the disruptions of globalization.[15] The real predictor of whether someone will vote for an extreme populist leader or party is whether they have an authoritarian personality, which they estimate to be a dominant personality trait in at least one-third of the population. They claim that the authoritarian personality is the most important cause of intolerance around the world. The rise of authoritarianism is not a temporary or sudden madness among the public. It is an eternal option in societies due to the persistence of the authoritarian personality.

Stenner and Haidt distinguish authoritarianism from "status quo conservatism" which, following Edmund Burke, values stability and tradition while resisting rapid change. Nor is it a laissez-faire conservativism which supports a free market and limited government. These conservatives might as well be called liberals or libertarians. Authoritarians demand restraint on the individual in all matters moral, political, and

14 Fuchs, *Digital Demagogue*, 53, 57.

15 See Stenner and Haidt, "Authoritarianism Is Not a Momentary Madness," and Stennor, *The Authoritarian Dynamic.*

racial. And, they are not necessarily opponents of government intervention in the economy or society. Authoritarianism is "an enduring (psychological) predisposition to favor obedience, conformity, oneness, and sameness over freedom and difference." It is a lack of "openness to experience" and cognitive limitations that reduce one's willingness and capacity to "tolerate complexity, diversity, and difference." They are inclined to anti-democratic and illiberal measures in times of stress, e.g., the expulsion of racial groups. They support ways of structuring society that minimize diversity.[16]

What arouses the authoritarian personality? Stenner and Haidt call this "the authoritarian dynamic." Intolerance of difference is caused by a combination of the authoritarian personality and a special type of trigger: the perception of a "normative threat." What is a normative threat? It is a threat to the continuing sameness of society by the introduction of difference and pluralism, e.g., an influx of immigrants of a different race or religion. This is normative because it is interpreted as a threat to conservative norms and how society ought to be. The perception of a normative threat awakens the authoritarian personality. People become more intolerant and rigid in their political views. Authoritarians become upset that their society is losing its shared values. They complain that leaders are out of touch with these values and the new citizens are "not our kind of people."[17]

In my terms, the authoritarian dynamic constructs the enemy stance based on the claim that certain groups promote dangerous and different values. It also fits my definition of extreme populism in *Ethical Journalism in a Populist Age*, as a political view which defines the people in narrow (and exclusive) racial or religious terms and opposes pluralism as a negative feature of society.[18] In a plural world where difference cannot be avoided, the idea of maintaining sameness is a reality-averse recipe for social conflict.

Stenner and Haidt's theory brings out the importance of social triggers, e.g., normative threats, which are, admittedly, somewhat more abstract than economic threats. Yet, as we saw with the German volk movement, one should not underestimate the power of a sense that one's group or nation is losing its deepest values. Nonetheless,

16 Sanders and Haidt, "Authoritarianism Is Not a Momentary Madness," 182, 183.
17 Ibid., 187.
18 Ward, *Ethical Journalism in a Populist Age*, 85–8.

their theory leaves some questions unanswered. It describes the authoritarian personality but does not explain why it exists. Why are some people authoritarian and others are not? Nor does the theory say much about how the authoritarian personality is related to other potential causes of intolerance, e.g., primordial, innate mechanisms or pre-existing conditions like paranoia. However, the theorists correctly underline how authoritarian intolerance is always a possibility in society. That fits with my evolutionary thesis about extreme traits being part of human nature.

My own view in these matters is easily summarized. I believe that there are personality types, although we may quarrel as to the correct categorization scheme. Having a personality is a psychic reality. Having an authoritarian personality is one of them. It seems clear that certain types of people are drawn more strongly to authoritarian leaders and types of society than other people. I regard authoritarian personality as one factor that encourages people to adopt the enemy stance. However, a full explanation will have to include the plurality of components in figure 11.1. An authoritarian personality is an important, but not the only, causal factor in the enemy stance. It is a pre-existing condition.

SECTION 3: COMMUNICATION VIOLENCE

Constructing the enemy stance is not the work of isolated individuals. It is a *social* process. My enemy stance is developed by my intolerant group and by leaders who feed on my vulnerabilities. Hence, communication plays a substantial role.

Irrational tolerance is spread through communication violence. This is the use of violent, prejudicial, propagandist, and hate messages – from verbal attacks and slurs to symbols of hate – to express and propagate the enemy stance.

Communication violence uses our susceptibility to be affected by what others say to develop group cohesion around extreme ideology and shared passions. This is public irrationality via media. Communication violence weakens democratic values and practices such as fair deliberation and respect for citizens who do not share my worldview. Communication violence is the use of authoritarian methods of communication to achieve undemocratic public ends.

Using my naturalist, evolutionary approach, I ask two questions: (1) what are the origins of communication violence in human history, and (2) what are the main communication strategies for persuading people to adopt the enemy stance?

Origins of Communication Violence

The origins of communication violence are to be found in primordial times, in the capacity (and need) of early humans to signal extreme aggression and hostility toward an enemy. Communication violence was another adaptation involving our Darwinian traits. Every tool that humankind has created since the emergence of the *Homo* genus in Africa has been used as a weapon, from the control of fire to the domestication of the dog, more than 15,000 years ago.[19] The tool of communication, spoken or written, was, and is, no different.

There are about 5,000 languages in the world. But we are not sure how these languages came to be. When did humans develop the anatomical capacity to make sounds, followed by the creation of symbolic language? Given the paucity of hard evidence, theories abound. Continuity theories think language, like the human eye, evolved gradually by natural selection.[20] Discontinuity theories think human language is so distinct that it occurred all at once due to a genetic mutation or some other mechanism.[21] Theories disagree on whether communication and language is innate, a product of social learning, or both.[22]

For our purposes, early communication includes vocalizations, gestures, body movements, singing, mimicking, and use of symbols, e.g., in art and ritual. We can divide language evolution into two giant steps: the evolution of pre-symbolic and symbolic stages of human communication. The pre-symbolic phase comes after early humans acquired a

19 Dogs were used in hunting and fighting and as an alarm system against wild beasts and human invaders. Harari, *A Brief History of Humankind*, 46.

20 Pinker and Bloom, "Natural Language and Natural Selection."

21 Structuralist Levi-Strauss, who believed that language was a formal system where no element has meaning except in relation to other meanings, said language had to arise "all at once." Levi-Strauss, *Introduction to the Work of Marcel Mauss*, 59–60.

22 On "both," see Tomasello, *Origins of Human Communication*.

basic anatomical capacity to makes sounds and vocalize, perhaps as early as 4.5 million years ago.[23]

Some researchers argue that *Homo sapiens* had a symbolic language during the Middle Stone Age in southern Africa (280,000 BC to 40,000 BC) due to the use of red ochre pigments in rock art, apparently for ritual and symbolic purposes, as found in the Blombos Cave, east of Cape Town, South Africa.[24] The oldest Ice Age cave art is a red disk at least 41,000 years old painted on a rock formation in El Castillo, Spain. Among the fascinating drawings of animals that appear on similar cave walls, researchers have also begun to pay attention to a core of thirty-two abstract signs or geometric forms, e.g., circles, triangles, lines, and dots that have been found in caves across Europe and beyond. The signs signal not only a symbolic mind at work but that humans engaged in art earlier than the conventional wisdom that human art began about 40,000 BC as *Homo sapiens* immigrated to Europa and began a cognitive revolution.[25]

Pre-symbolic communication probably began with bodily stances or gestures, e.g., pointing to game far off or suddenly freezing up to indicate to others behind you the proximity of a predator in the long grass. Darwin states, "I cannot doubt that language owes its origin to the imitation and modification, aided by signs and gestures, of various natural sounds, the voices of other animals, and man's own instinctive cries."[26] Humans probably used cries and sounds to alert band members to changes in the environment and to coordinate foraging. We know that chimpanzees in the wild today vocalize in sounds – answering calls with similar calls. The calls are graded in intensity to indicate the signaller's

23 One study found that a skull of *Ardipithecus ramidus*, from about 4.5 million years ago, is the first evidence that hominids at that time had vocal capacities exceeding nonhuman primates, perhaps similar to the vocal abilities of a human infant or very young child, including the capacity to modulate sounds, as we find today in singing. Clark and Henneberg, "*Ardipithecus ramidus* and the Evolution of Language and Singing."

24 Henshilwood and Dubreuil, "Reading the Artifacts."

25 An explanation of this research by Genevieve von Petzinger of the University of Victoria is "Why Are These 32 Symbols Found in Ancient Caves All Over Europe?," TED, August 2015, https://www.ted.com/talks/genevieve_von_petzinger_why_are_these_32_symbols_found_in_ancient_caves_all_over_europe.

26 Darwin, *The Descent of Man*, vol. I, 56.

state, such as its level of fear.[27] We also know that vervet monkeys have at least ten different vocalizations which warn other members about predators, e.g., an "eagle" call.[28]

There is a formidable gap between pre-symbolic communication and symbolic language. Pre-symbolic communication in humans and other animals is a finite repertory of calls (e.g., warnings about predators, sounds that signal a claim to territory) and an analog signal that registers the magnitude of some state (the livelier the bee dance the richer the food source). But symbolic language is infinite because it is digital and compositional. It is compositional because the meaning of wholes such as a sentence, paragraph, or text are built upon the meaning of its parts and the grammatical rules for arranging them.[29] There is no limit to the sentences we can construct. It is digital, not analog: sentences are constructed by re-arranging discrete elements in certain combinations. These differences have led experts to argue that the gap could not have been spanned by gradual evolutionary changes. This is too pessimistic. One might say the same about the human eye and be wrong. Moreover, as Pinker notes, natural selection is the only scientific explanation of adaptive complexity.[30]

So, nature *is* patient. But at some point, a significant change must have occurred to move human signalling across the threshold of language. One hypothesis is that human cognition, under pressure from a changing environment and made possible by a large brain, improved substantially. It could think abstractly about objects not present to the senses. Harari, for example, believes language emerged from a "cognitive revolution" in human evolution between 70,000 BC and 30,000 BC. Perhaps genetic mutations rewired the brain allowing humans to create an "altogether new type of language."[31] Whatever the account, few doubt the momentous difference that symbolic language made to human evolution. It allowed humans to trade, to cooperate, and to dominate other branches of the *Homo* genus. It allowed the construction of myths, supported by rituals, which led to religion and eventually led to modern ideologies.[32]

27 Arcadi, "Vocal Responsiveness in Male Wild Chimpanzees."

28 Seyfarth, Cheney, and Marler, "Vervet Monkey Alarm Calls."

29 Pinker, *The Language Instinct*, 334.

30 Pinker and Bloom, "Natural Language and Natural Selection," 454–5.

31 Harari, *A Brief History of Humankind*, 21.

32 Ibid.

Communicating for Violence

The origin of communication violence is to be located in these two giant steps in the evolution of human communication. But where? You will not find the answer in research about the use of language for peaceful, cooperative purposes.[33] You have to look at the role of language when humans employ their Darwinian traits. Communication violence began as a tool for warfare, for coordination when overrunning other tribes. The enemies of unreason sparked communication violence.

Examples are not hard to find. Above, I described the pre-symbolic capacities of early humans to issue cries and calls to alert group members of a threat. When it comes to bodily gestures, the breast beating by primates (and humans) is just one example of communication violence to display power and aggression.[34] Other signals would warn groups of the presence of rival human groups. *All* of these uses occur against a background of hostile, competitive primordial life. All occur where humans began to display their extreme traits. Nor did the role of communication violence move to the margins of society when humans became modern. The uses of communication violence have been central to empire building, maintaining a king in power, and eventually deluding the public through mass media propaganda.

What language would early humans, in Darwinian mindset, use? They would use the most aggressive, emotional forms of communication possible to express their extreme dispositions. In physical encounters, one's primordial fierceness would be shown by loud voicings, facial expressions that display no fear, aggressive stances and gestures, all in the cause of making oneself appear as big and dominant as possible. This communication fury arouses and is aroused by extreme behavioural responses. Once symbolic language arose, the content of communication violence became even more important. One made verbal accusations against the others (rather than just pointing one's finger); one used myths, superstitions, and rituals to communicate a negative stance toward others and to prime us for a confrontation with them. This

33 For a positive focus on cooperative communication, see Tomasello, *Why We Cooperate.*

34 On gestures, such as primate breast beating, as the origin of human language, see Arbib, Liebal, and Pika, "Primate Vocalization, Gesture, and the Evolution of Human Language."

capacity for violent language was so useful that it was favoured by natural selection and became part of human nature. These are the origins of modern propaganda techniques and group hate speech. Our modern penchant to swear at people, curse them, issue threats, and damn them to hell is an ancient legacy of early communication violence.

Unfortunately, like the extreme traits themselves, such uses of language in modern life can be maladaptive. Communication violence, as much as guns and napalm bombs, violates the peace, undermines reciprocity, destroys trust, prompts all groups to become defensive and uncompromising, and undermines the social virtues that make possible democracy. It is immorality in communication.

Peddlers of Communication Violence

Strategies of communication violence are a sub-species of strategies of persuasive communication. We actually know a lot about persuasive strategies because, since Aristotle, rhetoric and other means of persuasion have been studied by experts in logic, linguistics, rhetoric, political propaganda, commercial advertising, and mass media communication. There is no need to review all of this knowledge. Instead, we can focus on the persuasive strategies of communication violence. It helps to begin with a few words about persuasion.

Persuasion is an essential part of human life. As long as we live in groups, we will try to get people to see things our way. How we persuade takes innumerable forms: we can intimidate people with our academic degrees, the scientist's white gown, or similar displays of authority; we can point to what most people believe; we can point to facts, consequences, and cost–benefit analysis; we can use powerful images, symbols, nostalgia, or humour, to convey our message; we can use slogans, emotional words, misleading euphemisms, and twisted logic. We can persuade by applying group pressure, reminding people of their loyalty to us, the group.

Persuasion sometimes has a negative connotation, suggesting the manipulative messaging we see in television advertisements or during political campaigns. Some intellectuals feel that it is beneath them to engage in public persuasion. Facts, soberly stated, should speak for themselves. In the real world, this will not work. This leaves the field of public debate open to the distortions of skilled, intolerant persuaders. Aristotle put the matter clearly. He asks why a person should be able to defend themselves physically with their body but not be able to defend their ideas through persuasion and rhetoric. Why should falsehood alone enjoy the power of persuasion?[35]

Aristotle defined rhetoric as the "faculty of observing in any given situation the available means of persuasion."[36] A persuasive speaker has a skill, some might say a cunning, for sizing up their audiences and playing to their beliefs, emotions, and biases. Persuasion in public affairs involves three things. Using Aristotle, we can call them ethos, pathos, and logos.[37]

Ethos, normally, means the values and virtues of a group or community. But in persuasive communication, it refers more narrowly to the persuader's skill in impressing his audience with his moral character. The persuader presents himself to the audience as a person who not only has knowledge, skills, and energy but as someone who is honest, sincere, and hard-working. Often, the persuader portrays himself as a man of the people who comes from the same background as the audience (e.g., middle-class upbringing).

Pathos refers to the ability of the speaker to put the audience into a certain frame of mind. He stirs up people's emotions, attitudes, and biases. Pathos has been defined as "a rhetorically generated emotion aimed to induce audience judgment" or agreement with the speaker.

Logos (the Greek idea of explaining the world through rationality and language) means that persuasion employs an argument where there is no firm separation of reason and emotions. Rather, it is a form of heartfelt reasoning where speakers and their listeners draw inferences, consider their interests, become impassioned, and make plans.[38] Political rhetoric and many forms of drama, poetry, and journalism use heartfelt reasoning to stir the audience.

In summary, the successful persuader uses the tools of argumentation, understands human nature in general, grasps the psychology of specific crowds – their particular wants and beliefs – in concrete situations, and has an understanding of human emotions, especially their causes

35 Aristotle, *Rhetoric*, 1328 (1355b).
36 Ibid., 1329 (1355b).
37 Ibid., 1329 (1356a, 1–35).
38 On the definition of pathos and heartfelt reasoning, see Zhang and Clark, *Affect, Emotion, and Rhetorical Persuasion in Mass Communication*, 6.

and how to excite them. Rhetoric expert Chaim Perelman notes that the persuader can use high or low strategies. He may appeal to the audience's specific low biases, such as their fear of a local immigrant population, or he may appeal to high-minded principles that apply to everyone, telling the crowd the issue is the protection of their liberty.[39] From the crowd-pleasing sophists of ancient Greece to the stirring rhetoric of Martin Luther King Jr, acts of persuasion have joined ethos, pathos, and logos to hit their pragmatic target: to influence the audience and motivate them to act in certain ways.

The crucial skill, in my view, is not logos or even ethos. It is pathos. It is the capacity to recognize what people *really* want and believe deep down and what is *really* frustrating them. This is a skill because the deepest frustrations or fears may lay below the surface or are unexpressed for fear of social condemnation. For example, it has been argued that Donald Trump won the 2016 US presidential election in large part because he was able to win the white working-class vote by a 2–1 margin. Was the vote due mainly to a fear of losing jobs? Some research shows that this assumption is false. The deep reason was "white working-class Americans' fear of cultural change, not economic distress."[40] This is the authoritarian personality discussed above. This would explain Trump's continuing emphasis on dangerous strangers and terrorists invading America and his attacks on liberals. Trump tapped into a deep anxiety, ready to be manipulated.

Consider also the British political consulting firm Cambridge Analytica, which combines data mining, data brokerage, and data analysis with strategic communication during electoral campaigns. The firm became notorious when it was revealed that Cambridge Analytica had harvested the personal data of millions of people's Facebook profiles without their consent and used it for political purposes. In a private conversation recorded by British Channel 4's undercover journalists, Mark Turnbull, managing director of Cambridge Analytica, confirmed that his company's focus is on manipulating deep-seated voter emotion.

39 See Perelman, *The New Rhetoric.*

40 Zhang and Clark, *Affect, Emotion, and Rhetorical Persuasion in Mass Communication,* 1–2.

> The two fundamental human drivers when it comes to taking information onboard affectively are hopes and fears, and many of those are unspoken and even unconscious ... And our job is ... to understand what are those really deep-seated underlying fears, concerns. It's no good fighting an election campaign on the facts because actually it's all about emotion.[41]

It is important to note how *far* this view is from ideal theories of democracy. There is no talk here of reason, of a balancing of facts and views. No talk of anyone *changing* their mindset due to open deliberation. The goal is to manipulate existing prejudices. This is not a new idea, but modern media tools make manipulation even more effective and worrisome. Manipulating people's deep biases via media is now a worldwide industry. It can be used for any cause. Thus, we arrive at questions about the purpose of persuasion. Is the purpose of a moral nature, for example, to truly inform and to persuade people by rational, evidence-based argument? Or, is the purpose non-moral, i.e., to get people to believe something by any means to benefit an individual or their campaign?

The moral use of persuasion is tied to the idea of rational communication, a communication that respects the audience as autonomous rational beings. The non-moral use is tied to disrespect. In the former case, we argue *sincerely*, not deceptively, and we aim to arrive at well-evidenced conclusions that promote the common good. This is caring for *genuine rationality* in pursuit of morally good public ends – a rationally informed public. In the latter case, the immoral persuader does not care for reason or deliberation. Anything that *causes* someone to adopt a belief is good. Getting people to affirm some belief justifies the means. This attitude is disrespectful to individuals who should not be manipulated by communication techniques, bogus facts, and deceptive persuaders. This is *fake rationality* flying under the colours of genuine rationality, showing a false concern for truth, fact, and method, and other high values. It is the corruption of the idea of rationality and moral communication in the public sphere.

In *Prophets of Deceit*, a book on American agitators who incite hatred of Jews and other groups, Lowenthal and Guterman capture the essence of dubious public persuasion. Although published in 1949, the book's

41 Cited in ibid., 2.

tough-minded identification of the techniques of stirring up hate was ahead of its time. It starts by stating an important truth: agitators of hate translate "inchoate feeling into specific belief and action."[42] They are "peddlers of discontent" with expertise in verbal seduction. The agitator does not provide clear, specific answers to clear, specific problems. Rather, he is often content with "aggravation of the emotion itself." The emotion of being frustrated and discontented. He gives people "permission to indulge in anticipatory fantasies in which they violently discharge those emotions against alleged enemies." In the final analysis, the agitators appeal to the "irrational or subconscious at the expense of the rational and analytical." The persuader–agitator seeks to "lead the masses toward goals that run counter to their basic interests," which accounts for the "irrationality of demagogy."[43]

At the Nuremberg Trials, Nazi military leader Hermann Goring was asked why the German people followed Hitler into war. His answer spoke volumes about the strength of immoral communication. "Of course, the people don't want war," he said. "But … the people can always be brought to the bidding of the leaders. That is easy. All you have to do is tell them they are being attacked, and denounce the pacifists for lack of patriotism, and exposing the country to greater dangers."

Rhetoric of the Enemy Stance

These reflections apply to the rhetoric of the enemy stance, outlined by figure 11.1. This rhetoric, which also uses ethos, pathos, and logos, is a fake rationality of the worst kind – turning groups against each other. It is heartfelt reasoning gone wrong. The goal of leaders is to stir up the enemy stance. Yet the rank and file of extreme groups are not off the moral hook. They also promote the ideology through their own use of communication violence. There is satisfaction in indulging one's biases.

Here is a list of some of the strategies that the peddlers of communication violence use to create the enemy stance. It is written as a set of instructions. I will be brief because I have already explained these ideas.

42 Lowenthal and Guterman, *Prophets of Deceit*, vii.

43 Ibid., 11, xi.

UNDER PATHOS

Discover and tap into the deepest frustrations and wants of the audience, and then make their wants and beliefs extreme and uncompromising. Start with people who are confused, unmoored, vulnerable, or full of inner conflict. Validate these feelings. Like blowing on ashes in the fireplace, use strategies that inflame emotions, which are tinder-dry and ready to alight.

Connect inner conflict with social frustration. Explain inner problems as the result of external social problems. Stress the social malaise, the decline of culture, and the threats to the group to which individuals belong. Work upon such feelings and give them a direction.

Release frustration and anxiety by assisting people to project negative qualities on others. Provide a target for frustration in the form of scapegoats.

Create intolerant triggers where opportunities arise. For example, blame serious crime on a target group, such as claiming that immigrants are more violent than established citizens.

UNDER LOGOS

Create a distorted image of the enemy groups to justify hostility. Use whatever means are available, such as recycling ancient symbols of white supremacy or using false histories of peoples. Tell conspiracy theories about the enemy as potential witches, demons, or sub-human animals who contaminate good people.

Create an ideology that is absolute. The ideology explains in simple, extreme terms the problems of the world; it blames groups and stipulates what must be done to change the world. The ideology taps into the emotional needs of supporters, as determined under pathos. Create arguments, however specious, that support the ideology. Where possible, create a totalizing environment where members are controlled by cutting off access to reality.

Incite hope that the ideology and the leaders will remake the world. This may be done by constructing a belief in a utopian past and a utopian future, as found in millennial theories. Promise happiness or salvation, immortality in a great cause, or greatness.

Practise fake rationality. Use invalid reasoning techniques and limited facts; avoid full and rigorous rational critique. Care for victory in argument more than truth. Twist facts and logic to support one's ideology.

Undermine contrary views by attacking the persons who hold such views. Make all issues reducible to personality traits, interests, and biases while avoiding one's own biases.

Use all forms of public media. Use, especially, the new forms such as social media to spread the extreme ideology.

UNDER ETHOS

Create a great leader ethos. Support groups where a guru or great leader is revered and said to have special insights, strong moral character, and even a divine role. Demand utmost loyalty to the leader. Treat other leaders and other groups as enemies.

Emphasize a set of virtues that advance the group's extreme agenda. For example, develop a "bird of prey" or warrior morality. Downplay or dismiss other virtues.

Bulletproof Dogma

Before ending this chapter, I want to say more about the role of dogma and ideology in supporting the enemy stance and communication violence.[44]

The role of cognition in the enemy stance is to detect enemies and threats. Cognition develops a belief system that justifies the stance while protecting the mind from contrary views. To maintain a defensive, psychological cocoon, the enemy-stance person pays a high price in terms of cognition. They subscribe to a reality-averse view of life.

The dominant psychic forces in the enemy stance are not reason or objectivity or evidence-based cognition or science. The dominant forces are the need to transcend psychological discontent and the need to maintain the enemy stance, since it provides relief or distraction from discontent. The entire slate of capacities of human rationality – constructing beliefs, generalizations, reasoning, and observing facts – is energetically employed to reduce internal conflict and to prop up the enemy stance. The enemy stance still feels a need to justify itself to itself and to others. The best defence is bulletproof dogma immune to external doubt and contrary fact. The enemy-stance mind is like a castle in enemy territory, dependent on its protective walls.

44 Ideology goes back to the French Revolution where the term had a positive connotation. Antoine Destutt de Tracy defined ideology as the science of social ideals and ideas. Ideology's negative meaning, as delusional or rigid thinking, goes back to Marx and Engels, who challenged the ideology of capitalism as a tool to justify control of society. See Freeden, *Ideology*.

We have a word for this type of thinking in ordinary life: dogmatism. There was a time when dogmatism was a neutral word, derived from the Greek word for dogma (δόγμα) meaning literally "that which one thinks is true." Dogma referred to the main tenets of religions and philosophical schools. Today, dogmatism is a negative personality trait defined by *The New Shorter Oxford Dictionary* as "the tendency to lay down principles as incontrovertibly true, without consideration of evidence or the opinions of others." In everyday life, dogmatic people can be difficult co-workers and fellow citizens. They see things in black and white and presume they are right on most matters. No wonder dogmatism is a dirty word.

But in the enemy stance, dogmatism is more than an irritating trait. It is the cognitive platform on which extreme beliefs stand. It plays a crucial psychological role in political extremism, in authoritarian ideology, and in religious fanaticism.

Why are humans susceptible to dogmatic messages, psychologically? As Pinker says, the problem of ideology is "epidemiological." How can a toxic ideology spread like a virus from a few crazed zealots to many?[45] The answer was suggested earlier: the beliefs serve a crucial, irrational function for the person, connected closely to their vulnerabilities, delusions, and needs. Eliminate the delusions and the world of the extremist collapses like a house of cards. In such people, the cognitive need for belief security is an analogue of the physical need for bodily security. These powerful forces overcome the mind's original and biological function to accurately identify information about reality. The enemy stance perverts the mind's natural functioning.

When cognition serves the enemy stance, cognition is mental slavery. The rationality module of our minds is hijacked by the rest of our mind and made a slave to their purposes. The person with an enemy stance may cite facts. Some of their suspicions may have some basis in reality. They are usually not totally out of touch with reality. No matter how biased in politics, they get around in their environment. The malfunctioning occurs when they deal with social and political issues which touch on their interests. The thinking becomes charged with emotion, impulse, and defensive egoism. Cognition's role is reversed. Rather than present facts for the formation of true belief, cognition constructs

45 Pinker, *The Better Angels*, 557.

rationalizations that force facts to fit pre-existing prejudices. The latter is a hallmark of the enemy stance and the rigid ideologue. The former is a hallmark of rationality. Using logic and counterevidence to deflate the enemy stance will likely fail since such methods cannot break through the many-walled castle of the enemy stance, with its dense thickets of overheated ideas and emotions and primordial impulses.

Strozier, in *Apocalypse*, has found links between rigid thinking and intolerance in his study of religious fundamentalism.[46] Absolutism in fundamentalism – someone or some group is either good or evil – predisposes believers to intolerance. An extreme commitment to a set of religious belief makes sacred the difference between believer and nonbeliever. This religious commitment to a bulletproof dogma is a form a groupthink. In looking at foreign policy decisions, Janis described how groupthink can be a form of "group madness" or a "temporary derangement" of group decision making powers due to the pressure for conformity. Groupthink results in "a deterioration of mental efficacy, reliability testing, and moral judgment."[47]

The enemy image is a subjective invention and projection by people unable, or unwilling, to evaluate information on its own merits, apart from their emotions, needs, and biases. To borrow language from chapter 1, their mind is out of joint, or disordered. Ontological, epistemic, and social rationality have been weakened. The enemy image is ripe for abuse by leaders. It is a source of emotional release, a satisfaction of the desire for revenge, and the empowerment of groups turned mean, unreasonable, and predatory.

46 Strozier, *Apocalypse: On the Psychology of Fundamentalism in America.*

47 Janis, *Victims of Groupthink*, 3, 9.

EPILOGUE

The Fate of Democracy

An appalling and horrible thing has happened in the land: The prophets prophesy falsely and my people love to have it so.

Jeramiah 5:31

As stated in chapter 1, this is a philosophy book that has brought together diverse forms of knowledge to shed light on the worrisome phenomenon of irrational publics. During our journey through this book, I have, at various places, stopped to express concern about two things. One, the inclination of many people to not only adopt a hostile mindset toward others but to join intolerant groups whose tribalism has cost millions of lives. Two, the return of extreme irrationalism and intolerance into our contemporary democracies due to the use of powerful global media by fascistic groups and pseudo-populist leaders. I argued that such inclinations are part of human nature, so there can be no thought of *eliminating* them. The engines of unreason lurk within all of us.

The nature of these trends suggests that a society-wide response is necessary.

But how?

What can we do to restrain such trends? How to rebuild rational and tolerant publics?

I have no experience in practical social reform, advocacy, or activism. There are other people with such experience. My hope is they can provide suggestions on how to implement specific, practical measures, create new social programs, and draft new laws. What I can offer is a philosophical view of how to approach the rebuilding of rational publics, based on this book's understanding of irrationality.[1]

1 Some ideas in this epilogue have appeared in my previous books. For specific ideas on reform of news media and media ethics, see my *Objectively Engaged Journalism*, *Ethical Journalism in a Populist Age*, and *Disrupting Journalism Ethics.*

SECTION 1: STOPPING THE PENDULUM

This book has distinguished three senses of "irrational": First, the idea that we have capacities that stem from impulses, emotions, and imaginations that are not part of our rational faculty. This led to the distinction, in chapter 2, between rationalism and irrationalism, which differ on the value of our rational and irrational capacities. Second, the idea that we can use our capacities and resources irrationally to work against reason. Third, going against reason can become extreme, apart from reality, issuing into extreme intolerance. We can place the last two senses of irrationality into one category of working against rationality and reality.

Therefore, the fate of egalitarian democracy – a democracy that needs rational and tolerant publics – comes down to two large questions: (1) How can society establish the right balance between rationalism and irrationalism, allowing the expression of both sides of human nature, and (2) How can society maintain and encourage the development of rational and tolerant individuals, so that *these* citizens are greater in number and in social impact than the number and social impact of the extremists? This shows that social ethics is a project to maintain humane and just societies, and much of that project faces a problem of social design: how to design cities, educational systems, civic experiences, architecture, and moral norms so as to support and trigger the better traits of our nature, inherited from evolution.

This epilogue outlines possible responses by citizens, educators, and media practitioners.

Lessons Learned

An answer to the first question about the balance of rationalism and irrationalism should incorporate what we have learned about the swing of the pendulum in history.

The first lesson is that there is no room for complacency. As stated, social history does not move necessarily in a linear fashion towards greater progress and rationality. Historical patterns can be cyclical and rhythmical like the pendulum. Cultural decline and a move towards extremism is always possible. Vigilance is needed to ensure that democratic institutions and democratic forms of community are healthy.

The second lesson is that we should approach the problem of extremism with a realism about human nature. As I have argued throughout this book, we need to see our Darwinian self as an important part of our nature. In the nineteenth century liberals like Mill and Comte advanced ideas on reforming society based on an incomplete or too positive notion of human nature. The discovery of the unconscious and other complexities of human psychology still lay ahead. Today we need to take seriously Kant's notion that a radical evil exists. A "depravity ... the corruption of the human heart" is possible.[2]

The third lesson is that we should bear in mind that individuals and groups may, like the ancient Greeks or the German volk, return to the irrational in social practice and custom. Or they may be attracted to utopian ideals of a coming millennium, or a Third (or Fourth) Reich. We must remember the dangerous potential of a monistic, idealistic psychology which stresses one great value over all others, whether it be the romantic ideal of the great individual or the allure of the erotic absolute. This is moral fanaticism.

The fourth lesson is that we should be suspicious of perfectionism in political or social discourse. Much better for us to become imperfectionists and seek concrete, if partial, gains in society rather than seek a totalizing revolution based on some notion of a perfect society, cleansed of contaminating elements. We have seen the explosive tandem of paranoid and fanatical thinking, often with an apocalyptic aura. The totalizing approach to social engineering utilized by Stalin, Mao, and Pol Pot has been tested and shown to be an absolute, horrendous failure. It allowed brutal leaders to let slip the dogs of war, to wallow in dark irrationality and erotic absolutes, and to justify mass killings based on a crude consequential reasoning – and a narrow conception of human flourishing. Constructing society on one big idea, with no room for balancing values or rational criticism, is the most dangerous form of politics that humankind has ever invented.

In all things, the human and the humane is found in moderation, in compromise, in respect, and in give-and-take; in the transformations that come with communication and dialogue. In true learning. These are the formative experiences of the softer side of our nature. As a culture we need to learn to re-appreciate the importance of attempting

2 Kant, *Religion and Rational Theology*, 78.

to be rational *together*, through inclusive dialogue which stimulates the humane traits. Meanwhile, we should undermine tribalism by exposing ourselves, and our children, to other cultures and ethnic groups.

Rational and Irrational Capacities

To rebuild, we need to get the aim right.

The aim is not to swing society towards extreme rationalism or irrationalism. We want to stop the pendulum *somewhere in the middle* between these extremes. Human flourishing occurs at the convergence of rational and irrational capacities. As in the taming of the Furies, both sides of human nature need to be able to express themselves within society for there to be any reasonable peace and stability.

Society needs its rational side, whether it is healthy institutions of science or rational methods in the professions. In terms of education, a basic knowledge of the history of culture and ideas, including the social history of rationality and irrationality, should be considered important.

However, society also needs the irrational: emotive events, forms of public celebration and gaiety, Rabelais-like satire, freedom from excessive and intimidating bureaucracy and laws, and situations where citizens can express their irrational capacities in ways that are cathartic and self-fulfilling. There should be a social climate where citizens have the freedom to assent or dissent from current mores. In addition, society should give individuals and students a better chance to express themselves in the arts and in the humanities, not just in sports.

To have the opportunity to express one's irrational capacities, such as a chance to play music, dance, fall in love, adopt an alternate lifestyle, or participate in emotionally meaning activities is *not* the same as having the opportunity to express extreme emotions and intolerance tribalism. The latter are enemies of democracy. Given my explanation of the enemy stance, society needs to be conscious of the stance's triggers, such as hate speech. It should monitor and publicly criticize media sites with fake news and conspiracy theories. It should openly question or challenge political leaders and groups that display the enemy stance. For journalists, this means defining journalism as engagement for dialogic democracy, not a passive stenography of (presumed) fact.[3]

3 I explore the idea of democratically engaged journalism in *Objectively Engaged Journalism*.

SECTION 2: DEMOCRACY, RATIONALITY, AND OBJECTIVITY

Choosing Rationality

I conclude this book with a call – or a plea – for a revival of interest in notions of rationality and objectivity. I stress the social or political benefits of adopting an objective stance when we engage society as journalists.

Here, I explicitly extend that call to all citizens, as a duty, an epistemic duty owed to democracy and fellow citizens. We not only have ethical and social responsibilities to our country and world. We also have duties to adopt certain crucial epistemic attitudes and methods when we inquire into, discuss, and debate matters of importance to democracy.

Our society has lost faith in the ideals of rationality and objectively due to a corrosive postmodern scepticism towards any notion of truth or objectivity and the regrettable identification of rationality and objectivity with a narrow scienticism and technological capitalism. Rationality and objectivity are the very opposite of being mentally narrow. The use of rationality to dismiss rationality and its commitment to truth and objectivity is a socially dangerous, insidious attitude. It blurs the distinctions between fact and fake fact, rational persuasion and propaganda.

The ideal of objectivity in our society needs to exist because the public sphere features a clash of subjective views and interests, advanced by people or groups that have little interest in being objective. Objectivity is a crucial tool for discussing and evaluating the claims of these partisan people. Also, we need impartial professionals and officials every day in society to fairly adjudicate and peacefully resolve disputes between partial people, with their conflicting ideas about what actions or reforms are needed in a situation. Without objectivity, bias seeps into the decision-making process and destroys the credibility of important political offices and institutions. As a society where the pleasures of opining and unrestrained self-expression are highly prized, we are in danger of no longer understanding why there needs to be *self-imposed* limits to our partisanship and methods of persuasion.

The decision to adopt the disciplines and methods of objective rationality is a decisive choice by individuals, groups, and society at large. It is about the extent to which people are *willing* to adopt the rational, objective stance where it matters the most – in debates that affect the rights of citizens and minorities and in debates over the direction of one's nation. To what extent are journalists and citizens willing to encourage objective public reason in the public sphere? Whether they have such a will to be objective will depend on whether they have grown up in a society that encourages objective modes of thinking and respect for plural democracy, i.e., a society that supports the best side of human nature.

Rationality and objectivity, properly understood, is a bulwark against authoritarianism in belief and practice. It is a defence against an obscurantism that allows the clever to manipulate the naïve or vulnerable. The attitude of objectivity stands squarely against the many forms of obscurantism in our culture, propagating themselves through the media. It opposes irrationalism, emotionalism, extreme religious fundamentalism, occultism, and fraudulent mysticism. For all the faults attributed to a detached, cool objectivity, I fear more a mindless emotionalism and an inability to assess critically those beliefs inculcated by a media-saturated world. History, as discussed throughout this book, supports my fear as reasonable and not a matter of paranoia.

Educating Democratic Citizens

A major educational goal of rational democracy is the creation of rational citizens who are capable of, and prefer, public discussions that are tolerant and evidence-based. We want to educate students who have the tools of critical analysis so they are neither impressed nor recruited by utopian-wielding, charismatic, rhetoric-spinning extremists. But more than that, we want them to have the skills to construct their own rational, plausible perspectives.

What are we trying to avoid through education and other means? Irrational intolerance, a cognitive–emotive pathology where individuals or groups exhibit:

(1) *Reality-averse cognition*: (a) a dogmatic persistence in fixed and biased beliefs immune to counterfacts due to false reasoning or biased cognitive processes that resemble good reasoning but are in fact a fake rationality; (b) beliefs that are triggered and supported by extreme emotions of aggression, anger, or contempt.

(2) *Other-averse attitude*: Reality-averse cognition targets others in the public sphere. Individuals or groups adopt an attitude of prejudice, conceiving of the others in biased and inaccurate stereotypes. Myths, ideologies, and conspiracy theories abound.

Ward's Test for Irrationality

To detect such irrationality in oneself or others, ask the following five questions:

WHAT DO YOU BELIEVE?
The usual way to identify an irrational form of thinking is to note that it presumes the existence of dubious or delusional things, such as a coming millennium which requires mass suicide or UFOs awaiting your transport to heaven. Or, someone believes incorrectly that persons have highly negative properties, i.e., one is prejudiced, or that persons have highly positive properties, i.e., one indulges in leader worship. This is ontological irrationality.

HOW DO YOU BELIEVE?
People are also irrational in the way they hold their beliefs. I adopt a dogma that issued from questionable methods for belief formation. Moreover, my dogma is bulletproof. Resistance to rational methods is a key indication of irrationality.[4] This is epistemic irrationality

WHY DO YOU BELIEVE?
Do you believe something because of evidence and an impartial desire to know the truth? Or do you believe what you *want* to believe? Irrational intolerance is rooted in the latter. It needs to escape a heavy sense of vulnerability, inner conflict, and bitter frustration in life. Other factors are a desire to be great or to be immortal. To abandon the beliefs would threaten psychological stability.

HOW EXTREME ARE YOUR BELIEFS AND EMOTIONS?
Irrationality is linked with extreme beliefs and emotions. As we have seen, irrational people act according to extreme motivational systems which direct hate at groups. Emotional irrationality may be caused by an imbalance in emotions, a psychopath's lack of empathy, or the development of a love of killing and torture.

4 Sen defines rationality as the willingness to subject your beliefs and decisions to the "discipline" of reasoned scrutiny. Sen, *Rationality and Freedom*, 4.

WHAT ARE YOU PREPARED TO DO?

Social and moral irrationality are expressed by groups when they are willing to do grossly immoral actions, such as genocide, and to support leaders who go beyond law and morality. Social irrationality becomes public irrationality when people use communication violence to manipulate groups and to arouse hostility.

In the public sphere, much has been written of late about the surge in far-right extremism and fake news on social media. Detecting fakery in media – and not being impressed by its claims – requires new and strenuous efforts to develop media literacy programs for schools and colleges, including schools of journalism. So much of what we call reality today is constructed by the media we encounter. Media education should become *education for a democratic public*. This requires redesigning education to teach democratic principles and history, the role of media in democracy, and the media techniques of anti-democratic forces. There should be teaching about the social impact of technology, cultural and political differences among cultures, the influence of media on global issues, and the capacity of new media to radicalize young people.

Teaching the Objective Stance

One way to detect media fakery, and to detect one's own biases, is to practise what I call pragmatic objectivity.[5] It should be taught as part of media literacy courses and in schools of journalism. It is the deployment of a practical objective method in the use and analysis of media.

Pragmatic objectivity begins with the adoption of an objective stance. We develop in ourselves, conscientiously, a number of central cognitive virtues – dispositions that help inquiry. The virtues are open rationality, partial transcendence, a desire for disinterested truth, and integrity. Objective citizens practise open rationality by accepting the burdens of rationality – to listen to all sides, to learn from criticism, and to be accountable for public statements. They exhibit partial transcendence by putting aside, at least temporarily, their biases and parochial

5 For my full theory of pragmatic objectivity, see my *The Invention of Journalism Ethics*, chapter 8.

preferences. The objective citizen and journalist are disposed towards disinterested truth if they refuse to prejudge a breaking news story and follow the facts wherever they lead. Both the disinterested citizen and the journalist do not allow personal interests to overwhelm the passion for truth. They are willing to admit and correct errors. By following these virtues, the objective citizen acts with integrity and promotes informed democracy.

However, adopting the objective stance is not sufficient. The objective stance needs to evaluate news and information by applying a range of standards:

STANDARDS OF EMPIRICAL VALIDITY

Accuracy, verification, and completeness are prime empirical standards. In using media, accuracy calls for accurate quotations and paraphrases of statements and correct numbers. Citizens ask, what is the empirical evidence for the story? Are the facts carefully collected? Are counterfacts treated seriously? Verification means that citizens cross-check reports against original documents and reports by other news sources.

STANDARDS OF CLARITY, LOGIC, AND COHERENCE

Citizens check whether a report coheres with existing knowledge in the field. Is the newsmaker's interpretation logically consistent? Are concepts clear? Are fallacious arguments or manipulative techniques used?

STANDARDS OF DIVERSE AND TRUSTED SOURCES

The quality and diversity of sources are centre stage when we evaluate information. Are the sources reliable and, if they claim to be experts, are they truly experts in their field.

STANDARDS OF OPEN, PUBLIC SCRUTINY

This category reflects a concern for dialogic democracy. Are people ready to subject their opinions to the views of others? Are they prepared to alter their views? Does a report contribute to informing people in respectful ways or is it published to spark social tensions or aid extremists?

In summary, a report is objective to the degree that it derives from an objective stance and satisfies these standards.

Pragmatic objectivity is a tool for combatting fake news, while enhancing rationality.

Educating Moderate Patriots

The fate of egalitarian democracy in a global world depends on the ability of societies to develop the right kinds of political emotions in citizens. Ever since the French Revolution, Western nations have wondered how to create a unified body politic *not* based on the coercion of a monarch. Political philosophers from Rousseau to Comte have advanced various mechanisms to induce solidarity, such as a civic religion.[6] But too often their recommendations required sameness of ethical and religious belief to a degree that is incompatible with today's plural societies. How *can* there be "in many, one"?

One step involves teaching a moderate patriotism or love of one's country. Patriotism is a political emotion par excellence. A second step involves creating individuals who care for others, who go beyond their own self-interest and adopt the perspective of the common good – a difficult task in a world of my, me, mine. Civic education should overcome the gap between the interests of individuals and the interests of the populace and the gap between us and the nation-at-large. These steps would help to restrain the ever-dangerous emotion of extreme or tribal patriotism.

What form of patriotism we need depends on the type of democracy at which we aim. In other works, I have recommended dialogic democracy. A dialogic democracy is an ideal that purposely excludes extremes. It is a democracy whose decisions are based on rational, informed, and inclusive dialogue, open to all. Citizens meaningfully participate in the pursuit of a society that is just, tolerant, and reality-informed.[7]

The form of patriotism compatible with dialogic democracy is moderate or non-extreme patriotism. Extreme patriotism includes (1) a special affection for one's country as *superior* to others; (2) an *exclusive* concern for one's country's well-being and few constraints on the pursuit of one's country's interests; and (3) automatic or *uncritical support* for one's country's actions. Extreme patriotism prepares the ground for extreme nationalism until both are barely distinguishable.

6 On the importance of emotions to liberal democracy see Nussbaum, *Political Emotions*. On the problem of finding a new basis for solidarity, see her *Political Emotions*, 378.

7 For my notion of dialogic democracy, see *Ethical Journalism in a Populist Age*, chapter 4.

Moderate patriotism is a moderate loyalty to one's country. It consists of (1) a special affection for one's country; (2) a desire that one's country flourishes and prospers; (3) a special but not exclusive concern for one's country; (4) support for a morally constrained pursuit of national goals; and (5) conditional and critical support of one's country's actions.[8]

Moderate patriotism seeks to affirm a love of country but in a way that avoids superiority, exclusivity, and pressure to support one's country uncritically. The loyalty is genuine but limited. Moderate patriots have an inclusive attitude towards other nations. They eschew exaggerating the uniqueness and superiority of their country.[9] Moderate loyalty was rejected by the extreme political groups studied earlier in this book.

SECTION III: PATROLLING THE PUBLIC SPHERE

Macro-Resistance

To reduce the stream of polluted media information washing over us we need to organize a macro-resistance – a global collaboration of diverse organizations and publics who are concerned about their media and their world. Only macro-resistance can counter macro-corruption. It is time to create, at the centre of our media system, a networked core of groups that care about responsible communication for democratic community. Journalists, scientists, librarians, data workers, advocates, and others need to join in macro-resistance to fakery.

Here are a few ways to collaborate and to detox the media sphere.

NATIONAL COALITIONS

Journalists, with academics and media foundations, should build national coalitions for media accountability. I envisage a system of online, networked centres, independent of government or any one media organization, and plural – open to many approaches to media. Universities, journalism organizations, media ethicists, NGOs, media web sites, news

8 Nathanson, *Patriotism, Morality and Peace*, 37–8.

9 On how to teach moderate patriotism and a care for the common good, see Nussbaum's *Political Emotions*, chapters 8, 9, and 10.

councils, and citizens would create a high-quality resource for daily media discourse, evaluation, and promotion of excellence. It would be global in outlook, linked to coalitions in other countries.

The coalition would focus not only on the work of mainstream journalists. It would pay attention to the media practices of citizens, advocacy groups, and the so-called fifth estate – online critics of mainstream media. The coalition's functions would include fact-checking, exposure of dubious sources, debate on media ethics, and analysis of coverage of events. Crucial to the coalition is that it be *high-profile* – well-known to the public as a trusted place to check a media source and debate media policy. The hub of this network could be a school of journalism or a multi-disciplinary centre for democracy. Whatever its structure, it would be a place for macro-resistance, a centre of gravity amid the information wars that engulf us.

MEDIA ETHICS FOR EVERYONE

Macro-resistance will falter unless we make media ethics a more inclusive, important civic enterprise. Media ethics should be more than an online scolding of decisions made by mainstream newsrooms or the teaching of ethical case studies in journalism schools. One priority is to show students and citizens how to use media intelligently and ethically and how to evaluate the use of media by other people. Here, media ethics goes beyond the ethics of professional journalism to become a media ethics for everyone. It becomes a wide discussion of how media technology is to be used responsibly in life, from the issue of cyberbullying to the issue of sharing demeaning photos of vulnerable people.

Also, journalists should organize workshops on responsible news media for schools and social groups. This effort would be part of a larger project to help citizens distinguish responsible and irresponsible journalism. Journalists can use the workshops to explain journalism ethics and how the best democratic journalists work.

Further, we need a public revolution in how we "do" media ethics. We need the participation of publics in the formulation of media standards and in the monitoring of media performance. Rather than talk of media self-regulation we should think about a public-directed regulation of media ethics. By regulation I do not mean laws but ethical norms and processes that give the public a meaningful place in code revisions and debate on media issues. Maybe we should call it public-participatory ethics.

Neither individuals nor professional journalists alone can detox the media sphere. For citizens, there is no individualistic, technological fix to the problem of macro-pollution, e.g., to simply download a better anti-virus software. Government and society must take steps to address problems beyond what journalists can fix. Technology experts need to protect electoral systems from hacks; our education system needs to prepare digital citizens. Governments can pressure social media to identify fake news, refuse accounts to racists, and be transparent about who pays for ads.

Global Patriots

Finally, rebuilding rational publics should ground media norms, practices, and teaching in global ethics – principles that cross borders and seek flourishing for humanity at large. As long as citizens and journalists see their media duties as due only to the citizens in their country, the more likely is it that extremists can play the extreme patriotism card to arouse enmity to other cultures.

To transcend tribal ways of thinking, we should regard ourselves as global patriots, first; national patriots, second. A global patriot bases her ethics on what I call moral globalism. Her primary values are principles of human flourishing and human rights. The globalist promotes democratic institutions internationally and supports progress on global issues. Journalists, as professionals or citizens, see themselves as public communicators to the world, to a global public sphere. Global patriotism is loyalty to the largest group possible – humanity.

CONCLUSION: THE IMPORTANCE OF MINDSETS

In summary, to meet the threat of advancing authoritarianism and irrationality, what is vital is the learning and social reinforcement of democratic attitudes, habits of thought, and values. Rationality, fairness, moderation, and openness to other cultures is something that must be *learned*. And, what is learned in class must then be supported by civil society and social practices.

My recommendations deal with attitudes and the importance of education. But I do not think for a moment that this is *all* that must occur in society. For instance, groups will start being more tolerant of each other when the material conditions of society improve. For example, economic and social inequalities must be reduced for egalitarian democracy to be possible. But to explore these large questions would take me far afield.

In the end, however, the importance of material conditions does not invalidate attention to ideas and mindsets. People act on their mindsets no matter how they are generated.

As the many examples in this book have shown, if the enemy mindset prevails, if rationality and objectivity are belittled as myths, this will surely be the death of any democracy worth having. It would be a new slavery of the mind.

Bibliography

Abbate, Carolyn, and Roger Parker. *A History of Opera: The Last Four Hundred Years.* London: Penguin, 2015.

Adler, Alfred. *Understanding Human Nature.* Eastford, CT: Martino Publishing, 2010.

Adorno, Theodore. *Philosophy of Modern Music.* Translated by Anne G. Mitchell and Wesley V. Blomster. London: Sheed and Ward, 1987. Originally published 1973.

Adorno, Theodore, Else Frenkel-Brunswik, Daniel Levinson, and R. Nevitt Sanford. *The Authoritarian Personality.* New York: John Wiley and Sons, 1964. Originally published 1950.

Ackerman, Nathan W, and Marie Jahoda. *Anti-Semitism and Emotional Disorder: A Psychoanalytic Interpretation.* New York: Harper and Brothers, 1950.

Ackroyd, Peter. *Blake.* London: Minerva, 1996.

Aeschylus. *Oresteia.* New York: Penguin Classics, 1984.

Affron, Matthew. "Constructing a New Jewish Identity." In *Exiles and Emigrés: The Flight of European Artists from Hitler,* edited by Stephanie Baron, 113–19. Los Angeles: Harry Abrams, 1997.

Albrecht, James. *Reconstructing Individualism: A Pragmatic Tradition from Emerson to Ellison.* New York: Fordham University Press, 2012.

Albright, Madeleine. *Fascism: A Warning.* New York: Harper Perennial, 2018.

Allison, Dale C. *Jesus of Nazareth: Millenarian Prophet.* Minneapolis: Augsburg Fortress, 1998.

Allport, Gordon W. *The Nature of Prejudice.* Reading, MA: Addison-Wesley, 1954.

Anderson, Craig, and Brad Bushman, "Human Aggression." *Annual Review of Psychology* 53 (2002): 27–51.

Antliff, Mark. *Avant-Garde Fascism: The Mobilization of Myth, Art, and Culture in France, 1909–1939.* Durham, NC: Duke University Press, 2007.

Antliff, Mark, and Vivien Green, eds. *The Vorticists.* London: Tate Publishing, 2010.

Aquinas, Thomas. *Summa Theologica.* 5 vols. 2nd and rev. ed. Notre Dame, IN: Benziger Brothers, 1947.

Arber, Richard, ed. *Evolutionary Biology: Concepts and Theories.* Forest Hills, NY: Callisto Reference, 2018.

Arbib, Michael, Liebal, Katja, and Simone Pika. "Primate Vocalization, Gesture, and the Evolution of Human Language." *Current Anthropology* 49, 6 (2008): 1053–63.

Arcadi, Adam Clark. "Vocal Responsiveness in Male Wild Chimpanzees: Implications for the Evolution of Language." *Journal of Human Evolution* 39, 2 (August 2000): 205–23.

Ardrey, Robert. *The Territorial Imperative.* New York: Atheneum, 1967.

Arendt, Hannah. *Eichmann in Jerusalem: A Report on the Banality of Evil.* New York: Viking, 1963.

– *The Origins of Totalitarianism.* New York: Harcourt, 1976.

– "What Is Authority?" In *Between Past and Future*, 91–141. New York: Penguin, 1968.

Aristophenes. *The Birds.* Translated by Nan Dunbar. Oxford: Oxford University Press, 1991.

Aristotle. *Nicomachean Ethics.* In *The Basic Works of Aristotle*, edited by Richard McKeon, 935–1112. New York: The Modern Library, 2001.

– *Politics.* 2nd ed. Translated by Carnes Lord. Chicago: University of Chicago Press, 2013.

– *Rhetoric.* In *The Basic Works of Aristotle*, edited by Richard McKeon, 1325–451. New York: The Modern Library, 2001.

Armstrong, Donald M. *A Theory of Universals.* Cambridge: Cambridge University Press, 1980.

Arrow, Kenneth. *Social Choice and Individual Values.* New York: Wiley, 1951.

Asahara, Shoko. *Declaring Myself the Christ: Disclosing the True Meanings of Jesus Christ's Gospel.* Tokyo: Aum Publishing Company, 1992.

– *Supreme Initiation: An Empirical Spiritual Science for the Supreme Truth.* New York: AUM USA Company, 1988.

Asbridge, Thomas. *The First Crusade: A New History.* Oxford, 2004.

Ashley-Montagu, Montagne F. *The Nature of Human Aggression.* New York: Oxford University Press, 1976.

Attali, Jacques. *Noise: The Political Economy of Music.* Translated by Brian Massumi. Minneapolis: University of Minnesota Press, 2017. Originally published in 1985.

Auger, Montse. *Dalí's World.* London: Goodman, 2009.

Augustine. *City of God.* Translated by Henry Bettenson. London: Penguin Classic, 2003.

– *The Confessions of St. Augustine.* Translated by Rex Warner. New York: New American Library, 1963.

Auner, Joseph. *A Schoenberg Reader: Documents of a Life.* New Haven: Yale University Press, 2003.

Aunger, Roger, and Valerie Curtis, "The Anatomy of Motivation: An Evolutionary-Ecological Approach." *Biological Theory* 8 (2013): 49–63.

Aurelius, Marcus. *Meditations.* London: Penguin Classics, 1964.

Axelrod, Robert. *The Evolution of Cooperation.* New York: Basic Books, 1984.

Ayer, Alfred J. *Language Truth and Logic.* 2nd ed. New York: Dover Books, 1952. Originally published in 1936.

Bacon, Francis. *Of the Advancement of Learning.* Scotts Valley, CA: CreateSpace Independent Publishing Platform, 2017. Originally published in 1605.

Baigent, Michael, and Richard Leigh. *The Inquisition.* London: Penguin, 2000

Bakhtin, Mikhail. *Rabelais and His World.* Translated by Helene Iswolsky. Bloomington: Indiana University Press, 1984.

Ball, Susan. *Ozenfant and Purism: The Evolution of a Style 1915–1930.* Ann Arbor: University of Michigan Research Press, 1981.

Bandura, Albert. *Social Foundations of Thought and Action.* Englewood Cliffs, NJ: Prentice-Hall, 1986.

– *Social Learning Theory.* Toronto: Pearson, 1976.

Barkow, Jerome H., Leda Cosmides, and John Tooby, eds. *The Adapted Mind: Evolutionary Psychology and the Generation of Culture.* Oxford: Oxford University Press, 1995.

Barkun, Michel. *A Culture of Conspiracy: Apocalyptic Visions in Contemporary America.* Los Angeles: University of California Press, 2003.

– *Religion and the Racist Right.* Chapel Hill: University of North Carolina Press, 1994.

Baron, Robert A., and Deborah. R. Richardson, *Human Aggression.* 2nd ed. New York: Plenum Press 1994.

Baudelaire, Charles. *The Flowers of Evil.* Oxford: Oxford World's Classics, 1998. Originally published in 1857.

– *The Painter of Modern Life.* Translated by Jonathan Mayne. London: Phaidon Press, 1964. Originally published in 1863.

– *Salon of 1846.* Edited by David Kelley. Oxford: Oxford University Press, 1975.

Beck, Aaron. *Prisoners of Hate: The Cognitive Basis of Anger, Hostility, and Violence.* New York: HarperCollins, 1999.

Becker, Elizabeth. *When the War was Over.* New York: Simon and Schuster, 1986.

Becker, Jasper. *Hungry Ghosts: China's Secret Famine.* London: John Murray Publishers, 1996.

Benjamin, William E. "Abstract Polyphonies: The Music of Schoenberg's Nietzschean Moment." In *The Political and Religious Ideas in the Works of Arnold Schoenberg*, edited by Charlotte M. Cross and Russell Berman, 1–39. New York: Garland Publishing, 2000.

Berlin, Isaiah. "The Counter-Enlightenment." In *Against the Current: Essays in the History of Ideas*, 2nd ed., 1–32. Princeton: Princeton University Press, 2013.

– *The Crooked Timber of Humanity*, edited by Henry Hardy. London: Fontana Press, 1990.

– "The Decline of Utopian Ideas in the West." In *The Crooked Timber of Humanity*, edited by Henry Hardy, 20–48. London: Fontana Press, 1990.

– "Joseph de Masitre and the Origins of Fascism." In *The Crooked Timber of Humanity*, edited by Henry Hardy, 91–174. London: Fontana Press, 1990.

– *Political Ideas in the Romantic Age.* Edited by Henry Hardy. Princeton: Princeton University Press, 2006.

– "The Pursuit of the Ideal." In *The Crooked Timber of Humanity*, edited by Henry Hardy, 1–19. London: Fontana Press, 1990.

– "Two Concepts of Freedom." In *Political Ideas in the Romantic Age*, edited by Henry Hardy, 155–207. Princeton: Princeton University Press, 2006.

Berman, Marshall. *All That Is Solid Melts into Air: The Experience of Modernity.* New York: Simon and Schuster, 1982.

Bertrin, Georges. "Francois Rabelais." In *The Catholic Encyclopedia*, vol. 12, 131. New York: Robert Appleton Company, 1913.

Blumberg, Albert E., and Herbert Feigl in *The Journal of Philosophy* 28, 11 (21 May 1931): 281–96.

Boardman, John, Jasper Griffin, and Oswyn Murray, eds. *The Oxford History of Greece and the Hellenistic World.* Oxford: Oxford University Press, 1991.

Bossy, John. *Christianity in the West 1400–1700.* Oxford: Oxford University Press, 1989.

Bourke, Andrew. *Principles of Social Evolution.* New York: Oxford University Press, 2011.

Bouwsma, William J. *John Calvin: A Sixteenth Century Portrait.* Oxford: Oxford University Press, 1989.

Bowen, Barbara C. *Enter Rabelais, Laughing.* Nashville: Vanderbilt University Press, 1998.

Bowersock, G.W. *Martyrdom and Rome.* Cambridge: Cambridge University Press, 2002.

Bowles, Samuel, and Herbert Gintis. *The Cooperative Species: Human Reciprocity and its Evolution.* Princeton: Princeton University Press, 2011.

– "The Evolution of Strong Reciprocity: Cooperation in Heterogeneous Populations." *Theoretical Population Biology* 65, 1 (February 2004): 17–28.

Bowsky, William M. *A Medieval Italian Commune; Siena Under The Nine, 1287–1355.* Berkeley: University of California Press, 1981.

Bradley, Owen. *A Modern Maistre: The Social and Political Thought of Joseph de Maistre.* London: University of Nebraska Press, 1999.

Bremer, Francis J. *Puritanism: A Very Short Introduction.* Oxford: Oxford University Press. 2009.

Breton, Andre. *Nadja.* Translated by Richard Howard. New York: Grove Press, 1994.

– *Surrealism and Painting.* Translated by Simon Watson Taylor. New York: Harper and Row, 1972.

Brown, Donald E. *Human Universals.* New York: McGraw-Hill, 1991.

Broyles, J. Allen. *The John Birch Society: Anatomy of a Protest.* Boston: Beacon Press, 1964.

Bruck, Moeller van den. *The Third Reich.* Translated by E.O. Lorimer. New York: Howard Fertig, 1971.

Buenger, Barbara Copeland, and Keith Holz. "Antifascism or Autonomous Art?" In *Exiles and Emigrés: The Flight of European Artists from Hitler,* edited by Stephanie Baron, 57–73. Los Angeles: Harry Abrams, 1997.

Burgler, Roeland. *The Eyes of the Pineapple: Revolutionary Intellectuals and Terror in Democratic Kampuchea.* Saarbrucken, Germany: Beitenbach, 1990.

Burckhardt, Jacob. *The Civilization of the Renaissance in Italy.* London: Phaidon Press. 3rd ed. 1995. Originally published in 1860.

Burke, Edmund. *Philosophical Inquiry into the Origin of our Ideas of the Sublime and Beautiful.* New York: Simon and Brown, 2013.

– *Reflections on the Revolution in France.* Oxford: Oxford University Press, 2009.

Burke, Peter. *The Italian Renaissance: Culture and Society in Italy.* Reprint. Oxford: Polity Press, 1991.

Busoni, Ferruccio. *Selected Letters.* Translated by Antony Beaumont. London: Faber and Faber, 1987.

Buss, David M. *Evolutionary Psychology: The New Science of the Mind.* 6th ed. New York: Routledge, 2019.

– ed. *The Handbook of Evolutionary Psychology.* 2nd ed. Volume 1: Foundations. Hoboken, NJ: Wiley, 2016.

Calas, Nicolas. "Anti-Surrealist Dali." *View* 1, 6 (June 1941): 3.

Calinescu, Matei. *Five Faces of Modernity: Modernism, Avant-Garde, Decadence, Kitsch, Postmodernism.* 2nd ed. Durham, NC: Duke University Press, 1987.

Cameron, Norman. "The Paranoid Pseudo-Community." *American Journal of Sociobiology* 49 (1943): 32–8.

Camus, Albert. *The Myth of Sisyphus.* Translated by Justin O'Brien. London: Penguin, 2000.

Cannon, Walter. *Wisdom of the Body.* New York: Norton, 1963.

Carnap, Rudolf. *The Logical Structure of the World and Pseudoproblems in Philosophy.* 2nd ed. Translated by Rolf A. George. Berkeley: University of California Press, 1967.

– *The Unity of Science.* New York: Routledge, 2011. First published in English in 1934.

Carroll, James. *Constantine's Sword.* Boston: Houghton Mifflin Harcourt, 2001.

Casson, Lionel. *Everyday Life in Ancient Rome.* Baltimore: Johns Hopkins University Press, 1998.

Cecil, Robert C. *The Myth of the Master Race: Alfred Rosenberg and Nazi Ideology.* New York: Dodd, 1972.

Chandler, David P. *Brother Number One.* Boulder, CO: Westview Press, 1992.

– *The Tragedy of Cambodian History.* New Haven, CT: Yale University Press, 1991.

Chang, Jung. *Wild Swans: Three Daughters of China.* New York: Simon and Schuster, 1991.

Ch'en, Jerome. *Mao Papers: Anthology and Bibliography.* London: Oxford University Press, 1970.

Chisholm, Hugh, ed. "Vitruvius." *Encyclopedia Britannica,* 11th ed. Cambridge: Cambridge University Press, 1911.

Choron, Alexandre. "Introduction: Summary of the History of Music." In *A Dictionary of Musicians, from the Earliest Ages to the Present Time,* edited by John S. Sainsbury, 67–75. London: Da Capo Press, 1966. Originally published in French in 1810. The *Dictionary* was originally published in 1827.

Cinpoes, Radu. *Nationalism and Identity in Romania: A History of Extreme Politics from the Birth of the State to EU Accession.* London: Tauris Academic Studies, 2010.

Clark, Gary, and Maciej Henneberg, "*Ardipithecus ramidus* and the Evolution of Language and Singing: An Early Origin for Hominin Vocal Capability." *Homo* 68 (2017): 101–21.

Coffey, John. *Persecution and Toleration on Protestant England 1558–1689.* Toronto: Pearson Education, 2000.

Cohn, Norman. *Cosmos, Chaos and the World to Come: The Ancient Roots of Apocalyptic Faith.* New Haven, NJ: Yale University Press, 1993.

– *The Pursuit of the Millennium.* Rev. ed. New York: Oxford University Press, 1970.

Comte, Auguste. *A General View of Positivism.* Translated by John Bridges. New York: Robert Speller, 1957. First published in 1865.

– *The Positive Philosophy.* Translated by Harriet Martineau. New York: AMS Press, 1974. Originally published in 1830. Published in English in 1853.

– *System of Positive Philosophy, or Treatise on Sociology, Instituting the Religion of Humanity.* 4 vols. Translated by John Bridges. London: Longmans, Green and Co., 1875.

Conquest, Robert. *The Great Terror: A Reassessment.* Oxford: Oxford University Press, 1990.

Conrad, Joseph. *Heart of Darkness.* Edited by Leonard F. Dean. Englewood Cliffs, NJ: Prentice-Hall, 1960.

Coogan, Michael, ed. *The New Annotated Bible.* 3rd ed. Rev. standard version. Oxford: Oxford University Press, 1989.

Cornford, Francis. *The Unwritten Philosophy and Other Essays.* Cambridge: Cambridge University Press, 1967. Originally published in 1950.

Cottington, David. *The Avant-Garde: A Very Short Introduction.* Oxford: Oxford University Press, 2013.

Crisp, Richard J. *Social Psychology: A Very Short Introduction.* Oxford: Oxford University, 2015.

Cross, Charlotte M., and Russell A. Berman, eds. *The Political and Religious Ideas in the Works of Arnold Schoenberg.* New York: Garland Publishing, 2000.

Dachy, Marc. *The Dada Movement 1915–1923.* New York: Rizzoli, 1990.

Dalí, Salvador. *Diary of a Genius.* London: Creation Books, 1994.

– *The Secret Life of Salvador Dalí.* New York: Dial Press, 1942.

– *The Unspeakable Confessions of Salvador Dalí.* Translated by Harold J. Salemson. New York: Morrow, 1976.

Damasio, Antonio. *Descartes' Error: Emotion, Reason, and the Human Brain.* New York: Penguin, 2000.

Darwin, Charles. *The Descent of Man and Selection in Relation to Sex.* Vol. 1. Princeton: Princeton University Press, 1982.

– *The Origin of Species.* Edited by J.W. Burrow. New York: Penguin, 1984.

Daston, Lorraine. "Objectivity and the Escape from Perspective." *Social Studies of Science* 22, 4 (November 1992).

Daston, Lorraine, and Peter Galison. "The Image of Objectivity." *Representations* 40 (Fall 1992): 81–127.

Daub, Adrian. "Introduction." In *The Doctor Faustus Dossier,* edited by E. Randol Schoenberg, 1–30. Oakland: University of California, 2018.

Dawkins, Richard. *The God Delusion.* New York: Houghton Mifflin, 2006.

– *The Selfish Gene.* Oxford: Oxford University Press, 1976.

Debussy, Claude. *Debussy Letters.* Translated by Roger Nichols. Cambridge, MA: Harvard University Press, 1987.

Dennett, Daniel. *Darwin's Dangerous Idea.* New York: Simon and Schuster, 1995.

– *Freedom Evolves.* New York: Viking, 2003.

De Waal, Francs. *Primates and Philosophers: How Morality Evolved.* Princeton: Princeton University Press, 2006.

Dewey, John. *Art as Experience.* New York: Penguin, 2005. Originally published in 1934.

– *Experience and Nature.* New York: Dover Publications, 1958.

Dickson, Gary. *The Children's Crusade: Medieval History, Modern Mythistory.* London: Palgrave Macmillan, 2008.

Dodds, Eric R. *The Greeks and the Irrational.* Berkeley: University of California Press, 2004. Originally published in 1951.

Dollard, John et al. *Frustration and Aggression.* New Haven, CT: Yale University Press, 1939.

Dostoevsky, Fyodor. *Notes from the Underground.* Translated by Michael R. Katz. New York: Norton, 1989.

Duchting, Hajo. *Kandinsky: A Revolution in Painting.* Cologne: Taschen, 2017.

Dunbar, Robin I, and Susanne Shultz. "Evolution in the Social Brain" *Science* 317 (2007): 1344–7.

Eco, Umberto. *On Ugliness.* 6th printing. Translated by Alastair McEwen. New York: Rizzoli, 2018. Originally published in 2007.

Ehrenreich, Barbara. *Blood Rites: Origin and History of the Passions of War.* New York: Henry Holt, 1997.

Ehrman, Bart D. *A Brief Introduction to the New Testament.* Oxford: Oxford University Press, 2004.

Eksteins, Modris. *Rites of Spring: The Great War and the Birth of the Modern Age.* Toronto: Vintage Canada, 2012.

Eram, Cosana Maria. *The Autobiographical Pact: Otherness and Redemption in Four French Avant-garde Artists.* Charleston, SC: BiblioBazaar, 2011.

Fabre, Gladys, and Doris Wintgens Hotte, eds. *Van Doesburg & the International Avant-Garde: Constructing a New World.* London: Tate Publishing, 2010.

Faulkner, Jason, Mark Schaller, Justin H. Park, and Lesley A. Duncan. "Evolved Disease-Avoidance Mechanisms and Contemporary Xenophobic Attitudes." *Group Processes and Intergroup Relations* 7, 4 (October 2004): 333–53.

Feisst, Sabine. *Schoenberg's New World: The American Years.* Oxford: Oxford University Press, 2011.

Ferber, Michael. *Romanticism: A Very Short Introduction.* Oxford: Oxford University Press, 2010.

Ferguson, Niall. *The Ascent of Money: The Financial History of the World.* New York: Penguin, 2008.

Fichte, Johann Gottlieb. *The Vocations of Man.* Translated by Peter Preuss. New York: Hackett, 1987. Originally published in 1800.

Finlay, John. *Picasso's Life.* London: Goodman, 2011.

Forte, Allen. *The Structure of Atonal Music.* New Haven, CT: Yale University Press, 1977.

Foucault, Michel. *Discipline and Punish: The Birth of the Prison.* Translated by Alan Sheridan. London: Penguin Books, 1977.

– *Madness and Civilization: A History of Insanity in the Age of Reason.* Translated by Richard Howard. New York: Vintage Books, 1988.

Fox, Robin Lane. *Pagans and Christians.* New York: Viking, 1996.

Freeden, Michael. *Ideology: A Very Short Introduction.* Oxford: Oxford University Press, 2003.

Freely John. *Flame of Miletus.* London: I.B. Tauris, 2012.

Freud, Sigmund. "Beyond the Pleasure Principle." In *On Metapsychology.* Vol. 11. Translated by James Strachey, 275–338. London: Penguin Books, 1984.

– "Civilization and Its Discontents." In *Civilization, Society and Religion.* Vol. 12. Translated by James Strachey, 251–340. London: Penguin Books, 1991.

– *Dora: An Analysis of a Case of Hysteria.* New York: Touchstone, 1997. Originally published in 1905.

– "The Ego and the Id." In *On Metapsychology.* Vol. 11. Translated by James Strachey, 350–407. London: Penguin Books, 1984.

– "The Group and the Prima Horde." In *Civilization, Society and Religion.* Vol. 12. Translated by James Strachey, 154–60. London: Penguin Books, 1991.

– "Group Psychology and the Analysis of the Ego." In *Civilization, Society and Religion.* Vol. 12. Translated by James Strachey, 91–178. London: Penguin Books, 1991.

– "The Herd Instinct." In *Civilization, Society and Religion.* Vol. 12. Translated by James Strachey, 148–53. London: Penguin Books, 1991.

– *On Psychopathology.* Vol. 10. Translated by James Strachey. London: Penguin Freud Library, 1993.

– "Thoughts for the Times on War and Death." In *Civilization, Society and Religion.* Vol. 12. Translated by James Strachey, 57–89. London: Penguin Books, 1991.

– "Why War?" In *Civilization, Society and Religion.* Vol. 12. Translated by James Strachey, 341–62. London: Penguin Books, 1991.

Friedman, Michael. *Reconsidering Logical Positivism.* Cambridge: Cambridge University Press, 1999.

Fried, Michael. *The Moment of Caravaggio*. Princeton: Princeton University Press, 2010.

Fromm, Erich. *The Anatomy of Human Destructiveness*. New York: Holt, Rinehart and Winston, 1973.

– *Escape From Freedom*. New York: Avon Books, 1972. Originally published in 1941.

Fuchs, Christian. *Digital Demagogue: Authoritarian Capitalism in the Age of Trump and Twitter*. London: Pluto Books, 2018.

Galison, Peter. "Aufbau/Bauhaus: Logical Positivism and Modern Architecture." *Critical Inquiry* 16, 4 (Summer 1990): 709–52.

Garth, T. Rooster. "A Review of Race Psychology." *Psychological Bulletin* 27, 5 (1930): 329–56.

Geary, Patrick J., ed. *Readings in Medieval History*. Toronto: Broadview Press, 2003.

Getzfeld, Andrew R. *Essentials of Abnormal Psychology*. Hoboken, NJ: John Wiley and Sons, 2006.

Gibbon, Edward. *The History of the Decline and Fall of the Roman Empire*. London: Wordsworth Editions, 1998.

Giudice, Marco Del. *Evolutionary Psychopathology: A Unified Approach*. Oxford: Oxford University Press, 2018.

Gleason, Abbott. *Totalitarianism: The Inner History of the Cold War*. New York: Oxford University Press, 1995.

Glover, Jonathan. *Humanity: A Moral History of the 20th Century*. 2nd ed. New Haven, NJ: Yale University Press, 2012.

Godbeer, Richard. *The Devil's Dominion: Magic and Religion in early New England*. Cambridge: Cambridge University Press, 1992.

Goethe, Johann Wolfgang von. *Faust: A Tragedy – Part One and Two*. Translated by Martin Greenberg. London: Yale University Press, 2014.

Gold, Joel, and Ian Gold. *Suspicious Minds: How Culture Shapes Madness*. New York: Free Press, 2015.

Goldstein, Bluma. "Schoenberg's Moses and Aron: A Vanishing Biblical Nation." In *Political and Religious Ideas in the Works of Arnold Schoenberg*, edited by Charlotte M. Cross and Russell A. Berman, 159–92. New York: Garland Publishing, 2000.

Goldwag, Arthur. *Cults, Conspiracies, and Secret Societies: The Straight Scoop on Freemasons, the Illuminati, Skull and Bones, Black Helicopters, the New World Order, and Many, Many More*. New York: Random House, 2009.

Goodman, Nelson. *Ways of Worldmaking*. New York: Hackett, 1978.

Gottlieb, Anthony. *The Dream of Reason*. New York: Norton, 2000.

Gould, Stephen Jay. *Ever Since Darwin: Reflections in Natural History.* New York: Norton, 1979.

– "Sociobiology: The Art of Storytelling." *New Scientist* 80 (November 1978): 530–3.

Gould, Stephen Jay, and Richard Lewontin. "The Spandrels of San Marco and the Panglossian Paradigm: A Critique of the Adaptationist Programme." *Proceedings of the Royal Society of London*, B 205, 1161 (1979): 581–98.

Graves, Robert. *The Greek Myths.* London: Penguin, 1960.

Green, Donald P., and Ian Shapiro. *Pathologies of Rational Choice Theory: A Critique of Applications in Political Science.* New Haven, CT: Yale University Press, 1994.

Greene, Joshua. *Moral Tribes: Emotion, Reason and the Gap Between Us and Them.* New York: Penguin, 2013.

Gregor, A. James. *Phoenix: Fascism in Our Time.* New Brunswick, NJ: Transaction Press, 2009.

Guinn, Jeff. *The Road to Jonestown: Jim Jones and the Peoples Temple.* New York: Simon and Schuster, 2017.

Guterl, Matthew P. *The Color of Race in America, 1900–1940.* Cambridge, MA: Harvard University Press, 2009.

Guthrie, William. *The Fifth Century Enlightenment.* Vol. 3. *A History of Greek Philosophy.* 6 vols. Cambridge: Cambridge University Press, 1969.

Haack, Susan. *Philosophy of Logics.* Cambridge: Cambridge University Press, 1978.

Habermas, Jurgen. *The Future of Human Nature.* Cambridge: Polity Press, 2003.

Hacking, Ian. *The Social Construction of What?* Cambridge, MA: Harvard University Press, 1999.

– *The Taming of Chance.* Cambridge: Cambridge University Press, 1990.

Hahn, Peter, ed. *Bauhaus Berlin.* Weingarten, DE: Kunstverlag Weingarten, 1985.

– "Bauhaus Exile." In *Exiles and Emigrés: The Flight of European Artists from Hitler*, edited by Stephanie Baron, 211–23. Los Angeles: Harry Abrams, 1997.

Haidt, Jonathan. *The Righteous Mind: Why Good People Are Divided by Politics and Religion.* New York: Pantheon Books, 2012.

Haille, H.G. *Luther: An Experiment in Bibliography.* Princeton: Princeton University Press, 1983.

Hall, John R. *Apocalypse: From Antiquity to the Empire of Modernity.* Cambridge: Polity Press, 2009.

Hallowell, Alfred. I. *Culture and Experience.* Philadelphia: University of Pennsylvania Press, 1955.

Hamilton, George Heard. *Painting and Sculpture in Europe, 1880 to 1940.* Harmondsworth, Middlesex: Penguin Books, 1967.

Hamilton, William. "The Genetical Evolution of Social Behavior." *Journal of Theoretical Biology* 7 (1964): 1–52.

Hamlyn, David. *Bring a Philosopher: The History of a Practice.* London: Routledge, 1992.

Hansen, Chadwick. *Witchcraft at Salem.* London: Arrow, 1971.

Harari, Yuval Noah. *A Brief History of Humankind.* Toronto: Signal, 2016.

Hare, Robert D. *Without Conscience: The Disturbing World of the Psychopaths among Us.* New York: Pocket Books, 1993.

Hart, Bernard. *The Psychology of Insanity.* 5th ed. Cambridge: Cambridge University Press, 1962.

Hawley, Patricia. "The Duality of Human Nature: Coercion and Prosociality in Youths' Hierarchy Ascension and Social Success." *Current Directions in Psychological Science* 23 (2014): 433–8.

– "Ontogeny and Social Dominance: A Developmental View of Human Power Patterns." *Evolutionary Psychology* 12 (2014): 318–42.

Hayle, Joanne. *Lord Byron and Lady Caroline Lamb: Mad, Bad and Dangerous to Know – The Passionate and Public Affair That Scandalised Regency England.* New York: CreateSpace, 2016.

Hazlitt, William. *The Pleasure of Hating.* London: Penguin, 2005. Originally published in 1823.

Heath, Duncan, and Judy Boreham. *Introducing Romanticism.* New York: Totem Books, 1999.

Hegel, Georg Wilhelm Friedrich. *Aesthetics: Lectures on Fine Art.* Vol. 1. Reprint. Translated by T.M. Knox. Oxford: Clarendon Press, 1988. First published in 1835.

Heilbut, Anthony. *Exiled in Paradise: German Refugee Artists and Intellectuals in America, from the 1930s to the Present.* New York: Viking, 1983.

Henshilwood, Christopher, and Benoit Dubreuil. "Reading the Artifacts: Gleaning Language Skills from the Middle Stone Age in Southern Africa." In *The Cradle of Language,* edited by Rudolf Botha and Chris Knight, 41–61. Oxford: Oxford University Press, 2009.

Herder, Johann Gottfried. "Governments as Inherited Regimes." In *Another Philosophy of History and Selected Political Writings,* translated by Ioannis Evrigenis and Daniel Pellerin, 121–9. Indianapolis: Hackett Publishing, 2004.

– "Letters for the Advancement of Humanity." In *Philosophical Writings,* translated by Michael Forster, 370–9. Cambridge: Cambridge University Press, 2002.

Hesiod. *Works and Days.* Translated by A.E. Stallings. London: Penguin Classics, 2018.

Hewitt, Andrew. *Fascist Modernism: Aesthetics, Politics, and the Avant-Garde.* Stanford: Stanford University Press, 1993.

Hewitt, Paolo. "The Beach Boys Nearly Sign Charles Manson to Their Label." In *'Scuse Me while I Kiss the Sky*, 92–9. London: Quercus, 2011.

Heyworth, Peter. *Otto Klemperer: His Life and Times.* Vol. 2, 1933–73. Cambridge: Cambridge University Press, 1996.

Hilberg, Raul. *The Destruction of the European Jews.* 3 vols. Revised edition. New York: Holmes and Meier, 1985.

Hilton, Timothy. *The Pre-Raphaelites.* Oxford: Oxford University Press, 1970.

Hitler, Adolf. *Mein Kampf.* Boston: Houghton Mifflin, 1943.

Hobbes, Thomas. *Leviathan.* Edited by C.B. MacPherson. London: New York, 1985.

Hoffer, Eric. *The True Believer.* New York: Harper and Row, 1966.

Hofstadter, Richard. "The Paranoid Style in American Politics." In *The Paranoid Style in American Politics and Other Essays*, 3–40. Chicago: University of Chicago Press, 1979.

Hume, David. *A Treatise of Human Nature.* Edited by L.A. Selby-Bigge. 2nd ed. Oxford: Clarendon Press, 1978.

Hunt, John, and David Hodgson, "What Is Fitness and How Do We Measure It?" In *Evolutionary Behavioral Ecology*, edited by David F. Westneat and Charles W. Fox, 46–70. New York: Oxford University Press, 2010.

Hyer, Brian. "Tonality." *The New Grove Dictionary of Music and Musicians.* 2nd ed. Edited by Stanley Sadie and John Tyrrell. London: Macmillan Publishers, 2001.

Innocent III. *On the Misery of the Human Condition.* Translated by Margaret Mary Dietz. Indianapolis: The Library of the Liberal Arts, 1969.

Jabr, Ferris. "How Beauty Is Making Scientists Rethink Evolution." *The New York Times Magazine*, 9 January 2019.

Jacoby, Russell. *Bloodlust: On the Roots of Violence from Cain and Abel to the Present.* New York: Simon & Schuster, 2011.

James, William. *The Principles of Psychology.* Vol. 2. New York: Henry Holt, 1890.

– *The Varieties of Religious Experience.* London: Collins, 1979.

Janis, Irving. *Victims of Groupthink: A Psychological Study of Foreign-Policy Decisions and Fiascoes.* Boston: Houghton Mifflin, 1972.

Jay, Martin. "The German Migration: Is There a Figure in the Carpet?" In *Exiles and Emigrés: The Flight of European Artists from Hitler*, edited by Stephanie Baron, 326–37. Los Angeles: Harry Abrams, 1997.

Johnson, George. *Architects of Fear.* Los Angeles: Jeremy Thatcher, 1983.

Johnson, Ken. *The Rapture.* Scotts Valley, CA: CreateSpace, 2009.

Johnson, Paul. *A History of Christianity*. London: Simon and Schuster, 1979.

Joyce, Richard. *The Evolution of Morality*. Cambridge, MA: MIT Press, 2007.

Kafka, Franz. *The Metamorphosis*. Translated by Susan Bernofsky. New York: Norton, 2014.

Kahneman, Daniel. *Thinking, Fast and Slow*. Toronto: Anchor Canada, 2013.

Kant, Immanuel. "An Answer to the Question: What Is Enlightenment?" In *Toward Perpetual Peace and Other Writings on Politics, Peace, and History*, edited by Pauline Kleingled. Translated by David L. Colclasure, 17–36. New Haven, NJ: Yale University Press, 2006.

– *Critique of Pure Reason*. Cambridge: Cambridge University Press, 2007.

– *Religion and Rational Theology*. Translated by Allen W. Wood. Cambridge: Cambridge University Press, 2005.

Kaplan, David E., and Andrew Marshall. *The Cult at the End of the World: The Terrifying Story of the Aum Doomsday Cult, from the Subways of Tokyo to the Nuclear Arsenals of Russia*. New York: Random House, 1996.

Kaplan, Hillard, Michael Gurven, and Jane Lancaster, "Brain Evolution and the Human Adaptive Complex: An Ecological and Social Theory." In *The Evolution of Mind: Fundamental Questions and Controversies*, edited by S.W. Gangestad and J.A. Simpson, 269–79. New York: Gilford, 2007.

Karmen, Henry. *The Spanish Inquisition*. London: Weidenfeld and Nicolson, 1997.

Katz, Jacob. *The Darker Side of Genius: Richard Wagner's Anti-Semitism*. London: University Press of New England, 1986.

Keen, Michael. *The Penguin History of Medieval Europe*. London: Penguin Books, 1991.

Kennedy, Michael. "Atonal." *The Oxford Dictionary of Music*. Oxford: Oxford University Press, 1994.

– *Richard Strauss: Man, Musician, Enigma*. Cambridge: Cambridge University Press, 1999.

Kenrick, Douglas, and Victor Sheets. "Homicidal Fantasies." *Ethnology and Sociobiology* 14 (1994): 231–46.

Kershaw, Ian. *Hitler 1889–1936: Hubris*. New York: Norton, 1999.

Kierkegaard, Søren. *Concluding Unscientific Postscript*. Translated by David F. Swenson and Walter Lowrie. Princeton: Princeton University Press, 1968.

Kilduff, Marshall, and Javers, Ron. *The Suicide Cult*. New York: Bantam Books, 1978.

King, Dennis. *Lyndon LaRouche and the new American Fascism*. New York: Doubleday, 1989.

Kipling, Rudyard. *Just So Stories*. London: Macmillan, 1902.

Kirk, Geoffrey S., and John E. Raven. *The Pre-Socratic Philosophers.* Cambridge: Cambridge University Press, 1966.

Kirsch, Adam. "Assassin's Creed." *The New Yorker,* 30 September 2019, 81–5.

Kitto, Humphrey. *The Greeks.* Middlesex, UK: Penguin, 1973.

Klarman, Michael J. *The Framer's Coup: The Making of the United States Constitution.* Oxford: Oxford University Press, 2016.

Klineman, George, Sherman Butler, and David Conn. *The Cult That Died: The Tragedy of Jim Jones and the People's Temple.* New York: Putnam, 1980.

Kochin, Michael S. "How Joseph de Maistre Read Plato's Laws." *Polis* 19, 1–2 (2002): 29–43.

Koenigsberger, Hans, George Mosse, and George Bowler. *Europe in the 16th Century.* 2nd edition. London: Longman, 1991.

Koestler, Arthur. *Darkness at Noon.* Translated by Daphne Hardy. New York: Penguin Books, 1978.

Kohler, Wolfgang. *The Mentality of Apes.* 2nd ed. London: Routledge and Kegan Paul, 1927.

Kostof, Spiro. *A History of Architecture: Settings and Rituals.* New York: Oxford University Press, 1985.

Kraft, Viktor. *The Vienna Circle: The Origin of Neo-Positivism.* New York: Greenwood, 1969. Originally published in 1953.

Krausnick, Helmut et al. *Anatomy of the SS State.* New York: Walker, 1968.

Kravetz, Lee Daniel. *Strange Contagion.* New York: HarperCollins, 2017.

Lagarde, Paul de. *German Writings.* Paris: Ulan Press, 2012.

La Grange, Henry-Louis de. *Mahler.* Vol. 3, *Vienna: Triumph and Disillusion 1904–1907.* Oxford: Oxford University Press, 1999.

Laing, Ronald D. *The Divided Self.* London: Penguin: 2010.

Lake, Peter. "An Exegesis of the Radical Right." *California Magazine* 10, 4 (April 1985): 95–102.

Lambert, Gilles. *Caravaggio.* Cologne: Taschen, 2019.

Lambert, Malcolm. *The Cathars.* Oxford: Blackwell, 1998.

Langbehn, Julius. *Rembrandt as Educator.* Translator Alexander Jacob. London: Wermod, 2018.

Langdon, Helen. *Caravaggio: A Life.* New York: Farrar, Straus and Giroux, 1999.

Langer, Elinor. "The American Neo-Nazi Movement Today." *The Nation* (July 1990): 82–107.

LaRouche, Lyndon. *The Power to Reason.* Washington: Executive Intelligence Review, 1988.

Lauriola, Rosanna. "The Greeks and the Utopia: An Overview through Ancient Greek Literature." *Revista Espaço Acadêmico* 97 (June 2009): 109–24.

Lauryssens, Stan. *The Man Who Invented the Third Reich: The Life and Times of Arthur Moeller van den Bruck.* Stroud, UK: Sutton Publishing, 1999.

Law, Stephen. *Humanism: A Very Short Introduction.* Oxford: Oxford University Press, 2011.

Lea, Charles. *A History of the Inquisition in the Middle Ages.* Vol. I. New York: BiblioLife, 2009.

Le Bon, Gustave. *The Crowd.* London: Transaction Publishers, 1999.

Leighton, Alexander H., and Jane M. Hughes. "Cultures as Causative of Mental Disorder." *The Milbank Quarterly* 83, 4 (December 2005): 1–15.

Lemkin, Raphael. *Lemkin on Genocide.* Edited by Steven Leonard Jacobs. Lanham, MD: Rowman & Littlefield, 2012.

Lenin, Vladimir. *What Is to Be Done? Burning Questions of Our Movement.* Edited by Robert Service. London: Penguin Classic, 1990. Originally published in 1902.

Lenneberg, Eric, Noam Chomsky, and Otto Marx. *Biological Foundations of Language.* Vol. 68. New York: Wiley, 1967.

Lerner, Robert E. "A Most Holy War: The Albigensian Crusade and the Battle for Christendom (review)." *Common Knowledge* 16, 2 (2010): 292.

Le Roy Ladurie, Emmanuel. *Montaillou.* Harmondsworth, UK: Braziller Book, 1980.

Lessing, Gotthold Ephraim. *Laocoon: Or, the Limits of Poetry and Painting.* Translated by William Ross. London, Ridgeway, 1836.

Levi-Strauss, Claude. *Introduction to the Work of Marcel Mauss.* Translated by Felicity Baker. London: Routledge and Kegan-Paul, 1987.

Levitsky, Steven, and Daniel Ziblatt. *How Democracies Die.* New York: Crown, 2018.

Lévy-Bruhl, Lucien. *How Natives Think.* Translated by Lilian A. Clare. London: George Allen & Unwin, 1926.

Lewis, James R., and Jesper Aagaard Petersen. *Controversial New Religions.* Oxford: Oxford University Press, 2005.

Lewis-Kraus, Gideon. "Is Ancient DNA Research Revealing New Truths – Or Falling into Old Traps?" *The New York Times Magazine,* 17 January 2019.

Lewis, Wyndham. *Hitler, The Germans and the Jews.* Ann Arbor: University of Michigan, 1972.

Lifton, Robert Jay. *Destroying the World to Save It: Aum Shinrikyo, Apocalyptic Violence and the New Global Terrorism.* New York: Henry Holt, 2000.

– *The Nazi Doctors.* New York: Basic Books, 1986.

– *Revolutionary Immortality: Mao-Tse-tung and the Chinese Cultural Revolution.* New York: Norton, 1971.

– *Thought Reform and the Psychology of Totalism: A Study of Brainwashing in China.* New York: Norton, 1961.

Lingens-Reiner, Ella. *Prisoners of Fear.* London: Gollancz, 1948.

Linton, Ralph. *Culture and Mental Disorders.* Springfield, IL: Thomas, 1956.

Lloyd, George. *Magic, Reason and Experience: Studies in the Origin and Development of Greek Science.* London: Cambridge University Press, 1979.

Loptson, Peter. *Theories of Human Nature.* Peterborough, ON: Broadview Press, 1995.

Lorenz, Konrad. *On Aggression.* London: Methuen and Co., 1966. Originally published in 1963.

Lougee, Robert W. *Paul de Lagarde.* Cambridge, MA: Harvard University Press, 1962.

Lourié, Arthur. *Sergei Kousevitzky and His Epoch.* New York: Knopf, 1931.

Lovejoy, Arthur O. *The Great Chain of Being.* 14th printing. Cambridge, MA: Harvard University Press, 1978. Originally published in 1936.

Lowenthal, Leo, and Nobert Guterman. *Prophets of Deceit: A Study in the Techniques of the American Agitator.* New York: Harper and Brothers, 1949.

Ludwig, Emil. *Talks with Mussolini.* Boston: Little, Brown and Company, 1933.

MacDonald, David L. "The Erotic Sublime: The Marvellous in The Monk." *English Studies in Canada* 18, 3 (September 1992): 273–85.

MacDonald, Malcolm. *Schoenberg.* 2nd rev. ed. Oxford: Oxford University Press, 2008.

Mach, Ernst. *The Analysis of Sensations and the Relation of the Physical to the Psychical.* Translated by C.M. Williams. New York: Dover Publications, 1959.

Machiavelli, Niccolò. *The Prince.* Translated by Peter Bondanella. Oxford: Oxford University Press, 1990.

MacKay, Christopher S. *The Hammer of Witches: A Complete Translation of the Malleus Maleficarum.* Cambridge: Cambridge University Press, 2009.

Maes, Hans, and Jerrold Levinson. *Art and Pornography.* Oxford: Oxford University Press, 2012.

Mahler, Alma, *Gustave Mahler: Memories and Letters.* Translated by Basil Creighton. New York: Viking, 1969.

Mann, Thomas. *Doctor Faustus.* Translated by John E. Woods. New York: Vintage Books, 1997.

– *Frederick II and the Great Coalition.* Whitefish, MT: Kessinger Publications, 2005. Originally published 1915.

– *Stories of Three Decades.* Translated by Helen T. Lowe-Porter. New York: Knopf, 1936.

– "Von Deutscher Republik." Berlin: Bemuhungen,1925.

Marcus, Gary. "Survival of the Fittest? Just What Does Darwin Tell Us about the Human Mind?" *Psychological Science Agenda*, May 2009. At https://www.apa.org/science/about/psa/2009/05/sci-brief.aspx.

Marino, Adrian. *Modern, Modernism, Modernitate.* Bucharest: Editura Univers, 1970.

Martner, Knud, ed. *Selected Letters of Gustave Mahler.* Translated by Eithne Wilkins and Ernst Kaiser. New York: Farrar, Straus, Giroux, 1979.

Mason, Lorna L. *The New World Order: The American Patriot Movement, Globalization and Resistance.* Paper presented 31 July 2008 at the annual meeting of the American Sociological Association, Boston Copley Place, Boston, MA.

Mayr, Ernst. "How to Carry Out the Adaptationist Program." *American Naturalist* 121, 3 (1983): 324–34.

May, Rollo. *Man's Search for Himself.* New York: Delta Publishing, 1953.

Mazower, Mark. *Governing the World: The History of an Idea.* New York: Penguin Press, 2012.

McClary, Susan. "Afterword." In *Noise: The Political Economy of Music* by Jacques Attali. Translated by Brian Massumi. Minneapolis: University of Minnesota Press, 2017. Originally published in 1985.

McDonald, Melissa, Carlos Navarrete, and Mark Van Vugt. "Evolution and the Psychology of Intergroup Conflict: The Male Warrior Hypothesis." *Philosophical Transactions of the Royal Society B: Biological Sciences* 367 (2012): 670–9.

McDougall, William. *Outline of Psychology.* New York: Scribner's, 1923.

McHugh, David. "Conspiracy Theories Grow." *Detroit News and Free Press,* 29 April 1995, A1, A6.

Merleau-Ponty, Maurice. *Phenomenology of Perception.* Translated by Donald A. Landes. New York: Routledge, 2014.

Meyer, Leonard B. *Music, the Arts and Ideas: Patterns and Predictions in Twentieth-Century Culture.* Chicago: University of Chicago Press, 1967.

Mill, John Stuart. *On Liberty and the Subjection of Women.* London: Penguin Classics. 2006.

Mitscherlich, Alexander, and Fred Mielke. *Doctors of Infamy: The Story of the Nazi Medical Crimes.* New York: Schuman, 1949.

Moldenhauer, Hans, and Rosaleen Moldenhauer. *Anton von Webern: A Chronicle of his life and Work.* New York: Knopf, 1979.

Monk, Ray. *Ludwig Wittgenstein: The Duty of Genius.* London: Vintage, 1991.

Moore, John Clare. *Pope Innocent III (1160/61–1215): To Root Up and to Plant.* Boston: Brill Academic Publishers, 2003.

Moore, Robert I. *The Formation of a Persecuting Society.* Malden, MA: Blackwell, 2007.

– *The War on Heresy.* London: Profile books, 2014.

More, L.T. *Isaac Newton.* New York: Charles Scribner's Sons, 1934.

More, Thomas. *Utopia*. Translated by Paul Turner. Cambridge: Cambridge University Press, 2011.

Mosse, George L. *The Crisis of German Ideology: Intellectual Origins of the Third Reich.* New York: Grosset and Dunlap, 1964.

Mundy, Jennifer, ed. *Surrealism: Desire Unbound.* Princeton: Princeton University Press, 2002.

Murdoch, Iris. *The Sovereignty of Good.* London: Routledge and Kegan Paul, 1971.

Mussolini, Benito. *The Doctrine of Fascism.* Florence: Vallecchi Editore, 1935.

Nash, Ogden. *You Can't Get There from Here.* La Mesa, CA: Gargoyle Books, 1957.

Nathanson, Stephen. *Patriotism, Morality, and Peace.* Lanham: Rowman and Littlefield, 1993.

Nettle, Daniel. "Ecological Influences on Human Behavioral Diversity: A Review of Recent Findings." *Trends in Ecology and Evolution* 24 (2009): 618–24.

– *Evolution and Genetics for Psychology.* Oxford: Oxford University Press, 2009.

Nietzsche, Friedrich. *Beyond Good and Evil.* London: Penguin, 2003.

– *The Birth of Tragedy and the Case of Wagner.* Translated by Walter Kaufmann. New York: Vintage Books, 1967.

– "Nachgelassene Fragmente." In *Werke: Kristische Gesamtaugabe.* Berlin: Walter de Gruyter, 1877.

– *On the Genealogy of Morals.* Translated by Douglas Smith. Oxford: Oxford University Press, 2008.

– *Thus Spake Zarathustra.* In *The Philosophy of Nietzsche.* Translated by Willard Wright, 3–368. New York: The Modern Library. 1954.

– *Twilight of the Idols and The Anti-Christ.* London: Penguin, 2003.

– *The Will to Power.* Edited by Walter Kaufmann. New York: Vintage Books, 1968.

Nilsson, Martin P. *Greek Piety.* Translated by Herbert Jennings. Oxford: Clarendon Press, 1948.

Noys, Benjamin. *Georges Bataille: A Critical Introduction.* London: Pluto, 2000.

Nussbaum, Martha C. *Anger and Forgiveness.* Oxford: Oxford University Press, 2019.

– *Political Emotions: Why Love Matters for Justice.* Cambridge, MA: Harvard University Press, 2013.

– *Upheavals of Thought: The Intelligence of Emotions.* Cambridge: Cambridge University Press, 2008.

Ortega y Gasset, Jose *The Dehumanization of Art.* Translated by Helene Weyl. Princeton: Princeton University Press, 1968.

Orwell, George. *1984.* Toronto: HarperCollins Publishers, 2014.

Palmer, James T. *The Apocalypse in the Early Middle Ages.* Cambridge: Cambridge University Press, 2014.

Partridge, Christopher Hugh. *The Re-Enchantment of the West: Alternative Spiritualities, Sacralization, Popular Culture, and Occulture.* London: Continuum International Publishing Group, 2006.

Pascal, Blaise. *Pensées.* Translated by A.J. Krailsheimer. London: Penguin, 1995.

Passingham, Richard. *Cognitive Neuroscience: A Very Short Introduction.* Oxford: Oxford University Press, 2016.

Paxton, Robert O. *The Anatomy of Fascism.* New York: Vintage Books, 2005.

Payne, Stanley G. *Fascism in Spain, 1923–1977.* Madison: University of Wisconsin Press, 1999.

Peattie, Anthony. *The Private Life of Lord Byron.* London: Unbound, 2019.

Pegg, Mark Gregory. *A Most Holy War: The Albigensian Crusade and the Battle for Christendom.* Oxford: Oxford University Press, 2008.

Penrose, Roland. *Miró.* London: Thames and Hudson, 1970.

Perelman, Chaim. *The New Rhetoric: A Treatise on Argumentation.* Translated by John Wilkinson and Purcell Weaver. Notre Dame: University of Notre Dame Press, 1969.

Peters, Edward. "The Cathars." In *Heresy and Authority in Medieval Europe.* Philadelphia: University of Pennsylvania Press, 1980.

Petrarch. *The Sonnets, Triumphs, and Other Poems of Petrarch.* Scotts Valley, CA: CreateSpace Independent Publishing Platform, 2014. Originally published about 1351.

Pevsner, Nikolaus. *An Outline of European Architecture.* London: Penguin, 1990.

Phillips, John. *The Marquis de Sade.* Oxford: Oxford University Press, 2005.

Piaget, Jean. *The Origins of Intelligence in Children.* New York: International Universities Press, 1977.

Pierce, William. (Andrew McDonald, pseud.) *The Turner Diaries.* 2nd ed. Washington: National Alliance, 1980.

Pinker, Steven. *The Better Angels of Our Nature.* New York: Viking, 2011.

– *The Blank Slate: The Modern Denial of Human Nature.* New York: Penguin, 2002.

– *The Language Instinct.* New York: HarperCollins, 1994.

Pinker, Steven, and Paul Bloom. "Natural Language and Natural Selection." In *The Adapted Mind*, edited by Jerome H. Barkow, Leda Cosmides, and John Tooby, 451–93. Oxford: Oxford University Press, 1995.

Plantinga, Leon. *Romantic Music: A History of Musical Style in Nineteenth-Century Europe.* New York: Norton, 1984.

Plato. "Euthydemus." In *Complete Works.* Edited by John M. Cooper, 708–45. Indianapolis: Hackett Publishing, 1997.

– "The Laws." In *Complete Works*. Edited by John M. Cooper, 1318–616. Indianapolis: Hackett Publishing, 1997.

– "Phaedrus." In *Complete Works*. Edited by John M. Cooper, 506–56. Indianapolis: Hackett Publishing, 1997.

– "Protagoras." In *Complete Works*. Edited by John M. Cooper, 746–90. Indianapolis: Hackett Publishing, 1997.

– "The Republic." In *Complete Works*. Edited by John M. Cooper, 971–1223. Indianapolis: Hackett Publishing, 1997.

– *The Republic of Plato*. Translated by Francis Cornford. New York: Oxford University Press, 1968.

– "The Timaeus." In *Complete Works*. Edited by John M. Cooper, 1224–91. Indianapolis: Hackett Publishing, 1997.

Plotinus. *The Enneads*. Translated by Stephen MacKenna. Edited by John Dillon. London: Penguin Books, 1991.

Poggioli, Renato. *Theory of the Avant-Garde*. Cambridge, MA: Harvard University Press, 1968.

Polger, Thomas W., and Lawrence A. Shapiro. *The Multiple Realization Book*. Oxford: Oxford University Press, 2016.

Ponchaud, Francois. *Cambodia, Year Zero*. Translated by Nancy Amphoux. New York: Henry Holt, 1978.

Popper, Karl. *The Logic of Science*. 2nd ed. London: Routledge Classics, 2002.

Porter, Theodore M. *Trust in Numbers: The Pursuit of Objectivity in Science and Public Life*. Princeton: Princeton University Press, 1995.

Polybius. *The Histories*. Translated by Robin Waterfield. Oxford: Oxford University Press, 2010.

Pound, Ezra. "Arnold Dolmetsch." *Literary Essays of Ezra Pound*. New York: New Directions, 1968. Originally published in 1914.

– *Make It New*. New Haven: Yale University Press, 1935.

Prum, Richard. "Duck Sex and the Aesthetic Evolution." In *Life*, edited by John Brockman, 326–48. New York: Harper Perennial, 2016.

Putnam, Hilary. *The Many Faces of Realism*. La Salle, IL: Open Court. 1987.

– *Reason, Truth and History*. Cambridge: Cambridge University Press, 1981.

– "Peirce the Logician." In *Realism with a Human Face*, edited by James Conant, 252–60. Cambridge, MA: Harvard University Press, 1990.

Quine, Willard Van Orman. "On What There is." In *From a Logical Point of View*. 2nd revised edition, 1–19. New York: Harper Torchbooks, 1961.

– *Word and Object*. Cambridge, MA: MIT Press, 1960.

Quinn, Kenneth M. "Explaining the Terror." In *Cambodia, 1975–78: Rendezvous with Death,* edited by Karl D. Jackson, 215–40. Princeton: Princeton University Press, 1989.

Rabelais, Francois. *Gargantua and Pantagruel.* Translated by M.A. Screech. London: Penguin, 2006.

Rameau, Jean-Philippe. *Treatise on Harmony.* Translated by Philip Gossett. New York: Dover, 1971. Originally published in French in 1722.

Rank, Otto. *Beyond Psychology.* New York: Dover, 1958.

Rapoport, David C. "Some General Observations on Religion and Violence." In *Violence and the Sacred in the Modern World,* edited by Mark Juergensmeyer, 118–40. London: Frank Cass, 1992.

Reader, Ian. *Religious Violence in Contemporary Japan: The Case of Aum Shinrikyo.* Honolulu: University of Hawaii Press, 2000.

Reavis, Dick J. *The Ashes of Waco: An Investigation.* New York: Simon and Schuster, 1995.

Reich, David. *Who We Are and How We Got Here.* New York: Pantheon Books, 2018.

Reich, Willi. *Schoenberg: A Critical Biography.* Translated by Leo Black. London: Longman, 1971.

Reich, William. *The Mass Psychology of Fascism.* Translated by Vincent R. Carfagno. New York: Farrar, Straus, and Giroux, 1971.

Reiterman, Tim, and Jim Jacobs, *Raven: The Untold Story of the Reverend Jim Jones and his People.* New York: E.P. Dutton, 1982.

Reston, James. *Our Father Who Art in Hell: The Life and Death of Jim Jones.* New York: Times Books, 1981.

Reuth, Ralf Georg. *Goebbels.* Harcourt Brace, 1993

Ricoeur, Paul. *Interpretation Theory: Discourse and the Surplus of Meaning.* Fort Worth: Texas Christian University Press, 1976.

Riley-Smith, Jonathan. *The First Crusade and the Idea of Crusading.* Philadelphia: University of Pennsylvania, 1991.

Rimbaud, Arthur. *A Season in Hell.* New York: New Directions, 2011.

Ringer, Alexander L. *Arnold Schoenberg: The Composer as Jew.* Oxford: Clarendon Press, 1990.

– "Arnold Schoenberg and the Politics of Jewish Survival." *Journal of the Arnold Schoenberg Institute* III, 1 (March 1979): 11–48.

Robb, Graham. *Rimbaud.* New York: Norton & Co, 2000.

Robb, Peter. *M: The Man Who Became Caravaggio.* New York: Picador, 1999.

Robertson, Pat. *The New World Order.* New York: HarperCollins, 1991.

Robins, Robert S., and Jerrold M. Post. *Political Paranoia: The Psychopolitics of Hatred.* New Haven: Yale University Press, 1997.

Rodriques, Benjamin Olinda. "The Artist, the Scientist and the Industrialist." In *Art in Theory 1815–1900: An Anthology of Changing Ideas*, translated and edited by Charles Harrison and Paul Wood, 37–40. Oxford: Blackwell, 1998.

Rohde, Erwin. *Psyche: The Cult of Souls and Belief in Immortality Among the Greeks*. Vol. II. 8th ed. Translated by W.B. Hillis. Eugene, OR: Wipf and Stock Publishers, 2006. Originally published in 1890.

Rokeach, Milton. *The Open and Closed Mind: Investigations into the Nature of Belief Systems and Personality Systems*. New York: Basic Books, 1960.

Rosnow, Ralph L. "Poultry and Prejudice." *Psychologist Today* 5, 10 (March 1972): 53–6.

Ross, Alex. "As If Music Could Do No Harm." *The New Yorker*, 20 August 2014.

– *The Rest Is Noise: Listening to the Twentieth Century*. New York: Picador, 2007.

Rousseau, Jean-Jacques. *The Confessions*. Translated by J.M. Cohen. London: Penguin Classics, 1953. Originally published in 1781.

– *The Social Contract*. Translated by Maurice Cranston. London: Penguin Classics, 1968.

Rowell, Margit. *Joan Miró: Selected Writings and Interviews*. London: Thames and Hudson, 1987.

Runciman, Steven. *A History of the Crusades*. Cambridge: Cambridge University Press, 1954.

Ruse, Michael. *A Meaning to Life*. Oxford: Oxford University Press, 2019.

Russell, Frederick. "Children's Crusade." In *Dictionary of the Middle Ages*. Vol. 4. Edited by Joseph Strayer, 14–15. New York: Charles Scribner's Sons, 1984.

Sacks, Oliver. *The Man Who Mistook His Wife for a Hat and Other Clinical Essays*. New York: HarperCollins, 1985.

Saint Theresa. *The Autobiography of St. Teresa of Avila*. Charlotte, NC: Tan Books, 1997.

Sartre, Jean-Paul. *Essays in Existentialism*. Edited by Wade Baskin. Secaucus, NJ: The Citadel Press, 1972.

Schaff, Philip. *History of the Christian Church*. New York: Arkosc Press, 2015.

Schama, Simon. *The Power of Art*. London: Random House, 2009.

Schiller, Friedrich. "On the Art of Tragedy." In *Essays*, edited by Daniel O. Dahlstrom and Walter Hinderer, 45–68. New York: Continuum, 1993.

Schlick, Moritz. "The Turn in Philosophy." In A.J. Ayer, *Logical Positivism*, 53–9. New York: The Free Press, 1959.

Schmidt, Ulf. *Karl Brandt: The Nazi Doctor: Medicine and Power in the Third Reich*. London: Continuum, 2007.

Schmitt, David, and June Pilcher. "Evaluating Evidence of Psychological Adaptation: How Do We Know One When We Know One." *Psychological Science* 15 (2004): 643–9.

Schoenberg, Arnold. "Aphorismen." In *Schoenberg: A Critical Biography*, edited by William Reich, 56–7. New York: Praeger, 1971. Written in 1910.

– "Does the World Lack a Peace-Hymn?" In *Style and Idea: Selected Writings of Arnold Schoenberg*, translated by Leo Black, edited by Leonard Stein, 500–1. Berkeley: University of California Press, 1975.

– "A Four-Point Program for Jewry." *Journal of the Arnold Schoenberg Institute* III, 1 (March 1979): 49–67.

– "My Attitude to Politics." In *Style and Idea: Selected Writings of Arnold Schoenberg*, translated by Leo Black, edited by Leonard Stein, 505–6. Berkeley: University of California Press, 1975.

– "The Relationship to the Text." In *Style and Idea: Selected Writings of Arnold Schoenberg*, translated by Leo Black, edited by Leonard Stein, 141–5 Berkeley: University of California Press, 1975.

– *Style and Idea: Selected Writings of Arnold Schoenberg*. Translated by Leo Black. Edited by Leonard Stein. Berkeley: University of California Press, 1975.

– *Theory of Harmony*. Translated by Roy E. Carter. Berkeley: University of California Press, 1978.

Schoenberg, E. Randol, ed. *The Doctor Faustus Dossier: Arnold Schoenberg, Thomas Mann and Their Contemporaries, 1930–1951*. Oakland: University of California Press, 2018.

Schoenberg-Nono, Anna-Maria. *Schoenberg & Nono*. Florence, Italy: Olschki, 2002.

Schopenhauer, Arthur. *On the Will in Nature*. Translated by Madame Karl Hillebrand. Scotts Valley, CA: CreateSpace, 2010.

– *The World as Will and Representation*. Vol. 1. Translated by Judith Norman. Cambridge: Cambridge University Press, 2010. Originally published 1818.

Schorske, Carl E. *Fin-de siècle Vienna*. New York: Vintage, 1981.

Screech, Michael. *Rabelais*. London: Duckworth, 1979.

Scruton, Roger. *Beauty: A Very Short Introduction*. Oxford: Oxford University Press, 2011.

Scull, Anthony. *Madness: A Very Short Introduction*. Oxford: Oxford University Press, 2011.

– *Madness in Civilization: A Cultural History of Insanity, from the Bible to Freud, from the Madhouse to Modern Medicine*. Princeton: Princeton University Press, 2015.

Searle, John. *Rationality in Action*. Cambridge, MA: The MIT Press, 2001.

Seckel, Al. *Masters of Deception: Escher, Dalí & the Artists of Optical Illusion*. New York: Sterling Publishing Company, 2004.

Sell, Aaron. "Applying Adaptationism to Human Anger: The Recalibrational Theory." In *Human Aggression and Violence: Causes, Manifestations, and Consequences*, edited by Phillip R. Shaver and Mario *Mikulincer*, 53–70. Washington: American Psychological Association, 2011.

Sen, Amartya. *The Idea of Justice.* Cambridge, MA: Harvard University Press, 2009.

– "The Possibility of Social Choice." In *Rationality and Freedom*, 65–118. Cambridge, MA: Harvard University Press, 2002.

– *Rationality and Freedom.* Cambridge, MA: Harvard University Press, 2002.

Seyfarth, Robert, Cheney, Dorothy, and Peter Marler. "Vervet Monkey Alarm Calls: Semantic Communication in a Free-Ranging Primate." *Animal Behavior* 28, 4 (1980): 1070–94.

Shapiro, David. *Neurotic Styles.* New York: Basic Books, 1967.

Shaver, Phillip R., and Mario Mikulincer, eds. *Human Aggression and Violence: Causes, Manifestations, and Consequences.* Washington: American Psychological Association 2011.

Short, Philip. *Pol Pot: The History of a Nightmare.* London: John Murray, 2004.

Sibly, W.A., and M.D. Sibly. *The Chronicle of William of Puylaurens: The Albigensian Crusade and Its Aftermath.* Martlesham, UK: Boydell Press, 2003.

Sihanouk, Norodom. *War and Hope: The Case for Cambodia.* New York: Columbia University Press, 1980.

Skinner, Burrhus F. *Walden Two.* Indianapolis: Hackett Publishing Company, 2006. Originally published in 1948.

Slack, Corliss K. *Historical Dictionary of the Crusades.* 2nd ed. Lanham, MD: Scarecrow Press, 2013

Slonimsky, Nicolas. *Music Since 1900.* 4th ed. New York: Scribner's, 1971.

Snow, Robert L. *Deadly Cults: The Crimes of True Believers.* Santa Barbara, CA: Greenwood Publishing Group. 2003.

Sober, Elliott. *Philosophy of Biology.* Oxford: Oxford University Press, 1993.

Sontag, Susan. "Fascinating Fascism." *New York Review of Books*, 6 February 1975.

Sophocles. *Ajax.* Edited by David Grene and Richmond Lattimore. 4th printing. New York: Washington Square Press, 1973.

Speer, Albert. *Inside the Third Reich: Memoirs.* New York: MacMillan, 1970.

Speier, Jackie. *Undaunted: Surviving Jonestown, Summoning Courage, and Fighting Back.* New York: Little A, 2018.

Spence, Jonathan D. *The Search for Modern China.* New York: Norton, 1990.

Spinoza, Benedict de. *The Ethics.* In *The Chief Works of Benedict de Spinoza*, translated by R.H.M. Elwes, 43–271. New York: Dover Publications, 1955.

Spitz, Vivien, *Doctors from Hell.* Boulder, CO: Sentient Publications, 2005.

Stanley, Jason. *How Fascism Works: The Politics of Us and Them.* New York: Random House, 2018.

Starr, Kevin. *The Dream Endures: California Enters the 1940s.* New York: Oxford University Press, 1997.

Steegmuller, Francis. *Cocteau: A Biography.* Boston: Nonpareil, 1986. Originally published in 1970.

Stendhal. *Racine and Shakespeare.* Translated by Guy Daniels. London: Oneworld Classics, 2011. Originally published in 1823.

Stenner, Karen. *The Authoritarian Dynamic.* New York: Cambridge University Press, 2005.

Stenner, Karen, and Jonathan Haidt. "Authoritarianism is Not a Momentary Madness but an Eternal Dynamic within Liberal Democracies." In *Can It Happen Here? Authoritarianism in America,* edited by Cass Sunstein, 175–219. New York: HarperCollins, 2018.

Stephens, Mitchell. *A History of the News.* New York: Viking, 1988.

Stern, Fritz. *The Politics of Cultural Despair: A Study in the Rise of German Ideology.* Berkeley: University of California Press, 1974.

Stern, Joseph P. *Hitler: The Fuhrer and the People.* Glasgow: Fontana, 1971.

Stern, Kenneth. *A Force Upon the Plain: The American Militia Movement and the Politics of Hate.* New York: Simon and Shuster, 1996.

Stigler, Stephen M. *The History of Statistics: The Measurement of Uncertainty to 1900.* Cambridge, MA: Harvard University Press, 1986.

Strathern, Paul. *The Medici: Godfathers of the Renaissance.* London: Pimlico, 2005.

Strayer, Joseph R. *The Albigensian Crusades.* New York: The Dial Press, 1971.

– *On the Medieval Origins of the Modern State.* Princeton: Princeton University Press, 2016.

Strozier, Charles. *Apocalypse: On the Psychology of Fundamentalism in America.* Boston: Beacon Press, 1994.

Stuckenschmidt, Hans H. *Arnold Schoenberg.* Translated by Edith Roberts and Humphrey Searle. Westport, CT: Greenwood Press, 1979.

– *Arnold Schoenberg: His Life, World, and Work.* Translated by Humphrey Searle. New York: Schirmer Books, 1977.

Sumner, William. *Folkways. A Study of the Sociological Importance of Usages, Manners, Customs, Mores, and Morals.* New York: Ginn, 1906.

Sunstein, Cass R. *Can It Happen Here? Authoritarianism in America.* New York: HarperCollins, 2018.

Sussman, Robert, and Donna Hart. *Man the Hunted: Primates, Predators, and Human Evolution.* New York: Westview Press, 2005.

Szasz, Thomas. *The Myth of Mental Illness.* New York: Harper Perennial, 2010.

– *The Myth of Psychotherapy*. Syracuse: Syracuse University Press, 1988.

Tagg, Philip. "Harmony." *Continuum Encyclopedia of Popular Music of the World*. Part 1, *Performance and Production*, edited by John Shepherd, David Horn, David Laing, Paul Oliver, and Peter Wicke, 123–9. London: A & C Black, 2003.

Tajfel, Henri, and John Turner. "An Integrative Theory of Intergroup Conflict." In *The Social Psychology of Intergroup Relations*, edited by William G. Austin and Stephen Worchel, 33–47. Monterey, CA: Brooks, 1979.

Taruskin, Richard. "The Dark Side of Modern Music: The Sins of Toscanini, Stravinsky, Schoenberg." Review of *Music in Fascist Italy*, by Harvey Sachs. *New Republic* 199, 10 (5 September 1988): 28–34.

– *Music from the Earliest Notations to the Sixteenth Century*. The Oxford History of Western Music. Oxford: Oxford University Press, 2010.

– *Music in the Early Twentieth Century*. The Oxford History of Western Music. Oxford: Oxford University Press, 2010.

Taulbee, James L. *War Crimes and Trials*. Santa Barbara, CA: ABC-CLIO, 2018.

Taylor, Frederick H. *The Principles of Scientific Management*. Eastford, CT: Martino Fine Books, 2014.

Thagard, Paul. *Conceptual Revolutions*. Princeton: Princeton University Press, 1992.

Thomas, Keith. *Religion and the Decline of Magic: Studies in Popular Beliefs in Sixteenth and Seventeenth Century England*. New York: Scribner's, 1971.

Thomson, Nicholas D. *Understanding Psychopathy: The Biopsychosocial Perspective*. London: Routledge, 2019.

Tomasello, Michael. *Origins of Human Communication*. Cambridge, MA: The MIT Press, 2008.

– *Why We Cooperate*. Cambridge, MA: The MIT Press, 2009.

Tooby, John, and Leda Cosmides. "The Evolutionary Psychology of the Emotions and their Relationship to Internal Regulatory Variables." In *Handbook of Emotions*, 3rd ed, edited by M. Lewis, J.M. Haviland, and L.F. Barrett, 114–37. New York: Guilford, 2008.

– "Groups in Mind: The Coalitional Roots of War and Morality." In *Human Morality and Sociality: Evolutionary and Comparative Perspectives*, edited by Henrik Høgh-Olesen, 91–234. London: Palgrave-Macmillan, 2010.

Toynbee, Arnold J. *A Study of History*. Vol. 5. Oxford: Oxford University Press, 1961. Originally published in 1939.

Trilling, Lionel. "Freud: Within and Beyond Culture." In *Beyond Culture*. New York: Viking, 1965.

Trivers, Robert. "The Evolution of Reciprocal Altruism." *Quarterly Review of Biology* 46 (1971): 35–57.

Unger, Miles J. *Machiavelli: A Biography*. New York: Simon and Schuster, 2011.

Vitruvius, *On Architecture*. Translated by Frank Granger. Cambridge, MA: Harvard University Press, 1931.

Wagner, Cosima. *Diaries*. Vol. II: 1878–83. Translated by Geoffrey Skelton. San Diego, CA: Harcourt Brace Jovanovich. 1980.

Wagner, Richard. *Judaism in Music*. Wokingham, UK: Dodo Press, 2008.

Wakefield, Walter L. *Heresy, Crusade and Inquisition in Southern France 1100–1250*. London: Allen and Unwin, 1974.

Waldberg, Patrick. *Surrealism*. New York: McGraw-Hill, 1971.

Ward, Stephen J.A. *Disrupting Journalism Ethics*. New York: Routledge, 2019.

– *Ethical Journalists in a Populist Age*. Lanham, MD: Rowman and Littlefield, 2019.

– *Global Journalism Ethics*. Montreal and Kingston: McGill-Queen's University Press, 2010.

– *The Invention of Journalism Ethics*. 2nd ed. Montreal and Kingston: McGill-Queen's University Press, 2015.

– *Objectively Engaged Journalism: An Ethic*. Montreal and Kingston: McGill-Queen's University Press, 2019.

Webern, Anton. *The Path to the New Music*. Translated by Leo Black. Bryn Mawr, PA: Theodore Presser, 1963.

Weinger, Otto. *Sex and Character*. Translated by Ladislaus Lob. Indianapolis: Indiana University Press, 2005. Originally published in 1903.

Weir, David. *Decadence: A Very Short Introduction*. Oxford: Oxford University Press, 2018.

Welch, Robert. *The Blue Book of the John Birch Society*. Belmont, MA: Belmont Publishing, 1961.

– *May God Forgive Us*. Chicago: Henry Regnery, 1952.

Wen, Chihua. *The Red Mirror: Children of China's Cultural Revolution*. Boulder, CO: Westview Press, 1995.

West, Stuart, Ashleigh Griffin, and Andy Gardner. "Social Semantics: Altruism, Cooperation, Mutualism, Strong Reciprocity, and Group Selection." *Journal of Evolutionary Biology* 20, 2 (March 2007): 415–32.

Wicker, Tom. *Shooting Star: The Brief Arc of Joe McCarthy*. New York: Harcourt, 2006.

Williams, George C. *Adaptation and Natural Selection*. Princeton: Princeton University Press, 1966.

Wilson, Edward O. *On Human Nature*. Cambridge, MA: Harvard University Press.

– *Sociobiology: The New Synthesis*. Cambridge, MA: Harvard University Press, 1975.

Wolin, Richard. *Heidegger in Ruins: Between Philosophy and Ideology*. New Haven: Yale University Press, 2022.

Wordsworth, William, and Samuel Taylor Coleridge. *Lyrical Ballads, 1798 and 1802*. Oxford: Oxford University Press, 2013.

Wright, Lawrence. "Orphans of Jonestown." *The New Yorker* (22 November 1993): 66–89.

Wright, Robert. *The Moral Animal*. New York: Vintage, 1994.

– *A Short History of Progress*. The CBC Massey Lectures. Toronto: House of Anansi Press, 2004.

Yaeger, Carl. "Armageddon Tomorrow: The Posse Comitatus Prepares for the Future." TVI *Report* 1, 2 (1994): 16–20.

Zamoyski, Adam. *Phantom Terror: Political Paranoia and the Creation of the Modern State, 1789–1848*. New York: Basic Books, 2015.

Zee, Hugo J. "The Guyana Incident: Some Psychoanalytic Considerations." *Bulletin of the Menninger Clinic* 44 (1980): 345–63.

Zetkin, Klara. *Reminiscences of Lenin*. London: Chatto and Windus, 1929.

Zhang, Lei, and Carleton Clark, eds. *Affect, Emotion, and Rhetorical Persuasion in Mass Communication*. New York: Routledge, 2019.

Zhisui, Li. *The Private Life of Chairman Mao: The Memoirs of Mao's Personal Physician*. Translated by Tai Hung-Chao. New York: Random House, 2004.

Index